Telecommunications

Restructuring
Work and Employment
Relations Worldwide

Harry C. Katz, editor

Telecommunications

Restructuring

Work and Employment

Relations Worldwide

ILR PRESS

an imprint of CORNELL UNIVERSITY PRESS

ITHACA AND LONDON

First published 1997 by Cornell University Press.
Cornell International Industrial and Labor
Relations Report Number 32.

Printed in the United States of America

Library of Congress Cataloging-in-Publication Data
Katz, Harry Charles, 1951–
    Telecommunications : restructuring work and employment relations
worldwide / Harry C. Katz.
        p.   cm. — (Cornell international industrial and labor
relations report ; no. 32)
    Includes index.
    ISBN 0-8014-3286-3 (cloth : alk. paper). — ISBN 0-8014-8361-1
(pbk. : alk. paper)
    1. Telecommunication—Employees.   2. Industrial relations—Case
studies.   3. Telecommunication—Economic aspects.   I. Title.
II. Series: Cornell international industrial and labor relations
reports ; no. 32.
HD6976.T24K37   1996
331'.041384—DC20   96-32042

This book is printed on Lyons Falls Turin Book,
a paper that is totally chlorine-free and acid-free.

Contents

Telecommunications

*Restructuring
Work and Employment
Relations Worldwide*

Introduction and Comparative Overview

Harry C. Katz

This volume provides a comparative international analysis of the explosive changes under way in work and employment relations in the global telecommunications services industry.[1] Technological innovation and the disintegration of national product market boundaries have in the mid-1990s produced profound changes in employment levels, work organization, and employment relations in this industry of a sort that were unthinkable even a decade ago. When the United States began efforts to break up AT&T and the Bell System in the late 1970s, it was an anomaly; every other country in the world continued to operate telecommunications services as a public monopoly. In the post–World War II era, protection of the national telecommunications provider and public ownership of telecommunications were considered central to national sovereignty. Yet, the United Kingdom shortly followed the lead of the United States in deregulating its telecommunications industry and, as this book reports, other countries then followed to some degree the U.S. and U.K. model of deregulation and privatization.[2]

1. The author is grateful to Rose Batt, Fran Benson, Owen Darbishire, Anthony Ferner, and Lowell Turner for their helpful comments on earlier drafts of this chapter. Sincere thanks also go to Jackie Dodge for all her help in preparing this volume.
2. Evidence that the deregulatory approach found in the United States and United Kingdom is serving as something of a model for regulatory policy concerning the telecommunications industry in other countries is also provided in Bolton et al. 1993.

The telecommunications services industry is important because this industry provides the basic infrastructure for the information highway and thereby lies at the center of the economic changes that are occurring across the globe. Furthermore, telecommunications is an interesting industry because it is one of the few in which the United States (and the United Kingdom) have a leadership position in technology and provide a widely emulated model of industry restructuring. That model consists of deregulation and privatization of product markets and the redefinition of telecommunications from a natural public good to a global, customer-driven service.

As the chapters that follow show, a simple way to understand a country's telecommunications industry is to define where on the road of regulatory restructuring the country lies. The common starting point on this road was a telephone service that was either part of the post office or a heavily regulated public monopoly. Although the end point of the deregulation road is not yet visible in any country, the movement is clearly toward customer-oriented private telecommunications service companies who face intense competition from domestic and international rivals.

Yet, even in the face of the common trend toward deregulation and privatization, there is much variation in the focus of the restructuring occurring within national telecommunications industries. In the four Anglo-Saxon countries analyzed in this book, telecommunications restructuring is being driven by technological changes and market pressures. The large telecommunications companies in the Anglo-Saxon countries are using new technology to offer a wide variety of new products and to reshape their internal organizations. As the U.S., U.K., Australian, and Canadian chapters show, this restructuring has led to sizable employment reductions and cost-cutting efforts. In Europe and Japan, technological and market pressures have influenced telecommunications restructuring; yet this influence has been mediated and modified by unions and social concerns. A distinguishing feature of the restructuring occurring in the telecommunications industries in Europe and Japan is the extent to which labor unions are influencing the nature and extent of deregulation and lessening the scale of downsizing (in part by negotiating employment security guarantees). Labor's heavy influence in these countries also appears through the substantial adjustment assistance provided to telecommunications employees affected by corporate restructuring. In contrast, the restructuring of the telecommunications industries in Mexico and Korea is distinguished by the heavy influence exerted by the state (i.e., national government). In Mexico, for example, the federal government invited international telecommunications companies to become partners with domestic investors and it continues to guide the terms of the subsequent partnerships. In both Mexico and Korea the telecommunications industry has continued to grow in recent years in the midst of extensive modernization that has produced employment expansion, another contrast to the experiences in other countries.

In all the countries analyzed in this book the former telecommunications monopolists such as AT&T, British Telecom, Nippon Telephone and Telegraph, and Deutsche Telekom continue to play very large roles in the expanding and more diversified telecommunications service industry and retain sizable shares of total industry employment. That is why analysis of developments in the "former monopolists" constitutes a large part of each chapter. There is also probably an unavoidable bias built into the research that somewhat overemphasizes events in the former monopolists, given that is easier to gather information about them and more difficult to describe the work practices of the new entrants to the industry, who are often small, less unionized, and suspicious of researchers.

The recent news for the former telecommunications monopolists is mixed. On the one hand, the companies that traditionally provided telephone services clearly have a very central role to play in the emerging information age as the constructors and operators of the basic telecommunications information networks. Yet, these companies are in the process of redefining much of what they do, and this redefinition involves painful choices and strategic dilemmas with respect to where to invest, what products markets to enter, how to restructure, and how to reduce labor costs while retaining employee commitment and an appropriate skill base.

The corporate restructuring being driven by regulatory restructuring is in turn leading to significant changes in the employment systems of the telecommunications services industry. For example, in many countries the downsizing and "reengineering" of the former telecommunications monopolists are producing employment contractions and even greater adjustments in how and where employees work. The employees who work in the large telecommunications services firms thereby also face painful choices as a result of the extensive internal or external job transfers that are occurring or looming. These choices are influenced by the adjustment assistance provided to employees affected by corporate reorganizations. In those countries following a "labor-mediated" restructuring strategy this adjustment assistance is quite large. The scale of and cross-country variation in adjustment assistance are noteworthy as is the high degree of labor-management negotiation surrounding the provision of that assistance. These negotiations are propelling the unions representing telecommunications employees (particularly in the labor-mediated countries) into involvement in basic business and regulatory issues. Examining the implications of this shift in union roles and explaining the variations that are surfacing in union and worker involvement are among the key contributions of this volume.

In addition to downsizing, the telecommunications service companies have been altering their work practices and employment relations in many significant ways. Companies are applying concepts of employee participation, team-based production systems, total quality, and joint labor-management partnerships to the service jobs found in this industry. Because most prior research on these matters has focused on blue collar workers in manufacturing, a major contribution of this book is to expand our knowledge of the way work and employment relations are changing for white collar workers and managers. In point of fact, the chapters in this book provide the best available description of the specific tasks carried out by technical and other white collar workers in this service industry and analyze how firms are redefining these tasks in the context of industrial restructuring.

The Absence of a Japanese Lean Telecommunications Model

In the manufacturing sector over the last fifteen years there has been much discussion about the production methods and employment relations characteristic of the Japanese lean (or the Toyota) production system. In auto and many other industries around the globe, a key driving force for change in employment practices since the early 1980s has been management efforts to imitate this model (Womack, Jones, and Roos 1990).

As this book shows there is no analogous model in the telecommunications industry. That is, the United States and United Kingdom have taken the lead in restructuring, reversing the manufacturing pattern. However, the Anglo-Saxon countries at the forefront of restructuring have sought competitive advantage through technology and market strategies and not human resource strategies, as in the Japanese manufacturing case. Furthermore, there is little evidence that any one set of work practices or style of employment relations has performance advantages in the telecommunications services industry. Rather, there is a wide variation in the employment practices being adopted within and across countries. The concluding section of this chapter highlights the extent and nature of this variation.

To the extent that management in the telecommunications companies is emulating any one model of employment practices, the model is the cost-cutting and downsizing approach adopted by many of the U.S. and U.K. telecommunications firms. As Jeffrey Keefe and Rosemary Batt describe, this cost-cutting approach focuses on economies of scale, technological change, and work intensification, and contrasts with an alternative strategy that focuses on increased employee participation and job enhancement. The use of this approach is creating enormous tensions in employment relations as morale declines and employees fear even further downsizing. A critical question posed by the chapters that follow is whether this industry is trapped in the midst of a fundamental inconsistency because of the incompatibility that exists between the cost-cutting and participation-oriented employment strategies being pursued simultaneously within many of the same firms.

The ultimate consequences of the tension between cost-cutting and participatory-employment strategies is unclear at this time, in part because the direction of change in telecommunications service is so unclear. Uncertainty and confusion are rampant in part because the technological choices available to telecommunications firms are complex and rapidly changing, and these technological choices have important consequences for the organizational structure of the industry. In fact, only recently has it even become clear that the former telecommunications monopolists will play a central role in both constructing and operating the information highway. Earlier it appeared that new technologies based on microwave or radio transmissions might form the foundation of a largely wireless information highway and produce a dramatic decline in the role played by the wireline infrastructure of the old telecommunications companies (Chapter 1). Recent trends show, however, that the basic network for the information highway will be digital transmissions processed through a fiber optic network. Yet there remains much uncertainty regarding the extent to which cellular or radio frequency-based wireless communication will expand personal communication options and move the market away from the services provided by the older telecommunications firms and their subsidiaries.

There is also enormous uncertainty concerning the actual volume of consumer demand for all the services now being planned for the information highway.

The Public Sector Legacy

As this volume shows, significant public policy regulation of the telecommunications industry continues even in the face of the trend toward deregulation (what is referred to in Chapter 2 as "political contingencies"). This public-sector legacy contributes, for example, to the relatively high levels of unionization found in the industry, the extensive negotiations surrounding the adjustment assistance for displaced employees, and the cash reserves that allow companies to buy labor peace through generous severance packages. In the countries where restructuring is heavily "state-led," direct government intervention in employment relations in the former telecommunications monopolists continues to be particularly extensive. In Korea, for example, the governing board of Korea Telecom, on which government officials play a key role, must approve all major human resource management decisions (Chapter 10).

The restructuring of this industry has profound effects on citizens (consumers) as well as on employees, and current debates in every country involve redefining the role of government in the industry. In all the countries analyzed in this book governments have historically regulated telecommunications to ensure not only national security, but also universal and equitable access to services by all citizens. While everyone talks of deregulation and privatization, virtually every country is really in the process of defining the appropriate level and form of regulation. Because citizens as well as employees and investors have a significant stake in the future of the industry, restructuring has been and will continue to be complex and contested by a broad constituency of stakeholders.

The changes under way in the telecommunications services sector have been dramatic in part because they have been compressed into a relatively short time frame, which itself is a result of the fact that regulatory changes have been large and often sudden. These former public bureaucracies have had to learn fairly quickly how to be more competitive and "customer-oriented." Public employees working in large public bureaucracies had come to expect employment security for life; they also often chose government work because they wanted to serve the public. These public servants have been rudely shocked by the enormous downsizing and internal dislocation that are occurring in the large former telecommunications monopolists. The contrast between the former security and the current uncertainty may help explain the decline in the employees attitudes and morale problems that have surfaced among telecommunications employees in many countries.

One of the objectives of this research is to compare the changes under way in employment relations in the telecommunications industry to those that have been occurring in other industries. There has been much debate in recent years concerning the nature and extent of change in labor-management relations (Kochan, Katz, and McKersie 1994). In the face of substantial union concessions and the decline of union membership levels in nearly all countries, it is possible to see this era as one involving a fundamental deterioration in employment conditions and an erosion in the influence of trade unions. On the other hand, the emergence of worker and union participation programs and the spread of more direct communication between workers and managers suggest that a more positive transformation may be under way in the process and outcomes of labor-management relations.

To date, the rich debates about these trends have primarily relied on evidence drawn from changes that have been occurring in manufacturing industries. Furthermore, the evidence in these debates usually comes from only one country and focuses on changes that affect blue collar workers while conveying little about what is happening to the work and employment conditions of office, technical, or managerial employees. Given the dearth of previous research on this and other service industries, one of the central objectives of this volume is to provide a clear description of the specific job duties and tasks performed by employees in the telecommunications services industry and how these are changing.

By focusing on one industry, as this book does, the analysis controls for the influence of many common trends in technology and product markets. This allows the researchers to identify the critical variations that appear across countries (and across companies and regions within some countries) and the factors such as public policies, institutions, and managerial or union strategies that contribute to variations in outcomes.

Research Design

The chapters that follow focus on understanding the work practices in the telecommunications services industry: work organization, training, compensation, employment security, and workplace governance (including union membership, union strategies, and collective bargaining structure). The chapters analyze these practices and the extent and causes of their diversity within and across countries. The analysis includes comparisons between recent and traditional work practices, traditional practices being those that typically prevailed over the post–World War II period up to the mid-1980s. A key analytic question guiding the research involves explaining *why* practices have or have not changed. The work practices are defined more fully in the appendix to this chapter.

Analysis in this volume focuses on work practices in the following occupations with the respective basic tasks described below:

(1) Operators provide directory assistance and information to telephone callers.
(2) Field service technicians install, repair, and construct the telephone network.
(3) Customer service representatives are in charge of billing, taking orders, and responding to customer-reported problems.
(4) Computer technicians and network programmers are in charge of the software that runs the network and the internal information systems of the telecommunications services companies.
(5) Middle managers coordinate and oversee the activities of the above employees.

As is typical of service industries, many of the employees in the telecommunications services industry perform "white collar" tasks that involve a heavy dose of analytic skills and little manual labor. This is one reason why the traditional American-style distinction between "industrial relations" and "human resource management," the former concerning blue collar issues and the latter dealing with white collar and managerial issues, is not clearly drawn in this industry. At the same time, industrial relations issues narrowly defined (such as the extent of strikes and the structure of collective bargaining) still clearly do matter in telecommunications, in part because such a large fraction of the white and blue collar work force is unionized.

The authors of the country chapters are affiliated with the International Industrial Relations and Human Resource Network, a project organized by scholars at the Massachusetts Institute of Technology. The aim of the project is to make a comparative assessment of the evolution of employment relations with a particular focus on the interaction between economic restructuring and work practices. A description of the overall project and overview country analyses are provided in *Employment Relations in a Changing World Economy*.[3] The International Industrial Relations and Human Resource Network extended its initial national comparative program of research through projects on specific industries for such analysis provides the basis for clear international comparisons of the extent of change in work practices.[4]

The changes occurring in work practices in the telecommunications services industry are being heavily influenced by changes occurring in the economic and regulatory environment in each country. For this reason

3. See Locke, Kochan, and Piore 1995.
4. The other study teams are analyzing developments in the following industries: airlines, banking, motor vehicles, and steel.

each of the country chapters (and our overview of the key findings in the country reports) starts with a discussion of the changing nature of the telecommunication industry's environmental context.

The Changing Environmental Context: Regulatory, Market, and Technological Factors

Over the last ten years in all the countries a shift has been occurring away from the provision of telecommunications services by a monopoly and heavily regulated organization to a more competitive environment with a number of telecommunications service providers. Furthermore, in all countries (although in a variety of ways) the former monopolist is being privatized and diversified beyond voice into a range of telecommunications and information services.

In recent years the services provided over the telephone lines have broadened to include a wide variety of information services. Furthermore, the possibility of transmitting television signals along with telephone messages (and other information services) over a common line has led to merger discussions between companies that provide cable television and telephone services. The interactive capabilities of fiber optic network communication has also greatly expanded as a result of recent technological developments in network software.

Both the starting points and pace of deregulation vary across countries. In some countries (e.g., Germany) the starting point was a monopoly entity that formed part of the post office; in other countries (e.g., Korea, Mexico, and the United Kingdom), heavy government regulation of prices, investments, and market entry led to "political contingencies" in decision making of the sort well illustrated by the British case. As of the mid-1990s, international telephone services in each country are typically provided by a number of private firms, while the extent of recent new entry into the within-country telephone service market varies from substantial in the United Kingdom and United States to none (yet) in Germany, Italy, Korea, Mexico, and Norway. Simultaneously, new entrants and rapid growth have spread in the cellular telephone sector while competition and a very wide range of new products appear in the information services market.

The timing and degree to which markets have been opened varies substantially across countries and these variations affect the extent to which employment levels and work practices are being adjusted in the former monopoly telecommunications firms. Where competition has become particularly open, (e.g., United Kingdom and United States) greater change appears in employment relations processes and outcomes while in countries where the traditional monopolists retains substantial protection (as in Germany), there is less pressure for change. At the same time, even in Germany and in other countries where the telecommunications market is still relatively protected, pressures are mounting as privatization and freer entry to the industry are proceeding and further regulation is anticipated.

This association between the intensity of competitive pressure and the extent of change in work practices is similar to what occurred in manufacturing industries. However, as mentioned earlier, the international leader and the laggard countries in the telecommunications services industry are the reverse of the comparative ordering in manufacturing industries in the 1980s.

One contextual factor that varies across countries and exerts important consequences on employment adjustment is the regulatory policy that determines whether companies that provide telephone service are also allowed to provide cable TV. The contrasting extreme cases are the United Kingdom and Germany. In the United Kingdom, British Telecom (BT) is not allowed entry into the cable TV market while in Germany, Deutsche Telekom (DT) retains a monopoly on cable TV provision (and ranks as the world's largest provider of cable TV). With a sizable number of excess employees due to cost cutting and technologically driven productivity improvements, all telecommunications services companies have been under pressure to transfer employees either within the organization or to subsidiaries. As a result of its protected monopoly status, DT has the opportunity to shift redundant employees from its telephone service side to expanding cable TV operations and related subsidiaries. BT, on the other hand, has foregone such transfer opportunities and can only shift employees across a more limited range of service-related lines of business. In this way a regulatory policy exerts a crucial influence on employment security and transfer opportunities.

In all countries the spread of digital switching and fiber optics both facilitates the entry of new competitors and promotes the development and diversification of telecommunications service products. New technology also is spurring the centralization and consolidation of work as well as extending managerial control and electronic monitoring procedures. Even in the face of the construction of a number of digitized (often fiber optic) telephone networks by rival firms, the continuing importance of the telephone network exerts a critical centralizing influence on the industry and on corporate structure.

Faced with new competitors and with pressures for cost reduction and service quality improvements, the former telecommunications monopolists are altering their organizational structures in very similar ways across the ten countries. These firms typically have adopted a three-part structure with separate divisions providing telephone services to residential customers and business customers, and the third division concerned with the construction, operation, and maintenance of the core telephone network. In addition, the former monopolists have created new and often rapidly expanding business units that deal with cellular phones, international business, and information services.

A similarity also appears across the former telecommunications monopolists in the way they have been oscillating between organizational centralization and decentralization since the late 1980s. BT provides a particularly telling illustration of unsuccessful efforts to decentralize corporate structure, in that case down to the district level, and subsequent recentralization (Chapter 2). It was the continuing importance of the basic network and the resulting need to standardize and coordinate corporate policies that led to the subsequent recentralization of BT. This experience provides evidence of the important role that advances in network technology continue to exert as a force guiding corporate structures and strategies in the telecommunications services industry.

The Changes Occurring in the Five Key Work Practices

Pressure for cost savings, flexibility, and more customer-oriented service provision is shaping the changes occurring in work and employment relations. Our discussion of the specific changes that are being made to key work practices begins by examining employment security since this is such a critical issue in so many countries and interacts with other changes occurring in work practices.

Employment Security

Cost pressures are leading the telecommunications services companies in all countries to increase the pace and intensity of the work of managers as well as nonmanagerial employees. The ensuing productivity increases are in turn producing reductions in employment, although in a few countries continuing growth in the overall demand for services is leading to employment growth even in the face of work intensification (e.g., Germany, Italy, Korea, and Mexico). The more typical outcome of cost cutting is the downsizing of the previous monopoly carriers, and particularly large downsizing has been occurring in the United Kingdom and United States.

Downsizing is such a controversial issue in many countries because of the large numbers of employees involved and because it contrasts with the extreme employment security that telecommunications services employees had enjoyed for so long. In the traditional telecommunications monopolies employees had received "cradle to grave" employment security. Even where new technologies had in the past increased productivity and reduced staffing or employment levels (as had frequently occurred in operator services) growth in demand allowed companies to retrain and transfer employees into new occupations. However, by the late 1980s, large-scale employment reductions were occurring at companies such as BT and AT&T (and were beginning at the regional Bell operating companies (RBOCs) in the United States). It is interesting to note that even in the Anglo-Saxon countries, employment reductions have been, and continue to be, accomplished through early retirements, voluntary severance programs, and the expansion of internal transfers, with the exception of some involuntary layoffs at AT&T.

In Germany many DT employees benefit from the continuing civil service (Beamte) protections that prevent separations and limit transfers, while at Nippon Telephone and Telegraph (NTT) the enterprise union and management negotiated an employment security agreement prior to the start of privatization. The negotiated agreement in Japan includes a number of core principles, one of them being the continuation of employment security. While this agreement provides flexibility in the deployment of personnel by making internal transfers easier and allowing transfers to new subsidiaries, transferred employees are guaranteed maintenance of their pay level and many other employment conditions. Negotiated employment security agreements also appear in Italy, Mexico, Norway, and some U.S. RBOCs.

In all countries the number of internal transfers within the former telecommunications monopolists have been increasing dramatically and a sizable number of employees in these firms are being asked to transfer to new subsidiaries in information services and other new (or expanding) lines of business. An important employment relations issue is the extent to which union representation rights carry over into these new subsidiaries (policies vary within and across countries). In addition, unions spend much effort trying to keep earnings and other employment conditions in these subsidiaries at the same level as conditions in the former monopolists to prevent an undercutting of employment standards.

Where they are available, attitude surveys reveal that employees feel threatened by the increased employment and career insecurity and often resent management as a result (as in the Australia, Norway, and the United States). Statistical analysis of U.S. data shows that the understaffing and loss of job security associated with downsizing have significant negative effects on employee job satisfaction and employee commitment to the company (Chapter 1). Employee morale has declined even in countries such as Norway where employees did not face involuntary layoffs and the unions are provided with explicit consultation rights through national legislation.

Even in the face of the widespread deterioration in employee morale, however, there are no indications of increased voluntary quits, formal grievance filing, or wildcat strike action. Thus, although employees are clearly upset by insecurity and the adjustment costs they bear, firms are not confronting significant formal protests and other obvious direct costs as a result of their actions. This may help explain why telecommunications firms across countries continue to push the costs of adjustment onto employees and do not engage in radical efforts to redesign work in ways that make jobs more satisfying to employees.

Major strikes have occurred in a few instances, as at BT and NYNEX (a U.S. RBOC). Yet, there has been no sharp increase in formal strike action in the telecommunications services industry in recent years.

It will be interesting to see whether future research turns up evidence that declines in employee morale negatively affect productivity and if so, whether countries such as Germany benefit from the extensive employment security that is provided to their telecommunications services employees. At this point in time, data is not available to compare the size, causes, or consequences of declining employee morale across countries. Nevertheless, it does appear that the presence of downsizing and heightened employee insecurity run counter to, and to some extent undermine, employer efforts to solicit employee cooperation in productivity and quality improvement.

While the former monopolists are downsizing, the many new entrant firms to the telecommunications services industry simultaneously have been expanding employment. What has happened to total employment in the telecommunications services industry? Given the rapidly changing nature and boundaries of the information services side of the telecommunications services industry, it is difficult to define the industry precisely, let alone acquire longitudinal aggregate employment data for the industry. Nevertheless, figures in the country chapters suggest that total industry employment has been declining slightly over the last ten years as a result of technologically-induced productivity improvements (which, for example, dramatically reduced the need for operators) and productivity improvements achieved through reengineering and other workplace restructuring.[5]

Work Organization

Faced with pressure to reduce costs and assisted by technological changes, the former telecommunications monopolists are taking a number of steps to centralize and consolidate work. In most countries mega service centers have been created for operator services, network maintenance, and customer services. Technology often extends management's ability to monitor and control employee job performance (through, for example, handheld computers used by network technicians to input data as they complete projects). This also appears in the spread of electronic monitoring and automatic call distribution systems used for customer service representatives in many countries. No-fault and self-diagnostic digital switches require much less maintenance which produces declines in the number of field service technicians, a relatively highly skilled job. Furthermore, in many cases the network repair work that remains becomes more routine (through, for example, the introduction of plug-in replacement modules) and in some cases this work can now be performed by clerical employees. Technology also deskills the work of operators through the spread of expert systems, computer-generated voice messages, and "split calls" (in the latter example, one operator starts an informational request and then the call is passed on to another operator for the answer). Another example of deskilling is occurring in customer services through the splitting of sales and order tasks.

All of the above extends the previous tradition of highly fragmented, bureaucratic, and hierarchical work found in the telecommunications monopolists in the past. Keefe and Batt aptly refer to the "functional silos" that dominated the Bell System in the past and continue to play a significant role even in the face of some countermovements in work redesign. The other chapters in this volume point out that the functional-silo organizational structure was also typical of the telecommunications monopolists in the other countries in the past and continues to dominate.

Supervisors and managers receive increased monitoring and control responsibilities and their span of control (i.e., number of supervised employees) increases both via the changes in work organization described above and through the reductions in manning levels that are achieved through the reengineering of supervisory and managerial work. It is not

5. Evidence of this issue appears in the U.S. and Italian chapters.

surprising that the supervisors and managers that survive the headcount reductions experience significant increases in their own work pace. Where attitude surveys are available they show that supervisors and managers complain of overwork, resent higher managers, and express less confidence in the abilities of top management.[6]

This grim picture of increasingly fragmented and deskilled work does not describe the changes in work organization experienced by all telecommunications services employees. The country chapters cite a number of examples of movements in the other direction toward deeper skills and broader knowledge. For instance, Owen Darbishire reports that there is a wider variety of work and required skills for many technicians in Germany as a result of the proliferation of products. In some countries (such as Norway) the upskilling of customer service representatives has come through the introduction of "universal" representatives who handle a variety of tasks.[7]

Shifts in the composition of employment also have contributed to upskilling over the last ten years through increases in the number and share of computer technicians, managers, and professionals, as reported in Italy. Computer programming skills are increasingly required in "manual" and managerial jobs.

Increased concern for service quality and intensification of competitive pressures also are contributing to significant increases in the absolute number of, and share of, staff in marketing and sales. Even field service technicians are now expected to market products and services during their repair visits. While this example may involve increases in the pace of work for technicians, as they take on sales tasks along with the other things they are normally expected to do, this shift in work patterns also involves a broadening of job responsibilities.

The varied nature of the effects of technology and corporate and workplace reorganization on skill levels in this industry suggests that the search for a simple answer to the question of whether upskilling or deskilling is occurring is naive. In this industry, changes in skill level differ by job, occupation, location, and firm, and by industry segment. As the country chapters reveal, these variable effects are produced by the diverse

6. The deterioration of middle managers' morale in the face of downsizing and re-engineering is also reported in other industries. See Katz (forthcoming) for a review of the evidence.

7. In the United States the much-discussed experiment with universal customer service representatives at US West was actually never implemented in the face of downsizing and re-engineering at that company (see Chapter 1).

nature of technological and other structural changes and by diverse responses by managers and employees.[8]

In some cases the addition of new job tasks and skills is associated with the introduction of team forms of work organization. The chapters on Italy and the United States provide examples of the introduction of this work innovation for field service technicians and customer service representatives. There are numerous other less formal efforts to increase employee participation in decision making in many countries including Australia, Canada, Mexico, and Norway.

The chapters for Germany, Norway, and the United States reveal that field service technicians traditionally possessed a relatively high degree of autonomy and discretion in their work. Thus these workers always to some extent had team-like work relationships. This was particularly true for workers in rural and sparsely populated areas where it did not make economic sense to have a high degree of job specialization and direct supervision. At the same time, as the U.S. case shows, even for technicians the introduction of formal team systems does lead to a further broadening of job responsibilities and increases in worker autonomy. Team systems and other participatory processes also extend the amount of facilitating and coaching carried out by supervisors and thereby enlarge the skills required in those jobs.

The U.S. chapter provides evidence that workers (and their supervisors) generally value team systems and prefer that system to traditional work organization. Workers benefit from relief from the excessive supervision historically found in the industry; supervisors shed the more routine and monotonous parts of their jobs. The data also show that firms appear to benefit from teams both through better performance and cost savings. In multivariate statistical analysis, team membership is a significant predictor of work processes such as quality monitoring, internal group learning, and cross-functional problem solving. The performance effects of teams do appear to vary across occupational groups. Data from the United States shows that the objectively measurable effects of teams in customer services are through increased sales revenues, while network teams appear to absorb more supervisory functions, and this translates into indirect cost savings (Chapter 1). Future research is needed to see if these team performance effects generalize to other countries.

As the premium on service quality rises and the range of products and competitors increases, telecommunications services firms are striving for

8. See Milkman and Pullman 1991 for evidence of similar diverse effects from technological change in the auto industry.

ways beyond job reorganization to become more flexible and adaptable. To serve this end, firms are making greater use of subcontracting, outsourcing, and more flexible work schedules (for example, in Italy and the United Kingdom).

Training

The changes in work organization described above are leading to many changes in training. For example, firms have made substantial investments in total quality and customer awareness training; they are also expanding career planning and development courses to help employees deal with the increased insecurity in employment. Early retirement programs typically now include assistance in identifying appropriate openings elsewhere in the organization, or in some cases, outplacement assistance and tuition to train for new occupations. A number of companies have recently introduced skill banks and other systems to identify the current skill makeup and skill vacancies within organizations as a way of both meeting organizational needs and assisting internal transfers (for example, Italy and the United States). Many training programs now include training in "soft" or behavioral skills to extend total quality efforts, team working, or a customer orientation.

The digitalization of the network contributes to an increase in the importance of computer programming skills, as evidenced by the fact that employees in numerous job positions now have to acquire such skills in order to carry out their jobs, and training is often used to assist in that skill acquisition process. Technician training courses are being modified to help those employees adjust to a more rapid pace of technological change (see, for example, Chapter 2). The career paths of technicians also are being altered in some countries through an end to the previous practice of exclusive internal recruitment and the introduction of direct recruitment into openings that appear in highly ranked grades (as in the United Kingdom).

Compensation

Even where downsizing has been extensive, telecommunications services employees have received solid increases in their wage rates over the previous ten years. By contrast, in a number of countries fringe benefits, and particularly medical benefits, have been cut (as in the United States). The wage increases contrast with the wage cuts or pay freezes that occurred in manufacturing industries in many countries during the same time period. The relatively better treatment of telecommunications employees can be explained by the fact that the former telecommunications monopolists maintained a high degree of market power and continued to report positive profits in all countries. Unlike the manufacturing sector, the telecommunications services industry did not witness corporate bankruptcies; rather the widespread corporate downsizing and restructuring were preventative strategies adopted in anticipation of heightened competition. Furthermore, the telecommunications services industry is relatively highly unionized and even in the face of some erosion in their membership, the telecommunications unions remain quite strong and influential. In addition, the continuation of political contingencies and a strong public sector legacy contribute to the relatively favorable treatment received by telecommunications employees.

In most countries the use of performance-related ("contingent") pay has increased, although the extent of that increase, the form it takes, and the employees affected, all vary much across countries. In Australia, Germany, and Italy performance-related pay has been introduced for nonmanagerial telecommunications services employees during the previous ten years. Unions generally have opposed performance-related pay as a substitute for base pay increases, although the previous examples illustrate that union opposition to contingent compensation has not stopped its spread. In most countries only managers receive performance-related pay, often in the form of annual bonuses, profit sharing, and/or stock ownership. In all countries these pay methods apply most heavily to senior executives. Even where performance-related pay is provided to managers, and especially where it is paid to nonmanagerial employees, contingent pay has not become a large share of total employee compensation. Research assessing whether contingent compensation leads to improvements in service provision or motivation, as the companies hope, is not available.

In some countries firms are experimenting with "packages" of new work practices that include more contingent compensation, employee security, increased training, team systems, and increased union and employee involvement in shop floor decisions. This package appears in parts of the Australian, Canadian, Italian, and Norwegian, and United States (some RBOCs) telecommunications services industries. This new package is very similar to the package of new work practices that began to be introduced earlier into a variety of manufacturing firms and countries.

As in manufacturing, the new package of work practices being introduced into the telecommunications services sector has an internal logic—the new practices reinforce one another. For example, the use of work teams requires more extensive training and fits well with contingent compensation. Also, as in manufacturing, telecommunications employees appear to enjoy the new package although there are many adjustment problems and unions often struggle to find their place in the new workplace systems. At the same time, the use of these new practices is still highly experimental and the practices affect only a small fraction of employees in the telecommunications industry in any country.

The reasons for the slow diffusion of the new team and participation-oriented work practice packages in this industry appear to be similar to the explanations for the equally slow diffusion in manufacturing. These reasons include the short time horizons and financial pressures on senior managers as well as resistance from middle managers and difficulties in linking the new work practices with related changes in business practices. In telecommunications services, large corporate downsizings make the introduction of new team- and participation-oriented practices particularly difficult. Perhaps most importantly, the success experienced to date in the pattern-leading countries (the United Kingdom and United States) of a contrasting cost-cutting strategy diminishes managements' interest in team- and participation-oriented reform.

Governance

The telecommunications services monopolies in all the countries were heavily unionized in the past, and unions continue to play a major role among these firms in all countries. In a number of countries, unions represent nearly all employees below the ranks of senior management (as in Australia, Germany, Italy, Korea, and Norway). In the United States, in contrast, the "occupational" work forces of the telecommunications services companies (AT&T and the RBOCs) are nearly completely unionized, but computer technicians, and professional and managerial employees are not represented by unions. Union representation in this industry has declined in the United States as employment has shifted to the unorganized occupations; and some evidence exists that management also frequently reclassifies jobs in order to reduce union representation. That is, companies have sought to limit unionization of technical and professional employees by defining their jobs as "managerial" and therefore, by definition exempt from coverage by collective bargaining laws. Yet, even in the United States, which represents the low point in unionization across countries in the telecommunications services industry, union membership levels are high when compared to other industries, on average over 50 percent in the former Bell companies which continue to be the dominant employers.

Although the share of unionized employees in the telecommunications services industry remains relatively high, this share has declined over the least ten years in all countries, including those countries where the former telecommunications monopolist remains completely organized. This decline in representation has come through the entry and expansion of nonunion companies in the industry, including the growth of nonunion subsidiaries of the former telecommunications monopolists. Even in Japan some of the new subsidiaries of NTT are not unionized. Furthermore, many of the largest new entrant firms to the telecommunications services industry are not unionized. For example, in Australia, the United Kingdom, and the United States the large new companies providing international telephone services (respectively Optus, Mercury, and MCI) do not negotiate labor contracts with unions.

Australia provides an interesting illustration of how the new nonunion entrant, Optus, uses human resource policies that involve greater flexibility and a more individualized focus. Optus's policies include extensive communication between management and employees on an individual basis, a heavy role for performance appraisal, the linking of pay to company performance, relatively flexible job definitions, and the promotion of a strong corporate culture of employee loyalty and commitment. Optus thus possesses many of the characteristics of the sophisticated nonunion human resource management practices that appear in large corporations in Canada, the United Kingdom, the United States, and in other Australian industries. Thus the expansion of nonunion entrants is producing greater variation in employment practices in the telecommunications industry, not only because the new firms are nonunion, but because these firms' work practices differ from those used in the traditional union firms.

In a number of countries such as Australia, Italy, and the United Kingdom, unions have seen their influence decline through the growth of individual ("personal") contracts for managers and, to a lesser degree, for sales staffs—employees who previously had their compensation set through collective bargaining contracts. The telecommunications services firms also are promoting an individualization of employment conditions through more direct communication with employees; individual career planning; and the spread of performance appraisal, merit based, and other forms of individualized compensation.

More direct involvement in employment relations issues by operating managers is reported in many countries including Australia, Canada, the United Kingdom, and the United States. Operating managers are acquiring increased responsibility for employment relations in part as a result of the downsizing of industrial relations staffs and also as a consequence of efforts to decentralize decision making in organizations to make them more flexible and customer oriented.

The latter interact with efforts to shift decision making authority downward inside the former telecommunications monopolists. In the United States, for example, at AT&T under the banner of the "Future of the Workplace," operating managers now meet with union representatives (and employees) to discuss business-unit issues. Similar processes are mentioned in the Australian and Canadian country reports.

The emergence of these business-unit-level discussions of employment relations matters contributes to the decentralization that is occurring in the structure of collective bargaining in a number of countries. The decentralization of decision making authority is contributing to increased variation in work practices as localized decision makers derive particular solutions to the service problems they confront. A decentralization of collective bargaining also appears through increased variation in employment conditions across the subsidiaries of the former telecommunications monopolists and through increased site-by-site variation in collectively bargained outcomes across the unionized companies that provide telecommunications services (as in Australia, Canada, the United Kingdom, and the United States).

At the same time, although management often speaks about the need for wide variation in employment terms across business units and subsidiaries, they do not take advantage of more decentralized collective bargaining to push for variation as hard as one might expect from their rhetoric. In the United Kingdom early efforts at decentralized bargaining did not work out so favorably for management (particularly given the need to maintain a coordinated telephone network and standard services). Management at BT and elsewhere has come to appreciate more fully the stabilization and predictability provided by pattern bargaining and a continuing relatively high degree of standardization in employment conditions across workers and collective bargaining agreements. In particular, standardization (and centralization) satisfy the pressures for coordination and consistency arising from the continuing role played by the core telecommunications network.

Many of the telecommunications monopolists traditionally had maintained a geographic organizational structure that fit with their national provision of within-country telephone services. As part of reengineering initiatives, the organizational structures of the former monopolists are being reoriented away from geographically determined units and toward the basic three divisional and business-unit-oriented structure discussed earlier. In this process many of the former monopolists are consolidating former geographic units which, in turn, is leading to consolidations and centralization in the respective collective bargaining structures. For example, a number of the RBOCs in the United States have been merging state-based bargaining structures into regional ones. This centralization serves as a counter-movement that contrasts with the broader decentralization in bargaining structures discussed earlier.

The expansion of more direct forms of communication between management and employees, the increased role for operating managers in employment relations issues, and the decentralization of collective bargaining in the telecommunications services industry bears a strong resemblance to events that started to occur in manufacturing industries in many countries in the 1980s and continue in recent years. The outcome of these changes for telecommunications employees, as mentioned above, so far typically has been less severe when compared to the experiences of manufacturing employees, given the extensive voluntary severance payments and the absence of wage cuts in telecommunications firms.

The effects of corporate and employment relations restructuring, however, has been more troubling for telecommunications unions. The decline of union membership, the spread of more direct forms of communication between individual employees and management, and the use of personalized employment policies all raise the specter of a "marginalization" of union influence in the telecommunications services sector. This fear is elevated by union concerns that team and other new forms of work reorganization will either expressly or indirectly erode worker solidarity and union loyalty.

Although union marginalization, in fact, is occurring to some extent in Australia, Canada, the United Kingdom, and the United States, across countries there is significant variation in how unions are responding to managerial initiatives. In some countries unions are affecting the restructuring of the former telecommunications monopolists through political lobbying and involvement in strategic-level decision making. Union influence on corporate strategic plans is strongest in the labor-mediated countries and in Mexico. In Mexico, the unions' positive policies regarding the restructuring of the telecommunications industry are being hailed as a new model for union activism. While in Japan the telecommunications workers union continues to engage in extensive discussions with company and government officials regarding the nature and timing of industry deregulation.

Where the telecommunications services provider was formally a part of the public sector (Germany) or a quasi-private entity (Italy, Japan, and Norway), employment relations traditionally followed a public-sector pattern. As privatization has proceeded in those countries, the unions representing telecommunications services employees have been expressing differing preferences regarding whether they should continue to follow public-sector employment relations practices. In Japan, for example, the telecommunications union early on resented the fact that as part of the public-sector model the union was denied both the right to negotiate directly over pay rates and the right to strike. Privatization of NTT was attractive to the union in large part because it was viewed as a prerequisite for altering those rights. As the union hoped, with privatization the union at NTT has received the right to bargain over pay, and has succeeded in bringing wage rates into alignment with major private sector settlements in recent years. Along with the shift to private-sector employment relations status, however, the union has had to accept other features of Japanese private-sector employment relations, such as a heavy role for performance appraisal.

The German union representing employees at DT, in contrast, does not favor a shift to private-sector status, given the substantial benefits its members receive if they have civil service (Beamte) status and given the pay and other gains negotiated in recent years by the pattern-setting unions in the German public sector. Meanwhile, the union representing Korean telecommunications services employees has been expressing disfavor with their public-sector-like representation rights. It will be interesting to see whether, and if so, how, the representation rights of these unions change as deregulation of the telecommunications services sector proceeds even further.

Converging Divergences

A common (converging) tendency across the telecommunications service industries of the ten countries is increased variation (divergences) in employment relations. This concluding section draws from the evidence summarized above to examine the nature and consequences (particularly for employees) of the increasing divergences that appear in employment relations within and across countries and the role that institutions have played in shaping this variation.[9]

A key source of increased variation across countries in employment relations in the telecommunications services sector is the growth of non-

9. A comparison of the increased variation in employment relations that is appearing in telecommunications and other industries across countries is provided in Darbishire and Katz (in process).

union employment systems in an industry that traditionally was nearly completely unionized. The deregulation of telephone service provision has spurred the entry of nonunion competitors in a number of countries even in the core sections of the industry involved with the transmission of telephone calls. Examples of this trend are the entry and expansion of Optus in Australia, Mercury in the United Kingdom, and MCI in the United States. This is one of the ways the English-speaking countries have led the way in industry restructuring in telecommunications services. Yet, it is telling to note that even in Japan, where deregulation in the telecommunications service sector has been less extensive than that in the English-speaking countries, nonunion "common carriers" have greatly expanded and now provide a competitive challenge to NTT. The traditional telecommunications monopolists also have increased the outsourcing of service and equipment purchases in all of the countries analyzed in this volume and this provides another important avenue throughout which nonunion employment has grown as many of the suppliers to the former monopolists are nonunion.

It is not just the nonunion status of many of the expanding nonunion firms in telecommunications services that has led to increased variation in employment relations. In many ways the work practices in the nonunion firms differ from the practices found in the traditional monopolists and there is significant variation in the employment practices used *across* the growing nonunion sector in telecommunications services. Regarding the latter, on the one hand there are firms such as Optus in Australia that use extensive communication strategies and pay systems emphasizing individual contribution rather than pay systems based on the rule (and often seniority), which were characteristic of the unionized former telecommunications monopolists. There is also mention in a number of the country reports of small supplier companies in telecommunications services that utilize less sophisticated and more traditional "bureaucratic" personnel practices.

In a number of countries there is also an increased variety of work practices *within* the union sector.[10] For example, some of the RBOCs in the United States are pursuing participatory strategies (including experiments with team systems) in contrast to other RBOCs that have continued traditional work organization. Furthermore, wide variation in the tenor of labor-management relations appears across the union sector in Canada and the U.S. RBOCs.

10. Increased variation in the corporate and industrial relations restructuring strategies adopted across firms is noted in Locke 1992. More generally, my claims in this section provide an extension of the arguments raised by Richard Locke.

Increased variation in work practices also shows up in union and non-union telecommunications firms in the ten countries due to the increased variation in shop floor practices within and across firms. Some of this shop floor variation is associated with the spread of employee involvement processes and other informal communications policies that are shifting decision making responsibility downward to the workforce. In this industry, as in others, the decentralization of authority has spurred increased variation in work practices as workers now individually, or in some cases in groups, develop solutions to everyday work problems that are tailored to their needs or to the specifics of a problem (Katz 1993). Although there have been recent steps to recentralize the formal conduct of industrial relations in some of the former monopolists (as in Australia's Telstra), there is no evidence that this recentralization has slowed the growth in shop floor work practice variation.

Public policies and industrial relations institutions have shaped the extent and nature of the variation in employment relations across the telecommunications industries of the ten countries. Those countries with the most extensive deregulation of the telecommunications industry have experienced the greatest entry of nonunion firms challenging the former monopolists in the telecommunications services market. Furthermore, labor market policies also influence the extent of variation appearing in employment relations. In Germany, for example, national codetermination laws and provisions that extend collectively negotiated terms to nonunion firms have limited the degree to which low wage competition can challenge the former monopolist (DT). Similarly, in Australia, the legal framework of pay awards and wage tribunals limits the extent to which nonunion (or union) competitors can utilize work practices that differ from those used at Telstra.

Institutional factors also affect the work practices used within the still dominant former monopolists. For example, where a labor-mediated restructuring strategy dominates, employees in the former monopolists benefit from the employment security provided (in somewhat different forms) through either national legislation or collectively bargained agreements. In those countries, although employees have increasingly faced job and locational transfers, they have not confronted involuntary layoffs of the sort occurring at AT&T in the United States. And the terms of the increasingly common transfers and relocations vary significantly across the former monopolists. Employees in Japan, for example, are guaranteed no loss in earnings or deterioration in other benefits, a guarantee not afforded to all transferred employees in the United States.

Even in the face of the increased variation appearing within their telecommunications industries, in some of the countries the employment systems found in the telecommunications sector have become more similar to the employment relations found in the respective country's private sector (which has reduced the within-country variation in employment relations). In Japan, for example, the privatization of NTT has led to the introduction of performance appraisal and merit pay and thereby made NTT's work practices more similar to the practices found in large private-sector firms in Japan. Likewise, in Germany, where the employment practices at DT were special because of the influence of public-sector procedures, such as the protections afforded DT's civil service employees, the deregulation of telecommunications services is shifting DT's employment practices so as to make them more similar to those commonly found in the private sector in Germany.

There is even a limited degree of international convergence in work practices in the telecommunications industry. This convergence appears in the common development in all ten countries of a package of work practices that includes pay for performance, team systems, increased informal involvement of employees in decision making, and more extensive direct communication between management and employees.[11] The evidence from the ten countries is that while within some work sites (often only a relatively small share of the employees in a given firm) this new package has developed, there is a more dominant trend toward increased variation in employment systems of the sort described above. The new package has not spread enough to force an international convergence in work practices, and there is also substantial variation in the specific terms of the new package in those places in which it has been adopted.

The ten country chapters show that the telecommunications service sector continues to undergo extensive restructuring. Where all this restructuring will lead is not obvious. At this point it appears that the United States' model of technology and market-driven restructuring is serving as a pattern, although it remains unclear exactly where the telecommunications industries in the English-speaking countries themselves are heading, given the pace of regulatory changes, corporate mergers, and international alliances occurring in those countries.

Employment relations continue to be critically affected by the massive reorganizations occurring in industry and corporate structures and competitive relations. Some employees have faced increased job fragmentation and deskilling while others have seen their duties broaden. A number

11. The classic argument that convergence in employment relations is driven by industrialization is found in Kerr et al. 1964.

of employees have been induced to take early retirement or to pursue retraining as a way to improve their labor market prospects. Many employees are being asked to change what they do and often where they do it. Meanwhile, the traditionally strong unions in this industry have seen their coverage decline and their role challenged by new communication policies and new forms of work organization.

The uncertainty surrounding the structures and strategies within this industry make it especially difficult to predict the future of employment relations. At this point it appears that the variation in employment relations that has surfaced is likely to persist (and probably expand). Employees, unionists, managers, and government policy makers will have to make their way through this more diverse array of employment practices and decide whether, and how, to alter the growing variation in employment relations.

Appendix: Definitions of Key Work Practices

This appendix provides more detailed definitions and research questions for the five key practices analyzed in each of the country chapters.

Work Organization

The central question is whether work is organized in a narrow, tightly circumscribed "Tayloristic" or "job control" fashion or in a more flexible and group-based form. The former typically involves narrow job descriptions, clear lines of demarcation between individual jobs, and a separation of the execution of work from the conception of how the work is to be done. The latter often involves broader jobs and team work systems. The extent and nature of employee participation in decision making at the workplace is closely related to the question of work organization and thus data on participation processes are also analyzed.

Skill Formation, Training, and Development

This topic relates to the processes through which employees acquire skills on their jobs and over the course of their careers. The focus is on formal and informal training, career progression, and related organizational and institutional practices. Although the primary focus is on how skills are developed once individuals have completed their formal education and entered the labor market, the relationships between the formal education system and other institutions and practices involved in skill development also are considered. The extent to which training and skill development are transferable across jobs, employers, occupations, and industries also is assessed. Finally, the extent to which the skill levels of the workforce are keeping up with changes in demand is analyzed.

Compensation: Levels, Forms, and Structures

A central question is whether compensation is becoming more "flexible" or "contingent." Contingent pay involves various methods used to relate compensation to variations in individual or corporate performance through incentives, merit pay, pay for skills, or enterprise-based profit sharing or stock ownership. Important questions concerning the structure of wages relate to the size and degree of change in the differentials across classes of employees (blue collar, white collar, managerial, and high level executives).

Wage level issues include how the wages of workers in a country compare to those in other countries and the trends in real wages for workers within each country.

Employment Security/Staffing Arrangement

The key issue involves the extent to which employment is becoming more or less stable over time. Are long term attachments to firms increasing or decreasing? Is the "contingent" (part-time, temporary, contract, immigrant, etc.) portion of the labor force growing or declining? How are labor force adjustments made by individual enterprises? To what extent are layoffs, severance payments, early retirements, or social plans used? What are the labor market experiences of those who lost jobs due to cyclical or structural changes in the past decade?

Governance

The central issue is how employment relations policies and practices fit into firm-level governance structures. To what extent, and how, are employee interests articulated in the strategy formulation and governance processes in the enterprise? What roles, if any, are played by unions, works councils, co-determination, human resources managers, or other processes or institutions in corporate governance? How does the status of employment relations as a managerial function rank compared to other managerial functions in areas such as finance, marketing, or manufacturing?

PART 1

Technology and Market-Driven Restructuring

Chapter 1

United States

Jeffrey H. Keefe and Rosemary Batt

The U.S. telecommunications industry is in turmoil as formerly separate industries converge on the global information superhighway. As a multimedia market place emerges, market boundaries are eroding among diverse information service suppliers that include the publishers of newspapers, periodicals, and books; studios that produce movies and television programs; video game makers and software developers; data and information services; and burglar alarm and security firms. New wireless and cable transmission technologies are changing the relative economic and technical advantages among the common carriers in local and long distance telephone services, cellular communications, broadcast television and radio, and cable television. New digital technologies create the potential for a myriad of interactive multimedia products as they simultaneously destroy the value of traditional telephone and television transmission networks. State and federal regulatory regimes are being dismantled to eliminate cross-subsidies in rate structures and to promote innovation and market incentives, sometimes through competitive markets but more often through unregulated oligopoly, duopoly, and even monopoly market structures. In response to this changing environment, telecommunications firms are restructuring, vertically and horizontally integrating and disaggregating, allying with former competitors, competing with former allies, and vigorously lobbying and litigating for market advantage. For investors, uncertainty and risk have replaced stability and guaranteed rates of return.

This chapter examines the tumultuous restructuring of the U.S. telecommunications common carriers as they escape from rate and entry regulation and compete in traditionally monopoly markets. The first section discusses changes in product markets and technology; the second, business strategy and structure and union strategy; the third, labor-management relations; and the fourth, work reorganization and internal labor markets. In the first section, we argue that the chief cost advantages in the long distance, local telephone, cable TV, and wireless telecommunications markets derive from the integration of their network systems. Network integration can still generate substantial economies of scale and scope that produce lower unit costs; and consumers prefer integrated service delivery. While new technologies have a centralizing thrust, however, the ultimate structure of the industry is uncertain, and depends also on the outcomes of current political and economic battles over market deregulation and reregulation. In the second section, we discuss the business strategies of major telecommunications companies which have led them to restructure their organizations. They are consolidating and centralizing their network operations and customer service organizations to achieve scale economies at the same time that they are developing segmented marketing strategies. This organizational structure creates a basic tension between productivity-enhancing centralization and market-responsive decentralization.

These recent organizational and technical consolidations have resulted in substantial employee displacement in an industry that formerly guaranteed employment security through carefully managed human resource planning, which we analyze in the third section of this chapter. Since its 1984 divestiture, AT&T has eliminated nearly 150,000 union-represented jobs, accounting for 60 percent of its union-represented work force. Between 1984 and 1992, the regional Bell companies reduced employment in their regulated telephone subsidiaries by 28 percent, eliminating 158,281 jobs. As the deregulation of local telephone and cable television services continues in the wake of the 1996 Telecommunications Act, the seven regional Bells and GTE have announced plans to eliminate over 100,000 jobs, approximately 20 percent of local telephone service employment, including the first layoffs at some of these companies since the Great Depression. Downsizing has led to the demoralization of the survivor work forces. In response, employment security has become the major concern in collective bargaining, which remains relatively centralized.

In the fourth section, we analyze more closely the ways in which companies have reorganized work and the implications for internal labor markets. Specifically, we argue that two competing approaches to work reorganization have significantly changed the internal labor market rules for managerial and nonmanagerial employees alike. The first approach relies on employee participation and labor-management partnerships to improve service quality through the redesign of jobs and human resource practices. The logic of this approach is that employees will provide better service if they have the opportunity to offer innovative solutions (employee participation), if they have the autonomy to meet customer needs (job redesign), and if they have the appropriate skills (education and training) and incentives (career opportunities, employment security, compensation) to make a commitment to the company. This approach implies that commitment is a two-way street: if the company shows its commitment to enhancing employees' jobs and careers, then they in turn will increase their efforts to make the company competitive. This approach has a decentralizing thrust because it relies on the talent and creativity of employees at the point of customer contact.

The second approach focuses on realizing scale economies and cutting costs through consolidations, new applications of technology, reengineering, and downsizing. It begins at the macro organizational level and relies on top management, consultants, and engineers to develop system-wide innovations. This approach relies on centralized decision making rather than decentralized discretion. Because changes in the design of jobs and human resource practices flow *as a consequence* of new technologies and organizational restructuring, companies do not make prior commitments to job enhancement or employment security. The two approaches are, therefore, in conflict. As the statistics on widespread downsizing suggest, at AT&T and the regional Bell companies, the second approach has dominated, and often undermined, the first. This turbulent employment environment stands in sharp contrast to the stability that most incumbent employees came to expect from their employers.

AT&T Divestiture, Deregulation, and Industrial Restructuring

Throughout most of the twentieth century the telephone service industry was regulated as a natural monopoly in a two-tiered federal and state regulatory system. Under regulation, AT&T's Bell System achieved the goal of universal telephone service for Americans before any other telephone system in the world. Competition was largely repudiated as an effective public policy tool. Competition in an earlier period (1894–1907) had produced an unnecessary duplication of telephone plant facilities in urban areas and was thought to have slowed the diffusion of telephone service by raising the cost of capital and by preventing the realization of system economies, both of which allowed for lower prices for basic service. Regulation rather than state ownership was a uniquely American solution to the problems raised by competitive productive inefficiencies or the natural monopoly problem.

Regulators sought to achieve efficiency, reliability, and universal service. Efficiency was principally realized through network scale economies, the nonduplication of telephone facilities, regulatory review of costs, and regulated pricing. Reliable high quality service was provided through a highly integrated network and a service-oriented workforce subject to regulatory review and sanction. Universal service was accomplished by subsidizing the price of basic telephone service and rate averaging, which reduced the rates for residential and rural customers.

Under Federal Communications Commission (FCC) regulation, AT&T functioned as the public network manager (Stone 1989). It provided all local companies access to the long distance network. The Communications Act of 1934 required local operating companies to serve everyone within their region. Federal and state regulators established a fair and reasonable rate of return and prevented entry into the market. Under this system 92 percent of American homes had telephones, and most Americans were satisfied with their service.

Cross-Subsidy Problems and Strategic Entry

The cross-subsidies in the rate structure, however, made the Bell System vulnerable to competitive entry. Long distance service and business equipment rental rates were deliberately set above their costs. The revenue surpluses were used to reduce the price of basic telephone service below its cost. This cross-subsidized rate structure, designed to promote universal service, also created strong incentives for outside firms to devise ways to enter the high-priced subsidy-generating markets. It also stimulated large consumers of the high-priced services to seek alternative sources of supply. Specifically, a concentrated group of large businesses in financial and computer services increasingly subsidized local rates for residential users. These large users became well organized into political action groups that supported MCI's challenge to the Bell System's long distance monopoly and blocked AT&T's efforts at Congressional reform of the federal Communications Act.

During the post–World War II period, long distance rates increasingly cross-subsidized local service; this increasing subsidy was largely disguised by the rapid productivity gains in the long distance network. By the mid-1970s, long distance rates paid for one-third of the local plant costs, while long distance service accounted for less than 8 percent of local plant usage; by 1980, long distance rates contributed two dollars to the cross-subsidy for each dollar it cost to operate the long distance network. Largely as a result of the subsidy, the inflation-adjusted average monthly local telephone bill fell by 29 percent during the 1970s (Teske 1990). At the same time, the increasing subsidies stiffened the resolve of major corporate long distance users to escape from the Bell System monopoly and the cross-subsidized rate structure.

Over the objections of the FCC and AT&T, MCI gained entry to the publicly switched long distance market through a federal court ruling in 1978. Once MCI entered this market, the cross-subsidy rate structure was doomed. Between 1982 and 1992, as the cross-subsidies were eliminated, prices for long distance telephone service declined by 40 percent and long distance calling volume more than doubled, while basic local residential service rates increased by more than 60 percent from $11.58 to $18.66.[1] Deregulation led to substantial economic gains for concentrated large corporate interests that are major users of the long distance network and widespread losses for residential consumers and former Bell System employees (Teske 1990). Not surprisingly, public opinion polls at the time of AT&T divestiture indicated that over 70 percent of telephone customers opposed the Bell System breakup.

The AT&T divestiture and telephone deregulation eliminated cross-subsidies in long distance and telecommunications markets, while it is eroding the cross-subsidized rate structure in local service. Consequently, the principal beneficiaries of deregulation have been large corporate telephone consumers. The elimination of the progressive cross-subsidization of telephone service has redistributed income away from residential consumers to large corporations. Residential consumers pay relatively more for their telephone service than they would have under regulation; however, telephone rates continue to increase at a rate considerably below the rate of inflation. In the period 1982 to 1992 the average annual price increase in telephone service was 2.6 percent—considerably below the 4.7 percent average annual rate of increase for the Consumer Price Index (FCC 1994, table 8.2, p. 302).

1. However, telephone service has expanded to 93.8% of U.S. households and remains relatively fixed at 2% of consumer expenditures.

The Integrated System of Telecommunications Services Production

The production of telecommunications is inherently systemic in nature. The more participants in the telecommunication system, the more communications opportunities are afforded any participant. By providing universal communications services, a telecommunications network greatly enhances its value to all subscribers. However, to build such a network requires considerable technological integration and compatibility among all its elements (Rosenberg 1994). Each service innovation only becomes feasible when it can be technically integrated into the existing network in an economical way.

By continuously achieving new economies of system, the telecommunications services industry has led all service industries in productivity growth in the post–World War II period. During the Bell System era, between 1950 and 1984, labor productivity growth in telecommunications services averaged 6 percent annually, and during the last decade of the Bell System the annual rate of productivity growth rose to 6.9 percent. Pre-divestiture econometric studies consistently demonstrated overall economies of scale in the network, specific output economies of scale, single supplier cost advantages, and economies of scope at AT&T and Bell of Canada (Kiss and Lefebvre 1987), each contributing to lower unit costs and declining real prices of telephone services. Since 1935 prices for telephone service rose at half the annual rate of consumer prices (2.1% compared to 4.2%).

Since divestiture, however, productivity growth has significantly fallen below its postwar trend in telecommunication services. Using three different output measures, alternative calculations show that annual labor productivity growth has fallen from 6.9 percent annually to 3.5 to 4 percent annually (Keefe and Boroff 1994). The drop in the industry's productivity growth rate was due, we believe, to a loss of system economies and a substantial increase in marketing costs, both unintended consequences of competition, and was not simply a result of the disruption caused by restructuring.

Underlying the Justice Department's insistence on the AT&T divestiture was the belief that long distance service deregulation would usher in an era of competition utilizing relatively inexpensive and decentralizing technologies based on satellite and microwave transmission networks (Rosenberg 1994). Microwave network technology, however, was obsolete by the time the AT&T divestiture was implemented; and satellite communications have been since relegated to a secondary technology primarily used for communicating with remote areas of the world.

Divestiture, instead, accelerated the deployment of new digital switches, fiber optic network technologies, and cellular services. The "systemness" of these technologies demands even higher levels of network integration and interoperability than prior network technologies. Consequently, the new digital network systems exhibit greater economies of scale and scope than the analog network they have replaced. These economies, however, could not be fully realized because of the market separations contained in the 1983 AT&T Consent Decree and the resulting triplication of long distance network facilities, which has spawned over 500 companies that resell the services of the big three (AT&T, MCI, and Sprint). The current long distance oligopoly market structure has produced considerable excess capacity with sufficient facilities to serve many times the total needs of American consumers. For example, although AT&T accounts for 60 percent of the long distance traffic, AT&T's competitors alone could readily serve the entire nation's long distance demand (Allen 1993). In addition, the new competitive marketplace requires that long distance carriers devote an increasing proportion of their resources to advertising programs (over $3 billion in 1994) for "True Voice," "Friends and Family," and "The Most."

During the last decade digitalization of network switching and transmission has revolutionized telecommunication services. As network software replaces hardware as the principal source of value added, the telecommunications networks gain an increasing capability to offer a wide range of services and customization features. Common carriers working with manufacturers have created software-defined networks and software capable of delivering customized services for "intelligent networks." Advanced Intelligent Networks (AIN) will ultimately provide information suppliers with the flexibility to design their own service networks. New switching software will redefine interactive communications by delivering interactive voice, video, data, and imaging services simultaneously over a fully digital network. The new digital network systems have also created an exploding demand for software and software programmers to support flexible multi-product networks. Digital switches are designed with basic operating systems and software platforms that can be readily expanded. Each year new software upgrades are available to enhance digital switching capabilities, often allowing new services to be offered without making any hardware changes. Sales of system software upgrades to the regional Bells exceeded $1.2 billion in 1992.

A second technological revolution is underway in transmission systems. All major common carriers are transforming their analog transmission systems into broadband integrated services digital networks (ISDN).

ISDN is an engineering concept, not a technology; it signifies a digitally switched network that can simultaneously carry digitized video, voice, data, and imaging transmissions, and it requires a broad transmission band. Fiber optics is the preferred broadband medium for digital transmission. Light waves pulsed through an optical fiber can carry voice, data, imaging, and video transmissions simultaneously over the same strand (integrated broadband) without any electrical distortion or "noise." Fiber may make existing cable TV and telephone networks technically obsolete. It is currently deployed on most long distance and toll routes with growing application as local exchange feeder cable. About 90 percent of the potential circuit usage of fiber, however, is in the local loop, or what is referred to in the industry as the "last mile" (Bolter 1990:173). It is this last mile that represents the single largest obstacle to a national digital broadband network.

In the near term, the Regional Bells have opted for a less expensive broadband solution. It relies on a mixed system of fiber optic cable run from the central office to a local access point, where the lightwaves are converted into both digital and analog electrical impulses, which are carried to the home over coaxial cable. Lucent Technologies (formerly AT&T Transmissions Systems) has solved several technical problems that will permit the transmission of interactive communications over coaxial cable. The cost of this new mixed system is slightly more than half of a fully fiber optic system. This mixed system, however, has a narrower band width than a fully fiber system, which could potentially limit multimedia applications.[2] The regional Bells continue to scale back their plans for broadband deployment, as they devote more resources to wireless technologies.

Cellular telephone, an analog technology, grew from no subscribers in 1981 to 35 million in 1995. The next generation of wireless communications, personal communication services (PCS), a digital network technology, should substantially reduce the costs of mobile communications services and greatly accelerate the use of wireless communications for voice, data, and fax. Depending on technical innovations and economic

2. Several companies are also committed to fiber optic trials in the local loop. US West, for example, has undertaken a test in Omaha. It costs $1,500 to hook up a fiber optic subscriber compared to $1,200 to connect a regular telephone customer; however, projections indicate that the cost for fiber optic loops should fall to $1,000 within a few years as the technology advances with practical service experience. In addition, the major cable television interests, such as Tele-Communications, Inc., Time Warner, and major competitive access provider companies (such as Teleport and Metropolitan Fiber Systems), are battling to become major local ISDN suppliers.

feasibility, digital wireless technologies could account for half of all local access calling within ten years.

These new wire-based and wireless digital broadband network technologies, make obsolete entire sets of worker skills, while creating demands for computer and software diagnostic capabilities. At the same time, they permit companies to restructure operations by creating the opportunity to consolidate organizations into mega-centers for operations, repair, and customer service. The diffusion of these new technologies will create more opportunities for further integration that achieve even greater system economies of scope and scale; however, the pace of technological development and choice will be ultimately determined by market demand and by the economic feasibility of the new services. Optimistic projections about exploding demand for new integrated services in interactive video, data, voice, and imaging often lead to predictions about industrial convergence among computer hardware and software, entertainment, information, educational services, telephone equipment, telephony, cable and broadcast television, wireless, and other ancillary industries.

Is There a Convergence in Telecommunications Services Markets?

Forecasts of industry convergences, however, often tend to be premature. Convergence is often thought to arise solely from converging technologies. Regulatory, managerial, and economic constraints, however, greatly shape the viability of service market convergence. For example, at the time of the AT&T divestiture, the business press confidently predicted the imminent merger of the computer and telephone industries. In 1982, within hours of the AT&T divestiture agreement, the Justice Department also dropped its antitrust suit against IBM in part because AT&T was expected to become a major rival of IBM in the computer market. Additionally, industry analysts predicted that IBM would become a strong challenger to AT&T in telecommunications. IBM purchased a stake in Rolm, the business premises equipment company, then entered into an agreement with MCI, leveraging IBM's ownership stake in Comsat. These two industry leaders were supposed to tear down the wall between computers and telephony. AT&T lost millions on its investment in personal computers, however, and finally merged its operation into its acquisition, NCR, which it has now spun off as a separate company. IBM retreated from the telephone industry to focus on its imploding computer business. Although convergence between the telephone and computer industries is still likely, it remains a vision.

More recently, for a brief period in 1993, merger talks between the major cable TV companies and the regional Bells created the impression that the two industries would quickly converge through corporate mergers. Bell Atlantic's merger with TCI soon failed, followed by the collapse of the Southwestern and Cox cable merger plans, and by the renegotiation of deals between BellSouth and Prime, and Bell Canada and Jones Intercable. Although Southwestern Bell had already bought Hauser TV in suburban Washington D.C., it subsequently explored selling its interest. Only US West, which acquired Continental Cablevision in 1996 and owns 25.5 percent of Time Warner's stock, remains committed to convergence through corporate merger, although it has been embroiled in a bitter dispute with Time Warner over its acquisition of Turner Broadcasting.

At the time of the passage of the Telecommunications Act of 1996, the telecommunications services industry was divided into five major market segments: long distance, within state toll calls, local exchange service, cable TV, and wireless communications. The Telecommunications Act will unleash competition in the long distance and toll markets and will foster competition among the local access providers. In 1995, U.S. telephone service was supplied by over 160 million wire-based telephone access lines; the seven regional Bell companies and GTE provided 95 percent of the nation's local telephone access service through state-regulated monopolies. Cable TV supplied television signals to more than 60 million homes through local franchised monopolies. Between 1984 and 1993 cable TV operated without any regulatory oversight, allowing the companies to generate equity values four times their replacement costs. The Cable Act of 1992 brought cable TV under federal regulation, which will expire in 1999 under the new Telecommunications Act. The fastest growing local access providers are wireless communications companies that in 1996 supplied cellular services to 35 million customers through duopoly markets dominated by AT&T, Sprint, GTE, and the regional Bells.

As each type of local access service converts to a digital broadband technology, the providers plan to compete for customers with services currently offered by another existing technology. For example, modernization of the traditional telephone access lines will permit telephone companies to offer cable TV; digital upgrades in the cable TV network will permit internet access and voice communications; and new wireless technologies will improve voice quality and permit fax and data transmissions that will compete with telephone wire-based services. Each wire-based and wireless access service plans to create new interactive forms of communications. The Telecommunications Act anticipates that these new technologies will create a competitive market for local access services, progressively eliminating the basis for natural monopolies and the need for traditional regulatory oversight. Corporate planners, however, face increasing difficulty in forecasting market growth and potential competitive losses or gains to any of the alternative technologies, making investment choices in this capital-intensive industry very risky and expensive.

In 1995, long distance was the only developed marketplace in telecommunications services. AT&T (60 percent share), MCI (20 percent share), and Sprint (10 percent share) effectively divided the long distance market. By 1995 the long distance carriers had already gained the right to compete in 35 state area toll service markets. This allowed the long distance carriers to enter another market that historically subsidized local service and to compete directly with the regional Bells and GTE for market share. The Telecommunications Act of 1996 opened up the remaining intrastate toll markets to the long distance carriers, but at a substantial cost. The Act gives the regional Bells immediate entry into long distance markets outside their service areas and the regional Bells will likely gain the right to enter the long distance markets within their regions by 1999.

Although long distance market shares began to stabilize in 1992, as calling volume and profitability continued to grow, the entry of the regional Bells and GTE into this lucrative market recreates instability in the domestic industry. The major long distance carriers, thought to be the big losers in the Telecommunications Act of 1996, face several major issues beyond direct competition with the regional Bells and GTE. The first concerns the long distance access charges paid to local exchange carriers to guarantee universal service. In 1996, long distance carriers still paid 45 percent of their long distance revenues to GTE and the regional Bell companies for access and interconnection to the local exchange network, and these charges still subsidized basic telephone service rates. In 1995, AT&T, MCI, and Sprint were exploring options to enter local telephone service through alliances with cable TV companies, cellular carriers, and competitive access providers to drive down local access charges and deprive the regional Bells of a major revenue source. The Telecommunications Act of 1996 created a Federal-State Joint Board on Universal Service to define the scope of universal service and to propose mechanisms for federal support of universal service. The FCC will not decide the future of access charges and other mechanisms for supporting universal service until 1998 at the earliest; however, the future of access charges and other cross subsidies will significantly affect the financial health of long distance carriers and local access providers, as well as the cost to the consumer of basic telephone service.

Second, the Telecommunications Act of 1996 requires that local telephone exchange providers make available access lines at wholesale prices for resale. In theory, long distance carriers can lease these lines, which will provide them direct access to their customers. This direct access allows them to provide a comprehensive set of telecommunications services (one-stop-shopping) for their important clients. In an initial experiment AT&T leased lines from Rochester Telephone at a 5 percent discount, which AT&T found unprofitable, and then abandoned the experiment. Under the new Act, the state commissions will set wholesale prices. However, they confront a basic problem. The unsubsidized cost of a local access line is higher than the price charged to the consumer. The commissions confront a difficult issue in a cross-subsidized environment: what is the appropriate wholesale price, when the retail price is below both marginal and average costs? Depending on how local access wholesale prices are set, the long distance carriers may or may not be able to offer seamless comprehensive services, which they view as critical to their survival and growth.

Third, each major carrier is building international alliances with foreign long distance carriers. British Telecom has purchased 20 percent of MCI; German and French Telecom have jointly purchased 20 percent of Sprint. AT&T, while maintaining 70 percent of U.S. originated international revenues, is building its "World Partners" network; it already has ten participating telecommunications companies in Europe and Asia, who will market AT&T services. Each major U.S. long distance carrier is participating in the formation of a global oligopoly in telecommunications services. Will competition from the regional Bells upset the domestic and emerging international oligopoly market structure by creating more excess capacity in the network and shifting potential alliances?

Even before its enactment, the Telecommunications Act of 1996 produced corporate restructuring, once its basic elements became known. In September 1995, AT&T announced its trivestiture into the new AT&T, a telecommunications services company; Lucent Technologies, a telecommunications manufacturer and equipment supplier; and NCR, the former computer division of AT&T. The disaggregation of AT&T was largely propelled by a fundamental conflict between marketing telecommunications services and network equipment. As the Network Services Group within AT&T had escalated its direct competition with the regional Bells, the Network Equipment Group's largest customers, the same regional Bells became increasingly uncomfortable about buying their telecommunications equipment from their largest competitor. Equipment orders were canceled. Organizational walls were then built at AT&T between services and equipment to insure that information obtained in supplying equipment would not be used by the service divisions to compete with equipment customers. The advantages of vertical integration thus disappeared, leaving only its liabilities. In addition, the acquisition of NCR had failed to stop a decade of losses for AT&T in the computer business.

Within months of the AT&T trivestiture announcement and weeks after the Telecommunications Act of 1996 was signed into law, the number of regional Bells decreased from seven to five. Southwestern Bell Corporation announced plans to acquire Pacific Telesis, and Bell Atlantic announced its intention to merge with NYNEX. Both aggregations permit further system economies of corporate staff, network control operations, and customer service centers, while laying the financial basis to build stronger brand names both regionally and nationally.

The prospective deployment of digital cellular induced rapid changes in ownership of corporate assets that are symptomatic of future restructurings among local access providers. In 1994, AT&T merged with McCaw Cellular, the largest U.S. cellular company, putting AT&T into the local service business. McCaw was a highly leveraged company unable to undertake digital modernization of its network, and it was poorly positioned to acquire new PCS licenses. AT&T's massive financial resources instantly solved both of these problems. Additionally, McCaw's incipient national cellular network, Cellular One, gained instant visibility with the AT&T brand name. In response, US West's cellular subsidiary and Air Touch (the divested Pacific Telesis cellular company) merged. NYNEX and Bell Atlantic also merged their cellular operations. The latter four companies, then, formed a partnership that bid on the new PCS licenses. They also plan to collaborate on developing a national cellular network with brand name marketing to compete with AT&T's Cellular One. Sprint's joint venture with three major cable TV companies also bid on new wireless licenses, but encountered substantial internal problems.

Current trends strongly suggest that the local cellular wireless markets that are duopolies will restructure into a national oligopoly marketplace with well recognized brand name providers capable of supplying mobile voice and data services anywhere in the country. Over the next five years, all the major telecommunications companies plan to make substantial investments building digital PCS networks. The anticipated explosive growth of digital wireless, however, complicates the modernization of their wire-based networks. Telephone providers have difficulty forecasting how many wire-based customers they may lose to wireless services, particularly if cross subsidies for wire-based local access are phased out. Consequently, investment in cable modernization for residential service has slowed significantly.

The most anticipated restructuring in local services, however, still involves the local telephone and cable TV companies. The regional Bell companies are eager to enter cable TV markets, but they lack television broadcast experience. Several regional Bells have sought to gain this experience through their international investments. For example, NYNEX has made investments in Great Britain in order to offer both cable TV and local telephone service over its network in direct competition with British Telecom. The cable TV companies probably lack the financial resources necessary to compete with the regional Bells in interactive video or telephone. The highly leveraged cable TV industry earned revenues of $22 billion in 1993 compared to the $85 billion earned by local telephone service providers. Each of the major long distance carriers, however, has entered into discussions with cable TV interests as they seek to bypass the regional Bells and the cable TV companies seek investment to upgrade their networks to offer interactive switched services.

To upgrade their facilities for interactive media, the regional Bells will need to make massive investments. Their financial performance has been strong since divestiture, greatly assisted by lower interest rates and the 1986 changes in federal tax laws. Since divestiture shareholder wealth (share price plus reinvested dividends) has grown by more than 50 percent at each RBOC. Providing basic local service remains the regional Bells' single largest source of revenue ($40 billion), followed by the $19 billion paid by the long distance carriers in access charges to complete long distance calls. The intrastate toll service is the third largest source of revenue for the RBOCs, accounting for approximately 13 percent of their revenue. The regional Bells are also expanding into new unregulated businesses through fully-owned subsidiaries. These new businesses now account for 20 percent of the RBOCs' total revenues and are steadily growing in importance. The regional Bells' fastest growing new businesses are their cellular services and international operations.

Any excitement about an interactive global information highway, however, needs to be tempered. There are only a few new services that are in demand by residential consumers. Only a small segment of the consuming public may be interested in the new multimedia services that are being promoted to support the information highway. According to a 1991 AT&T study, for example, almost 40 percent of American households still use a rotary-dial telephone. In addition, although it is available to 90 percent of homes, less than two-thirds of American households purchase cable TV service. On the other hand, second lines for internet access have rapidly grown, producing a significant revenue source for the regional Bells.

Market Structure: A Matter of Legislative and Regulatory Uncertainty

In the post-AT&T divestiture period, the FCC and state regulatory commissions established very different levels and types of regulations for each telecommunications service market. In fact, regulatory oversight underwent a revolution during the last decade. Similar to the long distance market, state regulators eliminated some cross subsidies for regional Bell companies through rate reform and provisions for competitive entry in local markets. Incentive regulation, price caps on bundles of services, and deregulation virtually replaced all traditional rate-of-return regulation. Under incentive regulation, larger-than-targeted cost reductions can be kept by the local company, thus rewarding efficiencies by enhancing their profitability. Incentive regulation, however, may also reward companies for reducing the quality of service to improve earnings. A number of state commissions have held hearings and fined local companies for failing to provide adequate levels of service. One state, Oregon, abandoned its incentive regulation experiment to return to traditional rate and entry regulation to solve its service problems with US West. Also, bucking the trend toward deregulation, the cable TV companies, which had operated as local monopolies without regulatory oversight since 1984, were brought under FCC regulation in 1992; the FCC implemented two rate rollbacks, reducing cable TV revenue by an estimated $2 billion annually by 1995.

To implement the Telecommunications Act of 1996, federal and state regulators must develop rules to accomplish its intention to promote competition, to preserve universal service, and to support the development of innovative services. The Act does not mean the end of regulation; instead it will change the nature of regulation, shifting more responsibility toward the federal level and away from the states. Regulatory activity has increased to historically high levels and should remain high during the initial rule-making period under the Act, which should end by 1999.

Business Strategy and Structure

Given the turmoil and uncertainty created by new telecommunications markets and technologies, it is not surprising that organizational restructuring has occurred in fits and starts, with contradictory approaches and outcomes. Equally important in shaping business restructuring, however, are differences in the inherited positions of AT&T and the regional Bell companies. The interplay between market deregulation and institutional constraints on actors is the subject of the next section, which briefly outlines AT&T's and then the RBOCs' approaches to change.

AT&T: Global Telecommunications Systems

At divestiture in 1984, AT&T retained AT&T Long Lines, its long distance service provider; Western Electric, its equipment subsidiary; and Bell Labs, its research laboratories. The new AT&T employed approximately one-third of the former Bell System workforce at divestiture. The bulk of the service operations and two-thirds of the employees from the former Bell System remained with the local telephone companies, placed under the direction of the seven regional Bells. This division of labor has had some important consequences for business strategy. First, the "natural" extension of the long distance and the network equipment businesses has been international. Just as in the early part of the century, AT&T's strategy was to use its control over long distance service and network equipment to gain control over local service and create an integrated system, AT&T's post-divestiture strategy was to leverage its competitive advantage in long distance service and equipment manufacturing to become a dominant player in global networks. AT&T's strategy, first and foremost, was to reshape itself as a global corporation. And because so many global customers are multinational businesses, global service means providing an integrated set of voice, data, and video services through a seamless global network. Politically, AT&T has also been at the forefront of efforts to reduce international barriers to global communications and to push for deregulation of the public monopolies that have controlled most national telecommunications systems around the globe. While the regional Bell operating companies have also had international aspirations, they have entered international markets primarily by taking over or forming joint partnerships with national governments to improve basic domestic services within a country or by competitively entering cellular and cable TV markets.

Within the United States, the division of labor created at divestiture between AT&T and the RBOCs means that AT&T has only indirect contact—long distance service through access to the local phone companies—to the massive customer base. The local phone companies, by contrast, have had a direct and ongoing relationship with customers and are the ones responsible for maintaining the network infrastructure that provides basic service. While AT&T continues to be regulated by the FCC, the Bell operating companies continue mainly under the jurisdiction of state authorities. They have retained a regional embeddedness that constrains their behavior in ways that AT&T does not encounter. Their service base is geographically tied, their political orientation is to state authorities, their ability to restructure or move operations is limited to the states in which they currently operate. AT&T, by contrast, covers the entire country, and has taken advantage of this opportunity to consolidate operations and move them to whatever location offers the most economical choice.

A third difference is that AT&T began dealing with competition in long distance and equipment manufacturing prior to divestiture. It has responded rapidly and followed practices that rely on economies of scale and cost cutting, with labor costs a priority. In 1984, for the first time since the depression, AT&T employment fell. Post-divestiture AT&T eliminated over a third of its domestic workforce between 1984 and 1990, equal to its percentage of depression-era layoffs between 1929 and 1935 (Danielian 1939: 208). In the 1980s, network, manufacturing, and service workers bore the brunt of the layoffs: the nonmanagerial workforce dropped by 48.5 percent, while the managerial workforce rose by 4 percent. Additionally, to be competitive with MCI and Sprint, AT&T reconstructed its long distance network with fiber optic cable and invested heavily in new digital switching systems—technologies that have more capacity and provide better service and also need less maintenance. It cut costs and labor in part by consolidating operator and customer service offices to a handfull of mega-centers nationwide. This meant not only fear of job loss and demoralization, but repeated forced moves for survivors, an issue we discuss more fully in the next section of this chapter.

To deal with its antiquated organization of functional silos—AT&T was historically organized into departmental specialties and subspecialties such as network construction, installation, and repair; operator services; accounting, and so on—the company created a "decentralized" and "cross-functional" structure of twenty-two strategic business units based on national or international market segments. At the same time it committed itself to a focus on the communications business. Each business unit is largely responsible for all functions, from strategy and operations to marketing and human resources. It also expanded rapidly into new areas, partnering with Olivetti and then purchasing NCR as a computer subsidiary, creating AT&T Universal Card (financial services), acquiring McCaw Cellular, and investing heavily in global communications.

As AT&T lost the battle to keep the regional Bells out of the long distance market, until local service markets were opened and access charges eliminated, it launched an aggressive strategy to enter all service market segments with a comprehensive package of telecommunications services. This strategy made every service provider a potential competitor, which had immediate adverse consequences for its equipment business. As a supplier of network equipment and software, AT&T must have access to proprietary information of its customers to effectively support and update the network. As more customers came to see AT&T as a service competitor, they cancelled their contracts for AT&T equipment. For example, Sprint and MCI have never purchased an AT&T switch. The economies of scope were once again changing. In September 1995, AT&T announced that it would divide itself into three new companies. The telecommunications services company would retain the name AT&T and seek new integration and scale opportunities within the services markets; it accounts for two-thirds of AT&T's revenue, 80 percent of its profits, but less than 40 percent of its total former workforce. The AT&Ttelecommunications equipment company, formerly Western Electric, now Lucent Technologies, is one of the world's largest telecommunications equipment manufacturers, seeking to take market share from the crippled Alcatel. Finally, after losing billions of dollars in computers since 1984, AT&T spunoff the remnants of its ailing computer business as it once again exits the personal computer business.

Bell Operating Companies: Regional Services

The regional Bell companies have carefully watched and learned from AT&T's response to deregulation. They have moved more slowly largely because competition did not begin entering local markets in a serious way until the late 1980s. They are following a set of strategies similar to those of AT&T, but with somewhat different timing: slower entry of the regional Bells into new markets, slower restructuring and consolidation into business units, workforce reductions through attrition and early retirement buyouts spread over longer periods so that displacement and demoralization are less severe. Nonetheless, the workforce in the regulated telephone business of the regional Bells dropped by an average of 28 percent between 1984 and 1992. In the meantime, they began investing in those unregulated markets allowed by modifications in the divestiture agreement, such as information services or cellular, and international services. Deregulation in local services accelerated in the late 1980s as local access carriers such as MFS and Teleport were able to construct local fiber loops in metropolitan areas and skim the cream of the market by serving the more lucrative business customers. And cable companies, with coaxial cable access available to over 90 percent of the households nationally, may enter some local residential market as soon as legislative changes take place.

Under these circumstances the regional Bell companies began serious efforts in the late 1980s and early 1990s to cut costs and downsize, on the one hand, while trying to introduce workplace reforms to enhance the quality of service, on the other. It is this juggling of multiple reform agendas that has created tensions and conflicts because the agenda appears contradictory to employees.

Changes in strategy and structure among the regional Bell companies may be summarized as follows. First, they are shifting from being a regulated utility driven by a public service and an "engineering" mentality to a partially regulated private corporation driven by finance and marketing. Their financial decisions are now shaped much more by Wall Street than by federal and state regulators. Second, they have pushed for changes in state-regulated rate structures to allow "incentive" structures—structures that allow them to make a larger profit if they improve efficiency or productivity beyond a certain level.

Third, the Bells have shifted from a standardized high volume product market (voice) to a differentiated product market (voice, enhanced services such as voice messaging, data, video, image). To support this shift they have invested in fiber optic cable and integrated services digital networks (ISDN) to allow them to carry high speed data, voice, video, and imaging and remain technologically competitive. Similarly, they have used the cash generated in the regulated markets to expand in lucrative nonregulated markets such as information services, cellular, and international services. Regulated and nonregulated activities are carried out under separate subsidiaries.

Fourth, they have recognized that given new low cost entrants (competitors using the latest low-maintenance technology and lower cost, nonunion labor) they must cut costs; shedding labor has become a primary goal. While at AT&T nonmanagerial workers have borne the brunt of workforce reductions, the regional Bells appear to be reducing roughly proportionate numbers of managers and nonmanagers. For managers, this means the elimination of at least one level of management, and more importantly, significant increases in their span of control. But the RBOCs also realize that they cannot compete on cost alone—that their competitive advantage is in trying to hold on to and build their large customer base by improving quality and service. The cost of gaining back a customer who has left is four times that of keeping the customer in the first place, according to one company estimate (U.S. Congress 1993: 38). As a company executive noted, "We will be extremely sensitive to our existing customers because we know that our greatest strength lies in holding onto our $8 billion revenue stream" (Tom Bystrzycki, Vice President, Mass Markets and Operations, US West Communications, in U.S. Congress 1993: 37). To accomplish this business strategy, they are attempting simultaneously to implement cost-cutting and performance-enhancing strategies—on the one hand radically reducing size through workforce reductions and reengineering, on the other hand implementing total quality and employee participation and self-management programs that call on the commitment and discretionary effort of all employees to enhance service quality. This mixed strategy creates contradictory incentives for employees and the outcomes are unclear. The underlying theme is to shift from a public service culture to an "enterprise culture." While these contradictions have also existed at AT&T, the timing has been different: AT&T downsized substantially before trying to enlist the good will of employees. The RBOCs, by contrast, began with participatory approaches but subsequently embraced widescale downsizing.

Fifth, the RBOCs are restructuring their organizations in ways that centralize some functions while decentralizing others. On the one hand, strategic decision making has been centralized at the regional corporate level. Companies have then taken advantage of economies of scale by consolidating functions, offices, and staff from the state-level telephone company to the regional corporate entity. This centralization has required further standardization of most technological, organizational, and management practices. At the same time, to pursue differentiated product market strategies, the companies have moved network and customer service operational decision making from the state level (where it was traditionally located) to newly-created regional business units defined by market segment. These "customer-driven" entities are to include most functions necessary to meet customers' needs. In the past, by contrast, the state president of the telephone company was the key decisionmaker because the interface with the state public utility commission dominated operational decisions (for example, service standards). Departmental units (network operations, "traffic" or operator services, and customer service) were independent silos with local actors reporting up parallel chains of command to their counterparts at the state level.

At the same time that this centralization is occurring, companies are attempting to decentralize other areas of management decision making to the local or "district" level (the analogy in manufacturing would be the plant level)—in keeping with the recommendations of quality and excellence theorists that "empowering" managers to "get close to the customer" is the key to continuous improvement in service quality. The idea is to free up middle managers to be "entrepreneurs" and encourage greater cross-functional behavior to solve problems and improve quality and customer service. Part of the change also involves breaking down the command-and-control management style of prior eras and replacing it with a more participatory one of "coaching"—to "empower" workers to have more discretion in handling customer requests and problems. The direction of change, then, is to hollow out the old state organizations, with key operational decisions shifting either up to the regional business unit or down to the "district" or local managerial level. Responsibilities of frontline supervisors are in turn shifted to workers in self-managed teams. This is the vision of new work organization that firms are trying to implement. Table 1.1 outlines the shift in models of business strategy and structure under the old and new systems.

Restructuring, however, has also undermined the strong sense of moral purpose within these organizations. Since 1907 the Bell System promoted

TABLE 1.1. Telecommunications services: business strategy and production organization

Components	Old system	New system
Capital market	Regulated by FCC, State PUCs	Partially regulated: sensitive to stock market
Pricing mechanism	Regulated: Cross-subsidized (local/long distance) (resident/business)	Partially regulated: More competitive "Incentive-based" "Cost-based"
Product market	Standardized: Voice	Differentiated: Voice, data, video, image
Technology	Cable twisted pair copper transmission; Electric, analog, mechanical switching	Fiber optic transmission; digital switching
Competitive advantage	Low cost, scale economies	Cost, quality, customer service
Business strategy	Universal public service, "engineering driven"	Segmented service markets, "market driven"
Management structure	Vertical Bureaucratic Centralized	Horizontal Entrepreneurial Dual: corporate/business unit regional/local
HR/IR	Centralized	Dual: corporate/business unit regional/local

universal and reliable service as a public mission among its employees (Barnard 1938). The organizations instilled a "spirit of service" that created a powerful moral culture throughout the Bell System companies. The new financial and market-based decision making often collides with the deeply ingrained spirit of service. Although each of the major companies is grappling with a new moral purpose promoted through culture change programs, these new efforts do not resonate among employees, who still believe the traditional service culture is morally superior to the new culture of "greed" as it is often characterized. The loss of moral purpose has contributed greatly to the demoralization of former Bell System employees, a theme we discuss in more detail in the next section.

Labor-Management Relations after Divestiture

AT&T's business restructuring broke its historic social contract with labor on employment security. As indicated in the previous section, union-represented employment at AT&T declined from 250,000 at divestiture to 103,000 workers in 1994, representing a 59 percent reduction in union jobs. As downsizing continues, bargaining unit employment fell below 100,000 full-time jobs in 1995 (a 60% job reduction). If this trend of eliminating 1,000 jobs per month is not disrupted the bargaining unit will disappear at AT&T by 2004. By contrast, while the RBOCs downsized through attrition and voluntary separations until 1991, they have since announced workforce reductions of over 100,000; they project employment in 1996 to be 70 percent of their 1990 levels. As a result, it is appropriate to review the consequences of AT&T's downsizing strategy on workforce morale, productivity, and labor-management relations, the subject of this section.

As a consequence of AT&T's restructuring, employees became demoralized over the course of the 1980s and early 1990s. The October 1991 *AT&T Employment Security* survey, for example, found that bargaining unit employees had become profoundly pessimistic about their future employment prospects at AT&T.[3] In 1981, a Bell System survey found that 68 percent of nonmanagement employees felt that the company was providing job security and only 8 percent did not; by 1991 the numbers at AT&T had more than reversed themselves, with over 73 percent feeling

3. In 1991, we undertook an employee survey at AT&T to evaluate the effectiveness of the negotiated employment security programs. The survey was mailed on 24 September 1991 by AT&T Transtech to a stratified random sample of 8,100 AT&T bargaining unit employees. A total of 3,160 employees responded to the single mailing, yielding a response rate of 39%.

that there was little job security. In some business units, less than 4 percent of the nonmanagement employees felt there was any job security.
Less than 20 percent of the employees surveyed had confidence in management's ability to lead and solve the corporation's competitive problems. Over two-thirds felt they were unable to influence events that affect
their employment at AT&T. And, almost one-half of the employees surveyed had been surplused (had their jobs abolished) at least once. On
average, the surplused employee group had been surplused two and one-
half times.

When compared with attitude data collected at other traumatized organizations, the intensity of the pessimism of AT&T employees goes beyond the negative attitudes found in many of those organizations. There
are probably five reasons for these catastrophic-like responses. First,
many employees chose to work at AT&T because of the Bell System's
commitment to employment security, and now they face chronic insecurity. Second, downsizing has been a protracted ordeal that started in
1984 and continued over a decade later. Third, the average worker who
survived downsizing is immobile with family commitments; he or she is
white, forty-three years old, married with children at home, a home-
owner, a high school graduate with some college, and a CWA member
who has eighteen years of AT&T service and annually earns $26,000
with good benefits. Some 87 percent of the survey respondents wanted
to keep their current jobs until they retire, but less than 10 percent of
them believed that there were any opportunities for advancement at
AT&T. Although AT&T provides severance pay and on occasion induce-
ments for early retirements, few of the remaining workers can afford to
leave. Fourth, AT&T employees use the former Bell System employment
standards, which until recently have remained largely intact at the regional Bell operating companies, to judge the new AT&T's employment
practices. Fifth, AT&T conducts a continuous public relations campaign
emphasizing the strengths of the corporation; the campaign permeates all
corporate activities and appointments. In fact, the executive vice president for human resources has a background in public relations, not labor
relations or human resource management. AT&T is widely recognized
as a progressive, innovative employer for its retraining, out-placement
assistance, employee participation, and family leave programs. Many employees have found it difficult to reconcile AT&T's positive public image
with their recent personal experiences. Also, this positive image enables
corporate executives to engage in denial about the human consequences
of their downsizing decisions. Employees systematically underestimate

(by 60%) the amount of downsizing that has occurred at AT&T (Boroff and Keefe 1992).

Following divestiture, downsizing became an increasingly routine part of business operations. As a result, layoffs rather than voluntary separations have represented an increasing proportion of the terminations. For example, during the first two years of post-divestiture operations, AT&T reduced its overall head count by 56,000. This included 43,928 bargaining unit employees and 12,072 managers. The first downsizing, however, resulted in layoffs for only one-quarter of the total surplused population. The remainder left through attrition, voluntary severance, and early retirement programs, transfers within AT&T, or retreats back to the regional Bell operating companies. Between 1984 and 1992, a total of 107,291 AT&T union-represented employees were downsized (Internal AT&T document). Approximately 58 percent were laid-off, while 42 percent accepted "voluntary" severance packages. An additional 25,709 jobs were reduced by normal turnover. On January 2, 1996, AT&T announced that 40,000 jobs would be eliminated as part of trivestiture, most through layoffs. This announcement, which generated a huge public outcry, departed from prior downsizing at AT&T since it primarily targeted managers. Some 24,000 jobs to be eliminated in trivestiture are managerial, whereas 16,000 are union represented.

As part of the process to become more competitive, AT&T has been transforming itself from a predominantly unionized employer (67% organized) into a nonunion employer (42% organized in the U.S.). AT&T has acquired and launched nonunion businesses while downsizing its unionized core operations. AT&T developed two new major nonunion businesses, American Transtech, the largest U.S. telemarketing service, and AT&T Universal Card, the second largest credit card company. AT&T has also acquired two antiunion equipment manufacturers: Paradyne (data communications equipment) and, more recently, NCR. NCR is the sixth largest computer company with 1,300 locations in 130 countries. In 1990, AT&T classified 147,563 employees as nonmanagement; 97,206 were represented by CWA (66%) and 24,402 were represented by the IBEW (16%), which yields an 82 percent union density for the union-eligible workforce. The decline in union coverage at AT&T to only 42 percent of total employees, however, cannot be explained by the growth of new nonunion hourly employment nor the depopulation of traditionally unionized jobs.

Primarily, deunionization is occurring at the upper boundary of the bargaining unit, as management has expanded the scope of supervisory and managerial job titles and employment. Over 50 percent of AT&T

employees are now classified as either managerial or supervisory, compared to 29 percent in 1980. This trend is facilitated by U.S. labor law which excludes from protected activity supervisors, managerial employees, managers, and professionals who participate in the hiring or evaluations of their peers.

Industry Employment and Unionization

Although AT&T has aggressively downsized its workforce, employment in the telecommunications service industry declined in the first decade after divestiture by only 10 percent. In 1992, the industry employed 872,000 employees, down from its peak of 965,000 in 1983. Nonsupervisory employment fell to 649,000 a 7 percent decline since 1983. Slightly more than one-half of the employees in the industry are female, a proportion that has remained relatively constant over the last decade. Between 1984 and 1993 the RBOCs, the major employers in the industry, reduced their net employment by 12 percent or by approximately 72,000 jobs, employment in the regulated core businesses dropped by 28 percent, approximately 158,000 jobs, while employment in the nonregulated businesses expanded by over 300 percent.

Unionization has remained stable at the RBOCs, with two-thirds of all employees covered by collective bargaining agreements, although most of the new RBOC subsidiaries operate on a nonunion basis. Union coverage, however, in the overall telecommunications service industry fell from 67 percent in 1984 to 48.5 percent in 1994 (Spalter-Roth and Hartmann 1995). The 40,000 jobs generated by the growth of the nonunion long distance carriers, MCI and Sprint, is one major cause of declining union coverage in the industry. Also, the entry of 500 relatively small firms that resell long distance services and hundreds of firms that install customer premise equipment further erodes union coverage.

The convergence of cable TV and local telephone service creates some serious problems for both the IBEW and CWA. Although some local cable TV companies are unionized, CWA estimates that of the 108,700 union-eligible cable TV workers, only 5 percent are union members. The largest cable operator, TCI, is aggressively antiunion. Since 1990, TCI has sponsored six decertification elections—successfully decertifying CWA in four units. The substantial pay discrepancies between unionized telephone workers and nonunion cable employees creates the potential for whipsawing as the unionized employers compete for future cable modernization work.

The union/nonunion telecommunications wage gap increased from 8 percent to 20 percent between 1990 and 1995 (Spalter-Roth and Hartmann 1995). In sum, an antiunion environment increasingly surrounds the core of unionized telephone work. Management has steadily expanded its nonunion jurisdiction from above. New competitors, such as MCI and Sprint, have vigorously resisted unionization; competitive access providers Teleport and MFS remain nonunion; the cellular providers, even the AT&T and Bell subsidiaries, have kept union influence to a minimum; and cable TV operators remain solidly antiunion. In this environment, the unions have looked to build new relationships with traditionally unionized employers.

A New Relationship at AT&T

In 1992, AT&T stock soared by 30 percent, adding $17 billion in market value. The company's financial success reflected major improvements in its operating performance. Starting in 1991, AT&T stabilized its long distance market share, earning $30 billion in revenue on domestic long distance and $10 billion on its rapidly growing international service. AT&T also won three Malcolm Baldridge National Quality Awards, awarded to AT&T Universal Card, AT&T Transmission Systems, and AT&T Consumer Communications Services. AT&T's $12.6 billion purchase of McCaw Cellular, the nation's largest cellular company, put AT&T in the leading position in the cellular market with McCaw's Cellular One network. Strategically AT&T has defined itself as a networking company, where all lines of business must add value to the network and create value for the shareholders. AT&T's top strategic objective is to transform itself into a global corporation. To become a global competitor, the corporation planned to generate 50 percent of its earnings from international sales by the year 2000, up from essentially nothing at divestiture. AT&T employs 53,000 people or 17 percent of its workforce overseas.

During 1992, the relationships between AT&T and its two unions improved. They negotiated a three-year agreement that created a new framework for labor-management relations, called Workplace of the Future. The structure permits the unions to participate in Business Unit Planning Councils, and the contract requires that the unions select bargaining unit participants for the program. Through this involvement, the unions hope to develop plans to increase employees' discretion to provide quality service to the customer, influence restructuring and downsizing, and shape the structure and format for participative teams. If a Planning Council's program conflicts with existing contract language, it can apply for an exemption through the national Constructive Relationship Council. On 8 March 1993, the CWA and AT&T held a conference for one thousand managers and union representatives to kick off Workplace of the Future. An enthusiastic Secretary of Labor, Robert Reich, in his keynote speech commended the parties for their shared vision. AT&T and the IBEW held a similar conference in June 1993.

Other developments further encouraged the union leadership that AT&T was reversing its nonunion direction. Contract provisions negotiated in 1992 allow union members to transfer to nonunion subsidiaries—except NCR (renamed AT&T Global Information Solutions). The union also gained neutrality and card check provisions at some subsidiaries, and disputes over neutrality are arbitrable. In 1995, the company and unions negotiated contractual language that addresses union values.

Opponents of Workplace of the Future, however, remain in powerful positions at both unions and AT&T. As of 1996, four members of the CWA Executive Board continued to oppose the union's participation in the program. At AT&T, engineering and finance managers created labor-management instability through their ongoing commitment to major cost reductions, further downsizing, part-timing, and subcontracting of bargaining unit work.

Although negotiated in 1992, the Workplace of the Future process has diffused fully in only one business unit, the Network Services Division, the organization responsible for running the long distance network, where the union retains considerable strength. Union success in this joint program rests on the same foundation as successful collective bargaining, and that is bargaining power. Where the union is weak, labor participation in business decision making is often ephemeral or takes the form of post-decision-making consultations. For the union, decades of centralized collective bargaining have not prepared the secondary levels of leadership to participate in business decision making, because historically those issues were addressed at the top levels of the union.

Most importantly, however, when the CWA successfully organized a majority of potential members at American Transtech to sign union recognition cards, the company's neutrality pledge evaporated. Ignoring the neutrality provisions of the collective bargaining agreement, the president of American Transtech hired a law firm to engage in a full-fledged union suppression campaign and the union lost the representation election in 1995, souring the new relationship.

CWA's Strategic Responses to Industry Restructuring

The Communications Workers of America has been heralded as a union that engages in strategic planning (Dunlop 1990). Prior to divestiture, under the leadership of President Glenn Watts, CWA engaged in a systematic strategic planning process through the Committee on the Future, created in July 1981. In March 1983, a special convention adopted ten resolutions and two constitutional amendments proposed by the committee.[4] The administrative reforms improved the union's internal operations. In 1986 and 1987, to improve its operating effectiveness, CWA further streamlined its governing structure.

In the legislative arena, the CWA joined the RBOCs in promoting legislation that would allow them to enter the domestic equipment manufacturing business and long distance service—reforms that AT&T opposed. The CWA and the IBEW also supported the RBOCs effort to supply cable TV and information services. In addition, Morton Bahr, president of the CWA, sits on the national Democratic party's leadership committee and serves on Vice President Gore's influential council on the national information infrastructure.

At the state level, CWA policies on deregulation have varied by district. In the South, CWA District 3 supported deregulation, while in the Northeast, CWA Districts 1 and 2 opposed telephone deregulation. Since 1995, however, the CWA and the IBEW have been working together to form a coalition with consumer groups to contain the most damaging effects of deregulation, based on the twin goals of preserving union jobs and universal telephone service at reasonable rates.

CWA's major strategic goal is "Wall-to-Wall" unionization in the information industry. Since divestiture, CWA has added 85,000 new members in the telecommunications industry, primarily through mergers. Mergers with several Telephone Independent Unions after the divestiture announcement added 40,000 members. In 1987, CWA merged with the International Typographical Union, as America's oldest union (founded in 1852) grappled with declining membership as a result of the diffusion of computerized typesetting. In 1993, CWA merged with the National Association of Broadcast Employees and Technicians with members in the broadcast and cable TV industries; and in 1995 it merged with the Newspaper Guild.

Since divestiture CWA has organized 5,000 AT&T employees under neutrality provisions. CWA has been organizing at NCR and American Transtech, both AT&T subsidiaries. At NCR the CWA is organizing field engineers at twenty locations. For this national campaign the CWA set

---

4. However, the union's analysis of the changing environment was wrong. Following AT&T's lead, the CWA leadership thought that the newly competitive AT&T would be the dynamic growth area for employment and union membership, while the Bell operating companies would be relatively stagnant with declining employment and membership.

up the National Association of NCR Employees (NANE). By early 1994, approximately 400 field engineers had joined. The union runs an electronic bulletin board to keep members and organizers informed and to allow them to communicate with each other. CWA has also undertaken a corporate campaign to press AT&T for neutrality and access rights. NCR has vigorously resisted the organizing drive, hiring Jackson and Lewis, the well-known union-busting law firm, to organize their response.

By contrast, under the neutrality provisions contained in the 1992 collective bargaining agreement, CWA began organizing at Transtech. Transtech employs 1,500 managers, 600 regular workers, and 3,500 temporary employees. The Transtech Employees Association seeks to represent both the 600 regular Transtech employees and the 3,500 temporary employees at Transtech that are contracted through eight employment agencies. The temporary employees earn about eight dollars an hour with no benefits. They move from project to project for employment at Transtech. The union was demanding that these workers be made regular AT&T employees. Under the neutrality provisions of the AT&T collective bargaining agreement, the union thought it had gained managerial neutrality and access to non-work areas. Yet, as discussed above, once the election campaign began, Transtech management conducted an aggressive antiunion campaign, defeating the union in the election and poisoning the labor-management relationship.

Although the CWA and the IBEW have developed two sophisticated organizing departments, they have had little success in organizing the new aggressively antiunion competitors, such as MCI and Sprint, although the CWA has mounted another campaign at Sprint. At the local level, the two unions have organized some cable TV franchises, but the major cable corporations have maintained an aggressive antiunion posture. The growth of this nonunion sector has the potential to destabilize collective bargaining in the unionized core.

In collective bargaining, the CWA has sought to maintain a loose pattern on major economic issues and has generally succeeded. The union particularly wants to prevent any substandard agreements in the industry, which could then set patterns for other contracts. The CWA has been successful in keeping a pattern together. To advance its interest, the union has engaged in strikes, developed a member mobilization program, and used workplace campaigns. In 1983, 1986, and 1989 the CWA undertook strikes to oppose concessions in health insurance. Concessions are difficult to sell to the membership, particularly when the companies are earning higher profits than ever possible under the regulated Bell System.

The growth of nonunion competition in virtually every market segment, however, is putting downward pressure on wages and benefits.

In August 1988, CWA launched its Mobilization Program in preparation for 1989 bargaining. Mobilization is grass roots organizing that involves members in one-on-one communication on important issues at the work site. The program's basic aim is to involve all union members in actively representing their collective interest. The campaigns are designed to connect "the bonds of worker solidarity" through collective action. Mobilization tactics include petitions; one-on-one postcard messages; wearing common colors; expressing solidarity through rallies, arm bands, and stand-ups; work-to-rule campaigns; organizing nonmembers; on-site and electronic picket lines; community support activities; and strikes.

The mobilization programs have steadily improved in effectiveness since 1988 and were particularly useful in 1992 bargaining. Rather than strike, CWA continued to bargain after the contract expirations at AT&T, Bell Atlantic, Pacific Telesis, and US West. The membership mobilized to support the union's bargaining objectives. Electronic town meetings, conference calls, and taped telephone messages kept members involved and informed about bargaining progress. At AT&T the unions threatened an electronic picket line by getting all their supporters to pledge to switch their long distance phone service to another carrier until a contract was signed. Some CWA locals demonstrated their mastery of information technologies in getting the union's story out to their members and to management. CWA has also developed its in-workplace strategies. The union believes that these tactics will grow in power as employers rely more and more on a committed and involved workforce to provide high quality customer service.

In 1995, the union once again extended contract expiration dates and was able to achieve contracts without any strikes. At Bell Atlantic, however, the parties reached an agreement five months after the contract expiration date. The union won base wage increases of either 10.9 percent or 11 percent in each of the major contracts. Retiree health insurance will continue to be paid by the companies during the life of the agreement. Except for the NYNEX agreement negotiated in 1994 which limited layoffs, the other contracts did not limit the force reductions that the companies are undertaking. Most, however, improved transfer rights and/or severance benefits.

The industry-wide force reductions have serious implications for the stability of the CWA's internal governing coalition. The telephone installation and central office crafts have been the main pillar of political power within the union, often in coalition with operators. Each of these groups has experienced massive downsizing. Historically, local, district, and national leaders in the CWA came from the ranks of telephone installation and central office crafts, with one major exception, the president of the union. Joseph Beirne worked in Western Electric sales in New Jersey and New York; Glenn Watts started out representing the C&P Commercial Department in Washington, D.C.; and Morton Bahr began with the independent MacKay Radio, in ship-to-shore radio on Long Island. Because each of these leaders began in groups with little influence over union affairs, each became effective coalition builders. With the decline of the traditional union power bases, a new female leadership is emerging at the local, district, and national level. Secretary-Treasurer Barbara Easterling and District Vice Presidents Sue Pisha (District 7—US West) and Janice Wood (District 9—Pacific Telesis) are indicators of the changes underway inside CWA.

Local Unions

Grievance administration remains the primary function of the local unions in the telephone industry. The local unions' representation provides a buffer for workers who can easily be caught between the formal bureaucratic control system and the informal, but widely followed, work practices. Research evidence indicates that effective grievance representation, particularly winning grievances, remains the single most important activity in building the membership's commitment to the local union. Employee participation and other work innovation which reduce traditional methods of bureaucratic control and legitimize informal practices also have the potential to build the local union. Research also suggests that union participation in work reform improves member loyalty and does not undermine the union (Eaton, Gordon, and Keefe 1992; Vallas 1993).

The Post-Divestiture Collective Bargaining Process and Structure

Prior to divestiture, AT&T and its Bell operating companies bargained at two levels. At the first level, called "national bargaining," system-wide agreements covered wages, benefits, and employment security. As a result, a telephone technician working in New York City received the same relative wage increases whether he or she worked for the local operating company, New York Telephone, or for AT&T. The cents-per-hour component of the cost of living escalator tended to compress the wage structure throughout the Bell System (Keefe 1989). In a similar manner, vacations, pension benefits, health care coverage, and insurance benefits became more standardized across the system, regardless of the employing Bell company. This standardization aided human resource planning and force adjustments by facilitating personnel movement among the companies. At the second level of bargaining, "local" bargaining, the individual Bell operating companies bargained with local union leadership over work administration and work rules. Local bargaining issues included overtime policy, posting of schedules, steps in the grievance process, health and safety, and absence pay. Local bargainers, however, could not address issues that were on the national bargaining table.

With divestiture came a restructuring of labor relations. Shortly after divestiture, AT&T successfully removed itself from the common expiration dates established in telephone bargaining. AT&T and its unions renegotiated the termination date of its 1983 contract from 9 August to 31 May 1986. This removed AT&T from the contract termination deadline of 9 August 1986, faced by the RBOCs. As a result, cross-company comparisons would not be made, and the pressure to conform to a potentially more expensive RBOC pattern would be lessened.

Since the core business of the regional Bells had remained relatively unchanged, the expectations about bargaining were similarly unchanged. Initially, CWA sought to maintain a national bargaining structure (Koch, Lewin, and Sockell 1988). When the companies rejected that proposal, CWA pressed for continuance of the two-tier structure, with the first tier at the regional Bell-level and the second tier remaining at the local operating company level. Eventually, all the regional Bells opted for this two-tier structure, except for Ameritech which continued to negotiate at the local company level through 1992. Bargaining has taken place in this new structure in 1986, 1989, 1992, and 1995. Some companies, however, including BellSouth, US West, and NYNEX, expanded the scope of regional bargaining and standardized contract provisions across the local companies to improve operating efficiency.

With the restructuring of the RBOCs away from regulated state organizations toward market oriented businesses, pressures are building to change the two-tier bargaining structure. As former Bell companies reorganize along their lines of business (as discussed in the last section), we anticipate they will emulate AT&T and push for a new two-tier structure: one at the regional corporate level and the second organized around regional business units rather than local geography. AT&T's Workplace of the Future represents an interim step in a similar process, where the CWA and IBEW representatives meet with business unit executives in business unit planning councils to discuss workplace programs. US West and CWA already developed a separate agreement for its customer service division, Home and Personal Services Division in 1992; and in 1995, Ameritech bargained in a two-tier structure for the first time, agreeing to centralize bargaining at the regional level in exchange for union acceptance of local bargaining with business unit organizations. While local structures may continue to change, we believe that economic issues will remain relatively centralized in regional bargaining for the regional Bells and in national bargaining for AT&T.

Pressures for Pattern Bargaining

CWA maintains a loose pattern bargain across the industry on economic issues, receiving considerable assistance from AT&T and the regional Bells. Although the newly competitive AT&T was permitted to escape the common expiration date starting in 1986, it not only remains a participant in the loose pattern, but on some issues has become a pattern setter for the RBOCs, for example, on wages. Only NYNEX negotiations in 1989, 1991, and 1994 produced pattern-breaking agreements. AT&T and the regional Bells, however, faced different problems in the 1980s and early 1990s. Employment security has been the most difficult bargaining issue at AT&T, whereas health insurance has been a strike issue at four regional Bells. With state incentive regulation, employment security has become central to RBOC bargaining as well.

Because of increasingly stringent financial scrutiny by Wall Street and regulators, strategic economic issues have exerted a centralizing influence on the industry's post-divestiture bargaining structure. Deferred wage increases have averaged 2.78 percent annually, COLAs have been either eliminated or highly restricted, and each company has obtained some form of contingent pay, most commonly profit sharing. In either 1986 or 1989 all companies but NYNEX adopted preferred provider organizations to deliver their basic health insurance, a change that limits employees' choice of health care options. Most agreements contain expanded transfer rights, retraining, early retirement incentives, and severance pay enhancements to address employment security. Only Pacific Telesis and Southwest Bell, however, made no layoff commitments during this period. In 1994, NYNEX extended a new no-layoff commitment as part of its massive downsizing package, which is to be accomplished with voluntary separations.

In contrast, union institutional security and work administration issues arising from business reorganizations, new technologies, nonunion competition, and work restructuring exert a decentralizing influence on local bargaining structures. A 1992 CWA survey found that there were over thirty different local participative programs in operation at AT&T, the content of which we take up more fully in the fourth part of this chapter. Some of these programs had union participation and others did not. In the former Bell System companies, Quality of Work Life (QWL) became known as a "labor" program, since it was negotiated by labor relations. QWL always had union involvement, while Total Quality is often viewed as a management participative program, because it is not negotiated and rarely had union involvement (Batt 1993). All the regional Bells and AT&T have adopted workplace reforms such as QWL, quality teams, and self-managed teams; however, they have varied significantly in their degree of corporate commitment, on the one hand, and union involvement, on the other. The latest generation of joint involvement programs focuses most often upon continuously improving customer service. Strategically for the unions, retaining the loyalty of the embedded customer base is essential to preserving jobs in the newly competitive markets. CWA District 3 and BellSouth have been leaders in these joint labor-management, workplace redesign, and participative programs (see Batt 1993). Next to NYNEX (see below), BellSouth has agreed to the most far-reaching union security provisions in the industry, including broader bargaining unit recognition and accretion. Corporate commitments to union institutional security, employment security, and union and worker participation to improve performance are tied closely together in the industry. Security is exchanged for participation in improving performance (Batt 1993).

NYNEX Departs from the Pattern

NYNEX, the regional Bell operating company for New York and New England, appeared to be emphasizing a narrowly cost-cutting path in response to local competitors such as Teleport and MFS, until an historic turnaround in 1991. NYNEX has a history of the worst labor-management relations in the industry. The CWA waged a bitter seven-month strike at New York Telephone in 1971 over wages and union security; and in 1989, the CWA and the IBEW joined forces to win a four-month strike against NYNEX to maintain their health benefits. (NYNEX is the only former Bell company that has maintained its traditional health insurance coverage). As a result of the strike, NYNEX hired James Dowdall from AT&T to change its relationship with the unions; Dowdall's experience at AT&T provided him with considerable credibility with the unions. The subsequent round of negotiations covering 57,000 workers led to a new labor agreement eleven months early, settling in September 1991. The four-year agreement provided 4 percent annual wage increases over the life of the agreement, more than any other contract in the industry.

NYNEX has continued this new approach to labor-management relations even in the wake of announced downsizing. In 1991 and 1992, negotiated provisions for enhanced early retirement led 7,300 nonmanagement employees to take voluntary settlement packages, while some 3,400 managers were laid off. Similarly, in December 1993, the *Wall Street Journal* reported that NYNEX would reduce its workforce by 22,200 jobs over the next three years. Shortly thereafter, NYNEX entered into negotiations with the CWA, and the parties reached an agreement in March 1994, which extends the existing contract through August 1998. Contract provisions under the 1994 agreement contain the most far-reaching employment security framework in the industry. They include a special retirement incentive that adds six years to both service and age and a 30 percent social security supplement until age 62 or a $500 annual bonus, whichever is greater. The company estimated that the incentive program would lead to the voluntary elimination of 16,800 jobs at NYNEX at a cost of over $2 billion or $77,000 per participating employee.

While a major thrust of this program is to induce workers to leave the company voluntarily, other components seek to create a future for the surviving workforce. No worker can be laid off from NYNEX due to changes in organization, work process, or new technology. Layoffs are permitted only in response to volume reductions. A major innovation is the creation of a two-year associate's degree program in telecommunications technology, which is to open to all nonmanagement workers. The employees work four days a week and go to school the fifth day on company time during the academic year. The company pays all educational expenses. Employees begin receiving top craft pay upon entering the program. Upon graduation, employees receive an additional $50 a week increase. NYNEX recognizes that it is a high labor cost employer and hopes to offset this cost disadvantage with a highly educated, flexible, and productive work force.

In addition, all NYNEX employees with five years of service are eligible to take a two-year educational leave. They can receive up to $10,000 per year for educational expenses while retaining full benefits, seniority, and a guaranteed job when they return. The contract also creates a job bank and a new job-sharing provision. Union workers are guaranteed access to all new NYNEX ventures in the information industry. New subsidiaries start by offering union workers the opportunity to bid into the new jobs. Neutrality and card-check recognition apply in any nonunion NYNEX entity. Wage increases are 4 percent in 1994 and in 1995, 3.5 percent in 1996, and 3 percent in 1997, with an additional 3.23 percent in stock and cash bonuses over the term. Cost of living protection kicks in if inflation exceeds 8 percent. The fully paid medical plan continues for the life of the agreement.

While maintaining a traditional arms-length labor-management relationship, NYNEX and the CWA have created a framework that can dramatically turn around their relationship. Notably, it is not based on employee or union participation in productivity-enhancing partnership, but on creating a high-skilled future for the incumbent work force while humanely reducing employment. Through this formula, the parties hope to avoid the decade of employee trauma that AT&T has experienced.

Reorganizing Work and Internal Labor Markets

In the first section of this chapter we argued that the digitalization of the network has enhanced scale and scope economies, creating new opportunities for consolidation and centralization. At the same time market deregulation has led to market segmentation and fragmentation, a trend that lends itself to decentralized market-responsive strategies. We then outlined how these competing logics of centralization and decentralization have played out with respect to business strategy and structure and labor-management relations. This final section continues these themes at the level of distinct occupational groups in the Bell system. We show how the two competing approaches to restructuring have significantly altered the internal labor market rules that shape the jobs and careers of network craft workers, customer service representatives, operators, and managers of these groups.

Specifically, the first approach to reform uses union and employee participation to improve service quality through the redesign of jobs and human resource practices. According to this logic, employees provide better service if they have the opportunity to offer innovative solutions (employee participation), if they have the autonomy to meet customer needs (job redesign), and if they have the appropriate skills (education and training) and incentives (career opportunities, employment security, compensation) to make a commitment to the company. In this view, commitment is a two-way street; if the company shows its commitment to enhancing the jobs and careers of employees, then employees will commit themselves to making the company competitive. This approach has a decentralizing thrust because it relies on the talent and creativity of employees at the point of contact with the customer.

The second approach focuses on realizing scale economies and cutting costs through consolidations, new applications of technology, reengineering, and downsizing. It begins at the macro organizational level and relies on top management, consultants, and engineers to develop system-wide innovations. The approach relies on centralized decision making rather than decentralized discretion. Changes in the design of jobs and human resource practices flow *as a consequence* of new technologies and organizational restructuring. Because of this logic, companies do not make prior commitments to job enhancement or employment security. The two approaches are, therefore, in conflict.

At AT&T and the regional Bell companies, the second approach has dominated, and often undermined, the first. In 1984, AT&T began with the macro approach, and as indicated above, shed 60 percent of its domestic unionized workforce. It unilaterally introduced experiments with participation and teams in the late 1980s; but it was not until 1992 that it developed a joint union-management approach to job redesign which builds on the logic of decentralized participation. The regional Bells, by contrast, experimented more fully with participatory approaches in the 1980s, but by the early 1990s as local deregulation approached, they shifted gears, halted some of these experiments, and focused more fully on consolidation and reengineering.

While the shape of jobs and careers in the post-divestiture era is still uncertain, the evidence suggests that companies have chosen to focus on the benefits of scale economies and system integration. Two explanations are plausible, and both are probably at work. First, in the deregulated environment, the low-wage, nonunion option is available for the first time, and companies have taken advantage of what is a quick-fix solution to competitiveness—lowering costs and improving shareholder dividends at the expense of a weakened labor movement. Second, the integrated nature, or "systemness" of telecommunications services means that companies can continue to reap tremendous scale economies, particularly given the centralizing nature of new technologies, as discussed in the first section of this chapter. Both of these industry dynamics put at risk the participatory and job enhancing approach to quality service that total quality theorists and others advocate.

This section is divided into three parts. The first part briefly describes the pre-divestiture system of work organization and internal labor markets in the Bell System. The second part reviews trends in job redesign and shows how the competing logics of cost cutting versus job enhancement have played out for each of four occupational groups: network crafts, customer services, operators, and managers of these occupational groups. The third part outlines the new internal labor markets that are emerging.

Pre-Divestiture Work Organization and Internal Labor Markets

The stability of the AT&T work system prior to divestiture was one of its most salient characteristics. Its framework was largely set in place before World War I when AT&T used its control of patents and long distance service to purchase controlling interest in local operating companies around the country. Through license contracts with the operating companies, AT&T required the use of standardized technology (AT&T's equipment manufactured at its wholly-owned subsidiary, Western Electric, since 1881) as well as standard operating procedures—the Bell System Practices. AT&T's control created a functionally specialized, top-down, command-and-control organization early on. Corporate paternalism and implicit long-term employment relations also date to this period, when the company introduced the "American Plan" of benefits to build loyalty and long-term commitment to the firm. From World War I to 1937, AT&T successfully launched company unions as an alternative to independent trade unionism, and embraced the human relations movement, offering its Western Electric Hawthorne plant for Elton Mayo and F. J. Roethlisberger's experiments in industrial psychology (Roethlisberger and Dickson 1939). In the meantime, Chester Barnard, at that time president of New Jersey Bell, completed his theory of cooperative industrial organization—the corporation as a cooperative system with a moral purpose—based on his experience at New Jersey Bell (1938). Throughout this period, AT&T provided high and steady dividends to shareholders, and was minimally regulated by state and federal authorities.

In the post–World War II period, state and federal regulators put increasing pressure on the Bell System both to keep rates down and to expand universal service. AT&T developed two managerial strategies. First, to minimize costs and reap scale economies, it sought to apply new technologies that reduced the labor content of jobs. This strategy met with mixed success because some jobs (operator services) lent themselves to Taylorism more than others (customer services and network craft). The result was a very mixed production system that varied by occupational group, as we describe in greater detail below. Second, where technology did not pace labor, AT&T adopted a strategy of "management by numbers" to increase productivity and meet the monitoring requirements of regulators. The result was a phenomenal growth in bureaucracy as the managerial staff swelled from 13.5 percent to 29 percent of the workforce (AT&T 1982).

The functional organization of AT&T in 1980 closely resembled the company's framework in 1945 or in 1910. Both AT&T and the Bell operating companies had three basic components: Plant (network), Traffic (operator services), and Commercial (business office/customer service). Additionally, the General Department provided administrative support functions that included Accounting, Legal, Regulatory, and Personnel.

Each functional division, or occupational specialty, had a unique production logic. Network may best be compared to a continuous process industry in which highly skilled craft workers maintained the switching and transmission equipment needed for the continuous flow of dial tone (for a detailed discussion, see Keefe 1995). They did not produce a commodity, but maintained the infrastructure needed to transmit telephone communications, just as workers in oil refinery or chemical processing build and maintain the infrastructure through which liquids flow. Because of the nature of the work, throughout the post–World War II period, these jobs continued to require high skill, completion of a whole task (craft-like), and considerable autonomy for crews maintaining a highly geographically-dispersed infrastructure.

On the service side, customer services consisted of thousands of local business offices in which "universal" service representatives answered all questions and concerns of customers. Until the 1980s, jobs were quite varied and required considerable skill, and may best be thought of as providing highly personalized or specialized business services.

In contrast to network and customer services, operator services began as a mass production operation, with AT&T applying scientific management (Taylorism) to operator jobs by the turn of the century (Norwood 1990: 33–40). It was also unique because it was part of both network and services: operators were the "human switch" in the continuous process industry, making connections where machines could not; they were also the human face of the telephone company—the most frequent customer contact point in providing assistance or information. While operators' jobs were organized along industrial lines, however, they were classified as female service jobs for purposes of pay and promotion.

Changing employment levels of these occupational groups reflect differences in work organization. With the growth of the Bell System, the numbers of skilled workers in network and customer services steadily increased between 1950 and 1980—from 24 to 44 percent of the workforce (network) and from 5.3 to 11.1 percent (customer services). By contrast, the number of operators fell by fifty percent between 1950, when they comprised 47 percent of the workforce, and 1980, when they dropped to 16 percent (AT&T 1982).

Consistent with this unequal application of Taylorism to different occupational groups are trends in the ratio of supervisors to workers across departments. In operator services, the ratio increased from 1:6 in 1910 to 1:20 in 1980 as electronic monitoring absorbed supervisory functions. By contrast, the ratio in network craft occupations in 1980 was 1:6, and in customer service occupations, 1:10.

Within each functional division, the Bell system created additional subdivisions with occupational specialties and short job ladders (usually two steps in network and three in services). These functional divisions and job ladders are outlined in Figure 1.1. For female-dominated service jobs,

FIGURE 1.1.

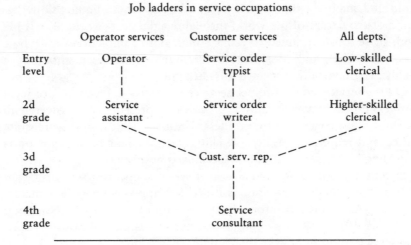

Job ladders in service occupations

	Operator services	Customer services	All depts.
Entry level	Operator	Service order typist	Low-skilled clerical
2d grade	Service assistant	Service order writer	Higher-skilled clerical
3d grade		Cust. serv. rep.	
4th grade		Service consultant	

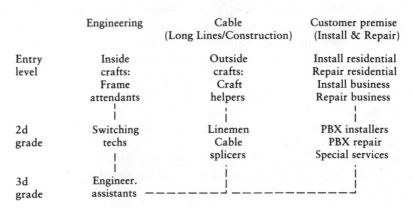

Job ladders in network occupations

	Engineering	Cable (Long Lines/Construction)	Customer premise (Install & Repair)
Entry level	Inside crafts: Frame attendants	Outside crafts: Craft helpers	Install residential Repair residential Install business Repair business
2d grade	Switching techs	Linemen Cable splicers	PBX installers PBX repair Special services
3d grade	Engineer. assistants		

low-level clerical or operator positions were the two ports of entry. From there, women could advance to skilled clerical work in different departments or to customer service jobs. The business office and repair service bureaus had three-tiered job ladders from entry clerical to customer service positions. The top job in the business office paid less than an entry level craft job.

In Network, subdivisions included Engineering, Construction (Long Lines at AT&T and Cable Construction and Maintenance at the operating companies), Central Office (switching and transmission equipment), and Installation and Repair (I&R) of customer premise equipment (CPE). Engineering consisted primarily of engineers who designed the network infrastructure, aided by the highest-paid craft job, engineering assistants, who usually came from the top crafts in construction or I&R. AT&T Long Lines built and maintained the long distance "trunk lines" connecting Central Office switches in different geographic locations to a long distance network controlled by toll switches. Operating company construction departments built and maintained the cables between the Central Office switches and the customer premises. Within Long Lines, there also were inside and outside crafts. Inside crafts consisted of entry-level frame attendants who ran wiring for each telephone number and installation and the higher-skilled central office switching technicians who maintained the electromechanical switches. Outside crafts included cable splicers' helpers (until the 1960s), higher-skilled linemen (line gangs) who built the pole lines and placed the cable, and higher-skilled cable splicers who spliced and repaired telephone cable. Installation and repair also had two grades: I&R (or service technicians) who placed and repaired the service wires and telephone sets on customer premises and PBX (private branch exchanges) or special services technicians, who installed and repaired PBX equipment in businesses and other special services such as data lines or fire alarms. Particularly in urban areas, companies further divided jobs within pay grades, with junior workers getting the less skilled and more difficult manual or "dirty work." Switching technicians specialized in particular switches; linemen would specialize in aerial, underground, or buried cable. The hierarchy of I&R service technician jobs was: residential installation, residential repair, business installation, business repair.

Historically, strong occupational subcultures emerged in these functional departments due to corporate policies of occupational segregation. John Schacht notes, "white-collar workers in the accounting and commercial departments looked down on both the traffic operator and the 'greasy plant man out there climbing poles, with creosote all over him.'

. . . In the commercial departments, particularly, insularity was encouraged by the company practice of paying monthly or bimonthly salaries, as distinguished from weekly wages in the other departments. Along with this practice went messages designed to nourished feelings of elitism, messages . . . that 'you [customer services] are the telephone company in the eyes of the public' and therefore 'the elite' " (Schacht 1985: 22). Network craft cultures also split along white collar (inside craft) and blue collar (outside craft) lines. Historically, network craft and operators organized separate union locals, while business and accounting resisted unionization. These subcultures continue to be robust. While the 1970s Equal Employment Opportunity Commission (EEOC) law suit against AT&T forced the opening of some craft jobs for women (for example, I&R jobs), occupational segregation has been quite resilient. At an early date AT&T also created a largely native white workforce, segregated from immigrants and Afro-Americans, through the high educational requirements and the entrance examinations for entry-level jobs. As early as the 1920s and 1930s, the median number of school years for operators was 11.8, compared to 10.8 for all U.S. female workers; comparable figures for AT&T network craft workers were 10.5 years versus 8.7 years for all U.S. males (Schacht 1985: 23–24).

Internal labor markets resembled the classic industrial markets described by Peter Doeringer and Michael Piore (1971). While the overwhelming majority of workers never rose beyond craft levels, they enjoyed lifetime jobs. Moreover, an important minority reached middle management positions during the growth years of the 1950s through 1970s. Paternalistic employment practices dated to 1913, when AT&T started introducing benefits policies (company-paid pensions, sickness and disability benefits, employee stock options, and an organization of retired and long-service employees); from the 1920s on, the company had seniority-based benefits and career ladders filled almost exclusively from within (Schacht 1985: 35–36).

The Bell System recruited first level supervisors either from the rank and file or from the external labor market. By the 1950s, those hired from the outside were usually college-educated; and until the 1960s or so, they were often placed in nonmanagement jobs for a year to learn the business. First level supervisors received considerable management training, primarily designed to separate managers from workers; and this was particularly true for workers promoted from within, who were encouraged to break all social ties with former coworkers. The advantage of promoting from within is that as former workers, supervisors had an intimate knowledge of the technology and job requirements.

The six levels of management above first level were filled exclusively from within. Informal sponsorship was extremely important for ensuring upward mobility; many also used the company's generous tuition-aid program to complete college courses and qualify for middle level positions. Bell companies encouraged college-educated hires to climb to higher levels of management, and they selected an elite group to be "fast-tracked" and groomed for top management. In a longitudinal study of managers at AT&T from 1956 to 1976, Ann Howard and Douglas Bray found that the modal level of achievement for non-college-educated managers was a level two management position, while that of college-educated managers was level three; while 5 to 10 percent of non-college-educated workers received promotions annually, 15 to 25 percent of college-educated managers did so (Howard and Bray 1988: 128–29).

In summary, the system clearly created middle-class jobs and management opportunities that otherwise would not have been available for a population dispersed in small towns, cities, and rural areas across the country. The AT&T internal labor market created a system of lifetime employment security unlike that provided by other large corporations because AT&T was guaranteed a rate of return by regulators and did not face business cycle fluctuations.

The Changing Nature of Jobs: Pre- and Post-Divestiture

If we consider the two competing approaches to work reform that have dominated post-divestiture efforts in the Bell System companies—job enhancement versus consolidation through technology and reengineering—the first approach is a break from the past, while the second represents a continuation. Moreover, while companies have undertaken job enhancement experiments in most occupations, they have occurred in "pockets" and affected only a minority of workers. New technologies and reengineering, by contrast, have affected the entire workforce in particular occupations, and therefore, have been more widely felt.

Job enhancement strategies since the 1980s are of four types: (a) those that involve workers in "off-line" problem-solving groups (Quality of Worklife committees, labor-management committees, quality improvement teams); (b) those that absorb supervisory tasks (task assignments, scheduling, monitoring, reporting), such as self-managed teams; (c) those that broaden jobs (job rotation, multitasking, job enlargement); and (d) those that deepen jobs (multiskilling, added quality control, and problem solving). By far the most common efforts have been of the first two varieties—both of which are directed at the problem of bureaucracy rather than, for example, the excesses of Taylorism. Early experiments in off-line groups focused on changing the style of management from a top-down military style to a more participative one. Later experiments in self-managed teams push this logic further, allowing workers to absorb supervisory tasks and firms to cut their indirect labor costs substantially. Workers and unions have supported self-managed teams as a way of reducing the excesses of heavy supervision, even though the teams must often absorb more work without additional time allocated to do it.

In contrast to these experiments which increase worker discretion, firms have expanded the labor-displacing technologies and the logic of mass production into new areas. In contrast to job redesign theories that emphasize the benefits of breadth and multiskilling, Bell companies have continued the pre-divestiture strategy of narrowing jobs and applying technologies that reduce the content of labor. In operator services, new software technologies or "expert systems" have *accelerated* labor-displacement and job fragmentation. In customer services, as a direct result of deregulation, companies have created detailed divisions of labor to separate out the sales function from other service functions; they have also introduced automatic call distribution and expert systems to pace work. Network digitalization has both decreased the demand for and changed the skill content of some network craft jobs; and new handheld computers represent the first introduction of electronic monitoring into outside crafts. The following section reviews these changes.

Network Crafts

As indicated above, by 1980, AT&T had created highly functionally-specialized occupations in network, but the jobs themselves remained craft-like. The jobs required electromechanical skills and the completion of a whole task; geographic dispersion reinforced autonomy. AT&T tried to compensate for its inability to control outside crafts by a management strategy of heavy supervision and individual responsibility for detailed quantitative performance measures (tasks or jobs per day). Job discipline based on these measures was an ongoing source of labor-management conflict.

It was not until the late 1970s and early 1980s that new technologies—particularly the digitalization of the network—began to reduce employment levels and change the skill content of network craft jobs.[5] The demand for skill has shifted from electromechanical to computer-based

5. AT&T has been four to five years ahead of the RBOCs in introducing these technologies. It introduced the first electronic switches that switched analog transmissions in the late 1960s. It introduced the first fully digital switches in 1983.

skills; the overall demand for labor decreased because systems needed less maintenance. This change was particularly significant because it represents the first time in the network's history that increases in productivity were not accompanied by increases in employment; instead, the relationship has reversed.

In the central offices, for example, switching technicians in the past had hand-wired and manually repaired the relays and switches. Failures were electrical and mechanical in nature. With electronic switches, by contrast, switching technicians use computers to test switches via remote work stations and write up orders for other technicians in the central offices to carry out. More recently, new advances in software programming make digital switches both self-diagnosing and "self-healing," further reducing the demand for traditional electromechanical skills of craft workers. A similar trend has occurred with the digitalization of PBX and other customer premise equipment, which may now be remotely tested and repaired.

The net effect of these changes on the demand for skill is mixed. On the one hand, some of the repair work formerly done by top craft workers is now done by clerks monitoring computers. For example, companies have created computer-based inventories of network specifications— information that used to be contained in blueprints. Engineering assistants who created blueprints of high-level circuit order layout designs have been replaced by clerks who do the same work at computers at roughly 60 percent of the craft pay. Similarly, historically "testmen" would manually test the line to identify the source of faulty transmission. In the late 1970s and early 1980s, the Bell System replaced testmen with "maintenance administrators," clerks who use computer systems to identify the problem. On the other hand, while the change eliminated a top craft job, clerks learned new software skills and were upgraded to a job at 80 percent of testmen's wages. In addition, companies have created a relatively small number of systems analyst and computer programming jobs.

The introduction of fiber optic cable in the short run has increased the demand for construction crews to replace copper wire, but in the long run reduces the demand for cable splicers because it is relatively maintenance-free. While AT&T and the RBOCs have substantially replaced their trunk lines and feeder cables with fiber, the "last mile" (the 90 percent of the network connecting the distribution cables in streets to the customer premise) continues to be copper.

Other changes in network crafts are the introduction of handheld computers which allow workers to input work reports as they finish them, a system which workers complain allows the company to monitor them electronically for the first time. Another dimension of change concerns the attempt of companies to turn network craft workers into a supplementary sales force. In Total Quality training, network craft workers are encouraged to use every opportunity to "meet customers needs," or sell. Craft workers have tended to resist this change, and its diffusion is relatively minimal because network craft workers consider sales to be demeaning, unskilled work.

AT&T and the regional Bell companies have also experimented with self-managed teams in network crafts, and generally find that workers successfully make the transition because they already have considerable autonomy and discretion. Self-management, according to some, formalizes preexisting informal arrangements. This is particularly true in rural areas, where large distances made heavy supervision infeasible, and workers retained not only greater autonomy but more varied skills. The evidence from interviews with teams, however, shows that the shift to formal self-managed teams changes the responsibilities of even the more autonomous rural workers, who absorb both the internal administrative duties of supervisors and the external duties of interacting with customers as well as other activities to get the job done. This includes ordering supplies, bringing in jobs, negotiating with parties over turf responsibilities, answering customer complaints, and working with engineers in the pre-survey stage. Craft workers now assume these responsibilities. In the language of quality consultants, craft workers interaction with both internal and external customers has grown.

Survey evidence supports these qualitative reports. A comparison of matched pairs of self-managed and traditionally supervised work groups in network crafts found that they differ significantly along a series of dimensions. Workers in the self-managed groups consistently showed higher levels of autonomy in their control over work assignments, tools, and pace of work; scheduling; and quality and safety inspections. They also show significantly higher levels of internal group learning and problem solving as well as more frequent cross-functional problem solving with managers and professionals outside of the group. While workers report consistently higher levels of job satisfaction and work group quality, they absorb the work previously done by supervisors in 25 to 30 percent less time, leading to dramatic savings in indirect labor costs for companies. The result is that this innovation has the support of the union and top management alike because it provides mutual gains—more rewarding jobs for workers, workforce reductions among managers rather than workers, and cost savings for management. As discussed in greater detail below, supervisors and middle managers suffer job loss under this model, but those who remain often experience job enhancement because they are relieved of mundane reporting and monitoring responsibilities (Batt 1995).

Customer Service

Customer service representatives (CSRs) are frontline employees who deal directly with customers over a range of issues, including sales, service orders, questions on service or billing, and collections on overdue accounts. Historically, telephone companies had "universal" service representatives who handled all customer requests and problems. Over the past decade, the companies and unions have debated the content of the service representative job, and the future is still uncertain. As a direct response to deregulation and the desire to increase revenues, Bell operating companies subdivided the service representative job into sales (CSRs) on the one hand, and services (collections representatives or credit consultants) on the other. The logic of the split job titles was to separate out interactions with customers that are "positive" from those that are "negative," thereby allowing CSRs to sell more. The split title allows companies to pay a lower hourly rate to the collections representatives (about 90 percent of what CSRs receive). On the billing side, some companies have further divided the job into those who handle active bills versus past-due bills.

According to workers, the split job functions confuse customers who want to get all of their business done with one call. It also has negative cost implications because CSRs feel pressured to meet their sales quotas and may sell to people who are poor credit risks. Collections representatives then find themselves dealing with repeat offenders.[6]

Companies have also divided service representative jobs by market segment—between those handling residential customers, small business, and large business accounts. While the first two job categories are narrower and involve only phone sales, account executives for large business provide one-stop-shopping for their clients. According to customer service workers, AT&T has developed an automated system that distributes incoming customer calls by their call volume, with high-end users forwarded to an account executive and mid-level users to a service representative, and low-end users to a recording and voice mail.

---

6. US West, for example, found that uncollectible payments, or net bad debt, had tripled in the five years after it split the titles, and this led them to create yet another job classification of customer credit approval (U.S. Congress 1993: 413).

In addition to the split titles in customer services, telephone companies have added telemarketing departments which handle only high-volume outgoing sales solicitation, usually follow-up calls to ad campaigns. Traditionally, telephone sales occurred primarily through incoming customer calls, handled by universal service representatives. To maximize sales, companies have dramatically increased their marketing budgets. Telemarketing jobs usually rely on a secondary, or low wage, high turnover workforce often under lease or subcontracting arrangements. The jobs resemble those of operators in terms of their low cycle time and repetitiveness, and use of expert computer systems to control the timing and script of calls.[7]

The job of CSR has also become more pressured, more specialized, and increasingly complex as telephone companies have developed differentiated products—a variety of enhanced services—to add value in saturated telephone markets. Most industry practitioners agree that service representatives have the most stressful jobs in the industry. Companies measure CSR performance by sales volume and/or achievement of sales quotas. Top sellers receive awards of cash or prizes. In many cases, companies also discipline CSRs who fail to meet adherence standards—schedules of 15 minute increments that indicate when CSRs are to be taking calls, on rest break, or at lunch.

To increase efficiency, companies have adopted new policies, both to reduce the amount of time that service representatives take between calls and to spread the distribution of calls more evenly. First, companies have introduced "automated call distribution" systems that pace work as well as expert systems that instantly supply customer background information, help identify selling opportunities, and electronically monitor the service representative. Second, they have shifted call distribution from a local level to a state level or beyond. While in the past, customers received specialized service from a local service representative whom they could come to know personally, automatic distribution systems now route calls to service representatives in consolidated offices around a state or region. For CSRs, this means they have a constant call-load, rather than a pace of work that varies over the course of a day. A third strategy has been to distribute calls over a longer period of the day—to establish 24-hour service with workers divided into three shifts for the first time.

7. Recently, at least two companies—US West and BellSouth—decided that they could improve quality by bringing telemarketing work in-house, and negotiated with their unions to "accrete" the telemarketing workers to the bargaining unit. In these companies, telemarketing jobs are now full-time with benefits.

At the same time that companies have introduced new systems that reduce CSRs' control over work, they have also tried experiments in "empowerment," in self-managed teams, and in job redesign to return to the "universal" approach. An example of the "empowerment" approach comes from total quality concepts initiated in several companies to give service representatives greater discretion to make nonroutine billing adjustments, a decision formerly made by supervisors.

In experiments with self-managed teams, service representatives absorb both the administrative tasks for the work group and the job of interfacing with "subject matter experts" in other departments to find out answers to nonroutine questions or problems that arise. This change requires managerial staff in other departments to give to workers the respect and credibility normally reserved for professional and managerial employees. Team members report that they enjoy the independence, the greater respect from managers, and the internal group cooperation that comes from working as a team. Group members also share knowledge in areas such as improving sales revenues, solving complicated billing problems, or handling difficult customers.

Quantitative analysis of survey and objective productivity data indicates that team membership significantly improves workers' job satisfaction as well as sales revenues. Multivariate analysis of sales data shows that members of self-managed teams achieve 17 percent higher monthly sales revenues, after controlling for variation in technology, markets, human resource practices, and demographic characteristics of workers (Batt 1995). As in the network teams described above, use of teams in customer services appears to produce mutual gains for workers and unions as well as management.

These findings are particularly surprising because self-managed teams are more difficult to establish in office settings. As already noted, automatic call distributors set the pace of work. Software technology allows companies to set call-loads at the state level or larger geographic region so that not even lower or middle level managers have discretion over scheduling and assignments. To give these workers the time away from the board needed to absorb supervisory tasks, supervisors may have to reduce the workload or call-load of the teams; many supervisors are unable or unwilling to do this either because they don't have discretion over call-loads, because workloads are already too heavy as a result of downsizing, or because giving "special treatment" to self-managed groups creates resentment from other workers.

In addition to self-managed teams, a number of companies have been rethinking the specialized job titles in customer services; and some have

made the decision to return to the concept of "universal service representative" or "one-stop shopping." The push for change has come largely
from workers who seek relief from monotonous jobs. The most extensive
experiment was a two-year joint labor-management job redesign effort
for 5,000 service workers at US West in 1992 and 1993. The job redesign, piloted in Phoenix, put an end to sales quotas. It envisioned a center
for customer service that reintegrated sales, credit verification, billing,
and collections, and ultimately, dispatch and repair services as well. Employees would be cross-trained in different functions and work as a team,
rotating jobs and gaining some choice in task-assignments. Additionally,
rather than using an automatic call distributor, the design called for an
"interactive work distributor" which would allow service representatives
to log on and choose the types of calls they would receive during a given
work period. The job redesign, however, was never implemented because
the company halted implementation in 1993 when it announced a company-wide consolidation (U.S. Congress 1993). Other companies, such
as AT&T, have piloted experiments in broader job design for service consultants serving small business clients; but by 1996, widescale implementation had not occurred.

Operators

Historically, the Traffic Department consisted of hundreds of thousands of operators tied to switchboards with supervisors or "service assistants" walking around behind them: operators were heavily
monitored, both physically and electronically. They were the "human
switch," manually making the connections between lines that would later
be made by electromechanical switching systems, and currently, digital
switching systems. The jobs were also complex and multiskilled—both
physically and mentally demanding, requiring intense concentration to
respond to signal lights, converse with customers and other operators,
plug in cords and time and record long distance calls (Schacht 1985:
31–32). Operator jobs are the female counterpart to auto assembly line
work, providing low discretion and high demands, an archetype of high
stress work.

Major technological displacement of operators occurred in the 1920s
and 1930s as dial tone (mechanical switching) made it possible for customers to dial their own local calls, and again in the 1950s, when
switches made it possible to direct dial long distance calls.[8] Digital sys-

8. One switchboard operator did the work of six manual operators, leading to the
displacement of some 50,000 operators in the 1930s (Danielian 1939: 210–12).

tems further eliminated operator work by letting customers use credit cards to direct dial. The new technologies also reduced the variety in operator jobs: eliminating the physical side of the job, reducing the types of calls, and eliminating the diagnostic work of identifying faulty telephone circuits (Kohl 1993:104). Companies first introduced automatic call distribution systems in operator services to increase the pace of work.

In the post-divestiture period, several changes have continued to displace and fragment operator jobs. First, using customer systems with enlarged computing power, "automated response systems" split long distance call-handling between two operators: the first punches in the numbers and goes on to another call while the computer makes the connection. The second operator comes on the line to ask if the collect call will be accepted. This "split" call-handling saves several seconds in an operator's handling of each call, and saves companies millions of dollars each year (Kohl 1993:105). These systems reduce call cycle time, increasing the repetitiveness and tedium of jobs. By the mid-1990s, directory assistance operators were handling approximately 1,000 calls per day.

Consistent with new technologies are new work procedures that limit the time operators spend with customers. Companies restrict operators, for example, from giving out more than two numbers at a time. According to one experienced operator, new work rules instruct operators to be more forceful in turning back callers and telling them to dial direct or to use a credit card.

Another change is the now widespread use of computer-generated voice messages, primitive voice recognition systems or "robot operators," which instruct callers to enter a series of numbers in order to place a call or obtain billing or other information. Another automated procedure is automatic calls to customers to remind them their bill is overdue. Companies continue to develop and test ever more sophisticated voice recognition software designed to reduce the labor content of operator services. This technology allows computers to recognize key words and to handle a greater variety of calls (collect, person to person, third party billing) as well as to recognize different languages.

In contrast to the thrust of new technologies and work methods which reduce the discretion of operators, companies have also experimented with self-managed teams or "team-centered management" in operator services. AT&T's Eastern Region of Consumer Customer Services (formerly Operator Services) introduced self-managed teams in 1988, and the program subsequently expanded throughout the region. "Teams" of twelve to twenty-five operators would meet on a monthly basis to discuss performance objectives, results, and appraisals. In addition, smaller teams of six to ten employees would absorb the administrative tasks previously handled by managers and take responsibility for problem solving and conflict resolution. Multiple purposes of the effort include reducing management ranks and increasing their span of control, improving employee morale and involvement in decision making, and improving labor-management trust. The new system covered 5,000 employees, before it began to unravel in 1994 as a result of a another round of downsizing in operator services coupled with the departure of the top manager, Dana Becker Dunn, who had spearheaded the team-based system.

Managers

In the pre-divestiture period, managerial jobs in the Bell System were highly regimented and functionally specialized—resembling much more the Taylorism of industrial labor markets (Doeringer and Piore 1971) than the breadth commonly associated with managerial markets (Osterman 1988).[9] Managers rose in functional silos through seven layers of management leading up to officers in the Bell System; those groomed for top management were rotated across departments. Observers described the AT&T system as a military one: "A traffic manager in the smallest of Bell offices reports to the traffic manager directly above him in the next largest office area to district to regional to operating company and ultimately to 195 Broadway [AT&T's 'Pentagon']—just as an Army G-1 officer has counterpart from battalion level all the way up to the Defense Department" (Goulden 1968:17).

The primary role of supervisors and managers was to meet productivity goals. AT&T embraced the 1960s fad of management by objectives. And because the Bell System measured the performance of managers as the aggregate of the performance of workers under them, the system provided incentives for heavy monitoring of workers and enforcement of work discipline. If top management demanded better numbers, middle and lower managers felt squeezed, and in turn, pressured workers. Standard operating procedures set at the top, however, often made the jobs of responsible managers more difficult: they had to act as if they were following orders while working around them to get the job done. The system of functionally-specific measures reinforced separation and "turf" competition between managers in different departments. Maximizing efficiencies in one department, however, often undermined efficiencies in another. Maximizing tasks per day, for example, creates incentives to

---

9. This section summarizes the more detailed analysis of changing managerial jobs and careers found in Batt (1996).

find quick fixes to problems, which may result in repeat repair calls for repair technicians, or long-term network deterioration requiring replacement.

In the post-divestiture period, changes in managerial jobs have drawn on ideas of employee participation and total quality, beginning with "participatory management" to change the military-style command-and-control nature of managerial jobs. The changes for managers stressed new *behaviors* rather than new *skills* in the narrower sense of the term. Management training emphasized a "softer" approach of listening more than dictating. Middle and lower level managers had to learn to discuss ongoing problems with union leaders, rather than only in the context of grievances. The use of self-managed teams, still in its infancy, is a logical extension of this approach; and where teams have been introduced, they particularly change the jobs of first-line supervisors, who become "coaches." Coaches are supposed to "lead rather than command, inspire rather than demand obedience," according to industry practitioners and consultants.

The effects on first-line supervisors of the shift to teams appears to be complex. One multivariate analysis of the determinants of the work attitudes of supervisors found that supervising self-managed teams had a significant negative effect on supervisors' job satisfaction, but a significant positive effect on their organizational commitment. These findings are consistent with qualitative evidence from the same study: supervisors noted that the shift to self-managed teams was necessary for the company to streamline management ranks and increase the span of control of supervisors (from a traditional ratio of 1:6 to 1:20 or more) (Batt 1995). In effect, while supervisors felt threatened by the changes, they signaled their commitment to the company by supporting an innovation that they viewed as necessary for competitiveness.

The response of supervisors also appears to be contingent upon how management redesigns the job responsibilities of supervisors. As companies attempt to increase the span of control of supervisors, the supervisors will simply experience greater workloads unless they are relieved of some of their prior responsibilities. By shifting the more mundane reporting and monitoring responsibilities to workers while increasing the coordinating and developmental functions of supervisors, their jobs may actually be enhanced.

According to one company-sponsored survey of network supervisors, two-thirds of the supervisors were dissatisfied with their traditional job responsibilities; one-third said they would return to craft (nonmanagement) jobs if given the opportunity. The company found that traditional supervisors spent 60 percent of their time doing administrative work and less than 10 percent of their time in the field monitoring or training workers. The company subsequently used the experience from self-managed teams to develop a new supervisor job description. Under the piloted job redesign, coaches spend fifty percent of their time in the field—a dramatic improvement from the perspective of the supervisors who express dislike for "paperwork."

For middle level managers responsible for local or district level operations (responsible for a county or portion of a city, the equivalent of a plant manager in manufacturing), companies have also applied total quality concepts to decentralize responsibility and create "ownership." The idea is to create small business units in large organizations.

In one company, for example, to break from the past when local managers had little discretion and reported through department hierarchies to state operations managers, the company created cross-departmental "district operations councils" for integrated problem solving at the local level. The district councils, local geographic units established at divestiture and made up of local managers from different departments, had functioned in the 1980s primarily as vehicles for public relations, employee involvement in community affairs, and the telephone company's interface with the regulatory environment. Local managers maintained departmental turf and interacted little beyond monthly council meetings. Under the total quality program, the new role for the district operations councils was to improve service quality, maximize revenues, and control costs. Legislative and regulatory duties became secondary; coordination of community activities was discontinued. Councils took responsibility for initiating quality action teams to solve particular problems or initiate workplace innovations such as self-managed teams. Newly revised customer service reports provided data at the local level, rather than at the state level as had previously occurred.

Conceptually this reform represents a change not only from centralized to decentralized, and functional to more collaborative ways of operating, but from a focus on *public* service to *individual customer* sales, from actions such as community service that present the collective face of the company, to actions designed to maximize sales. For middle managers, this requires a shift in skills: away from the regulatory environment and toward business, marketing, and human resource management. More importantly, it represents a break from the moral purpose of the organization as put forth by Barnard (1938)—and many workers and managers alike resent this change as a violation of their ethical standards. From the viewpoint of the customer, the effects of this change are unclear. To the extent that employees focus on improving customer service, the public indeed will benefit. To the extent that companies pressure employees to meet demanding sales quotas, customers may be negatively effected. They may face heavy-handed marketing, or as has occurred in at least three states (Florida, Pennsylvania, and California), employees may feel pressured to engage in questionable sales practices such as assuming levels of enhanced services for customers without their full knowledge or explicit agreement.

Finally, companies have initiated changes in human resource policies that uniquely affect managers. Whereas workers are covered by collective bargaining contracts and unions to date have successfully avoided major restructuring of compensation systems or benefit plans (with the exception of co-payment plans in health care), companies have unilaterally introduced changes in performance appraisals, compensation, and benefit plans for managers.

A representative example comes from one regional Bell company that has reclassified jobs and introduced new measurement and compensation systems in order to increase competitive behavior. To match jobs more closely with the external market, managerial job classifications dropped from 3,600 to 2,000, largely by eliminating departmental distinctions and creating short descriptions of broad responsibilities. The new job classifications drive changes in performance measurement and compensation, and link pay scales more closely to the external market. A forced distribution system to promote pay-for-performance has replaced across-the-board pay raises. Under the new system, managers receive between 80 percent and 120 percent of their grade, but a forced distribution means that superiors must differentiate more between high and low performers among their subordinates. An additional 10 percent of salary is at risk (an innovation since divestiture), with group payouts dependent upon firm performance. Additionally, the company has altered its promotion policies to allow external recruitment to "fill skill gaps." The question for current managers is what constitute skill gaps and to what extent they will be allowed to train and skill up in new areas before external recruits are added.

Post-Divestiture Internal Labor Markets

The most significant change for workers and managers alike under the new internal labor market rules is the break in the historic commitment to long-term employment contracts. Companies have continued with relatively high wages and benefits, education and training opportunities remain above average, and companies have increased opportunities for retraining in some cases. Use of two-tier wage structures or part-time and contingent workers remains relatively marginal; however, subcontracting has expanded. The commitment to downsize has at least three significant effects. First, in the absence of successful reengineering projects, employees have simply absorbed the work that was previously done by a larger number of people. One survey of employees at a regional Bell company found that 69 percent of workers and 93 percent of managers said their workload had increased over the last two years. Forty-eight percent of workers and 60 percent of managers said they were always or quite frequently understaffed. Sixty-three percent of all managers (68% of network and 52% of customer services) said they worked ten hours or more each day, and over 60 percent said they had more overtime or take-home work than they wanted. For managers, these higher workloads are reflected in increased spans of control. Seventy-two percent of all managers say that their span of control has increased, with a significantly greater percentage (82%) in customer services than in network (67%). Almost 40 percent of those with larger spans of control now supervise three to five additional workers; another 37 percent manage between six and fifteen additional workers (Batt 1995; Batt 1996).

Downsizing has also reduced overall mobility throughout the workforce. In most cases, job ladders created under the old Bell System continue in place; but mobility has virtually ceased. In the same survey, 83 percent of workers and 89 percent of managers indicated that opportunities for promotion had declined; 72 percent of workers and 78 percent of managers said opportunities for lateral transfer had declined.[10] Only 5 percent of managers at the company were promoted to higher pay grades in 1990, a fraction of what existed during the 1950s through 1970s when the Howard and Bray study (1988) was conducted. Moreover, approximately the same number of managers received promotions in 1990 as in 1991 through 1993. A large minority of managers (38%) said they had had to relocate in the past three years as a result of organizational restructuring (Batt 1995; Batt 1996).

Third, the ongoing downsizing undermines morale. The upheaval and dislocation is reflected in employee dissatisfaction over particular aspects

10. Interviews with managers indicate that downsizing also reduces requests for lateral transfers: managers don't want to risk losing their "sponsorship" and joining a new department where they will be the new person, a relative unknown to a new supervisor who will evaluate them. Interviewees also related stories of managers reluctant to take advantage of opportunities for mid-career educational programs or international experience for fear that ("out of sight, out of mind") their departments would have learned that they were dispensable.

of their jobs that have been most affected and of corporate leadership more generally. Whereas Keefe's study found widespread demoralization at AT&T as we discussed in the second section above, Batt's study finds growing discontent at an RBOC. The RBOC study found that 86 percent of workers and 92 percent of managers said job security had decreased in the last two years. Whereas over two-thirds of workers were satisfied with their jobs, benefits, and pay, only 14 percent were satisfied with their opportunities for promotion and 27 percent were satisfied with their job security. The pattern was similar among managers: whereas 70 percent or more were satisfied with their jobs, pay, and benefits, less than 20 percent were satisfied with their employment security or opportunities for advancement. In sum, employees continue to like the work they do and the skills they use and have very low absentee rates. Most score high on commitment measures such as their willingness to work harder for the company, their pride in working for the company, and the loyalty they feel. But they are critical of top management's commitment to them: to employment security and advancement, to providing adequate resources for getting the job done, and to taking into consideration the interests of employees when making technological and organizational decisions (Batt 1996).

Conclusions

The ultimate outcome of industrial restructuring in U.S. telecommunications is still uncertain and likely to remain so for several years. Several patterns, however, emerge from our analysis. First, at the level of the industry, the centralizing thrust of network technologies compete with decentralizing market strategies. Changes in productivity growth reflect this mismatch. The rate of productivity growth has declined in the 1980s because of the overcapacity generated by multiple players. More significantly, the historic positive relationship between productivity growth and employment growth has reversed itself in this decade. The extensive activity of mergers, acquisitions, joint ventures, and deal-making has netted few new permanent or productive alliances.

At the firm level, companies have created cross-functional business units that do away with the worst information problems associated with functional silos. This restructuring enhances the managerial jobs that remain, but downsizing increases workloads and spans of control. While these reforms reduce bureaucracy, they do not attack Taylorism or functional specialization at the nonmanagement level, which has, in fact, accelerated. Pockets of innovative experiments in self-management or multiskilled teams have been overshadowed by cost-cutting benefits associated with reengineering and the application of new software technologies such as automated call distribution systems for service workers. Companies in this sense have continued to implement labor-displacing and deskilling technologies that are much more consistent with pre-divestiture past practices than not. As a result, the tensions, disagreements, and lack of trust between labor and management have increased in an industry historically known for cooperation between the parties. Ironically, this shift is occurring in a period in which most management and industrial relations scholars alike call for reduced adversarialism if U.S. firms are to be globally competitive. While it is surprising that corporate restructuring to date has not produced more outright conflict, it appears that unions have accepted at least some labor displacement as an inevitable outcome of deregulation and have made the strategic decision to negotiate generous severance packages, retirement buyouts, and retraining-replacement programs as the best alternative for members' welfare. What remains unclear is whether companies can continue to pay the generous settlements that have bought labor peace and whether continued downsizing will erode the embedded skill base that historically provided high productivity growth for these companies.

Chapter 2

United Kingdom

Anthony Ferner and Michael Terry

(with Jon Berry, Mark Gilman, Benson Maina, Athina Nicolaides, and Yee Mei Tong)

This chapter deals with developments in industrial relations in the British telecommunications services industry over the past decade or so.[1] Deregulation has brought new players into the game. Nonetheless, the former state monopoly supplier, British Telecom (BT), remains the major actor, responsible in 1995 for the great bulk of the telephony market and of employment. BT dominates the agenda and the strategy of telecommunications in Britain, and sees itself as one of the top four or five telecommunications companies in the world. The chapter therefore concentrates on developments in BT.

The Context of Industrial Relations in Telecommunications

This section provides an overview of the context: the move from public corporation to privatized company; the environment of regulation; the

---

1. The chapter draws on a long experience of research on BT conducted by the authors (Batstone, Ferner, and Terry 1984; Ferner and Colling 1991; Smith and Terry 1993), supplemented by more recent fieldwork in 1993–94. In the summer of 1993, Jon Berry, Mark Gilman, Benson Maina, Athina Nicolaides, and Yee Mei Tong researched various aspects of BT's industrial relations for their Masters' dissertations; their work has made a useful contribution to the present report and they are cited as co-authors. The authors are very grateful to Owen Darbishire, Enrique de la Garza, and Harry Katz for their detailed and constructive comments on earlier drafts. We also thank the representatives of BT manage-

growth of competition; and BT's globalization. It goes on to describe the key organizational changes that have taken place in BT in response to the changing environment. Subsequent sections examine developments in industrial relations since privatization.

Privatization, Regulation, and Competition

Privatization. In 1984, BT became the first major public corporation to be privatized[2] by the Conservative government, in the teeth of bitter opposition from the trade unions and the Labour party.[3]

Privatization was to transform the way in which BT managed its business and specifically its industrial relations. As a nationalized industry it had operated in an environment conditioned by political factors. It had a formal responsibility to the minister and thence to Parliament; there was detailed ministerial oversight of board appointments, investment plans, and rates of return. The corporation had a high political profile as a major state-owned infrastructural service and as one of the largest public-sector employers. This "political contingency" (Batstone, Ferner, and Terry 1984) strongly influenced the conduct of industrial relations— encouraging centralization, bureaucratization, stability, detailed joint regulation of work, and an emphasis on consensus and negotiation. It also facilitated direct government intervention in areas of industrial relations such as pay determination.

Privatization meant the end of direct political control, although a sort of "arm's-length" political contingency was established through the framework of regulation described below, and a more diffuse political pressure continued, not least because BT was regarded as the flagship of the government's privatization program and could not therefore be seen to falter. Some of BT's industrial relations policies can be seen, partly at least, as responses to this political context. For example, cost-cutting programs (including workforce reductions) were directed at shaping political perceptions of the company's efficiency and adaptability, and hence deflecting political pressures for further tightening of regulation.

ment and unions who gave their time to be interviewed and in some cases to comment on drafts of this chapter, particularly John Ainsley of the NCU who provided extremely helpful comments and advice at several stages of drafting.

2. For analyses of privatization of BT and the evolving telecommunications market, see Vickers and Yarrow 1988: chap. 8; NCU 1992; NCU 1993; Noam 1992: chap. 8; Souter 1993. On the impact of privatization on industrial relations in BT and other former public corporations, see Ferner and Colling 1993 and Colling and Ferner 1992.

3. The original flotation disposed of only 49% of BT shares; subsequently, further tranches were offered, the last block of shares being sold in 1993.

Privatization also had the consequence of replacing ministerial control by shareholder control. The influence of investors, as mediated by the reports of financial analysts and movements in the BT share price, became a significant factor in managerial calculations, reinforcing pressures on management to "pare away the fat" of public ownership, and particularly to reduce the size of the workforce, which was judged by analysts to be excessive in comparison with those in other telecommunications companies abroad. Such international productivity comparisons came to form part of a new environment of managerial decision making in BT, and of pressure on the unions.

Competition. From the early 1980s the government progressively relaxed BT's near total monopoly of services, including the supply and installation of customer equipment. Competition was allowed in the apparatus market, and in 1982 Mercury Communications was licensed to operate a second fixed-link network in competition with BT. Private operators were permitted to provide mobile communications networks. From 1987, cable television companies entered the market for local telephony services; the sector, though small, was growing very rapidly, signing up around 50,000 BT customers a month by 1995. In the mid-1990s BT continued to dominate the telephony market, although Mercury had made significant inroads particularly in the major financial centers and in international traffic. In 1994, BT had some 95 percent of the residential call market, but its share of the national business market had slipped to 83 percent, and of international calls to 72 percent. Mercury's workforce grew rapidly, from about 1,500 in 1987 to around 10,500 in 1994 (although it was subsequently cut back significantly).

A major review in 1990–91 led to the ending of the BT—Mercury "duopoly," and in the early 1990s several new companies were granted licenses to operate fixed-link networks, including major international players such as AT&T. Liberalization has given Britain the most competitive telecommunications market in Europe, and one of the most open in the world. As a result, it is estimated that BT's market share will fall significantly, particularly for international and long distance traffic (Souter 1993).

Regulation. The act which privatized BT also created a framework of regulation by setting up the independent government agency, the Office of Telecommunications (Oftel). Regulation was premised on the need to supply artificial competitive elements in a sector dominated by a near-monopoly supplier. The role of Oftel was thus to regulate competition in the industry, notably by advising the minister on the granting of licenses to operators, and setting the formulae governing the prices that BT may charge for core services (which are about 70 percent of the total). As with other privatized utilities, BT faces price caps linked to inflation. The basic formula is RPI (retail price index) minus x, where x is a variable percentage by which BT must reduce prices annually. Successive formulae have raised the value of x from 3 percent for 1984–89 to 7.5 percent for 1993–97. (Inflation in 1994 was around 2 percent per annum.)

The history of Oftel has been dominated by efforts to constrain the activities of the dominant player, BT, and to boost the competitive position of new entrants. This has provoked hostility on the part of BT, which repeatedly demanded a "level playing field" and a much lighter regulatory regime. Among the most contentious issues was the "asymmetry rule" excluding BT from the provision of broadcast "entertainment services" over its main network. This put BT at a disadvantage in relation to cable television companies which were seen as subsidizing their entry into local telephony through their monopoly on local TV franchises.

The overwhelming thrust of regulation has been to pin back BT in the home market. BT argued that capping prices imposed a penalty on it of around £0.5 billion a year, and used this to justify cost cutting and employment reduction. It was also convinced that the government and the regulator were determined to favor its competitors until it had lost a very substantial slice of the market, perhaps as much as 50 percent. This gave a further impetus to job cuts to scale BT down to a size commensurate with a much lower market share at the end of the century.

Diversification and Globalization

Privatization provided the opportunity for BT to diversify into new areas, both sectoral and geographical; while regulation of the "core" service combined with increasing competition provided the spur for it to do so. BT thus gave high priority to looking for newer areas of operation within its core activity, the provision of telecommunications services. Its vision was "to become the most successful worldwide telecommunications group," or as it was more succinctly put, to become a "top Telco." (It is currently among the largest three or four carriers in the world, with outgoing traffic of around 2.2 billion minutes in 1992.)

BT focused its global strategy on the major developed blocs in the world economy, North America, Western Europe, and the Pacific Rim, which it saw as having a higher long-term potential for growth and profitability than the regulated domestic market. In a key move into the increasingly competitive global telecommunications market, it set up a billion-dollar joint venture with MCI to provide "outsourced" telecommunications services to multinational corporations worldwide. Within the European Union (EU), BT hoped to take advantage of gathering moves toward deregulation which will force EU states to end public telecommunications monopolies over the next few years; for example, in 1995 BT was developing joint ventures in Germany, Italy, Spain, and Sweden.

The industrial relations consequences of diversification and globalization are likely to become increasingly important. First, several thousand people are now employed in dozens of subsidiaries in Britain and overseas. In 1993, BT employed around 6,000 outside the United Kingdom, about half in BT plc and half in subsidiaries. Second, the workforces in subsidiaries are likely to be managed differently from those in the core company, especially where they are operating in very different institutional frameworks such as the United States. In the 1980s, unions in the United Kingdom fought unsuccessful battles for recognition in a number of subsidiaries. Although these were sold off when BT divested itself of its manufacturing interests, there was still a union fear that subsidiaries might be used as a "test bed" for developing novel personnel and industrial relations policies, which then might be imported back into the core company. Unions also feared that BT might transfer activities to its peripheral operations where they would be less subject to the collective influence that still remains significant in the main company.

Organizational Structure

BT's organizational structure has gone through radical transformations as the company has struggled to adapt to the new environment. There have been two basic thrusts to the changes. First, BT has moved to a structure based on key customer segments. Second, there has been an oscillation between centralization and decentralization of authority to the local operating unit, with the pendulum currently swinging decisively back to centralized management control.

The major reorganization of 1991, known as Project Sovereign, created a divisional structure based on customer groups. Business and domestic markets were the responsibility of the Business Communications (BC) and Personal Communications (PC) divisions respectively. The network infrastructure for all BT's activities became the responsibility of a new division, Worldwide Networks (WN). (Subsequent further reorganization has led to the partial merger of PC and BC in the United Kingdom Customer Field Service [UKCFS].)

The second element driving corporate change—the tension between devolved managerial power and central control—has been manifest since the early 1980s when the geographical operational units, that is telephone "districts," were given much greater authority, in an effort to generate more flexible, commercial, and responsive behavior by local line managers and to "get close to the customer." The new structure had widespread repercussions for industrial relations; for example, negotiations on the implementation of higher-level "framework" agreements were devolved to districts. District managers never gained full command over their own resources; with centralized pay bargaining, they had little control over their labor costs, for example. They were, however, encouraged by the new corporate culture to "extend the bounds of the possible" and assert their authority within the existing framework.

The key problem for corporate managers was the effect of devolution on service provision. "Getting close to the customer" at local level sometimes meant a greater variability of quality and performance across the country. This was unacceptable in an organization whose revenues depended disproportionately on large companies who expected uniform standards of service and proper coordination between different parts of the network. Moreover, undue service variations had a disproportionate influence on BT's public standing and image, and on the attitude of the regulator (Ferner and Colling 1991).

The response to these problems was a broad recentralizing movement in BT, embodied in Project Sovereign, which set up the new divisions and ended the autonomous power of the districts. Each major division was divided into operational "zones" and districts, but these were operational entities rather than profit-responsible business units. However, the center appears to have found it difficult to apply consistent policy guidelines across the divisions, and to bring divisional interests into line with strategic corporate objectives. As a result, it is unlikely that the present structure represents the end point of BT's organizational odyssey.

The New Context and Changing Industrial Relations in BT

This new environment of privatization, competition, and regulation conditioned the context of industrial relations strategy in BT, and gave rise to a new, if still shifting, array of priorities. First, it greatly increased pressures for cost cutting and in particular for reductions in the labor force: such forces reflected, as described above, the entry of competitors into the previously monopolistic market for BT services; the need of management to satisfy the new (and often short-termist) preoccupations of shareholders and the stock market; and the determination of the regulator to reduce prices of core services in real terms, and to reduce substantially BT's share of the market in the medium term. Second, however, many of the same pressures pointed to a different strategic imperative for

BT's industrial relations: to establish a high quality, customer-oriented culture of service, based around employee skill and commitment. Associated with this is the need to increase the flexibility with which work is organized, so as to respond to rapidly-changing markets and accommodate the massive introduction of new technology (itself undoubtedly hastened by the impact of a more competitive environment).

However, the development of industrial relations strategy in response to these impulses from the environment was not straightforward. The new environment gave rise to sometimes conflicting demands on BT management; cost cutting and labor reduction, for example, sat uncomfortably with the need for greater workforce commitment, not least for managerial staff whose relationship with the company was undergoing some of the most dramatic changes. The result was a switching between key priorities in different phases. Likewise, organizational change was driven by conflicting imperatives: for example, by the need to "get close to the customer" while satisfying the regulator on overall standards. This was one factor behind the oscillation in corporate structure between centralization and decentralization, each with its distinctive consequences for industrial relations management. Tensions over the management of industrial relations were evident not just in the relationship between the corporate center and the local operating units, but also, more recently, between the center and the business divisions.

Third, the nature, and especially the timing, of management's responses to the new context were influenced significantly by the continuing strength and presence of organized labor in BT, despite an increasingly inhospitable climate for British trade unions in general. Thus the implementation of management's agenda has been a phased process, concentrating in one period on cost cutting, in another on securing more flexibility in work organization or the reform of payment systems.

The remainder of this chapter examines in more detail the processes and outcomes that marked BT's adoption of these changing priorities.

Work Organization and Participation at the Workplace

BT's traditional system of work organization was conditioned by an elaborate negotiated system of rigid job grades and hierarchies, rules of transfer and promotion, staffing ratios, supervision, working methods and workloads, and procedures for introducing change (Batstone, Ferner, and Terry 1984: chap. 6). A uniform national grading was determined for each new job by a national grading committee composed of management and union representatives. This process could take up to eighteen months (IDS 1988: 27).

The past decade or so has witnessed several initiatives to break down the rigidities of the grading system. Technological modernization demanded far-reaching changes in the nature of the work performed, particularly in telephone exchange maintenance. There was also an attempt by BT to meet customer service requirements by introducing more flexible hours of work, particularly for the technicians, the Engineering Technical Grades (ETGs). These developments are discussed in turn.

Functional Flexibility

In 1986–88, the so-called repatterning agreement redefined engineering jobs to allow staff to carry out a wider range of tasks within their existing skills (IDS 1988). For example, staff could be scheduled to work on either installation or maintenance, according to operational need. Fixed staffing ratios between higher and lower grade staff in work teams were abolished, allowing staffing to be adapted to variations in local circumstances (Tong 1993: 48–49). Technicians' activities were classified into a hierarchy of broad "work communities," such as the internal network; "skill families," such as installation and maintenance of business equipment; and specialisms, such as digital equipment maintenance. The intention was to allow job definitions sufficiently broad to encompass new activities as they emerged.

The different BT divisions also sought flexibility to organize work according to their own business needs. A 1992 agreement between the technicians' union, the National Communications Union (NCU), and the Personal Communications division adopted division-wide guidelines for grading. The division had responsibility for a comparatively narrow spectrum of the market—residential apparatus and external plant—making "a consistent national approach viable and desirable." Moreover, BT faced intense competition in the residential apparatus market, and the agreement was seen as a way of maximizing the effective utilization of ETG skills (BT 1992: 3). The 1992 agreement created the category of Customer Service Engineer covering broad areas of work in the installation and maintenance of customer apparatus and of external plant, and capable of moving between them for operational reasons (Tong 1993: 34). There were also trials of the centralized allocation of work previously controlled from three different control centers (repair, for customer apparatus and line, installation for extension fitting, and external plant maintenance for underground faults). According to Owen Darbishire (personal communication), such moves were accompanied by a tightening of direct supervisory control of ETGs; this was encouraged in the case of ETGs working outside of exchanges by the introduction in the early 1990s of the new role of "field manager." This has been described as "basically a foreman with technology." Usually recruited from the ranks of senior technicians, field managers performed a role previously done by first line managers. They operated in the field, using computers to maintain contact with their managers; this allowed closer control of ETGs than was the case with office-bound managers. Moreover, the introduction of performance-related pay for field manager, linked to the performance of ETGs under their control, provided an added incentive for the close supervision of ETGs.

As Yee Mei Tong (1993: 36–37) argues, skill requirements, and hence the need for multiskilling, were likely to vary significantly between BT's three main divisions, PC, BC, and WN. While PC was concerned with flexibility, WN required a high level of firm-specific skill, and the training costs were such that it was not in the company's interests to have skilled staff perform other tasks; thus the functional flexibility of key workers in WN was likely to be limited. Similarly, multiskilling was limited for the most highly skilled, specialized technicians who were expected to spend the great bulk of their time working on their primary specialty (e.g., exchange maintenance); its main application was for less qualified staff working under the supervision of more senior technicians.

The Organization of Work

New technology has been the major factor permitting changes in the way work is performed. This applies most strikingly to technicians' work, but also to clerical and operating staff.

By the early 1980s, the replacement of electromechnical by semi-electronic systems was having a significant impact on exchange maintenance (Clark et al. 1988: chap. 6). The introduction of the fully electronic System X from the mid-1980s saw further, even more radical and rapid, changes. In March 1987, under 2 percent of subscribers were linked to System X exchanges, compared with 42 percent semi-electronic and 57 percent electromechanical. By 1994, around 75 percent were System X exchanges, and electromechanical connections had fallen to less than one percent.

The new technology's high fault tolerance, combined with the capacity for the remote supervision of exchanges, made possible also the centralization of maintenance at a single point servicing several exchanges (Clark et al. 1988: chap. 7). Component design meant that there was no longer any need for on-site repair. Remote control centers monitored groups of System X exchanges, analyzing bulk fault data, coordinating day-to-day maintenance, and providing diagnostic fault programs to field engineers.

With the pooling of staff to cover a group of exchanges, supervision became more direct, and management achieved greater flexibility over the deployment of staff. The high proportion of routine faults not requiring skilled intervention by technicians led management to press for a relaxation of staffing ratios for senior to junior technicians, and hence a reduction of maintenance costs. This was one of the major factors in the 1986–87 engineering strike in BT (Smith and Terry 1994: 258).

Technology also changed the nature of other technical work. On external work, for example, some of the old skills of underground fault tracing were rendered obsolete by more sophisticated testing equipment and reliable fiber optic cables. Cable pressurization kept water out and hence reduced maintenance needs. Managerial control of external work, traditionally lax, was tightened by the introduction of two-way radios and pagers for technicians (Penn 1990: 140–41). In business customer premises, the traditional skills of fault diagnosis and repair were sidelined by the reliability of modular electronic PaBXs (ibid.).

Advances in the computerization of management information systems also led to changes in work management, particularly under the so-called field effectiveness program in the early 1990s. There were trials of integrated systems whereby computerized information on customer requirements from customer service centers (see below) was automatically supplied to field technicians via computer terminals, providing them with a continually updated work schedule according to customer demand, the skill requirements and priority of a job, the location of the work, travel time, and so on. This reduced technicians' discretion, since they were given batches of jobs to do, with standard times attached, and divergences from scheduled timings had to be explained to the field manager.

Clerical work was significantly affected by BT's emphasis on customer service as the crucial function: 80 percent of customer contact was estimated to be with a clerically graded employee. The use of computer systems and data entry on visual display units brought certain engineering tasks—for example, in fault reporting—into the sphere of clerical work. The key role of the "customer interface" prompted the increase in clerical staff—the only growth area among major staff groups in BT—by some 6,000 to 7,000 in 1993.

Work was influenced by technological developments such as the computerization of service and management control systems. The principle of a single point of contact for customers was established in the so-called

Customer Service Centres set up in the 1980s. Call logging equipment permitted automatic recording of answering times and other aspects of performance, calls were automatically distributed among staff, and supervision could be carried out remotely. The system was also used to log and monitor customer complaints. The pace of change and pressures of work created morale problems for clerical staff. In an NCU survey (NCU 1993a) of 2,600 employees in service centers, a high percentage complained of the pressure and alleged that there was inadequate consultation and training when new methods or technology were introduced.

Operators were the group most severely affected by changes in technology and work organization. By the late 1980s, manually controlled switchrooms had been entirely replaced by modern digital technology, and numbers fell from around 40,000 in the 1970s to some 6,000 in 1995. Most operators were women, many of them working flexible part-time hours. The bulk of remaining operator work concerned directory inquiries, where despite the introduction of charging the volume of work rose. Directory inquiries were computerized: a screen and keyboard replaced "hard copy" telephone directories. This both reduced transaction times and (as with clerical staff) permitted automatic monitoring of performance. As a result, the organization of the service was restructured and a tier of supervision removed (Nicolaides 1993). Operator centers were rationalized, and many sites are now remote from the calls they handle, often in greenfield locations. In October 1993, BT announced the closure of a third of the remaining centers.

Some common trends were therefore visible among the different groups of staff. Skills were not necessarily downgraded, but technological development tended to diminish the scope for individual discretion and to allow a closer monitoring of performance. There was also some evidence of contrary tendencies. For example in late 1994, BT began trials of the so-called high performance teams under which small groups of ETGs would have "day-to-day responsibilities for managing themselves and their work in order to satisfy customers" (BT internal document). Team members would be in charge of work scheduling, customer contact, quality responsibilities and team performance. It was not clear, however, how comfortably work teams would coexist with the closer supervision implied by the introduction of field managers.

In clerical and operating work individual discretion was always limited. What was new was the technological potential for greater managerial control of the work of technicians. Particularly in activities such as exchange maintenance where the software facilitates centralized control, the traditionally large measure of individual autonomy of technicians became more circumscribed. The reorganization of work allocation for technicians under sophisticated computerized systems and the introduction of performance assessment for field managers will tend to encourage such developments.

Attendance Patterns

One of the key issues in the organization of work in BT in the 1990s was the flexibility of attendance patterns for technicians. Rigid attendance arrangements had grown up locally in the wake of a 1978 agreement for a shorter working week. This was particularly a problem for the Personal Communications division: with increasing residential customer demand for service outside normal working hours, the cost of service provision escalated, and local managers attempted to "claw back" flexibility against the strong resistance of the ETG workforce. More flexibility was also needed to meet the challenge of the cable companies.

In 1993, therefore, under the "Customer Service Improvement Programme" BT proposed extending the standard cover time, making starting and finishing times flexible, and introducing a standard seven-day working week so that normal weekend working would be rostered in to attendance patterns. Following considerable union and work force opposition to management proposals, an agreement was eventually reached in late 1994. It applied to around 23,000 technicians in UKCFS and PC. Staff were offered incentives to transfer voluntarily to one of the new flexible working patterns. The great majority of technicians signed up for transfer, the bulk of them to one of two options for four ten-hour days rostered over either six or seven days of the week (IRS 1995).

Employee Participation in Decision Making and Problem Solving at the Workplace

Employee participation was traditionally based on joint regulation through formal consultation and negotiation. After privatization, management increasingly placed the emphasis on individual relationships with employees, rather than on collective relationships with the unions; and in the latter sphere, there was a move to broader, less rigidly defined agreements leaving more space for local managerial autonomy. In addition, traditional collective relationships were eroded by human resource innovations such as Total Quality Management (TQM) which BT introduced in the mid-1980s, based on the slogan of "meeting the customer's agreed need, first time, every time." An organizational structure responsible for the quality program was established throughout the company, with quality trainers and "facilitators" reporting to line managers. (Subsequently, the quality structure was generally merged into line management organization.) One impact of TQM was to challenge union control over issues of work organization by giving the work group, under the oversight of the supervisor, a role as a forum for thinking through and acting on work practice issues.

TQM could be seen as one tool for gaining employee commitment in BT. With the downgrading of collective relations, BT struggled to square the circle of ruthless cost cutting and employment reductions on the one hand, and maintaining a highly productive, well-motivated, and flexible workforce on the other. The company placed an increasing emphasis on direct communications with the individual employee: it made increasing use from the mid-1980s of employee attitude surveys (the so-called CARE [Communications and Attitude Research for Employees] surveys), and its communication programs propagated messages about "working as one team" and "winning matters." A key initiative of employee involvement at the workplace was the system of team briefings for employees at all levels (Nicolaides 1993: 39–41). Evidence from BT and NCU surveys suggests that they were valued by employees (NCU 1993a). Around three-quarters of employees attended briefings, which dealt with topics relating to the work unit's performance, and would also cover more general issues such as management's proposals on hours of attendance.

But at the same time the CARE surveys revealed plummeting morale in the early 1990s in the face of great job insecurity, disappearing career opportunities, and increasing pressures of work. A large majority found the changes taking place not only bad for themselves but for the company as well. Even where there were good working relationships with first-line managers, and a commitment to the immediate work team, this was not translated into a commitment to BT itself (see NCU 1993a).

Skill Formation and Development

BT undertook a huge training program, spending around £200 million in 1994 on some 840,000 days of training—an average of around five days for every employee. New technology generated changes in training and skill requirements in BT, particularly for ETGs, but also for clerical staff and others. At the same time, the effort to build a new corporate culture and organization created its own training demands, as for example in the TQM program, and in training for managers expected to assume new responsibilities in a period of rapid organizational change. One aspect of this was the emphasis on "personal development plans" for managers, based on their identified training needs within the context of career development. A further development was the outsourcing of training as a measure to reduce BT's non-core activities,: the aim was to limit centrally delivered management training to high-skill courses and those where technology conferred economies of scale; large investments were made in distance-learning (Lee 1990).

The ETGs experienced major changes in skill requirements and hence training. Traditionally BT technicians—from the semiskilled Technician IIB through skilled Technician IIAs to highly skilled Technical Officers (TOs)—progressed through the grades as part of an established career pattern, and there were jointly agreed restrictions on direct entry at higher levels. But in the early 1990s, BT opened up the TO grade to direct recruitment, arguing that insufficient posts were being filled internally, and inter-firm competition for such skills increased following deregulation.

In recent years technological change has led to an enlargement of the competencies required of ETGs, in part because of the overlaying of different generations of technologies. In addition, ETGs were increasingly seen as requiring skills in staff management and in problem solving in the context of new market and business demands. The penetration of computers into all aspects of BT's work led to an increased demand for computing and software skills. At the same time the automatic diagnostic facilities of System X, which allowed routine maintenance and repairs to be identified and handled by the system, altered the nature of the skills required. The increased reliability of the System X exchanges meant that certain faults were now so rare that maintenance staff faced problems in retaining learned skills (Maina 1993).

Technological modernization and changing customer requirements prompted a major overhaul of the technical training system. Prior to 1989 technical training was provided through a Trainee Technician (Apprentice) Scheme which allowed for study over three years, the third designed to qualify staff for the Technical Officer post. This was a classical apprenticeship scheme, based purely on technical training, and designed with a view to advancing ETGs through the career grades. In 1989 a new Technical and Commercial Trainee Scheme (TACT) was introduced, directed primarily but not only at school-leavers. It was designed to equip technicians to adapt to rapid technological change throughout their careers, and allow them to "relate to customers in a knowledgeable and caring way" (BT internal document). Importantly, this was no longer a scheme directed purely at ETGs; it was intended to develop staff who were "adaptable in their career progression," training Sales Support Officers, Commercial Officers, and Marketing Service Representatives in addition to TOs. However, the very rapid rundown in technical staff numbers in the early 1990s hindered the operation of the TACT scheme.

Pay and Payment Systems

Since privatization, wage payment systems have been stable. The major exception was the rejection by BT of collectively bargained pay and conditions for certain categories of white collar and managerial and professional staff, and their replacement by individual contracts and/or pay increasingly based on assessed individual performance.

Internal relativities for key BT grades such as Technical Officer and Clerical Officer remained remarkably stable between 1984 and 1993, more so than in the economy as a whole. Two changes were visible, however. First, union data suggest a small but significant falling-behind of BT staff compared to external comparator groups. Second, salaries and other benefits paid to BT directors increased very much faster, and indeed, were the subject of press and political, as well as union, criticism. Table 2.1 shows these developments in summary form.

The rapid increase in directors' salaries reflected BT's view that they were competing for top managers in a world market and that their desire to become a world leader required them to match the best international rates. By contrast, the (slight) decline in engineering and clerical rates against averages for the economy as a whole may be a reflection of BT's long-term objective of reducing direct labor costs. Certainly there was a view in the unions that BT wished to move away from being a wage leader, especially with regard to its managerial grades.

TABLE 2.1. BT plc pay since privatization (1984 = 100).

	Engineering (TO)	Clerical (CO)	Male manual	Female non-manual	RPI	MPG index	Directors emoluments
1.7. 1984	100	100	100	100	100	100	100
1.7. 1985	107	107	106.9	108.8	106.9	107	164.18
1.7. 1986	112.42	112.38	113.5	117.4	109.6	112.4	231.92
1.7. 1987	118.69	118.54	121.75	130.5	114.2	113.5	260.07
1.7. 1988	128.91	127.35	131.28	144.9	119.5	127	265.15
1.7. 1989	140.51	138.81	145.1	160.5	129.4	136.5	359.43
1.7. 1990	154.57	152.69	158.87	173.03	142.0	150.3	430.72
1.7. 1991	165.85	163.85	169.99	189.42	150.3	174.6	531.54
1.7. 1992	173.48	171.29			156.2		614.67

Source: BT Annual Report and Accounts.

Engineering, Clerical, and Operator Grades

Wage structures for engineering, clerical, and telephone operator grades remained broadly unchanged. Most continued to be on salary scales through which progression was at least semiautomatic. For such grades, BT's pay policy was to agree annual or two-yearly increases at or slightly above the inflation rate. The picture overall was thus one of stability. In particular there is no evidence to support a prediction made at the time of privatization in 1984 that pay awards would increasingly reflect both skill levels and market forces and thus show greater variations between grades than in the past (cited in Smith and Terry 1993: 234), although there is anecdotal evidence suggesting that local managers used the grading system to pay more to recruit and retain staff in tight local labor markets.

However, pay has been a central tool in BT's drive for rationalization and greater flexibility in that virtually every set of pay negotiations since privatization has been accompanied by discussions on matters such as grading structures, repatterning of work, and so on (for the period 1984–89 see Smith and Terry 1993: 233–38 for more details). For example, alongside pay negotiations in 1985, issues such as the introduction of the new computerized customer services system were discussed with the clerical group of the NCU. In 1987, the union agreed to a pay increase in exchange for efficiency measures for its clerical members, and the traditional pay link between managerial staff and engineering grades was broken. Two years later, there was an agreement on new shiftworking patterns under which technicians could be required to work longer continuous periods without earning overtime pay.

From 1990, however, pay awards tended to be "without strings." This apparently reflects the overwhelming priority that BT gave in the early 1990s to cutting the workforce rather than to changing working practices. BT had no desire to lower morale further among staff by awarding small increases, and the unions had little credible bargaining power with members queuing up to accept redundancy terms. Indeed, during these years bargaining over terms and conditions for staff in post almost took second place in union priorities to negotiating the terms of severance. Generally, therefore, for such grades, pay has been used more as a lubricant for securing union and employee agreement to change than as a means to alter the relationship between pay and performance. In the spring of 1992 BT announced a scheme for awarding small gifts to employees whose behavior and performance were seen as implementing BT values (*Financial Times,* 9 May 1992), but individual performance-based measures have not been introduced, in contrast to the position of managerial and professional grades.

Managerial and Professional Staff

Since the early 1980s BT has carried out a more radical reassessment of the reward system of managerial staff, introducing pay progression based on individual performance appraisal, and replacing collectively bargained terms and conditions of employment by "personal contracts." The latter move was widely seen by the management union as intended to weaken or destroy its influence. BT stressed the need to replace seniority-based pay progression along scales collectively negotiated with trade unions with a payment system that rewarded initiative, attention to quality, problem-solving and decision-making skills.

In BT such schemes have a history of just over ten years. (The following account draws heavily on Gilman 1993, and on documents of the management union, the Society of Telecom Executives, STE.) In 1983 a new ten-band structure for Managerial and Professional Staff (M&PS) and a Senior Band (XJ), were introduced. Between 1984 and 1987 staff moved through these bands on the basis of annual increments, technically based on performance appraisal, but in practice automatic except in the case of unsatisfactory performance. The scales themselves and, where appropriate, individuals' pay, were increased through negotiation with the STE. There were four appraisal categories, with 80 percent of staff being rated 1 or 2 (fully acceptable performance or better).

In 1987 a new system replaced service-based with appraisal-based progression, to run alongside a continuing system of "across-the-board" awards paid to all. The system was based on the existing appraisal categories, but the speed of progression through the pay range would vary with the category. The size of the award depended on the category, with 6 percent for the highest; there was some senior management discretion to increase the size of the award for good performers and to pay up to 10 percent above the range maxima.

In 1992 BT announced its intention to move from a system of two increases each year—one from the performance-related scheme and one from collectively bargained increases—to a single increase based on appraised performance scores against targets. In the same year the existing pay scales were frozen. The net effect, according to the STE, was to lengthen the time it would take the "average" performer to move through the scale from six to eight years. In 1993 the previous four appraisal categories were extended to six and the targets against which performance was to be rated were extended from seven criteria to fifteen "competencies," covering "operational performance," "people management," and "change management."

In 1994, however, BT unilaterally suspended the pay scheme when it became clear that the proposals agreed would breach its target 2.3 percent increase for managerial staff for 1994. More fundamentally, there appears to be a clash, at least in the short term, between the operation of the scheme and BT's publicly stated intention to "move down the market" in its managerial pay; in particular to stop paying in the upper quartile for managerial staff in the United Kingdom. BT's internal pay comparison study, it is claimed, shows that BT pays its managers 11 to 14 percent more than comparable staff in other enterprises; a study considered by the STE to be "deeply flawed."

Finally, in addition to appraisal-based progression there has been since 1983 a system of bonus payments. BT's intention was that bonuses should only be paid to a minority of managers, although about half of Managerial and Professional Grades (MPG) staff and almost all Personal Contract Grades (PCG) (see below) received them (Gilman 1993:20). Bonus payments were unconsolidated and non-pensionable, and were limited to 10 percent of pay in any year. Bonus payments appear to be contentious (Gilman 1993: 33) and managers remained deeply suspicion about performance-related pay. An STE survey in 1992 found that only 7 percent of managers felt that it had improved their performance. Sixty-six percent thought it was applied unfairly compared to 34 percent who thought it rewarded individual effort. Nearly 72 percent felt the bonus payments to be discriminatory, and over three-quarters that they discouraged teamwork. These findings, confirmed by Mark Gilman's survey, are not broadly disputed by BT. One consequence of the new system is that it is very difficult to obtain accurate data on pay movements for the staff affected, because of the increasing individual variation (made more problematic by job loss and reorganization). Thus far it is unclear whether the scheme improved recruitment and managerial performance. It may have succeeded, however, in reducing the rate of increase of the managerial pay bill by moving from two increases to one per year (*Financial Times,* 2 February 1994). With the likelihood of continuing large reductions in managerial staff, the use of performance appraisal to determine candidates for compulsory redundancy cannot be ruled out.

In 1983 the most senior managers were taken out of collective bargaining and put onto personal contracts, a move opposed by the STE. This process went a great deal further when in 1989 BT proposed taking several tiers of middle managers onto personal contracts with pay increases awarded purely on the basis of appraised performance and bonuses. Although managers were originally offered a "free choice" of accepting this change or remaining on collectively agreed terms, the 200 staff who opted for the latter were later told that their pay would be frozen unless they agreed to the change. In September 1991, BT moved to end collective bargaining for the 1,400 people in its field sales force. BT argued that such a change would allow it to retain key staff by being able to respond more quickly to market conditions. By March 1992 BT claimed that of the 4,000 middle managers to whom personal contracts had been offered in 1990 only 200 remained on STE-negotiated terms and conditions (*Financial Times*, 11 March 1992).

According to Jane Pickard (1990: 44) the move to personal contracts also enabled BT to offer a range of "perks" such as company cars and private health insurance without concern that it would be extended through collective bargaining to other groups. Managers who accepted the transfer to personal contracts were offered these, plus an increase of £1500, despite the fact that an STE survey suggested that around 80 percent of those affected would rather remain on collectively bargained terms.

According to the STE, "informal" promotion of bright staff into PCG (Personal Contract Group) grades was widely used by local managers as a means of retaining staff when there was in effect a freeze on MPG pay. The union estimates that there were as many as 1,200 such "backdoor" promotions in 1992–93, without any union input.

Conclusions

Since privatization, BT has been concerned to reduce its labor costs. Primarily this has been done through job loss, but there have also been small downward pressures on the pay of all but the highest-paid directors and managers. For nonmanagerial grades pay has been used as a tool to secure consent to change rather than as a specific stimulus to improved performance. For managerial grades, by contrast, pay systems have been fundamentally restructured to engender greater efficiency and commitment, although their success in doing so is not yet clear.

Employment Security and Numerical Flexibility

Downsizing

BT remains one of the largest private employers in Britain, with around 137,000 staff at the end of financial year 1995. However, it has been reducing staff very rapidly and over a decade will have cut numbers by more than half.

The trend in employment in BT since privatization illustrates well how the different pressures from regulation, competition, and technological change have impacted on the company. As may be seen from Table 2.2, there was a gradual decrease in the workforce over the first part of the 1980s, followed by a slight but significant rise at the end of the decade in response to the quality of service crisis of the mid-1980s, and to the "bulge" in work on exchange modernization; the end of the 1980s witnessed employment levels as high as at privatization. From 1990, however, the fall in numbers was dramatic. Around 94,000 left the company between 1990 and 1995, including thousands of managerial staff. The trend is expected to continue for some years, with an estimated workforce of 100,000 or fewer by the end of the century.

The sharp fall in numbers reflects two main forces: the virtual completion of the exchange modernization program, and the projected loss of up to 50 percent of BT's business market to competitors by the year 2000. In the short term, the company also faced pressure from Oftel for cost cutting; staff costs (including redundancy costs) were still around 40 percent of operating costs in 1994. In addition, share price considerations meant that efforts were made to reduce lines-per-employee ratios by subcontracting areas of work (see below).

Within the overall fall, some groups were more affected than others. The Engineering Technical Grades retained their proportional weight in the workforce of just under 50 percent. Clerical and administrative employees increased somewhat, from 14 percent to 18 percent between

TABLE 2.2. Employment in BT, 1981–1995 (thousands)

1981	253.1
1982	251.7
1983	246.0
1984	241.1
1985	235.2
1986	239.2
1987	223.1
1988	225.1
1989	232.0
1990	231.5
1991	215.4
1992	199.3
1993	165.2
1994	156.0
1995	137.5

Source: BT Annual Report and Accounts.

1990 and 1993, reflecting their importance in customer service, while operators as a proportion of the workforce were more than halved over the same period. Managerial and professional employees remained around a fifth of the total.

BT had a history of avoiding compulsory redundancy, and it generally retained its commitment to voluntary severance. The costs of redundancy amounted to around £2.4 billion just for the three-year period 1993–95. There was also a virtual freeze on recruitment in the early 1990s. With natural wastage of 5,000 to 10,000 a year, this had a considerable impact on job levels. Under the redundancy scheme Release '92 (see IRS 1993), around 29,000 employees left the company. The massive response— 45,000 employees applied for voluntary redundancy—and the loss of more employable staff led management to specify groups of staff that were unlikely to be accepted for redundancy, notably those with scarce skills and employees at customer service centers. Informally, managers were encouraged to reject those with potential for promotion and those with longer service (and hence more expensive), leading unions to complain that individuals were being penalized for loyalty and ability (*Financial Times,* 17 August 1993). Enthusiasm for voluntary redundancy partly reflected relatively attractive severance terms, with payments averaging around £35,000 a head. BT signed agreements with employment agencies guaranteeing a number of the leavers minimum periods of temporary work with BT or other telecommunications companies (IRS 1993: 15).

In general, the traditionally strong internal labor market in BT was weakened, by "delayering" of management and the decline of company-specific skills, and as a result of direct recruitment into certain technical grades. Nevertheless, average length of service remained high, especially for engineers, managers, and professionals. A third of engineering grades had twenty years or more years of service in BT. Of the 6,000 or so senior managers in PCG grades, and the 32,000 middle managers and professionals, as many as 44 percent had twenty years or more of service. This suggests that the model of the "one-company" manager in BT was still reasonably strong.

Numerical Flexibility: Contract Work and Part-time Employment

Around 4 percent of BT's workforce was employed part-time in the early 1990s, a figure which had changed little since the beginning of the 1980s. Part-time work was, however, a fairly significant proportion of female employment (almost 14 percent in 1992). In some areas, the employment of part-timers is likely to increase as management pursues greater flexibility. Thus PC proposed an increase in part-timers to service payphones, where the bulk of usage and faults tends to be at weekends, and to staff 24-hour fault reception centers which have an evening peak in work.

The great majority of part-time employees were female, around half in operator grades and the bulk of the rest in clerical and "other" grades. Women formed around 30 percent of the BT labor force, a proportion which had not varied much since the beginning of the 1980s. The main categories of female employment were operators, clerical, and catering and cleaning staff, where women made up around four-fifths of the workforce. In the traditionally male bastions of middle and higher management, and engineering grades, there were significant increases in women employees over the decade, although levels of female employment remained very low; for example, the proportion of female ETGs rose from 0.6 to 2.9 percent between 1981 and 1992.

Other nonstandard forms of contract such as temporary employment were uncommon. However, when BT was faced by sharp but transitory increases in labor requirements in the mid-1980s, there were increased pressures for the appointment of temporary staff. Subsequently, sharply falling employment reduced the company's need for such staff.

More significant were developments in the sale or contracting out of activities. Equipment manufacturing subsidiaries were sold off. Catering, which employed 2,500 in 1990, was subcontracted, as were other peripheral services such as cleaning and other office services. Contractors had always been used in BT to carry out "external" ETG work (Tong 1993: 5). In the mid-1980s, driven by skill shortages, quality of service problems, and the modernization program, BT looked to expand its use of contract staff in areas such as maintenance of the old electromechanical Strowger exchanges. According to one key respondent, BT was increasingly using contracting in "internal" work (i.e., inside exchanges) of high skill and high value, where traditionally it had been rarely used. This brought it into repeated conflict with the NCU (Tong 1993: 26–29). BT's policy was that as much work as possible should be done by "BT people," but that contractors should be used to meet peaks in short-term demand, provide specialist skills, and meet competitive pressures. Accurate figures for the use of contractors are hard to come by, although Yee Mei Tong's rough estimate is that there were 6,000 to 8,000 in the ETG area in 1993, a figure that was expected to fall to around 4,000 by 1994 or 1995 (1993: 35–36). Another new area for the use of contractors was managerial and professional work. According to union sources, BT had over 1,000 contracted staff doing managerial jobs in 1993, mostly in development, computing, and procurement. A proportion of them were former BT employees who took redundancy under the Release schemes and returned under arrangements with employment agencies.

This emphasis on contractors thus partly reflected a desire to improve flexibility and adaptability. It also derived from BT's desire to concentrate on its core activities, hence the divestment of manufacturing activities. European Union regulations requiring open competition in public procurement may also force the company to divest itself of equipment repair activities. But there is some evidence that contracting of work was also being used to accelerate the fall in BT employment figures: this was largely in order to reassure financial analysts, whose concerns about international productivity comparisons in terms of lines per employee tended to be reflected in share prices. The evolution of lines per employee is shown in Table 2.3.

In the future, the role of contracted work may be even more prominent, for two reasons. First, the notion of BT's core workforce will be progressively refined, with less core work more likely to be contracted out; on some estimates, BT's workforce could be reduced to as low as 65,000 by such means (Darbishire 1993: 111–12). A two-year consultancy project, Operation Breakout, was set up in 1993 "fundamentally to change the way the company operates" according to BT's annual report. It aimed to challenge accepted definitions of BT's work and how it was done. One idea mooted was the contracting out of entire functions such as personnel (with around 4,000 employees in 1994) or finance (3,000), leaving only small strategic policymaking units. Cutting out sup-

TABLE 2.3. Exchange lines per employee, 1981–1994

1981	68.6
1982	74.4
1983	78.0
1984	82.2
1985	87.3
1986	88.9
1987	98.2
1988	100.7
1989	102.3
1990	107.1
1991	117.8
1992	128.4
1993	157.9
1994	170.5

Source: BT Employment Statistics.

port functions was seen as a way of bringing unit costs down to compete with leaner operators in North America and the Far East.

Second, the notion of core *activities* may diverge from that of core *employees*. On one reading, BT would see as part of its core workforce all those essential to provision of its service, particularly those with high skills that were specific to BT (e.g., network maintenance) (Darbishire 1993: 111). But on another, the trend already visible to the use of contract workers in core engineering functions (cf. Tong 1993: 37) may be extended. One possibility worrying BT unions was the spread of "franchising"—with, for example, "an engineer sitting in a van, doing installations or repair work, but working on their own account, not employed by BT" (field notes, union respondent). Whatever the final outcome, one consequence is likely to be the "awkward coexistence" in the future of stable, highly skilled jobs in one business division, and of "sharp insecurity" in others (Darbishire 1993: 112).

Workplace Governance

The Structure and Strategy of the Personnel and Industrial Relations Function

As a nationalized industry, BT had a personnel function geared to the management of a stable bureaucratic structure of employment, and to the conduct of equally stable and highly formalized industrial relations (Batstone, Ferner, and Terry 1984). After privatization, BT attempted to forge a function more in tune with its changing corporate goals.

A new personnel structure emerged from the Project Sovereign reorganization of the early 1990s. Its key aspect was that at Group level the responsibility for devising industrial relations strategy was separated from the actual negotiating role. Thus policies on "remuneration, attendance patterns, grading, employment, resourcing, and performance" were developed by the Personnel Policy Division (see Darbishire 1993: 93), while the Employee Relations Division was responsible for negotiation, consultation, and communication with the unions.

The objective of the split was, in the words of one senior manager, to "render dispassionate" the interaction with the unions; management negotiators, it was felt, tended to become excessively understanding of the union point of view. The split therefore signaled a move away from the old public service ethos of joint regulation and bargained change, and toward "more employee-centred" approaches to issues. The change also had a more immediate spur in the imperative to cut the costs of collective agreements. The operation of the split gave rise to some problems, however. The unions were frustrated by it, seeing it as a "defensive posture" of management frightened of giving too much away. But it was also frustrating for managers. It proved difficult to accommodate more cooperative policies on the part of the unions, since if the unions did come up with a good idea, management negotiators would have to go back to more senior managers and "sell" the idea to them.

In addition to the strains at the corporate center between policy making and negotiation, there were also important tensions between the personnel function in the center and in the divisions. BT was subject to pressures for central control and coordination that were much stronger than in the average decentralized multidivisional company (see Colling and Ferner 1992). As described above, the early post-privatization devolution of responsibility to operational units had subsequently been reversed, largely because of the need to plan and coordinate service delivery on a uniform basis across the country. Personnel policies were also governed by this pressure for consistency. A key experience was the 1986 ETG repatterning agreement which created national guidelines, leaving detailed implementation to negotiation at district level, with uneven results for management (see below). Thus the divisions were not seen as having autonomy in the personnel sphere: "they do not 'own' their own personnel" (senior manager) as they might in a typical multidivisional company, even though each division had its own personnel director reporting directly to the divisional managing director. One of the reasons for the split between industrial relations policy formulation and negotiation was, according to BT, to enable the divisions to be consulted before policy was decided, while making clear that the resultant policy applied to the entire company and was the property of the center.

Although management at BT Group level was "in the long-term business of reining-in the divisions," there was a degree of conflict between the center's desire for consistency and the divisions' need for operational flexibility. In any case, the divisions' control over resources and information made the imposition of central control a difficult task. Senior management conceded that there was significant variation between divisions in areas where there was scope for individual judgement. For example, the STE complained that annual performance reviews (APRs) were being implemented inconsistently in different divisions, despite the despatch of "very robust" central guidelines on such reviews. BT's own monitoring of APRs showed that one division put significantly more of its employees in lower categories. The application of central policy was monitored through various systems of audit and post-implementation review, although BT was trying to reduce central bureaucratic intervention.

Collective Relations and the Machinery of Collective Bargaining

BT continued to accept collective bargaining as the most important means of regulating the terms and conditions of its staff. Up to 1995, it officially recognized three trade unions for collective bargaining purposes. The largest, the National Communications Union (NCU) had two sections: the engineering (NCU(E)) representing engineering and technical grades, and the clerical (NCU(C)) representing clerical and secretarial staff. The second largest, the Society of Telecom Executives (STE), represented middle and senior managers. The Union of Communication Workers (UCW), whose principal membership was among postal workers, represented the dwindling number of operators. It also recruited cleaning, catering, security, and other staff, although much of this work had been contracted out. In January 1995, the NCU and the UCW merged to form a new union covering posts and telecommunications, the Communication Workers Union (CWU). While each union traditionally negotiated separately with BT, certain matters of shared interest, such as facilities, discipline procedures, superannuation, and "London weighting" (that is a supplement to pay rates for employees in the capital) were negotiated jointly.

The first Thatcher government, elected in 1979, had a clear view that collective bargaining machinery in the British public sector was cumbersome, centralized, inefficient, and essentially served the protected interests of unions and management. "A cosy collusive relationship" was how it was perceived by one government minister. One consequence was that policies designed to weaken traditional collective bargaining arrangements were implemented in many parts of the public sector. These included decentralization, which caused serious problems for traditionally centralized trade unions; the reduction in the use of arbitration as a means of dispute resolution; and the reassertion of managerial control over the pace and allocation of work and over the introduction of new technologies. During the mid-1980s all these trends were visible within BT. But at no time did they amount to an all-out assault on collective bargaining itself. With the significant exception of the derecognition of the STE for collective bargaining purposes in respect of senior management grades, BT did not try to replace union-based bargaining and consultation with nonunion alternatives. Structures of formal joint consultation continued to operate at divisional and at corporate level, providing the unions with information on matters such as financial performance, capital expenditure programs, quality of service, and so forth. But they underwent substantial reform. BT had criticized a "heavily centralized and formalized joint consultative process which subjected virtually every aspect of Company policy to interminable joint committee debates and considerable procrastination" (cited in Smith and Terry 1993: 243). Consultation routinely shaded into de facto negotiation.

In the wake of the Project Sovereign reforms of the early 1990s, management introduced new principles of consultation (Barrett and Heery 1995). It took control of the consultation agenda, refashioning it according to managerial priorities, and linking the timetable of joint meetings to the calendar of corporate decision making. The number of tiers of consultation was cut to three, eliminating the local level. The number of meetings was reduced, and timetables for consultation were speeded up: the unions complained that in some of the new joint consultative committees at divisional and "zonal" level, they were required to give "authoritative responses . . . within two weeks" (NCU document). Senior management stressed that the role of the new consultative bodies was to deal with policy and strategy issues and with business performance, rather than function as de facto negotiating forums. Indeed, the emphasis was on informing, rather than consulting, the unions about management strategy and the company's performance, although management also tended to use them to sound out the unions on new initiatives, such as those emerging from Operation Breakout. Finally, the higher levels of the consultation system were no longer to serve, as they had in the past, as "a court of last resort" for minor issues and individual grievances referred up the consultative hierarchy from the local level.

In general, there was a widespread feeling within the unions that the (intended or unintended) consequence of the TQM program and other HRM initiatives was a gradual marginalization of union influence and collective bargaining. Even where formal structures remained in place, there was a change of management style. The new approach was to accelerate the process of negotiation and to implement change unilaterally where agreement could not be rapidly achieved (Berry 1993: 33).

The inter- and intra-union tensions that had been a feature of BT industrial relations persisted, and BT made use of the multiplicity of bargaining units to pursue what was sometimes seen as a policy of "divide and rule." During the 1987 technicians' dispute, for example, settlements with the UCW and, more important, the STE, left the NCU somewhat isolated. The Conservatives' industrial relations legislation, in particular the prohibitions on supportive or secondary action during industrial disputes, made the problem more complex.

Despite their loss of political influence and their feeling of being under constant attack by an unsympathetic management, the unions were of the view that they were still able to influence BT. One example from the early 1990s concerned a BT proposal to introduce a form of points ranking system as a guide to selection for redundancy. The union responded rapidly, issuing threats of strike action, and the decision was modified. Examples like this persuaded unions—the NCU in particular—that they had a role to play in identifying employee grievances and assisting management in avoiding bad decisions and taking good ones.

Pay bargaining. Pay bargaining remained centralized,[4] but the tradition of identical settlements with the same implementation dates for different groups (engineering, clerical, managerial, and so on) was broken (Darbishire, 1993: 63) as BT started to insist on separate negotiating dates, and small differences began to emerge in the size of settlements. This further weakened the unions' ability to coordinate pay claims. According to Darbishire (1993: 109) there was no apparent desire for any moves to divisionalized bargaining. However, there was a trend to separate negotiations for BT's other businesses. In 1991 the NCU agreed that it would negotiate separately for BT's individual companies, although the key negotiations centered on the largest, BT plc. At this time the NCU was involved in sixteen sets of negotiations with settlement dates from April to October. Clearly this has implications for union tactics, structures, and allocation of resources.

Decentralization and recentralization: the rise and fall of the districts. While company-wide national structures of bargaining and consultation persisted, the drive in the mid-1980s was, as mentioned, to reduce the scope of national bargaining and enhance the authority and discretion of district managers. Bargaining on work reorganization took the form of "framework agreements" for detailed implementation at local level to suit local conditions. On occasions, elements of the pay package were made conditional on successful local implementation. The clearest example was the ETG 1987 "repatterning agreement" which provided for district-level supplementary bargaining to implement the changes within national guidelines. Local bargaining also covered issues such as the employment of temporary and part-time workers and the use of subcontractors, training arrangements, promotion, job-share arrangements, and the introduction of new technology (Darbishire 1993: 57–58). BT argued that organizational change was not a subject for negotiation but that the staffing implications of change were.

---

4. For a short period from 1989, bargaining was carried out by the largest division on behalf of the corporation as a whole, but since Project Sovereign, pay negotiations have been relocated at corporate level.

The process of implementation revealed the tensions between central control and local managerial discretion described above. On the one hand, local managers wished to implement their own local "vision." Darbishire (1993: 55–56) describes a picture of substantial local variation, with district managers seeking to introduce, often against union opposition, proposals that fell outside the nationally-agreed framework. The increasingly heard union view was that, despite the rhetoric, meaningful bargaining was being replaced by unilateral managerial implementation of change. "In the districts we at first created a macho culture. Personnel managers interpreted that as seeing the unions perhaps once a year" (senior manager interview).

On the other hand, central corporate management did not want to risk either local strikes or excessive local variation. The activities of district managers were being carefully monitored centrally, and corporate industrial relations staff would intervene in local bargaining if they perceived the risk of a strike, or of the propagation of practices that were at odds with corporate personnel policy. Intervention was justified on the grounds that "line managers often underestimated the strength of local union representation, overestimated their own negotiating powers, and could not handle incidents such as strikes effectively" (Colling and Ferner 1992: 217). Many district-level managers did not have the necessary bargaining skills and tended to hide behind national agreements; indeed, they had to be coaxed into action, partly by direct central encouragement to treat at least some elements of national agreements in a flexible way (Colling and Ferner 1992: 215).

The decentralization of bargaining caused problems also for the traditionally centralized BT unions, nervous about local "macho" management "forcing unsatisfactory agreements on local unions, creating 'downward emulation' pressure from management" (Colling and Ferner 1992: 218). Their reaction was to coordinate union district responses, thereby reducing regional variation and, according to some union sources, contributing in turn to central coordination of district bargaining by BT itself.

A multiplicity of forces were thus combining significantly to restrict the degree of bargaining decentralization in practice. Limited decentralization operated in the sense that negotiations could take place at divisional level with central approval, although as suggested above, it was not always easy for the center to impose its own discipline on the divisions.

The unions were ambivalent about recentralization. Although they were happier to see a more centralized structure, they complained that new joint structures below corporate level (at divisional and zonal or operational unit level) were increasingly "skeletal and more consultative than collective bargaining, defining rights of access and a minimum floor of joint consultative arrangements" (interview with senior union official). They were also frustrated at being unable to locate those managers with formal responsibility for certain decisions and policy issues; they increasingly resorted to informal approaches and soundings. They were critical of what they perceived as divisional "barons" ignoring, or failing to implement properly, agreements reached at corporate level.

The future of collective bargaining. The unions, especially the STE, were fearful that the long-term intention of BT was to manage without them. Senior managers acknowledged that such a policy was unfeasible, at least as long as BT failed to win employee commitment and loyalty. While managerial discussions concerning derecognition did continue, there was a view that a combination of size and the persistence of public service traditions made this impractical for the present, at least in respect of NCU-represented grades.

However, collective bargaining was constantly under review "at the margins." The derecognition of the STE in respect of its senior managers was the clearest example (see the section on pay). This was the practical implementation of a philosophy which perceived a fundamental incompatibility between managerial loyalty to the company and loyalty to the union. There were fears within the STE, and debates within the senior management, concerning the further downward extension of this principle. At the same time, collective bargaining was becoming increasingly concentrated on BT's core activities. In the more peripheral areas, including some BT contractors, unions were finding it hard to gain recognition. In Mercury, BT's major competitor, there was no union recognition and no role for collective bargaining. Mercury's human resource policy focused on the individual employee relationship, with individualized pay for all employees and annual pay rises based on individual performance (IRS 1994). In 1994, there were some 900 NCU members out of Mercury's total workforce of 10,500. Although the NCU claimed members in over 100 companies—and recognition agreements in around 30 (IRS *Employment Trends,* December 1993: 10–12)—the fragmentation of the structure of the industry as a result of competition and deregulation was making union organization increasingly difficult. Despite the relative stability at BT plc, therefore, within the telecommunications sector as a whole collective bargaining was certainly in decline.

Conclusions

Like most other telecommunications authorities, BT operated in a context of rapidly changing technology, which affected the organization of work and skills, and the size and composition of the workforce. In addition, however, its management structures and its operating environment were transformed by the transition from public corporation to private sector multinational company. In this respect it was unlike other European telecommunications companies, although some of the continental European companies are now going down the same road. The change in ownership per se has generally been seen as a relatively minor influence on management strategy compared with increasing competition and technological change. Yet the move from political control to shareholder control influenced the ethos of management in BT: manifested for example in the determination to relegate the role of management unionism. It also meant the end of direct government intervention in areas of pay determination and productivity characteristic of the public sector (although a more diffuse influence persisted). The regulatory framework which was an inherent accompaniment of privatization also had its specific impact, notably through the pressures of the price control formulae on labor costs.

Moreover, the dynamic effects of privatization cannot, in practice, be separated from those of increasing competition. Although in theory market structure issues are distinct from those of ownership, there is no doubt that privatization gave a massive impetus to competition in the peripherals market, in the provision of value added services, and indeed in the basic network. The competitive potential made possible by technological advances was as a result realized earlier in Britain than elsewhere in Europe. Competition—and the fear of still more competition in the future—was driving some of the changes in employment relations, particularly the massive cuts in the workforce, and it was equally behind the move toward flexibility in work organization in customer service functions (notably hours of attendance for the Customer Field Service).

Ownership factors combined with competitive and regulatory ones to encourage BT's move toward the global market. One of the key questions for future industrial relations is how a much more fragmented and dispersed labor force will be managed, and whether a diversity of patterns or models of industrial relations will emerge. Already it is possible that within the core BT Group, the different business divisions are developing approaches to industrial relations that suit their particular needs and interests, according for example to how close they are to the customer, how skilled the work content, how company- (or division-) specific the skill requirements, and so on. Such divergences raise the familiar question of central control versus local, or divisional, autonomy. How far can the center continue to exert its influence over increasingly disparate divisions, let alone over much more segmented subsidiary and overseas operations? We have repeatedly emphasized the strains between the desire to encourage more dynamic managerial behavior at the operational level, and the need to provide uniform standards of customer service in an integrated national telecommunications network. A similar tension may be observed in the desire both to encourage flexible and responsive teamworking among groups of technicians, and simultaneously to subject them to more detailed supervisory scrutiny and more rigid job descriptions.

Yet, despite the changes in industrial relations and personnel management, the legacy of the long public sector tradition lingered powerfully. Machinery of negotiation and consultation had been slimmed down, speeded up; issues once handled by collective determination were now part of managerial prerogative; bargaining was becoming more fragmented (both between central and local negotiations, and between Group and subsidiaries). A range of managerial techniques were deployed containing no explicit role for the unions, for whom much of this appeared to constitute hostility toward established practice. But bargaining remained important. Management continued to show a preference for change through negotiation rather than imposition. Derecognition of nonmanagerial unions was not on the agenda. Indeed, below the managerial grades, unionism was in relatively good shape, exceptionally so compared with the situation in much of the rest of British industry. This may largely reflect the pragmatism and responsiveness of the NCU, which was prepared to pay the price of its continued influence.

A major question is whether in the future the balance that management has assiduously sought to adjust—between collective and individual employee relations—will shift more decisively in favor of individualism. This will depend partly on the dynamics of relationships within BT—the continued compliance of the NCU, the success or failure of BT's employee commitment programs. A question mark must hang over the possibility for engaging employee commitment at a time of such unremitting upheaval and continuing job losses. "Delayering" of management, for example, has severely eroded the premises of the old internal labor market, leading to a mismatch between career aspirations and opportunities (Newell and Dopson 1995). The evolving balance between individualism and collectivism will also depend to an extent on uncertain external developments: the growth of competition, the impact of European regulation, changes in the governing party and hence, for example, the pervasive climate of antiunionism. One possibility is an increasing dualism. A core of stable industrial relations based on collective bargaining and consultation, combined with a degree of employment predictability if not stability, may still be found a decade from now. But it may be increasingly confined to a redoubt of activity in the provision and maintenance of the network. Elsewhere, that is in areas more closely related to the customer, a more individualized system of relationships may predominate. Indeed, a model of franchised indirect employment may grow. Outside the current mainstream BT activity, in the subsidiaries and abroad, the divergences may be even greater.

Chapter 3

Australia

Greg J. Bamber, Mark Shadur,
and David Simmons

In Australia, as in some other industrialized market economies, there is continuing deregulation in the telecommunications industry, and convergence between it and other industries, including news media, entertainment, and information technology.[1] There is increasing international competition and much change, not least in terms of human resources (HR) and industrial relations (IR). Against this background we examine changing management strategies, organizational structures, and employment relations (HR and IR) in Telstra, Australia's largest and oldest telecommunications service corporation, and Optus, Australia's main alternative provider.

As in many other countries, a government telecommunications monopoly operated for many years, but in 1991 a second carrier license was awarded to Optus. While confronting its new circumstances, Telstra is experiencing a great deal of change. It is trying to move from being an

1. We are indebted to those managers, union officials, and others in the Australian telecommunications industry who have spared the time to be interviewed. We much appreciate the help of Owen Darbishire, Glenda Kann, Harry Katz, Rene Kienzle, Jan Nixon, John Rice, John Rodwell, Stephen Teo, and several others. Our research is greatly facilitated by specific financial support from the Australian Research Council, which also founded the Australian Centre in Strategic Management at the Queensland University of Technology, the base for each author when the research was conducted and when this chapter was written.

inward-looking, technically oriented bureaucracy towards an outward-looking and more market-oriented enterprise. The aim of the restructuring is to make Telstra more competitive by "flattening" its organization, so that it will be "leaner" and will respond to customer needs more efficiently and effectively. There has been rationalization of its collective bargaining arrangements and downsizing of the enterprise.

Optus entered the duopolistic market claiming that it would provide higher levels of customer service than Telstra does. As a relatively new enterprise, Optus aimed to select its employees carefully. Senior management explains this process in terms of building a strong and cohesive organizational culture, as articulated in the mission of Optus. Optus management attempted to adopt a strategic approach to HR, which included efforts to integrate approaches to HR with broader business strategy.

These events parallel developments in many other industries in which changes in the macro environment and changing internal approaches to HR/IR have led some commentators to argue that approaches to HR/IR are undergoing a process of transformation (Kochan, Katz, and McKersie 1994). This process includes the transition from an industry to an enterprise focus to collective bargaining (Katz 1993), the development of a human resource management focus to employment relations (Storey 1992) and an increase in flexibility and broader approaches to work systems that involve the participation of employees (Buchanan 1994; Geary 1994).

The chapter illustrates some of the tensions in telecommunications in Australia. The industry's economic, political, and technological environment is changing. While we focus most of our attention on Telstra, we also draw comparisons between the different approaches of Telstra and Optus and put these into a context of debates about organizational change and whether current developments represent a marked departure from past methods of organization and HR/IR.

The Australian Context

Telegraph services were operating in Australia in the 1850s, and telephone exchanges were introduced to Australia in the 1880s (CITCA 1980: 372). Yet in the 1990s telecommunications is by no means a mature industry. On the contrary Australian telecommunications is experiencing rejuvenation and a great deal of organizational and technological change.

In Australia, moreover, telecommunications is seen as a particularly important industry. Perhaps this reflects the "tyranny of distance" in two senses. First, Australia is a long way from most other countries. Nonetheless, its population includes a high proportion of recent migrants who have family and friends overseas. In addition, its business community includes a high proportion of overseas-owned multinational enterprises. Hence international telecommunications services are widely seen as vital. Second, Australia is a large country with relatively few people (about 18 million). In sparsely populated rural communities, the telephone is a vital means of communication with relatives, neighbors, and commercial and public services. People appear to rely on the telephone to communicate with others to a greater extent than in most other countries.

In this context the Australian government has often intervened in the industry. For example, most local phone calls have always been untimed. Previously there was a proposal to introduce timed local calls, which elicited storms of protest. The issue was settled when the Prime Minister and federal cabinet rejected timed local calls. While future intervention has not been ruled out, the type of intervention may change. The Australian Government has announced a review to consider changes in policy, legislation, and regulation, following the expiration of the current duopoly arrangement in 1997 (Lee 1994).

The Australian government took steps toward dismantling its long-standing telecommunications monopoly in the late 1980s. Policies were altered and in 1989 and 1991 legislative changes were enacted to allow limited competition in telecommunication services. Value added network services were deregulated in the late 1980s and the reforms eventually enabled Optus Communications to be granted a second carrier license (Bureau of Industry Economics 1995: 33). Telstra and Optus then each attempted to adopt a more strategic approach to managing HR and IR than had generally been found in Australia. These trends mirror developments in other countries.

Overview of the Industry

The Main Services and Products of the Industry

There are two main subsectors in telecomunications: services and equipment. This chapter focuses on services. The services provided include local, trunk, and international networks, and mobile telecommunications. Services are provided by three carriers: Telstra, formally Telecom (which is 100% owned by the Australian federal government) the main player,[2] Optus, the second player, and Vodafone, which at present is limited to mobile communications.

For many years, Telstra has been one of the largest employers in Australia. Telstra was formed by merging the former Australian Telecommunications Corporation (Telecom) and the Overseas Telecommunications Corporation (OTC), which were both state-owned enterprises. In the past, Telstra has also manufactured some of its own equipment. Since the 1980s, however, it has generally seen its "mission" as a supplier of services and has bought equipment from other suppliers who provide a wide range of products including cabling, optic fiber cabling, and analog and digital communications and switching devices.

Trends in demand. Demand for telecommunications services and equipment has grown strongly and this trend is likely to continue. There has been an upsurge in the variety of services provided in recent years with electronic data transfer and mobiles, in particular, becoming more popular. Cellular services, for example, commenced in 1986. There has been a faster take-up rate for mobile phones in Australia than any other country except Sweden (Bureau of Industry Economics 1995: 14).

Competition. In the 1996 federal election, telecommunications policy was one of the major differences between the main political parties. The conservative coalition parties proposed to privatize one-third of Telstra, while the incumbent Australian Labor Party's official policy was that the government should retain ownership. The former won the election. Therefore it is probable that Telstra will be at least partly privatized within the next few years.

Internationally, there is a trend toward such privatization for at least three reasons. First, governments (e.g., in Britain and New Zealand) can raise a huge income by selling their telephone companies. In the Australian context, the coalition government has promised to use some of that income to protect Australia's natural environment. Second, especially in a period of scarce resources, governments seem unable or unwilling to supply the investment capital that might be necessary for telephone companies to compete with their international rivals (which

2. Although it has used other trading names, we generally use the current name Telstra when referring to the post-1991 period. We use Telecom (or OTC as appropriate) when referring to the pre-1992 period. If referring to phone service providers more generally, we use the term telecommunications companies or TelCos.

enjoy considerable deregulation, especially in overseas markets) particularly since there is a great deal of technological innovation taking place. Third, in the face of such competition and innovation, there is an influential "rational-economic" view that, other things being equal, public-sector enterprises are less innovative and less likely to be competitive and flexible than their more entrepreneurial private-sector counterparts.

The arguments of opponents of privatization include that: first, a private-sector company would kill an Australian "sacred cow," untimed local calls; second, it would not maintain full services to remote locations and payphones which are not profitable, but hitherto were cross-subsidised by Telstra; and, third, would reduce levels of employment and unionization, but increase prices.

Even though it has not yet been privatized, Telstra's major predecessor began to behave more like a private corporation after it was "corporatized" in the 1970s. Since the 1980s, in particular, its senior executives have sought to restrict the role of government. Nevertheless, they have had only a limited success in this regard, for some of its stakeholders (including unions, customers, suppliers, and even competitors) have continued to seek government intervention to promote their own interests.

Until the 1990s, government-owned monopolies prevailed in the Australian telecommunications services sector (e.g., Telecom, OTC, and Aussat—the government's communications satellite). In the 1990s Australian governments have sought to deregulate the market to increase competition as a means to improve services and enter overseas markets, particularly in the Asia-Pacific region. In 1991, Optus purchased Aussat's operations and their satellites for A$800 million.

At present the government is proposing to deregulate the market further in 1997. The Australian telephone service carriers are monitored to some extent, by an independent regulator Austel. It has been severely criticized for not taking a tougher stance on a range of regulatory and policy issues (*Australian Financial Review*, 29 July 1993). Austel appears to be weaker than its counterparts in the United States or United Kingdom, for example. But the Australian Competition and Consumer Commission may also intervene in Australia. In addition, the federal government asked the three players to establish a Telecommunications Industry Ombudsman scheme.

Starting in 1993, independent ballots were held in Australia's major cities whereby customers could chose their preferred long distance carrier, Telstra or Optus.[3] Unlike the customer ballots carried out in the United States, the Australian customer ballot surveyed at least 90 percent of customers' lines in each charging area, and Telecom and Optus were the only options on the ballot. Telecom was limited by price caps, and no subsequent interconnect price had been agreed in Australia (Forster 1993). In the initial ballots, Optus secured 14 percent of the votes as the preferred long distance carrier in Melbourne and 18 percent of the preferred long distance carrier vote in Sydney. The ballots were accompanied by massive advertising campaigns by both players. Each accused the other of having an unfair advantage and using "dirty tricks." There was a view in the private sector business community that, on average, Optus's prices would be at least slightly lower and Optus would maintain less complicated pricing structures and discounts. Further, Telstra incurred unfavorable publicity in the early 1990s following a campaign by some aggrieved small businesses that claimed to have suffered from phone faults, so that their businesses were "casualties of Telstra." On the other hand, the unions tended to favor Telstra as it was much more highly unionized and was owned by the Australian government. In particular, they assumed that reductions in Telstra's employment would be correlated with the success of Optus in winning market share. One senior union official commented that the competition "was fabricated," with the playing field "sloping" to provide "obvious advantages for the new player" (interview, 5 May 1993).

Deregulation in the Organization for Economic Cooperation and Development (OECD) countries is leading to more global competition. Continuing regulation of domestic carriers has been leading them to seek overseas markets in order to expand as has been the case with the U.S. "baby Bells." Since the two old U.K.-based carriers, British Telecom and Cable and Wireless were privatized in the early 1980s, they have also been expanding internationally. Several OECD telecommunications com-

3. Austel conducted a public information campaign for the ballot process. Probably inertia contributed significantly to the large share won by Telstra. Results of the initial ballots were as in the following table.

	Canberra	Sydney	Melbourne	Mornington	Geelong
Response rate	52%	58%	56%	50%	55%
Optus share	12%	18%	14%	10%	10%
Telstra share	88%	82%	86%	90%	90%

Source: Austel.

panies were looking to the Asia-Pacific countries as a major region for investment, especially given the high growth rates and the increasing demand for urban and international services. Telstra and Optus are facing tight competition in their efforts to enter such overseas markets (Allen Consulting Group 1991: 35). Telstra has had some offshore successes, for instance, winning a major service contract in Saudi Arabia and the sale of satellite-based services in Indochina.

Productivity and quality. Spurred by more competitive markets, telephone companies are paying more attention to international benchmarking, for instance, in relation to productivity and quality. By Telstra's own admission, competition has led to improved levels of productivity and customer satisfaction. Nevertheless analysis of some performance indicators suggest that Australian telecommunications services fall well behind international benchmarks (Bureau of Industry Economics 1992, 1995). On productivity, for example, one study indicates that Australia is ranked 19 out of 27 countries in terms of revenue per employee, 26 out of 30 on lines per employee, and last out of 11 countries on partial labor productivity. Quality also appears to be low with Australia ranked 15 out of 19 on fault clearance and 15 out of 24 on international direct dial (IDD) completion rates. On the other hand, however, Australia performs better in terms of many pricing categories including 1 out 24 for the international call basket, 4 out of 24 in the mobile basket and, 14 out of 23 in the national basket (Bureau of Industry Economics 1995: xiv).

There are also important *caveats* with these data. Caution should be exercised, for example, in terms of economies of scale. With its low and sparse population and large geographic network coverage, Australia could not be expected easily to reach the levels of network productivity as in more densely populated countries such as Japan, the Netherlands, and Switzerland. Telstra has subcontracted network construction and maintenance to a lesser extent than TelCos in many other countries with which Australia is being compared; this may distort labor productivity measures. Furthermore, Australian TelCos are currently undertaking major capital development programs including digitalization and optical fiber deployment. These programs have a negative impact on current capital expenditure and operating expense, but may provide long-term benefits in terms of lower cost structures, and Australian telecommunications services are among the most advanced in the world.

Many TelCos are trying to adopt Total Quality Management (TQM). Telstra has initiated a high-profile internal TQM program, whereby sections of the company compete with each other to win recognition and prizes. Sections of Telstra also compete in the Australian Quality Awards (which have some parallels with the U.S. Baldrige awards).

Optus did not initially adopt a formal TQM program. Many of the espoused practices of the company, however, such as team working and an organization-wide commitment to customer service, are similar to the basic tenets of TQM. Optus measures the quality and effectiveness of its organization relative to customer satisfaction. It has attempted to measure its performance against several accepted measures of service quality (cf. Parasuraman et al. 1985) and benchmarks its performance against "world best practice".

Labor Markets and Industrial Relations

Telecommunications services include a series of technical and electronic processes and skills concerned with installation and maintenance of complex equipment. Many such skills are industry specific; they are not readily transferable to or from other industries. The links between skills and technological change have been particularly controversial. In brief, there are examples of new technologies being used to deskill some jobs, but to reskill others (cf. Zuboff 1988). Technologies and skills can be shaped by the relative power and knowledge of the relevant parties.

Telstra's predecessors developed well-defined internal labor markets, with occupationally based unions, some of which were industry specific. Traditionally, Telstra relied on its internal labor market for recruitment and promotion. Optus is smaller and newer, so the internal labor market is less well developed and greater reliance is placed on the external labor market. Optus drew certain senior management from Cable and Wireless and from BellSouth; many of its core engineering staff came from Aussat. Optus has also recruited extensively from universities and has a relatively young workforce (average age 28 in 1994).

Significant rationalization among Australian unions in general led to amalgamations in the early 1990s between the Public Sector Union (PSU), Professional Officers' Association (POA), and others to form the Community and Public Sector Union (CPSU).[4] There have also been significant amalgamations between the Australian Telecommunications Employees' Association/Australian Telegram and Phonogram Officers' Association (ATEA/ATPOA) and Australian Postal and Telecommunica-

---

4. Although the unions have all used other names in the past especially before the early 1990s' series of amalgamations, to simplify the text we generally refer to unions by their 1995 names wherever possible.

tions Union (APTU) to form the Communication Workers' Union (CWU). The CWU linked with the Telecommunications Officers' Association in early 1994, and subsequently merged with the Telecommunications Officers' Association and the Electrical, Electronics, Plumbing, and Allied Workers' Union to form a new large federation, the Communications, Electrical, and Plumbers Union (CEPU) covering the communications and electrical industries.

The CEPU is an active member of the Postal, Telegraph, and Telephone International (PTTI), an international trade union secretariat based in Geneva.[5] In view of the rapid moves toward globalization of this industry and of the similar issues faced by telecommunications workers in other countries, the CEPU sees the PTTI as a significant source of information and contacts.

Telstra and Optus

Until 1975, Telecom was part of the federal government's Postmaster-General's Department and was part of the public service. From 1975 the Australian Telecommunications Commission operated separately from postal services. Following the Australian and Overseas Telecommunications Corporation (AOTC) Act (1991), Telstra's immediate predecessor, known for a short while as AOTC, was incorporated in 1991 and began trading in February 1992. Telstra became the new official name of AOTC in 1993.

In 1990–91 the government made decisions to partially deregulate the telecommunications sector. In 1991 the government awarded Optus a carrier license, and by mid-1994 Optus employed slightly more than 2,600 employees. This is expected to grow to approximately 5,000 employees by the year 2000.

Optus is owned by a consortium comprised of two insurance companies: the Australian Mutual Provident Society and National Mutual, and a transport company, Mayne Nickless, which, together, own 51 percent, together with BellSouth (U.S.A.) and Cable and Wireless (U.K.), which own 49 percent. Initially, Optus offered alternative services in trunk, international, and mobile networks. Its next aim was to compete also in the market for local calls and multimedia cable TV in a joint venture with Continental Cable (U.S.A.) and an Australian television network (the Nine Network). Optus owns 46.5 percent of the joint venture. Optus

---

5. On international trade union secretariats, see Bamber & Lansbury 1993: chap. 11 (by O. Clarke).

aimed to "piggy-back" local telephone services on its incipient pay-TV cable network.

One year after entering the Australian market, Optus had won 18 percent of Telstra's mobile phone and international markets, but only 7 percent of its domestic long distance market. Optus had built up an A$600 million business, while the drop in revenues for Telstra prompted it to cut investment by 10 percent (*Australian Financial Review*, 4 Aug. 1993). By 1995 Optus had won more than a third of the mobile phone market and had increased its share of domestic long distance calls.

Operating profit for Telstra after tax to 30 June 1995 was A$1,753 million (see Table 3.1). Telstra's total assets in 1995 were A$24,083 million. Telstra makes a significant value-added contribution to the Australian economy; for the year ended 30 June 1995 this was A$8.78 billion, or 2.2 percent of Australia's gross domestic product (Telstra 1995a: 6, 13). Telstra's major investments have included the roll out of fiber optic cable and its "fibre to the kerb" goal in most suburbs. Current investment plans envisage an outlay of A$3.9 billion in the four years 1996–99 to provide a fiber optic and coaxial cable network that will enable four million homes to be connected (Telstra 1995a: 10). Telstra's fiber optic network is opening strategic opportunities to expand its range of services and to generate revenue.

By 1994 Optus had spent A$1 billion establishing its fixed and mobile networks. Optus reported its first net profit (A$7.1 million) for the six-month period 30 June to 31 December 1995. Its senior management claim that Optus will add, directly and indirectly, at least A$2 billion to Australia's GDP by 1997.

Industrial Relations and Human Resources

Corporate Structure

In the 1970s and early 1980s Telecom had a functional corporate structure (e.g., accounting and supply, commercial services, network en-

TABLE 3.1. Operating profits and total assests, Telstra, 1990–1995

Financial statement items	1990/91 (A$M)	1991/92 (A$M)	1992/93 (A$M)	1993/94 (A$M)	1994/95 (A$M)
Operating profit (after tax)	1,240[a]	300	905	1,699	1,753
Total assets	24,036[a]	22,827	23,160	21,139	24,083

Source: Telstra Annual Report 1995 and earlier years.
[a]Totals derived from addition of Telecom Australia and OTC Limited Statistical Summaries.

gineering, personnel), together with state managers who also had a functional structure. The state managers held considerable power. In the late 1980s and early 1990s, following recommendations by McKinsey & Co., Telecom introduced a divisional structure based on different segments of the product market. With increasing competition, efficient operation and cost containment became priority issues for Telstra's management. To accompany the rationalization of activities and subsequent reduction in employment levels, Telstra moved toward flatter organizational structures. Telstra attempted to introduce multiskilled teams of people, focused on specific markets and with the ability to respond quickly to changing demands. The changes also meant a major reduction in the power of the state managers.

Telstra aimed to create "semi-autonomous business units, each with its own customers, its own assets, its own team of employees and, indeed, its own culture consistent with the overall Telstra culture" (AOTC 1992: 11). The 1992 restructure resulted in six business units and a services group. For IR negotiations, however, Telstra was further divided into twenty-two bargaining units, and management sought to decentralize IR negotiations to these units in 1992–93 in an effort to achieve greater flexibility. However, there were very few different outcomes from this approach. For example, there were no major pay differentials across the units and the most notable achievements were some variations in working hours arrangements such as start and finish times. Similarly, gainsharing negotiations resulted in differences across the bargaining units of only a few hundred dollars per annum for comparable employees. The unions did not support decentralized bargaining because this might result in a lack of equity ("equal pay for work of equal value" is an oft-used rallying cry for Australian unions). In addition, the unions wanted to avoid the logistical difficulties of bargaining in many units. Management also became disenchanted with decentralized bargaining since it engendered pressures for leap-frogging of wages and increases in job classifications across different parts of the enterprise. Also the more complex decentralized organizational structure and IR bargaining units were not conducive to driving the change program through the organization. Accordingly, in the mid-1990s Telstra reverted to more centralized bargaining arrangements.

In terms of corporate culture, a large proportion of Telecom's long standing senior executives had a technical background. They took pride in engineering achievements. But in the 1990s, Telstra is attempting to reorient itself to focus to a much greater extent on marketing to customers. Telstra employees are encouraged to provide excellent customer service as an overriding priority. The focus, then, is shifting from an internal producer view to an external consumer view.

Optus has the advantage of being a new enterprise. According to one Optus manager, this "enables the company to start from scratch, unencumbered by an existing network base consisting of several generations of technologies." This comment refers to specific telecommunications technologies, and also reflects the ability of Optus to tailor its corporate structure to meet the perceived needs of the market. It adopted a relatively flat organizational structure unlike more traditional bureaucracies. Corporate culture is frequently mentioned by Optus executives, with one senior manager stating that attention to customer satisfaction is the most important element of the Optus culture. According to the Customer Focus and Communications Manager, "the Optus culture promotes the idea that all Optus employees and strategic partners are customer service people." This approach is promoted by a procedure for dealing with customer concerns that was initially developed for the Optus Customer Service Centre, but is being promoted for use among general staff and helps to support the espoused culture. "Culture" is often discussed with staff, in newsletters and videos, and in general day-to-day communication.

According to a senior manager, "the original organization structure was established to provide a functional focus and specific project management capability." This approach reflected a perceived need to establish market share quickly. Optus has also adopted a regionalized organizational structure. This strategy was designed to make Optus "closer to the customer" and to combat the customer perception that decisions are made remotely (Optus, *Billabong Magazine*, July 1993: 4).

Management has attempted to foster cross-functional interaction. Optus has an open plan office for managers and they claim to use a central clerical pool. According to Bob Mansfield, Optus's first chief executive officer, the open plan office design was also necessitated by a need to get Optus up and running quickly: "We couldn't afford to have executives cloistered behind closed doors, isolated from our staff. We wanted an open culture that would talk about issues before they became problems, so we [top executives] had to include ourselves in that. The example must come from the top tier" (Plunkett 1993).

This office design encourages the flow of communication between departments. Without a tradition of demarcations, and given the explicit efforts from the outset to promote communication flow between departments and the relatively small size of the organization, there is easier communication flow between functions at Optus than at Telstra. For example, to deal with customer queries the customer service function invariably works across many areas of the business.

Employment Relations at Telstra

As a large public-sector employer, Telstra has long been highly union-ized at all levels of its organization. Until the 1990s, only twelve jobs in Telecom were exempt from industrial awards[6] and union coverage. These were the CEO and those positions that reported directly to the CEO. Most of the unions were originally occupational. In 1987, twenty-eight unions had members at Telstra, though five unions represented 91 per-cent of all the union members there (Davis and Lansbury 1989: 17). By 1992, more than 95 percent of Telstra employees who were union mem-bers belonged to either the CPSU or CEPU (AOTC 1992: 34). Typically, most operatives belonged to the CEPU (which in mid-1993 had about 45,000 members in Telstra), while most clerical and supervisory staff be-longed to the CPSU (which then had about 13,000 members in Telstra).

Traditionally, people who joined Telstra saw it as a "job for life." Tele-communications was not subject to the "booms" and "busts" that char-acterized some other industries (cf. mining, manufacturing, and construction). For many years Telstra's forerunners were steadily recruit-ing (and promoting) more people, rather than engaging in periodic re-trenchments (cf. car manufacturers).

Further, Telstra generally appeared to have had a relatively harmoni-ous relationship with the unions. It spent a lot of time and money on communicating, consulting, and negotiating with union representatives. This pattern did not apply only at the national level, but was also at state and local levels even though most of Telstra's job regulation was centralized and governed by federal awards. In short, employment and industrial relations at Telstra and its predecessors could perhaps be seen as approximating an "indulgency pattern" (cf. Gouldner 1954).

Cooperation and Conflict

The telecommunications industry has undergone fundamental changes in recent years. Nevertheless, in this period there has not been serious industrial action. By contrast and in spite of the above generalization about relative harmony, in the 1960s and 1970s against the background of technological change, there were some significant disputes between Telecom and ATEA. In the 1960s, there was conflict about the mainte-nance arrangements for the then new "crossbar" exchanges. In the 1970s, the issue was similar, but involved Ericsson's ARE II exchanges.

---

6. An *award* is a legally enforceable determination of employment terms and conditions in a firm or industry, which has been arbitrated or certified by an IR commission. For an introduction to Australian industrial relations, see Bamber and Sappey 1996.

ATEA led a strike to counter Telecom's renewed attempt to centralize maintenance. The upsurge in militancy was particularly apparent in the eastern states: Queensland, New South Wales, and Victoria. This "celebrated 1978 strike" precipitated "a novel settlement" that involved a series of trials of two different ways of introducing technological changes. The first approach was joint management-union consideration of proposals for change (including those submitted by unions) before a firm decision had been made. The second approach was employer provision of information and resources to unions to enable them to make accurate assessment of the implications of the employer's proposals. Independent experts used six criteria to evaluate the outcomes (Lansbury and Davis 1984: 140–41). The findings were considered by what later became known as the Australian Industrial Relations Commission (AIRC). "The manner of settlement was as innovative as the strike itself, for it represents one of the few occasions when competing claims about the social impact of technology have been evaluated through controlled experiment" (Matthews 1987: 143; see also Muller 1980).

This dispute in 1978 prompted the government to establish the Committee of Inquiry into Technological Change in Australia (CITCA 1980: 367–97). In 1983 the parties (Telecom and the unions) concluded a landmark Technological Change Agreement that helped to settle conflict over the introduction of new technology and was widely cited as a benchmark by unions in other sectors (Davis and Lansbury 1989a and 1989b).

As was the case for many other Australian enterprises, until the late 1980s for the most part Telecom's usual approach would be characterized as rather reactive in relation to union claims. Since the late 1980s, however, Telstra has taken initiatives in IR/HR to a greater extent. "Now, we're actually serving it up to the unions with quite proactive plans of our own saying: it's no longer acceptable to say you guys work this way, this is the way the business has got to work in order to make money. Here's how we want the arrangements changed. It's quite a culture shock for them and for us" (interview, 3 May 1993).

Before mid-1992, Telecom conducted separate negotiations with some 15 different unions or groups of unions:

Communication Workers Union
Public Sector and Broadcasting Union
Metals & Engineering Workers' Union
Telecommunications Officers Association
Association of Professional Engineers and Scientists Australia

Senior Managers' Association
Australian Journalists' Association
Australian Nursing Federation
National Union of Workers
Operative Painters & Decorators Union of Australia
Electrical Trades Union
Amalgamated Society of Carpenters and Joiners of Australia
Federation of Industrial Manufacturing Engineering Employees
Building Workers Industrial Union of Australia
Plumbers & Gas Fitters Employees' Union of Australia (*Our Future,*
    7 Dec. 1992: 2).

Telstra was prompted to accelerate a rationalization of its bargaining arrangements by Optus and CEPU having agreed to a single-union enterprise award in 1992. Therefore, Telstra sought assistance from the Australian Council of Trade Unions (ACTU) in moving Telstra itself closer toward such an enterprise award with CEPU and CPSU. Subsequently, the Australian Manufacturing Workers Union (AMWU) is the only other union that Telstra negotiates with. (It has about 2,000 members in Telstra.) Under the revised arrangements, the AMWU speaks on behalf of all of the other minority unions. After 1992, then, Telstra negotiated with only three separate unions. For most purposes Telstra's dealings were with only two main unions: CPSU and CEPU.

Nonetheless, Telstra is aiming to encourage even more rationalization of its bargaining arrangements. Telstra has 24 separate awards and numerous industrial agreements (which are generally less formal than awards). In the mid-1990s, Telstra and the main unions tried to rationalize all of these into a "single, common core" enterprise award which may have more specific business-unit industrial agreements as supplements. In view of the accelerating rate of change that is being experienced, the parties also agreed to reconsider the 1983 Technological Change Agreement.

The merger between Telecom and OTC, and the restructuring and deregulation process had an enormous impact on employees. The CEO, Frank Blount, acknowledged at this time that the "change process . . . has had and is having a traumatic effect on many of the people. . . . They feel uncertain about the future and about the overall direction of the Company" (AOTC 1992: 11). He elaborated:

I'm not surprised people are unsure about their future—so much has happened to this company in a short time. We've experienced more change and stress in the past 12 months than most companies experience in several decades—a merger, a restructure, job losses, a change in leadership and exposure to full scale competition.

The issue of job security dangles above people's heads and I can well understand that this is reflected in their confidence in management leadership and career advancements. (*Our Future,* 7 Dec. 1992: 1)

These changes were not accompanied by a return to the confrontation between Telstra, the unions and employees that characterized changes in the 1970s. But the process was certainly testing the patience of all parties. The CEPU leadership generally adopted a moderate policy of trying to accommodate and influence the changes, for they are generally seen as inevitable. However, there was a growing chorus of disquiet and of vocal dissent from militant CEPU factions, which argued in favor of more oppositional policies. Such dissent is understandable in view of the trauma that CEPU members were experiencing at this time. As one senior union official put it: "unfortunately some of the organizational changes are contradictory . . . the management oscillates between centralization of functions and decentralization. People lose confidence that management know where they're going . . . [and if] they're genuinely concerned for the customers" (interview, 5 May 1993).

Even though its members are generally higher in the employment hierarchy, in the 1990s the CPSU has sometimes adopted policies that are less accommodative to Telstra. Such stances are explicable in at least two ways. First, the CPSU is less of an industry- or enterprise-specific union than the CEPU. The CPSU has only a small proportion of its members in telecommunications, is more "open," and tends to identify with the public service more generally, unlike the CEPU, whose Communications Division is a relatively "closed" union; most of this CEPU division's members are employed either in Australia Post or Telstra, with just a few in Optus (cf. Turner 1962; Hughes 1967; Bamber 1986).

Furthermore, in the early 1990s, Telstra threatened the CPSU's organizational security. The new regime at Telstra removed the most senior 1,000 jobs out of coverage by awards and unions. It then sought to remove another 4,000 senior executives from the coverage (which primarily affected the CPSU) and to shift them on to more individualized employment contracts which included performance-related pay with possibilities for higher earnings, but less job security. Telstra's aim was that managers paid above about A$45,000 per annum would all be exempt from awards. Telstra held that it could not manage its managers in the new competitive environment if their jobs were rigidly prescribed and they were on "paid-rates" awards. A Telstra executive elaborated the nub of the issue:

> Rigidity versus market driven flexibility . . . management needs to deal with managers and not have a union in the middle or the . . . Commission. We can't afford to run a business where we're subject to—every time you want to change something at that level—some collective negotiation or re-arrangement or leaving open the capacity for them to serve a log of claims on us and drag us back into some compulsory arbitration and for us to finish up with the result that we don't want. And so, it's not about de-unionization. Quite frankly, we couldn't care if people maintain their membership of the associations or not. It's about not having prescribed conditions and not having to deal with a third party. (interview, 3 May 1993)

But the CPSU successfully opposed this aim, partly by seeking government intervention to prevent what it saw as de-unionization. In some other countries' TelCos, employees have been moved to new, possibly nonunion, subsidiaries to avert involuntary retrenchments. Telstra also formed a new subsidiary, Visionstream, for special projects relating to rolling out fiber optic cables. This mechanism ensures that there is no expectation of permanent employment once the project is completed, but unions have successfully insisted that these employees remain union members. Telstra has also used Skilled Engineering, a separate private subcontracting company, to supply temporary employees to work alongside Telstra staff, for example, laying cables; however, these temporary employees must also be union members.

Generally, however, Telstra is aiming to introduce more flexibility into its remaining industrial awards, with fewer classifications and better designed jobs. In one award Telstra managed to reduce 100 job classifications to around six, though there are pressures to reintroduce one or two additional classifications. To use a current notion, it wishes to become "leaner" (cf. Womack et al. 1990; Shadur and Bamber 1994). This is an underlying rationale of its management strategies, as well as of its current enterprise bargaining agenda.

Employment Relations at Optus

Optus has adopted an HRM and enterprise focus to its employment relations. The CEPU is the only union that has any coverage in Optus. Union membership density, however, is less than 10 percent. In 1994 Optus became among the first Australian enterprises to implement a new-style nonunion enterprise flexibility agreement (EFA). The 1994 EFA recognizes the need to continue implementation of appropriate levels of minimum income and working conditions and includes guidelines to achieve these. Under the 1994 EFA, management and individual employees deal directly with each other on employee relations matters, without the involvement of a union. Since its inception, Optus has tried to integrate its HR function with its broader business strategies. This reflected a belief among its senior management that the HR function could play a major role in driving the espoused customer-oriented culture.

The 1994 EFA sets the tone for employment relations at Optus. The EFA builds upon a 1992 enterprise agreement that Optus concluded with the CEPU. The CEPU accepted the 1992 agreement as it provided for up to 50 percent higher pay in return for such concessions as longer hours and more flexible work practices. This resulted in differences between Telstra and Optus; for example, regarding working hours (Telstra 36.75, Optus 38 hours per week) and leave provisions (family leave provided by Optus but not Telstra), but the general view of the union is that conditions between Optus and Telstra remained reasonably comparable.

Employees voted directly for the 1994 EFA without direct union involvement. Approximately 85 percent of eligible Optus staff voted in the EFA ballot; 89 percent of these voted in favour of the EFA and 10 percent voted against. The EFA was subsequently approved by the AIRC. Referring to the EFA, the HR director at Optus claimed proudly that "this has put us [Optus] at the forefront of the Australian scene in employee relations. This result underpins the strong commitment staff share with us to talk directly with our staff regarding their terms and conditions of employment." (*Billabong*, Aug. 1994: 1).

The EFA covers many issues, but, in particular, it provides Optus with considerable flexibility to change work arrangements, provided changes are agreed to by employees and that employees are not worse off under the changes than they were under the conditions set out by the EFA. The agreement covers such issues as contracts of employment, hours of work, job classifications, remuneration (compensation), leave provisions, and issue prevention and resolution.

Many of the employment relations initiatives are expressed in terms of the corporate values espoused by Optus, which include attention to customer service, empowerment, and teamworking. Optus had employed a management consultant to help develop these values and strategies. Despite what may perhaps be considered a "soft" approach to employment relations, the HR department relies on many specific procedures. Performance appraisal, for example, is an important tool to give feedback to employees and reinforce the culture. There is a performance-based pay system for all levels of employees at Optus, unlike at Telstra where only senior executives have performance-related pay.

Employees in all job categories at Optus are appraised on a five-point rating system and this is used to calculate annual salary increases and bonus payments. Performance appraisal is fundamental to the corporate policy of rewarding individual performance. Optus management sees this as a major factor in facilitating a positive work culture. However, the union is critical of this reward system. It claims that there is a forced distribution following a bell-curve, so only a minority can receive the highest ratings (e.g., about 5% receive the top rating of 5, and 25% receive a rating of 4). In addition, the rating system places pressure on employees to perform beyond what the union considers normal work levels (e.g., arriving early, finishing late, working through lunch). According to the union, this encourages a workforce that is compliant, since those who speak out tend not to be rewarded.

Optus has attempted to reward performance (which includes the behavior of employees). Recruitment was also seen as an important part in the process of building a culture. Optus attempted to select employees with values and personalities that could be assimilated with the views of Optus. Optus adopted a behavioral approach to recruitment. Among the elements of this process is a teamworking exercise that attempts to gauge the ability of potential recruits to work effectively in a team (Simmons et al. 1996).

The HR department played an active role in designing work organization throughout the enterprise and took an active part in most facets of managing employees (cf. Schuler 1992). This approach was adopted to provide coherence in working conditions and standards. Optus has had some success in this endeavor. Its 1993 employee survey reported a high level of commitment in the responses of employees. According to the consultant who managed the survey, there was a high degree of consistency among managers and staff, and men and women. In the employee opinion survey, employees rated most elements of the organization as highly favorable. It was elaborated:

> This suggests a strong overall culture and set of work practices have been achieved which influence all employees, and compensate for variation of experience that might be caused by individual managers or the work practices of a particular unit. The uniformity of response indicates an organisational-wide understanding of the vision and values [of Optus], backed by a fairly strong and uniform management style, rather than a narrow, work-unit driven experience

with differing individual approaches (*Optus Employee Survey Results* 1993).

Union leaders argue, however, that the practice has fallen short of the promise of a positive work culture for Optus employees. One union leader stated that "The honeymoon with employees is nearly over and there are now cracks that are emerging which expose an underlying adversarial approach" (interview, CEPU official, March 1995). According to this view, employees' expectations were raised during the recruitment process but later they find that promotion opportunities have not always fulfilled these expectations. Similarly, the flexible remuneration package has been criticized by the union since the prospect of high bonuses has not always flowed to employees in practice, as the bonus system appears to follow a bell curve so that only a minority receive the high bonus. Union sources suggest that labor turnover is increasing through dismissals and as employees move on when they become disenchanted. Optus disagrees with this interpretation, but concedes that people may leave if they do not fit in with the strong corporate culture.

Work Organization at Telstra and Optus

As a large and bureaucratic public-sector enterprise whose predecessors began in the nineteenth century, Telstra and the unions harbored many demarcations and traditions of fragmented Taylorist work organization. Nevertheless, in the early 1990s the parties reached agreement to reduce the incidence of demarcations among jobs and promote more flexible working arrangements. The 1992 Enterprise Agreement (on Business Improvement and Future Growth) enabled mobility of staff across the business units, and recognised that multiskilling should be further developed. An Understanding on Customer Services was part of the 1992 Agreement and attempted to enhance the provision of customer service, such as specific measures to reduce demarcations.

Work practices have changed considerably at Telstra. Staffing levels have been cut in many areas and technology is changing so that different or additional roles must be conducted by remaining staff. In Network Operations, for example, there were about 200 district telephone exchanges around the country. Telstra has been centralizing these functions into main centers in each state which implies substantial staffing cuts. Staff in these main centers will be largely devoted to analysis and software maintenance and these roles will be reduced in the district exchanges. While the skills of some staff will be enhanced, union leaders see such changes as decreasing the multiskilled aspects of work for many employees (interview with a senior CEPU official, March 1995).

To gauge employee opinions, Telstra commissioned an international consultancy company to undertake a survey of the workforce in 1992. With responses from 36,330 people, it was the largest employee opinion survey ever conducted in Australia. Some broad comparisons between Telstra attitudes and national norms can be inferred from the consultant's surveys; these are indicated in Table 3.2 and these results are discussed in the sections that follow. The same consultant has conducted similar surveys in AT&T (U.S.A.) and Mercury (U.K.), so it also has international benchmarks from the telecommunications industry.

Results of the 1992 employee survey indicated that 56 percent of Telstra staff viewed their work organization (item 1) arrangements favorably, a little lower than the national norm (64%). The questions in this category related to, for example, the clarity of employees' job responsibilities, the efficient organization of work, and the provision of sufficient staff to handle the work load. A high proportion (81%) of respondents were satisfied with their physical work conditions, and this was above the national average. Overall job satisfaction (item 3) was 64 percent which was below the typical responses in Australia (72%). "Working relationships" refers to the respect employees are accorded and cooperation between the employees' own branch and other sections of Telstra. These relationships were positive (68%), though lower than the norm (74%). In spite of the large amount of time and money spent on employee communications, however, their satisfaction with communications (item 5) within Telstra was low (34%). The national average on this category was also low (42%).

TABLE 3.2. Telstra employee opinions in 1992 compared to national averages (Percentage giving favorable responses)

		Telstra	National norms
1	Work organization	56	64
2	Working conditions	81	75
3	Job satisfaction	64	72
4	Working relationships	68	74
5	Communication	34	42
6	Training and development	40	52
7	Career advancement	28	50
8	Pay and fringe benefits	36	47
9	Job security	34	71
10	Management	33	59
11	Supervision	62	68

Source: AOTC Employee Survey, 1992.

Following that employee survey, Telstra took steps to improve the areas that appeared to have the worst results. As part of a program to improve communications, for instance, Telstra has held a series of "front-line link-ups" in which the CEO and top managers give presentations and answer questions from employees of all levels. These are broadcast simultaneously on televised links. Typically, more than 2,000 employees attend the link-up at venues around Australia; audience feedback indicated that 75 percent of attendees considered that the presentations were "open, honest, and addressed real issues" (*Our Future,* 24 March 1995).

Another employee opinion survey was conducted at Telstra in 1995. While full details are not yet available, there has been a significant improvement in the results. The survey consultant compared Telstra results with those of other TelCos who were its clients. By 1995, Telstra claimed that its employees recorded a higher approval rating than those in overseas TelCos in relation to, for example: personnel policies and procedures, job security, communication, management, working relationships, working conditions, and supervision. The 1995 employee survey showed improved results with Telstra employees' satisfaction with communications above the national norm and 6 percent above that in the other TelCos (Telstra 1995a: 33).

From its inception Optus has attempted to design work organization flexibly. Jobs have been designed to give a holistic span of control that focuses on the process and not individual tasks. This strategy is supported by a relatively flat hierarchy and open-plan offices. A senior HR manager stated that this was epitomized by work organization in the customer service department. Customer service representatives handle customer queries or complaints, from initially speaking with the customer to the resolution of the issues. The primary objective of this strategy was to improve customer satisfaction and make individual employees accountable for specific processes. This accountability reflects senior managers' attempts to extend to more operational areas what they see as "a managerial approach" to work organization. In the view of Optus executives, such a managerial approach reflects a commitment to the organization and a willingness to perceive "ownership" of work.

Optus has attempted to decentralize decision making. This approach extends to operational levels, such as in the customer service area discussed above, and there is also a decentralization of decision making to the different Optus regions. This strategy has been promoted to increase the speed and flexibility of decision making, especially as it impinges upon customer service. For example, according to the Mobile Sales Manager: "I can tell customers that the decision makers are sitting in the same room. . . . That allows us to make decisions quickly, and we can set up special purchasing arrangements there and then. Customers respond to that" (*Billabong*, July 1993: 4).

Skill Formation at Telstra and Optus

Telstra has long had a reputation for providing a great deal of technical training and development for its employees, who could look forward to good prospects of promotion from the operative level through supervision and even into management. In the 1990s Telstra has implemented a further series of programs that it claims will boost employees' skills. Among these is a Skills Management System that is aimed at identifying the skills and expertise of the staff, and aids in competency modelling, succession planning for senior staff, and for extending the competency-based assessment and training programs (AOTC 1992: 32). The training budget is much higher than the government training levy, which, until 1994, applied to employers that spent less than 1.5 percent of their total payroll costs. Telstra claims to spend closer to 5 percent; typically around A\$200 million annually on training and skills development.

In addition to technical training, Telstra also provides programs on management development, TQM, marketing, and customer service. Its Employee Support Policy distributed A\$1 million in 1991–92 to allow staff to take external courses such as those at institutions of higher education. This program provides study leave, reimbursement of tuition fees, and scholarships in selected areas.

Critics of Telstra's training counter that, in the past, it lacked focus. One senior executive asserted that much of the training expenditure was wasted. In other words, employees and managerial staff could undertake a wide range of training, but it did not necessarily relate clearly to their current or immediate future jobs or the needs of the business. For instance, most supervisors could benefit from more training in people-skills, though much of it was focused on technical subjects.

Despite spending more money per employee on training than nearly all other Australian enterprises, Telstra learned from its initial employee survey that only 40 percent of its employees were satisfied with the adequacy of training (item 6) provided to them and the efforts made to familiarize them with activities in their business unit and in Telstra as a whole. This response was considerably below the national norm (52 percent). Training remained an issue in the 1995 survey with Telstra employees' approval rating slightly below that of employees in other TelCos. In 1992, there was a lack of satisfaction with career advancement at Telstra (28 percent) which was well below the national average (50 percent).

After the earlier program of staff reductions, the 1995 employee survey showed much improved results regarding career advancement with Telstra employees recording a higher approval rating than the national norm (Telstra 1995a: 33).

According to the Optus EFA, training is "directed towards facilitating the required implementation of leading edge technology by the development of a highly skilled workforce which is receptive to technological and operational change" (EFA 1994: 16). Optus has attempted to deliver broad-based training, to support a flexible approach to work organization. Optus has attempted to adopt a strategic approach to training, and the majority of training has been focused on facilitating the specific business objectives of Optus. In its 1993 employee survey, 79 percent of employees were satisfied with the level of commitment to training at Optus.

Employee Involvement

For many years Telstra encouraged various forms of employee participation and industrial democracy. In 1992 Telstra undertook to maintain consultation to promote productive relationships. Management agreed that unions "will be informed of proposed changes at the formulative stage," and union views will be objectively considered. But final decision-making authority rests with management (Enterprise Agreement 1992: 4). Telstra's current TQM program includes avenues for employee involvement such as the Staff Suggestion Scheme that began in 1991.

Optus management argues that employee involvement is part of the corporate culture and is expressed in the Optus values of teamworking and empowerment. As at Telstra, efforts have been made to involve employees in the process of decision making. These efforts do not resemble the industrial democracy and participative schemes that have been tried at Telstra (see below, Enterprise Governance), but instead employees are encouraged to influence their own work on an individual or team basis at the point of production (Geary 1994: 638).

Remuneration and Compensation

In 1991 the AIRC endorsed Telecom's move toward a new executive structure which meant that senior management positions were no longer subject to industrial awards. Telstra's Board subsequently approved a management incentive plan and a flexible remuneration scheme for executives who move to performance-based employment contracts, with the potential for considerable pay increases.

Earnings for the majority of Telstra employees have been set by awards that are negotiated before and established by the AIRC. Telstra's 1992

Enterprise Agreement included an immediate 3 percent increase in award rates of pay, a further 3 percent increase subsequently subject to completion of the business unit agreements (described below), and an additional 2 percent after 31 December 1993 subject to continued productivity gains under the business unit agreements. In return for these increases, the unions agreed not to pursue further pay claims during the period of the agreement. In addition, the parties agreed that two "one-off" payments of A$500 and A$1000 would be paid in the next two years to all employees, subject to "significant productivity and performance gains" linked to specified customer satisfaction and performance targets (*Our Future,* 7 Dec. 1992: 1). Before any lump-sum payment could be made the net profit must reach a specific level. If this is achieved then each employee would receive A$100 for each of the five targets that are met, for example, a 63 percent very good-to-excellent customer rating on service installations. Telstra had not achieved initial targets set under an innovative pay-for-performance scheme. In its place, however, an A$200 "recognition" payment (less tax) was made to staff on 15 July (*Our Future,* 14 July 1993: 1). Telstra's 1994 Enterprise Agreement adopted a similar approach but endorsed a new "Participative Approach" (discussed later).

Telstra's 1995 Enterprise Agreement further developed the earlier agreements. In addition, it included in total an 11 percent pay increase in four stages over a two-year period. This agreement advocated significant improvements in customer service operational flexibility and work processes, with unit cost reductions. It included also a new dispute avoidance/resolution process. Telstra has tried to move in the direction of productivity-based pay increases, but this is a gradual process and is applied alongside across-the-board increases.

The initial Telstra employee survey showed a relatively low level of satisfaction with pay and fringe benefits (36 percent), compared with national norms (47 percent). The questions in this category asked respondents to assess the degree to which the pay system is easy to understand, and to compare their pay and fringe benefits with those of other nongovernment organizations, and other employees at Telstra. Respondents expressed particular dissatisfaction with Telstra's provision of fringe benefits in comparison with those in the private sector. The 1995 employee survey suggested that Telstra employees' satisfaction with pay was similar to or slightly higher than that of employees in the overseas TelCos included in similar surveys.

The award to Telstra technicians specified a nine-day fortnight, 36.75-hour week, four weeks' annual leave, three months' service leave after ten years' service, and a superannuation scheme that enables retirement at fifty-five years old. Similar technicians in the United States do not receive such a level of fringe benefits. By contrast, their pay levels are higher. This difference implies that Australian workers and their unions put a higher value on leisure.

At Optus the 1992 Enterprise Agreement provided for higher than "award wages" in exchange for more flexible working hours and work practices. The 1994 EFA included a 2.5 percent increase in wage rates. Optus employees are entitled to overtime if it has been directed and is more than 38 hours per week. Pay supplements are given for work done outside of the 7 a.m. to 7 p.m. "core working hours." Employees are entitled to four weeks' annual leave, and long service leave is in accordance with state or territory legislation. Leave loading (holiday pay supplement) is incorporated into the salary structure.

Optus' HR director claimed that, as of June 1995 pay rates at Optus were still higher than comparable Telstra rates. The union disputed this claim, and argued that while average rates at Optus at its inception were higher than at Telstra, the gap has been substantially closed, and pay levels at Optus had not kept pace with productivity improvements in the industry or wage increases at Telstra.

Employment Security

The telecommunications services sector has been undergoing dramatic change not least in terms of its levels of employment. Telstra's total full-time staff declined from a high of over 94,000 in 1986 and, in spite of the merger with OTC, to 67,000 in 1993. A Redundancy Agreement was implemented in January 1992 to regulate reductions in employment. The parties agreed to limit as far as practicable the effects on current employees by, for instance, minimizing external recruitment and the use of consulting firms, retraining existing employees, and using natural attrition and voluntary redundancy programs. Involuntary redundancy was to be used only as a last resort. But given the rate of retrenchment and the uncertainty within Telstra, it is not surprising that the first employee survey showed a very low level of satisfaction with job security (34 percent) compared to the national average (71 percent). One comment on the survey form was: "It is impossible to retain dedication and loyalty to a company when the main topic of conversation at any gathering is redundancies and how much each one would get if they (sic) left" (*Our Future*, 7 Dec. 1992: 3).

Between 1994 and 1995, Telstra's total workforce increased again to 73,000, not least in view of its huge investment in new technologies and "pay TV." Hence feelings of insecurity abated considerably; the 1995 employee survey indicated that Telstra employees' satisfaction with job security was 8 percent higher than employees in the consultant's overseas TelCos (Telstra 1995a: 32–33). By mid-1996 resellers were confronting Telstra with tough price competition, partial privatization was on the horizon, and further deregulation was imminent; therefore, there were continuing pressures for Telstra to cut costs, and further employment reductions were initiated. In September 1996, Telstra announced that 22,000 jobs would be eliminated in the 1997–99 period.

Significant changes have also taken place at Telstra's management level. There has been a high level of turnover, particularly at the senior levels. (Most of the incumbents of the top 24 executive roles were changed in the 1992–95 period.)

After its start up, Optus increased its full-time staff at a rate of more than 120 employees per month. The growth in employment at Optus contrasts with the downsizing at Telstra and other major Australian enterprises. This relative security helped to foster positive attitudes among employees at Optus.

Enterprise Governance

Members of Telstra's main Board of Directors are appointed by the federal government. One of the non-executive directors on the Board was an assistant secretary of the ACTU. He had previously been the General Secretary of ATEA and had earlier been a Telecom employee. He was appointed to the Board under the federal Labor government. The 1996 federal conservative coalition government terminated his appointment along with other Labor government appointees.

Nevertheless, employees were less than satisfied with arrangements relating to enterprise governance at Telstra in the early 1990s. The 1992 survey results showed that only 33 percent of the sample made favorable responses to issues such as the extent of interest management has in the well-being of employees, the fairness of decisions and the perception that branch managers understand the problems of employees (item 9). There was a major gap between Telstra and the national average (59 percent) on this issue. There was, however, a smaller gap between Telstra employees' satisfaction with their supervision (62 percent) compared to employees nationally (68 percent). Items in this category include the extent to which supervisors engender teamwork, are receptive to ideas, understand technical aspects of the work, and develop people's abilities.

The HR and IR functions have a prominent place in Telstra. In the early 1990s, the Director of Human Resources and the Director of Industrial Relations each reported directly and separately to the CEO. Both of the incumbents were changed in 1993–94. Following the departure of the latter in 1993, and the release of these survey data, Telstra brought in a high-profile consultant, Ian MacPhee, a former Liberal Party federal cabinet minister with an IR portfolio, to become Acting Director of Industrial Relations and to induce a program of further change. Subsequently Telstra amalgamated its IR and HR functions under a new Employee Relations portfolio in October 1995 and Mr. MacPhee left Telstra in December 1995. These changes represent a recentralization of and a departure from the earlier attempts to decentralize HR and IR to the divisions and business units. In the meantime, the other major development in corporate governance supported by MacPhee—"the Participative Approach" continued to influence labor-management relations. In the early 1990s, relations between unions and management were strained due to downsizing and management's attempt to introduce performance pay and individual contracts. A conference of 120 managers and union leaders was held in March 1994 and the parties agreed to adopt the Participative Approach to IR based on several principles, including viewing "unions and management as equal and independent parties," and stating that unions would have "involvement in the early stages of strategic and all other levels of planning and change processes" (Telstra 1994: 1). A framework was developed to implement these principles and involved an extensive consultative structure at all levels of the corporation, commitment to consultation on changes, and best practice trials in four selected locations to test the introduction of the participatory principles. Management takes the view that the Participative Approach marks a departure from adversarial industrial relations based on bargaining and a "trade-off mentality" (Telstra 1995b: 3). It is not yet clear to what extent management and the unions are committed to the Participative Approach in the long term. It is supported by corporate rhetoric, although not all senior managers and unionists are staunch supporters of this approach (interviews with senior managers and union officials, May and August 1995).

The HR function at Optus plays an important role in the governance of Optus. Its HR director reports to the CEO and is involved in the strategic direction of the enterprise. The importance of the HR function reflects the HRM and enterprise approach to employee relations at Optus. Enterprise governance is influenced by the regional structure of Optus and efforts to tailor service to customers and empower employees. It does not have a distinct IR section and does not use the term IR. In so far as there is specific IR management, it is handled by the HR function.

HR at Optus appears to be less centralized than at Telstra, with some

HR responsibilities being pushed down to the supervisor level. Optus' middle managers, under the supervision of HR staff, conduct performance reviews of their direct reports. A senior Optus HR manager argued that managers were "empowered" to perform HR tasks, such as performance reviews. However, the unions claimed that Optus managers were not properly trained to perform these HR responsibilities, and in some cases managers' assessments of performance were quite subjective.

Productivity

Although TelCos generally employ a large number of people, they have substantial continuing capital requirements to fund the development and modernization needed for the delivery of future telecommunications services (AOTC 1992: 9).

The parties have begun to negotiate productivity and efficiency improvements at business-unit level in Telstra. These negotiations will cover a broad range of issues but they generally should not lower the current standard pay levels or depart from standards enshrined at the AIRC relating to hours of work and leave provisions (Enterprise Agreement 1992: 8). The aim is to tailor agreements to the needs of business units rather than relying solely on organization-wide programs which lack specificity. One of the issues that arises from the decentralization of bargaining will be ensuring consistency across the business units, particularly given the agreement to facilitate the mobility of employees across the units. It is likely that consistency and equity versus specificity and efficiency trade-offs will be a point of continuing negotiation between the parties.

Concluding Comments

The above discussion illustrates the dynamics and tensions in Australian telecommunications. Its economic, political, and technological environment is turbulent. The industry's main player, Telstra, is trying to transform its employment relations policies and practices. It is aiming to implement rather more proactive and innovative approaches than had been apparent hitherto with regard to human resource issues (e.g., improved training and succession planning) and industrial relations (e.g., bench marking to international best practice, surveying employee attitudes, and introducing novel enterprise bargaining arrangements).

Optus has the advantage of being much smaller and being still in a growth phase, building from a foundation that was almost a "greenfield enterprise." It has attempted to adopt a strategic approach to its human resources that has been reflected in its 1992 enterprise agreement and subsequent 1994 EFA that was established directly with employees.

In the 1990s, Telstra was wrestling with increasing competition. This induced corporate downsizing, rationalization, and reorganization, including attempts to flatten hierarchies, reduce demarcations, introduce TQM, and improve customer service. In the face of controversies in the late 1990s about further downsizing and privatization, it remains to be seen to what extent Telstra's latest participative approach can succeed and whether its apparently increasingly positive employee attitude survey results will be maintained.

Simultaneously, the new entrant, Optus, began by trying to win market share and occasionally to recruit key employees from the main player (though most of Optus's employees came from other backgrounds). Typically, the new entrant had certain handicaps and advantages. The handicaps included the lack of physical infrastructure (no network or local exchanges); so it rented facilities from the main player and other sources. In some ways this lack was an advantage, for most of Telstra's customer complaints and bad publicity concerned its local facilities. Optus's other advantages included the potential to design new human resources and industrial relations arrangements, without having to overcome an inheritance of long-standing demarcation lines or other restrictive practices.

With regard to international comparisons our tentative conclusions are that, in spite of the contrasting patterns of ownership and public policy in other countries, there are similarities in the relevant corporate strategies and tactics of the main players across the largest English-speaking countries. In particular, Telstra's behavior appears comparable to that of AT&T and BT. There are also similarities in the strategies of the new entrants. Optus's behavior appears comparable to that of Sprint and MCI in the United States and that of Mercury in the United Kingdom. We would begin to explain these similarities in terms of two complementary questions: first, are the enterprise leaders making appropriate strategic choices in the face of similar technological and other contingencies; and second, are enterprises imitating each other (or following the same management fads)? We could answer "yes" to the first question, and also to the second, because there are more and more linkages between these enterprises, for instance, in the form of joint ventures, strategic alliances, cross-share holdings, and mobility of executives (either following an employer-initiated secondment or an individual job change). One goal of our continuing research is to refine such comparisons and explanations by relating our empirical findings more explicitly to suitable analytical apparatus at the national, industry and enterprise levels, and by engaging in more thorough and systematic international and comparative analysis.

On the other hand, there appear to be some key contrasts between the telecommunications companies in the English-speaking countries and, for example, Japan, Germany, and the Scandinavian countries. In Scandinavian telecommunications companies, in contrast with those in the English-speaking ones, there has been much less emphasis on redundancies and downsizing, and usually a more sustained emphasis on employee participation.

Perhaps these contrasts illustrate strategic choices of the Scandinavian telecommunication companies, but also the importance of the political, economic, and social context. In Scandinavian telecommunications companies, the decision makers have chosen a different path to organizational change. Arguably this path reflects rather different policies at a national level, where, unlike their counterparts in the English-speaking countries, recent governments have been less likely to embrace "supply side" economics and privatization. To an extent, this contrast reflects a distinction between what have elsewhere been characterized as Type I and Type II countries' industrial relations systems (Bamber and Lansbury 1987: 23ff).

Joint ventures between Telstra and News Ltd, and also with IBM, and between Optus, Continental Cable and Australian TV networks exemplify telecommunication companies moving quickly to form strategic alliances with news media, entertainment, and information technology firms. In the expensive race between Telstra and Optus to cable Australia's streets, there were very high stakes; some commentators predicted that since Australia has a relatively small population there would be only one winner in this competitive market; the loser might not survive.

What are the implications of our analysis for employment relations? Which forms of organizational change are heralded by these strategic alliances? We are proceeding to explore such erosion of the boundaries between what were, hitherto, separate industries and to consider the consequences in terms of human resource and industrial relations innovations. There are powerful legacies of custom and practice in Telstra, and in Australian industrial relations and human resource management, therefore, some continuity is likely. None the less, we infer that Telstra will continue to change not least in view of the increasing threats to its traditional markets, which are inducing a sense of crisis in this large enterprise. Current trajectories are tending toward significant changes from past employment-relations policies and practices by the telecommunications enterprises and governments, and even by the unions. Such transformational tendencies are likely to be reinforced by the relatively new economic, political and technological circumstances facing this industry.

Chapter 4

Canada

Anil Verma and Richard Chaykowski

Almost since the invention of the long distance telephone call in Ontario in 1876, the Canadian telephone industry has consisted of regulated monopolies. This arrangement was considered "natural" because of the high cost of establishing a network and of meeting the public policy goal of universal service. Canada enjoys one of the most modern telephone networks in the world and a penetration rate of 99 percent of all households and businesses, a rate that exceeds even that of the United States (Verma and Weiler 1992: 406). Many would argue that the system of regulation was largely responsible for this achievement.

Employment relations in this almost completely unionized industry have also benefited from the regulated monopoly regime. Employment security in the industry has been historically high. Collective bargaining has functioned well and resulted in very few strikes relative to many other industries. The workplace is characterized by high technology and continually higher skills over time. The regulatory regime allowed Canadian firms to make steady investments in new technology in order to upgrade services continuously.

Some parts of the industry, such as terminal equipment, have been gradually deregulated since the 1970s. The big change in industry regula-

The authors gratefully acknowledge partial financial support received from the Social Sciences and Humanities Research Council of Canada. We also thank Ella Patel for valuable and thorough research assistance.

tion came in 1991 when the CRTC, the federal government's chief regulator, decided to open up the market for long distance services. Since then more markets have been opened up with further deregulation being actively considered.

This change in the regulatory makeup combined with advances in new technology causing convergence across telephone, computer, and broadcast technologies is resulting in severe pressures for change in the employment and employment relations system. Firms are downsizing as well as reorganizing work, sometimes with the help and involvement of employees and unions, and sometimes on their own. In facing these changes labor-management relationships can potentially draw on the foundation of joint forums and committees built up over the past fifteen years. However, the danger of slipping into a more traditional and adversarial relationship is quite real.

In this chapter we first describe the structure of the Canadian telephone industry. This is followed by a brief account of the development of the regulatory regime. In the third section, we profile the major firms in the industry, followed by an account of employment trends in the fourth section. The fifth section describes collective bargaining and key outcomes including changes in the workplace. The final section focuses on Bell Canada, the largest of all Canadian telephone companies.

The Structure and Development of the Canadian Telephone Industry

The Canadian telephone industry began with the establishment of the Bell Telephone Company of Canada under Royal Charter of 1880 (Babe 1990). Although Bell operated with a complete monopoly in the early years, by the early 1900s several competitors had emerged. The original company lost control of its operations in both Western and Eastern Canada and consolidated its position in central Canada (Verma and Weiler 1992: 411–12): in the late 1880s Bell divested itself of operations in the province of British Columbia while in 1908–9 the governments of Alberta, Saskatchewan, and Manitoba nationalized its telephone operations and created Crown corporations. Bell also divested itself of ownership of telephone companies in the Eastern provinces of Nova Scotia, New Brunswick, and Prince Edward Island but gradually bought significant interests in each of them. Despite an unambiguous start in the industry, Bell Canada became the dominant firm in Ontario and Quebec and in the larger Canadian telephone industry.

As a result of the original divestiture and nationalization of the various provincial operations of the Bell Telephone Company of Canada, the industry developed in a highly concentrated manner with relatively few monopolistic firms dominating each region supported by a large number of very small firms that provided services in small towns and cities and that were owned by the municipalities. Figure 4.1 illustrates the changes in the number of firms and employment in the telephone industry over the period from 1978 through 1992.

Overall, the number of firms has declined significantly in the past several decades. In 1978 the industry consisted of approximately 260 firms but, by 1992, this number had declined to only 60, largely as a result of corporate consolidation. Even so, employment levels, while fluctuating throughout the period, have remained between 90,000 and 100,000 workers. Industry employment increased during the economic expansion of the late 1970s to a peak level of 105,000 in 1982, then declined during the economic downturn of the early 1980s before increasing again to a high of roughly 99,000 in 1989. Employment again declined during the deep recession of the early 1990s, with a substantial drop at the trough of the recession in 1991–92. The largest firms in the industry have continued to downsize their workforces through 1995.

All of the major telephone companies provide both local and long distance services, although long distance business accounts for the majority of their revenue. In fact, while the combined number of residence lines has remained roughly constant between 1978 and 1992 at 15 to 16 mil-

FIGURE 4.1. Canadian telecommunications industry systems and employment

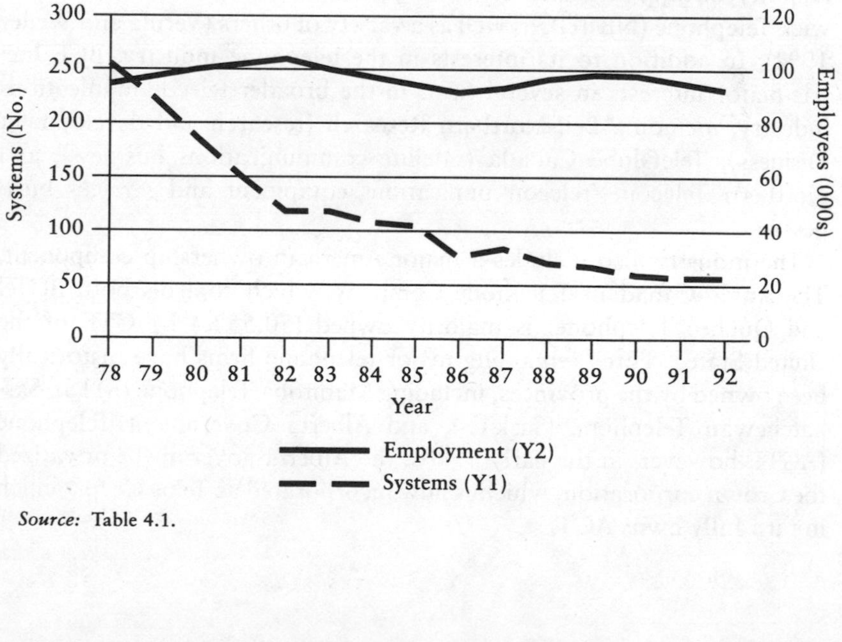

Source: Table 4.1.

lion lines, the number of toll calls has tripled from approximately 1.08 billion calls in 1978 to 3.35 billion calls in 1992. (Table 4.1 provides industry trends in customer lines and toll calls.)

Figure 4.2 presents the number of toll calls and total revenue in the Canadian telephone industry over the period from 1978 through 1992. As expected, changes in toll call activity roughly track changes in the Canadian business cycle. In marked contrast, total industry revenue has increased steadily and substantially over the entire twenty-year period. Since each of the major telephone firms operates as a regional monopoly, the rate structures have been controlled through government regulatory agencies. Consequently, changes in the rulings on the rates are a significant determinant of the growth in total revenue in the industry.

In 1992, the 60 firms in the industry together generated total revenue of $13.73 billion and employed approximately 96 thousand workers. In 1992 the top ten telephone firms accounted for roughly 98 percent of total industry revenue while the three largest firms in Canada, including Bell Canada, BCTel, and AGT, accounted for approximately 82 percent of industry revenue.

With 1993 revenues of just over $20 billion, BCE Inc. ranked number one in revenue among all firms in Canada and holds a dominant position in both the telephone and broader telecommunications industry (the Globe and Mail 1994: 65). In the telephone industry, BCE Inc. wholly owns Bell Canada (Bell Canada 1994). BCE Inc. also holds a controlling major interest in Maritime Tel and Tel (MT&T) (which in turn holds a majority interest in Island Tel), Newfoundland Telephone, New Brunswick Telephone (NB Tel), as well as a variety of others (Verma and Weiler 1992). In addition to its interests in the telephone industry, BCE Inc. has major interests in several firms in the broader telecommunications industry, including Bell-Northern Research (research and development business), TeleGlobe Canada (satellite communications business), and Northern Telecom (telecommunications equipment and services business).

The industry also includes a major American ownership component. The Anglo-Canadian Telephone Company, which controls both BCTel and Québec Telephone, is majority owned (50.55%) by GTE of the United States. Three remaining major telephone firms have historically been owned by the provinces, including Manitoba Telephone (MTS), Saskatchewan Telephone (SaskTel), and Alberta Government Telephone (AGT); however, in the early 1990s, the Alberta government privatized the Crown corporation, which is now incorporated as Telus Corp., which in turn fully owns AGT.

TABLE 4.1. Canadian telephone industry, 1978–1992

Year	Telephone systems (number)	Residence lines (millions)	Business lines (millions)	Wire KM (millions)	Toll calls (billions)	Employees (000's)	Total revenue (billions)	Cost of plant (billions)
1978	260	10.6	4.5	155.8	1.08	92.9	4.58	16.03
1979	223	11.1	4.8	162.9	1.21	96.5	5.34	17.75
1980	183	11.5	5.0	172.2	1.34	100.1	6.18	19.74
1981	153	11.8	5.2	180.4	1.45	102.6	7.38	22.30
1982	120	11.8	5.0	187.1	1.48	105.1	8.32	24.47
1983	119	11.7	4.9	190.0	1.54	100.6	8.97	25.92
1984	112	11.7	4.7	184.2	1.64	96.6	9.70	27.31
1985	106	11.3	4.6	201.3	1.79	94.1	10.33	28.48
1986	75	NA	NA	207.9	1.96	91.7	11.03	29.99
1987	81	10.0	3.5	216.6	2.21	92.7	11.47	32.11
1988	69	10.2	3.7	227.5	2.53	96.1	12.13	35.12
1989	66	10.6	4.1	236.3	2.85	98.6	12.90	37.69
1990	62	10.9	4.4	244.2	3.09	98.2	13.56	40.35
1991	60	11.1	4.7	251.7	3.26	95.7	13.73	42.49
1992	60	11.4	4.9	252.9	3.35	92.3	14.10	44.65

Sources: Statistics Canada. 1994. *Telephone Statistics 1992.* (March 1994) Catalogue 56-203. Ottawa, Ont.: Minister of Supply and Services Canada. Table 1, p. 16.
Statistics Canada. 1993. *Telephone Statistics 1991.* (January 1993) Catalogue 56-203. Ottawa Ont.: Minister of Supply and Services Canada. Table 1, p. 16.
Statistics Canada. 1988. *Telephone Statistics 1986.* (April 1988) Catalogue 56-203. Ottawa Ont.: Minister of Supply and Services Canada. Table 1, p. 18.

FIGURE 4.2. Canadian telephone industry toll calls and total revenue

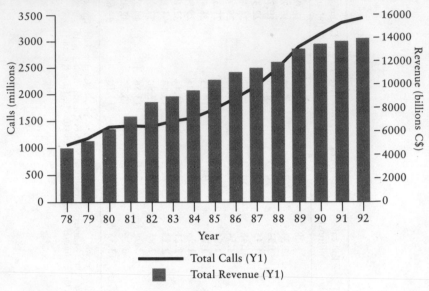

Source: Table 4.1.

Although these patterns of corporate ownership reflect the high degree of concentration in the industry, there remains a significant number of smaller telephone firms, particularly in Ontario. Two important developments have emerged to affect the business relationships among the firms in the industry as well as the degree of competition. The first factor is increasing convergence of communication technologies creating an overlap of telephone, computer, and broadcast industries. This has brought the activities of these large, traditionally regulated, telephone monopolies into contact with firms providing other forms of telecommunications services, notably in the areas of wireless communication, cable, and computer-based services.

The second factor has been a rapid shift in the regulatory environment toward permitting higher levels of competition in a wide range of telephone services such as terminal equipment, long distance services, data networks, and since 1994, the local telephone service. In the early 1990s, changes in regulatory and broader governmental public policies have rapidly advanced the prospect of direct competition between telephone and cable companies. As a result of these pressures, and as many of the established telephone firms have entered new service areas (e.g., cellular communications, data processing services), firms have begun to reposition themselves by divesting non-core operations and increasing investments in new technology and product lines to better reflect the increasingly less regulated nature of the industry.

Regulatory Developments in the Canadian Telephone Industry

The history of the development of the regulatory environment in the Canadian telephone industry may be characterized as beginning with a prolonged *regulated monopoly* period which is progressing through the current period of *restrained competition* toward the beginning of a new era of full competition leading to *convergence*. The evolution of the regulatory environment has been shaped both by the significant transformation in telecommunications technology in the broader industry as well as by the evolving public policy objectives of greater competition and less regulation.

Under regulation, firms were allowed to operate as regional monopolists. This era extended from the origins of the industry at the turn of the nineteenth century through to the late 1980s. During this period, the telephone industry has operated as a regulated monopoly in which several provincial governments and the federal government exercised regulatory jurisdiction. Until recently, each of Québec Telephone, SaskTel, and Manitoba Telephone were regulated under provincial jurisdiction, whereas Bell Canada, BCTel, and AGT are all covered under the federal jurisdiction. In addition, most smaller firms, include New Brunswick Telephone, Maritime Tel & Tel, and Newfoundland Telephone were also covered under federal jurisdiction (Verma and Weiler 1992:409–410, table 11.2). The federal government thus exerted the broadest regulatory influence, and through the federal regulatory body, the Canadian Radio and Telecommunications Commission (CRTC), later played a major role in opening the industry to the second phase of restrained competition in the early 1990s.

Up until the late 1980s, the regulatory regime had been guided by several broad principles (Verma and Weiler 1992: 412–13): first, the need to support telephones as regional "natural monopolies"; second, the desire to promote universal access to "affordable" telephone service; and third, the attempt by telephone firms to maintain so-called system integrity by providing high quality equipment and services throughout the system. Taken together, these principles provided some guidance during much of the period up to the 1980s, although the notion of "system integrity" was successfully challenged before the courts and CRTC as early as 1975.

Although changes in the regulatory framework were gradual, by the

1990s the principle of competition in the industry had begun to shape regulatory policy (Verma and Weiler 1992: 416). While the CRTC had allowed resellers to operate as early as 1984, the 1990 CRTC ruling that expanded resale was probably more significant in contributing to increased competition in long distance services (Surtees 1994: 195). The second period of development in the regulation of the telephone industry really commenced with the 1992 CTRC decision to end the monopoly of the telephone companies in the long distance market by opening the door to new service providers and by ensuring "equal access" to customers choosing different carriers (Surtees 1994: 277–78). This meant that customers did not have to dial extra digits to access competing long distance services. Moreover, the CRTC ruling facilitated the initial entry of firms into the long distance marketplace.

As the industry was gradually deregulated, a number of Canadian and American firms entered the long distance market and began to position themselves to provide services in several areas of telecommunications that have traditionally been partitioned, but which are expected to converge in the latter half of the 1990s. Unitel is the largest of the new competitors entering long distance services. Unitel is owned 48 percent by Canadian Pacific Ltd., a large Canadian conglomerate with interests in transportation, resources, and manufacturing; and 20 percent of Unitel is owned by the U.S. multinational AT&T, the maximum allowed under current rules for foreign ownership. Most of the remainder (29.5%) is owned by Rogers Communications, a Canadian firm with major interests in cable, satellite communications, and by Cantel, provider of cellular phone services (OECD 1992; Surtees 1994). Other United States-based long distance companies have also joined the competition by aligning themselves with Canadian firms. Sprint of the United States owns a 20 percent interest in a Canadian firm, Call-net, through its subsidiary Sprint Canada. United States-based MCI has formed an alliance with Stentor which is jointly owned by all the monopoly telephone companies in Canada led by Bell Canada. Among other services, these alliances produce a seamless cross-border 800 service for businesses.

Coincident with the opening of this new period of restrained competition, federal authority in the regulation of telecommunications was asserted regardless of whether or not a telephone company is provincially owned. Under a 1989 ruling (in *Alberta Government Telephones versus CRTC*), the Supreme Court of Canada established federal authority to regulate telecommunications under the Constitution. This decision effectively cleared the way for the federal government to begin to develop a more national telecommunications policy (Verma and Weiler 1992: 416).

In 1993 the federal government enacted the Telecommunications Act, which reaffirmed that the CRTC had regulatory authority over all telecommunications carriers and which contained provisions in the following key areas: empowering the federal government to guide the CRTC in relation to public policy; empowering the CRTC to determine whether domestic regulation is necessary in the presence of international competition and to decide the means of regulation (BC Telecom 1994: 37).

In the fall of 1994, the CRTC further opened up the market for local telephone services, effectively allowing cable companies to offer local telephone services through its cable network. It is expected, however, that competing local telephone services will not be offered to households until late 1995 or 1996 because of the high capital cost of creating the basic infrastructure. A number of telephone resellers were already offering local area network services by early 1995, to corporate offices and condominiums in major downtown areas.

The CRTC began regulatory hearings in March 1995, to consider the issue of direct competition between telephone and cable companies. At issue is the desire of telephone companies to enter the broadcast market and thus directly compete with cable companies. Under current rules, telephone companies are prevented from acting as broadcasters. Bell Canada and other monopoly telephone companies in their submissions to the CRTC, argued that since cable companies were now allowed to enter the local and long distance phone markets, the telephone companies should have reciprocal rights to enter the cable business (Vardy 1995). Bell Canada estimates that it could begin offering combined cable and phone and other services within eighteen to twenty-four months of deregulation.

The federal cabinet identified several key issues to guide the CRTC in its deliberations over the extent and timing of further deregulation: the preservation of Canadian content under a competitive regime, ensuring fair and affordable access, and the scope of the definition of "broadcasting" (Surtees 1995a: B2). Clearly, these are significant developments in the history of the industry as well as the Canadian economy and society. It is widely expected that the CRTC will rule in favour of greater competition even if the precise rules and the timetable for deregulation are not entirely to the liking of the companies or the consumers.

Profile of the Major Operating Companies

The major telephone firms in the industry, their ownership, employment levels, major unions, and total revenue are provided in Table 4.2. Each

TABLE 4.2. Major telecommunications firms, 1993

Firm	Ownership[a]	Employees[b]	Major unions[a,c]	Total Revenue[b] (billionsC$)
AGT[d]	Telus Corp (widely held)	6,946	IBEW	1.167
Bell Canada[e]	BCE Inc. (100%)	50,982	CEP—Craft & operators CTEA—Clerical	7.957
BCTel[g]	Anglo-Canadian Telephone Co. (majority owner: GTE, 50.5%)	13,478	TWU	2.209
Island Tel[g]	MT&T (52%)	329	CEP	0.057
MTS[g]	Province of Manitoba (100%)	4,408	IBEW—Craft CEP—Operators	0.538
MT&T[e]	BCE Inc. (34.5%)	3,736	AC&TWU	0.473
NBTel[f]	Bruncor Inc.	2,283	CEP	0.355
Newfoundland Telephone[e]	NewTel Enterprises	1,672	CEP	0.274
SaskTel[d]	Province of Saskatchewan (100%)	3,517	CEP	0.556
Quebec Telephone[g]	Anglo-Canadian Telephone Co. (majority owner: GTE)	1,709	SCFP	0.243

[a]*Sources:* Annual Reports 1993; Verma and Weiler (1992:409–410, table 11.2).
[b]*Source: Statistics* (Annual: 1993) Ottawa, Ont.: Stentor.
[c]Unions:

AC&TWU	=	Atlantic Communications and Technical Workers' Union
CEP	=	Communications, Energy, and Paperworkers Union
CTEA	=	Canadian Telephone Employees' Association
IBEW	=	International Brotherhood of Electrical Workers
TWU	=	Telecommunications Workers Union

[d]Does not include directory or cellular operations.
[e]Includes directory operations.
[f]Includes cellular operations.
[g]Includes both directory and cellular operations.

of the major firms is concentrated in a geographic region defined largely by provincial boundaries. As noted in the discussion of the organization of the industry, there is a high level of corporate concentration. With total revenue and employment levels greater than the combined revenues and employment of the next five largest telephone firms, Bell Canada dominates the Canadian telephone industry. Bell Canada is the telephone services arm of BCE Inc., a telecommunications conglomerate whose manufacturing arm is Northern Telecom, a multinational telecommunications equipment manufacturer, and the research arm is Bell-Northern Research. As the leading firm in the industry, the operations of Bell Canada will be profiled separately below.

Selected operating indicators for six major firms in the industry are provided for the ten-year period from 1984 to 1993 in Table 4.3 (Total revenue in panel A; Total capital expenditures in panel B; Long distance calls in panel C; and Employment in panel D). Interestingly, each of the firms experienced strong growth in revenues, not only through the period of rapid economic expansion of the mid to late 1980s, but also through the deep recession of the early 1990s. This consistent growth in revenue was driven largely by the steady growth in long distance traffic, which forms the primary source of revenues. Although capital expenditures may be influenced by changes in the business cycle, capital expenditure patterns are likely to be more closely associated with technological changes in the industry, such as the need to upgrade to fully digitized switching systems and to expand fiber optic networks.

Employment levels at six major firms rose gradually during the 1980s, but around 1991 began to decline steadily. The combined impact of the recession and the introduction of competition in the long distance market in 1992 created pressures on firms to focus on improving productivity and reducing costs. The entry of major domestic and foreign-based competitors is expected to increase significantly these competitive pressures. In March 1995, Bell Canada announced its intention to cut employment levels by roughly 10,000 jobs over the next three years (Surtees 1995b). The cuts were to be achieved through incentives to leave, normal attrition, and early retirements but the company did not rule out involuntary layoffs, which, if they did occur, would be the first in the company's 115-year history. Significant employment cuts at all of the major telephone firms are expected to be a feature of the remainder of the 1990s.

With operations concentrated in Ontario and Quebec, Bell Canada is the largest telephone firm in Canada and, with 1993 net income of $870 million on total revenues of nearly $8 billion, Bell ranked number one in profit in Canada (Bell Canada 1994; Globe and Mail 1994:70). Bell Canada provides roughly 58 percent of all service lines in Canada. Bell's core business is the provision of local and long distance telephone services. As have most telephone companies, Bell has diversified into related areas through a variety of subsidiaries; Bell Sygma Inc. (100% interest) provides data processing and other information services; WorldLinx Telecommunications Inc. (100 percent interest) offers "high-end" services such as desktop teleconferencing and electronic messaging services; and Bell-Northern Research Ltd. (30% interest) engages in research and de-

TABLE 4.3. Operating data for major Canadian telecommunications firms, 1984–1993

Year	Bell	BCTel	AGT	MTS	Sask Tel	NB Tel
A: Total Revenue (billionsC\$)						
1984	5.140	1.148	0.963	0.320	0.382	0.300
1985	5.566	1.211	1.054	0.343	0.424	0.244
1986	5.946	1.341	1.026	0.373	0.500	0.256
1987	6.169	1.481	1.048	0.398	0.470	0.278
1988	6.372	1.521	1.070	0.455	0.513	0.284
1989	6.989	1.562	1.164	0.512	0.554	0.305
1990	7.328	1.712	1.175	0.537	0.574	0.324
1991	7.729	1.936	1.186	0.527	0.568	0.336
1992	7.863	2.037	1.200	0.527	0.621	0.349
1993	7.957	2.210	1.167	0.538	0.355	0.556
B: Total capital expenditures (millionsC\$)						
1984	1,285	344	207	97	94	60
1985	1,363	344	175	130	109	60
1986	1,582	361	225	116	145	67
1987	1,981	303	288	164	154	77
1988	2,197	392	419	160	163	84
1989	2,326	451	443	170	178	92
1990	2,337	409	497	189	156	106
1991	2,295	448	331	193	107	103
1992	2,686	379	348	172	114	107
1993	2,105	515	315	170	74	93
C: Long distance calls (millionsC\$)						
1984	845	217	247	84	92	50
1985	927	238	236	92	100	55
1986	1,028	262	248	110	106	67
1987	1,192	298	265	100	NA	76
1988	1,382	328	290	109	119	86
1989	1,586	359	327	110	128	96
1990	1,702	357	370	117	139	107
1991	1,758	394	391	135	153	119
1992	1,758	424	421	147	165	131
1993	NA	520	469	157	179	150
D: Total employment						
1984	49,807	13,973	11,660	4,635	4,382	2,411
1985	48,807	13,777	11,092	4,814	4,434	2,455
1986	49,459	13,361	11,220	5,064	4,713	2,530
1987	52,159	13,549	10,942	5,041	4,786	2,571
1988	53,448	12,713	11,430	5,212	4,831	2,592
1989	55,942	12,852	11,902	5,462	4,745	2,651
1990	54,568	13,367	11,584	5,626	4,557	2,628
1991	54,632	15,015	9,439	5,549	4,289	2,432
1992	52,897	14,524	9,037	5,338	4,134	2,348
1993	50,982	13,478	6,946	4,408	3,517	2,283

Sources: Statistics (Annual: 1984–1990), Ottawa, Ont.: Telecom Canada; *Statistics* (Annual: 1991–1993), Ottawa, Ont.: Stentor.

Note: All 1993 data listed for BC Tel refers to the parent BC Telecom; consequently, these figures overestimate BC Tel operations that year.

velopment in the telecommunications industry (Bell Canada 1994). In 1994, another subsidiary company, MediaLinx, was formed to enter the newly emerging markets of "info-tainment" and "edu-tainment" made possible through the integration of entertainment, communications, computers, and educational products and markets.

Over the period from 1984 through 1993, Bell has experienced strong growth, with total revenues increasing from $5.1 billion to roughly $8.0 billion. Most of Bell's revenue (81% in 1993) is generated through the provision of local and long distance telephone services (Bell Canada 1994); from a base of 845 million calls in 1984, long distance calling activity doubled to roughly 1.8 billion calls in 1993 (see Table 4.3). Despite revenue growth, Bell Canada's profits declined in 1994 to $721 million and were expected to drop further to about $500 million in 1995. Much of the decline in profits was directly attributable to the deregulation of the long distance market.

The growth in Bell Canada's telephone services has been facilitated by its substantial investment in new technologies. Between 1984 and 1993 Bell's expenditures on capital nearly doubled to $2.1 billion (Table 4.3). Currently, 99 percent of Bell's switches are digital. Between 1988 and 1993, the number of optic fiber kilometers tripled to 640 thousand in 1993 (Bell Canada 1994; Stentor 1994).

Figure 4.3 depicts Bell Canada employment levels and total payroll as a percentage of total operating costs. Employment levels increased during the late 1980s to a peak of 56,000 in 1989, declining thereafter to around 51,000 workers in 1993. While the recession of the early 1990s may have had some initial influence on employment levels, the major pressure has been the increasingly competitive business environment brought on by the deregulation of the industry, particularly in long distance markets. Bell Canada's share of the long distance market has declined by around 18 percent since the industry was deregulated (Bourette 1995: B4). In fact, after 1991 the number of long distance calls leveled out at approximately 1.76 billion (see Table 4.3), so that the contribution of toll and network services to total operating revenue declined from roughly 49 percent in 1990 to 44 percent in 1993 (Bell Canada 1994). However, payroll as a proportion of total operating costs has remained at roughly 50 percent; the modest decline in employment levels in the early 1990s did not result in any meaningful decrease in the relative size of the wage bill. Clearly there is pressure to make more substantial cuts in the size of the workforce of the sort announced in March 1995, when Bell Canada announced that it planned to reduce overall employment levels by up to 20 percent (Bourette 1995). In a later section, we discuss the responses

FIGURE 4.3. Bell Canada—employment and labor costs

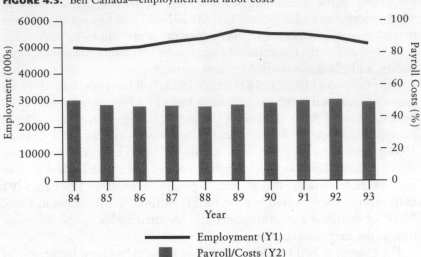

Sources: Statistics (Annual: 1984–90) Ottawa, Ont.: Telecom Canada; *Statistics* (Annual: 1991–93), Ottawa Ont.: Stentor.

of Bell's two unions to this move. Briefly, both unions expressed dismay and vowed to fight involuntary layoffs.

Employment Profile and Trends

The shift in technology and the regulatory environment caused some shifts in employment patterns in the 1980s and the 1990s. Some of the employment trends were obvious by 1995, while others had just begun to surface given the continuing pace of regulatory reform and the lowering of trade barriers in both telecommunications services and equipment. We discuss both these trends in turn.

Total employment for all firms declined over 1981–93 as shown in Table 4.3. A more detailed examination shows that employment for most firms did not decline much in the 1981–88 period. In fact, it went up for several firms. Much of this decline over 1989–93 coincided with the anticipated and actual effects of deregulation. In order to understand this decline, we break down employment into the four major occupational groups: operators, technicians, sales, and clerical staff. Table 4.4 shows the pattern of unionization for these groups, while Table 4.5 shows employment trends.

The operators group suffered the biggest losses in employment ranging from a low of 22 percent at BCTel to a high of 58 percent at SaskTel

TABLE 4.4. Membership of major unions in the Canadian telecommunications industry, 1994

Union	Membership[a]	Affiliation
Atlantic Communications and Technical Workers' Union (AC&TWU)	2,370	Independent
Communications, Energy, and Paperworkers Union (CEP)	22,810	Independent
Canadian Telephone Employees' Association (CTEA)	18,522	Canadian Labour Congress
International Brotherhood of Electrical Workers (BEW)	6,730	AFL-CIO/Canadian Federation of Labour
Telecommunications Workers Union (TWU)	11,700	Canadian Labour Congress
Telecommunications Employees Association of Manitoba (TEAM)	900	Independent

Source: Human Resources Development Canada. 1995. *1994–1995 Directory of Labour Organizations in Canada.* Ottawa, Ont.: Minister of Supply and Services.
[a]With the exception of AC&TWU, membership is based on membership at NB Tel, MTS, SaskTel, AGT Ltd, BCTel, and Bell Canada.

(Table 4.4). For this group, the decline had set in even before 1989 and was clearly driven by technology. This group provides services such as directory assistance, operator-assisted long distance calls, and conference calls. Many of these services were gradually automated, a trend that was still visible in early 1995. The operators are unionized in most Canadian telephone companies and were historically mostly female although more men began to apply for these jobs beginning in the 1980s.

The technician group provides maintenance and installation services for much of the hardware used in a telephone company. This group is responsible for switches, transmission lines from switches all the way into the customer premises, wireless stations, and so forth. This group is almost always unionized and is predominantly male. The employment in this group also declined over 1989–93 after having remained somewhat stable over the earlier period. The decline was not as steep, however, as the one for the operator group. The decline was largest for AGT because the company divested some operations over this period. BCTel had the smallest decline, perhaps because the population of British Columbia grew relatively rapidly during this period.

The clerical group consists of all employees working in the office environment who are not managers. They are mostly female and they tend to be less unionized than the previous two groups. In some companies like Bell Canada, this group is represented by an independent enterprise-level

TABLE 4.5. Employment

Category	1989	1993	% change 1989–1993 (annual avg.)
Operators			
NB Tel	242	121	−50%
MTS		570	NA
SaskTel	610	270	−58%
AGT	1302	859	−34%
BCTel	1532	1199	−22%
Bell Canada	5071	3717	−27%
Technicians			
NB Tel	804	690	−14%
MTS		1540	NA
SaskTel	NA	1160	decreased
AGT	3515	2453	−30%
BCTel	5136	4860	−5%
Bell Canada	16380	13389	−18%
Sales			
NB Tel	69	66	−4%
MTS			
SaskTel	NA	NA	slightly increase
AGT			
BCTel	NA	114	increase
Bell Canada	624	769	+16%
Clerical			
NB Tel	665	659	−1%
MTS		1506	NA
SaskTel	NA	NA	decreased
AGT	3052	1792	−41%
BCTel	4537	3892	−14%
Bell Canada	19198	17753	−4%
Total Employment			
NB Tel	2651	2283	−14%
MTS	5462	4408	−19%
SaskTel	4745	3517	−26%
AGT	11902	6946	−42%
BCTel	12852	13478	+5%
Bell Canada	55942	50982	−9%

Source: Data provided by companies and unions named above.

union. Employment in this group declined the least of all these three groups (with the exception of AGT). Larger declines may be in store for this group between 1995 and 2000 as deregulation takes hold.

Lastly, the sales group either declined very little (4% at NB Tel) or increased at several companies between 1989 and 1993. The explanation for this increase lies in the deregulation process that has increased competition and, consequently, forced companies to invest more in the sales effort. This upward trend may continue through the 1990s. This group is not always unionized and was historically dominated by men although the numbers of women increased between 1985 and 1995.

In summary, it can be seen that employment declines in the core telephone business began in the early 1990s and is likely to continue into the second half of the 1990s as a result of technological change as well as competition in core businesses such as local and long distance telephone services. Meanwhile, some occupations such as sales will likely grow moderately in number while employment will also increase in new services such as cellular phones, other cordless services such as PCS, and delivery of data and pictures through telephone networks.

Collective Bargaining and Outcomes

The Legal Framework for Labor Relations

Under the Constitution Act, 1867, matters of private and public sector labor relations are largely included under provincial jurisdiction (Labour Law 1991: 64). However, the federal government retains authority over the conduct of labor relations in several key industries, notably transportation (including airlines, rail, ports) and telecommunications (Labour Law 1991: 64). Labor relations in the telecommunications industry fall under the federal Labour Code, which in 1995 was undergoing broad governmental review to consider such issues as ways in which to improve the operation of the Canada Labour Relations Board, the role of the Federal Mediation and Conciliation Service, and more specific labor relations issues such as the use of replacement workers. While substantial changes in these areas could have a considerable impact on the conduct of labor relations, these changes would only be expected to take effect toward the year 2000.

Labor relations in the federal jurisdiction have for the most part followed the original framework set out in PC1003 in 1944, which essentially established key elements of the U.S. Wagner Act framework of industrial relations in Canada. Collective bargaining has largely followed typical business unionism objectives and has been conducted in a adversarial tradition common in North America. However, several major firms, including AGT and Bell Canada, have introduced interest-based bargaining approaches in an attempt to move away from the more conflictual bargaining toward a broader cooperative approach to union-management relations.

Patterns of Unionization

Most of the unions in the telephone industry trace their origins to employee associations. These associations were converted to trade unions after the enactment of the federal labor code in 1949, which established collective bargaining rights in the federal jurisdiction (Verma and Weiler 1992). The industry has remained very highly unionized, although the structure of employee representation has changed substantially from 1950 to 1995. Many of the early unions that developed out of the original employee associations were established as independents that remain as significant players in the industry today.

No single union dominates the Canadian telephone industry. There were three types of unions representing workers in telephone companies. First, there were independent enterprise unions such as the Canadian Telephone Employees' Association (CTEA). Historically, these unions were the first ones to take root within the industry and they were not always completely independent of employer meddling (Kuyek 1979). Another type of union was the Telecommunications Workers' Union (TWU) at BCTel which was an enterprise-level union but was also affiliated with labor federations outside the firm. The third type of union was the national or international union such as the Communications, Energy, and Paper (CEP) Workers Union and the International Brotherhood of Electrical Workers (IBEW). The CTEA represented roughly 18,500 clerical and sales workers in Ontario and Quebec in two bargaining units at Bell Canada, the largest group of workers within a company represented by a single union. The largest union in the industry was the CEP representing roughly 20,500 workers in several companies (Table 4.6).

During the 1970s and 1980s, labor-management relations in the telephone industry had the benefit of a prolonged period of growth and prosperity. As a result, the Canadian telephone industry prospered under the relative business protection conferred upon it by its status as a regulated monopoly. These economic conditions provided an industrial relations environment that was in marked contrast to the experience in steel, airlines, and rail; major firms in these industries experienced severe economic crises during the late 1980s, which in turn placed substantial strains on labor relations (Chaykowski and Verma 1992). Consequently, during the 1980s telephone labor relations evolved relatively gradually without the pressure of increasing competition or a financial crisis, and with the benefit of substantial resources with which to meet union wage demands and develop human resource programs, particularly in the area of training (Verma and Weiler 1992: 405). However, changes both to the

TABLE 4.6. Industrial relations profile

Company	Union	Bargaining unit size (1993)
NB Tel		
operators	CEP	115
technicians	CEP	675
clerical	Nonunion	659
sales	Nonunion	66
MTS		
operators	CEP Local 55	570
technicians	IBEW	1540
clerical	CEP Local 7	1506
sales	TEAM	NA
SaskTel		
operators	CEP	270
technicians	CEP	1160
clerical & sales	CEP	1680
systems	CEP	390
AGT Ltd.		
operators	IBEW	846
technicians	IBEW	2530
clerical	IBEW	1814
sales	Nonunion	NA
BCTel		
operators	TWU	1199
technicians	TWU	4860
clerical	TWU	3778
sales	TWU	114
Bell Canada		
operators	CEP	3631
technicians	CEP	12813
clerical	CTEA	17753
sales	CTEA	769

Source: Data provided by companies and unions named above.
Note: At NB Tel, SaskTel, and BCTel all unionized groups are represented by one bargaining unit. At AGT, technicians are in one bargaining unit while clerical employees and operators are in another bargaining unit. At MTS, clerical employees and operators are in one unit, the technicians are in another unit; and, sales staff are part of a larger white collar union. At Bell Canada, each group has its own separate bargaining unit.
CEP—Communications, Energy, and Paperworkers Union
CTEA—Canadian Telephone Employees Association (an enterprise union)
IBEW—International Brotherhood of Electrical Workers
TEAM—Telecommunications Employees Association of Manitoba (an enterprise union)
TWU—Telecommunications Workers Union (an enterprise union)

regulatory environment and to national policy in the 1990s have increased competition in the industry and created pressure on management to improve productivity and customer service, and pressured unions to obtain greater employment security as firms attempt to reduce the size of their workforces.

Bargaining Structure

At some companies such as SaskTel all groups of employees, operators, technicians, clerical, sales, and (computer) systems are in one bargaining unit. At Bell Canada, there are four bargaining units, one each for operators, technicians, clerical, and sales. Bargaining is generally centralized at the firm level. There are over fifty collective agreements in effect, covering more than 60,000 workers. Of these, twenty cover 500 or more workers according to Labour Canada's collective agreements file. The largest bargaining unit in 1993, a CTEA local, covered roughly 17,750 clerical workers in Ontario and Quebec.

Bargaining Priorities

To put in perspective the changes that have occurred in workplace practices, we asked the companies to rank their priorities in bargaining for two employee groups: operators and technicians. These results, shown in Table 4.7, not only reveal the emphasis placed on each bargaining objective but also the relative priority across the two groups. For both groups, the companies placed high priorities on obtaining new flexibilities: flexibility in scheduling work time, in performing work across trades or jobs, and in reducing restrictive workrules. Flexibility in job assignment was slightly less important for operators (1.83) than for the technicians group (2.33) because of greater skill variety in the latter group.

There were several areas where bargaining priorities differed across the two groups. For example, use of part-time employees was a higher priority in the case of operators than for technicians. One of the underlying reasons is that technicians' job out in the field is harder to manage through part-time employees. On the other hand, operators' work is performed round-the-clock and it goes through many daily, weekly, and seasonal highs and lows. Use of part-time employees helps the companies balance the work load.

Reduction in job classifications received a very low priority for the operators' group but a much higher priority for the technicians' group. This can be explained in light of the greater skill variety in the technicians' work, which has historically resulted in a large number of job classifications, many of which are in skilled trades. This is of little consequence for operators whose work tends to be less skilled and less varied.

Use of subcontracting was expectedly low in priority for the operators' group since much of the need for flexibility was taken care of by use of part-time workers. It was relatively higher in bargaining priority for the

TABLE 4.7. Rating the importance of firm's bargaining objectives

	Operators							Technicians						
	NBTel	MTS	SaskTel	AGT Ltd.	BCTel	Bell	Mean	NBTel	MTS	SaskTel	AGTLtd.	BCTel	Bell	Mean
Lower wage costs	1	1	1	2	2	3	1.66	1	1	1	1	3	3	1.66
Lower benefits costs	1	1	1	2	2	3	1.66	1	1	1	2	2	3	1.66
Flexibility in pay systems	2	1	1	3	1	3	1.66	2	1	1	3	3	2	2.00
↑ use of part-time employees	2	2	3	3	1	3	2.33	1	2	1	1	3	2	1.66
↑ use of contracting out	1	1	1	1	1	1	1.00	1	1	2	1	3	3	1.83
↑ flexibility in scheduling hrs.	2	2	3	3	3	3	2.67	2	3	3	3	3	2	2.67
↑ intro. of new production technologies	1	1	3	2	1	2	1.66	1	1	2	3	1	1	1.50
↓ # of job classifications	1	1	1	1	1	1	1.00	1	3	3	3	1	2	2.17
↑ flexibility in performing work across trades/jobs	2	1	2	3	1	2	1.83	3	3	3	3	1	2	2.33
↓ in restrictive work rules/practices	1	2	2	3	3	3	2.33	2	3	3	3	2	3	2.67

Note: Responses were based on the following scale to rate what bargaining objectives were most important to the firm:

1—Not at all important
2—Somewhat important
3—Extremely important

technicians group where a number of jobs such as repair, painting, and fabrication of small or large parts, can be performed by a subcontractor often at a lower costs.

Four areas of bargaining were shown to be of medium priority and the priorities were the same for both groups: lower wage costs, lower benefit costs, flexibility in pay, and introduction of new technologies. These results suggest that some bargaining priorities may be linked to industry characteristics. For example, there is relatively low priority on cutting wages or benefits. Industry wages and benefits are characterized by uniform unionization across the country and by pattern bargaining. Most wages have historically varied within a narrow range (Verma and Weiler 1992). Also, telephone wages are not among the highest or the lowest in the economy. The competition in the long distance market, although present in 1995, was still a minor factor relative to the (former) monopoly telephone companies. Further, with the exception of some salespeople in the industry who are paid on commission, another long-standing tradition is to pay relatively fixed as opposed to contingent wages.

Lastly, workers in these companies tend to be familiar with new technologies and with the continuous upgrading of technology that has occurred gradually over the decades. Worker resistance to new technology is lower (relative to some other less technology-intensive industries) and, hence, not such a high priority in bargaining for the employers.

Strikes

With only a few exceptions, the industry has not seen many strikes since its inception. Between 1980 and 1994, there were only a handful of strikes. Some companies such as AGT have not had a major strike in the last eighty-five years.

BCTel has had a long history of conflict both in its early years as well as between 1960 and 1981 (Bernard 1982). The conflict at BCTel peaked in 1981 when workers occupied a number of telephone exchanges on Vancouver Island and in Vancouver. The work stoppages at BCTel could be attributed partially to poor employment relations and in part to the polarized nature of politics in British Columbia. As described elsewhere, the parties attempted to build a better relationship in the 1980s and succeeded in reducing strikes (to none in the 1980s and 1990s) and in using mutual negotiations, arbitration, and joint labor-management committees to settle differences (Verma and Weiler 1992).

At SaskTel labor-management relations were a bit rocky in the 1980s. In the early 1980s, there were no major strikes except for some "study sessions" that lasted a day or half-day. When the contract at SaskTel expired in 1986, both sides were poised for a fight. There followed a two-year period during which there were strikes, lockouts, violence on the pocket lines, and numerous unfair labor practice and other statutory charges filed with the Labour Relations Board. The number of grievances going to arbitration rose steadily. A two-year collective agreement was signed followed by a year during which there was no contract. In 1988, a new three-year contract was concluded. In late 1990, with the contract due to expire in 1991, the parties negotiated a new agreement. It was ratified by the workers but rejected by the company's board of directors as unacceptable. This unprecedented action by the company was another indication of the political conflict (between the conservative government in the province and the socialist alliance of the New Democratic party and the labor movement) in which labor relations at SaskTel had become entangled. After reaching a low point in 1987, relations improved gradually in the early 1990s.

Bell experienced two major strikes in 1979 and 1988. In 1979, there was a one-month strike by craft workers. It was a rotating strike and, hence, the company had little trouble in maintaining full operations throughout the strike period. The operators went on an all-out strike at about the same time (late 1979 and early 1980) for four months. The second strike in 1988, by two CWC bargaining units representing craft workers and operators, lasted for seventeen weeks. Despite this lengthy strike, the employer managed to keep operations near normal with the help of managers and supervisors. Two factors helped the company in maintaining services to the public. First, the rapid computerization of exchanges and other equipment made it easier for a replacement crew to take over the operations. Second, Bell's tradition of long-term service and promotion from within created a managerial cadre familiar with skills in most jobs in the company. During the strike, managers worked long hours to install phones, climb telephone poles, and staff operator services.

We may conclude that strikes and lockouts have never been prominent in industrial relations in the telephone industry. Advances in technology have further reduced the effectiveness of strikes as an economic weapon by enabling managers to maintain near normal operations during a work stoppage. Lastly, one effect of deregulation may be to discourage use of strikes because the competition can take away business from a company during the strike. On the other hand, deregulation can lead to major workforce reductions forcing the parties to an impasse and leaving them to resolve difficult disputes through work stoppages.

Work Reorganization

Work reorganization was a major theme in both Canadian and U.S. industrial relations through much of the 1980s. Much of the literature has focused on the manufacturing industry in describing the reorganization of work (e.g. Katz 1985; Kochan, Katz, and McKersie 1994; Walton, Cutcher-Gershenfeld, and McKersie 1994). The nature of work in the telephone industry is somewhat different from the typical manufacturing firm. For this and other reasons such as the regulated nature of the industry, there were few changes in work organization in the Canadian telephone industry in the 1980s. By early 1990s several companies began to negotiate changes in the job structure through collective bargaining. Other related changes, not always the subject of collective bargaining, such as multiskilling, cross-training, use of work teams, quality and/or continuous improvement programs accompanied the thrust for greater flexibility through work reorganization.

Reduction in Job Classifications. The changes did not affect all groups of employees uniformly. The operators group were not spread across many job classifications to start with and, hence, there were not many changes for this group. However, the nature of their work did change to allow for greater flexibility in assignment. For example, the older practice was often to subdivide the operator group into directory assistance and long distance services. These distinctions were merged in many companies in the 1990s without the need to redefine job classifications.

The number of job classifications for technicians was reduced drastically at most companies. The reductions were in the order of 50 to 60 percent. At SaskTel, the number of job classifications for technicians was reduced to seven from twenty-two. These changes increased flexibility but also increased the need for multiskilling and cross-training. A typical installation and repair worker, circa 1995, would carry a handheld computer which identifies his schedules and jobs for a particular shift. The worker need not go to the office to get work assignments. The worker commutes to the work site directly from home, performs the tasks, and reports on the handheld computer. The worker may perform repairs, install new lines or services, and also support the sales effort with specialized knowledge of the company's line of products and services.

In most companies these changes were negotiated through collective bargaining and, hence, the union was always fully involved in the decision process even though they frequently disagreed with the thrust of these initiatives.

Multiskilling and Training

Most companies reported that as of early 1995 employees received between 40 to 80 hours of training per annum on an ongoing basis. The focus of such training changes over time depending on the changes in business conditions. During the period from 1985 to 1995, training was associated with work reorganization, introduction of new products and services, and downsizing of the workforce.

As job classifications were reduced, there was a need to train workers in additional duties. Training for new skills introduced by new technologies was also a constant need. In the post-deregulation period, the pace of introduction of new services increased, which meant further training for employees. Most companies introduced "smart" services such as call waiting, call screening, and voice mail, which required employees in all groups to become familiar with the features of these new services. In many companies these changes were accompanied with downsizing, which required employees to learn the skills of their laid-off colleagues.

Work Teams

The introduction of work teams varied widely across the firms in our sample. At NB Tel and Bell Canada, there was a fairly high degree of experimentation with teams in a number of areas over several years. At BCTel and at MTS, a more limited set of initiatives had been undertaken but had not diffused widely across the company. These initiatives were not very significant in terms of their impact on work and work relations. At AGT and SaskTel, there was no development in this area although discussions had taken place about the possible introduction of these ideas.

In a few departments at Bell Canada, such as a group responsible for in-house printing and another that receives bill payments from customers, jobs were redesigned along socio-technical lines to become broader in scope. Workers learned multiple skills and rotated across jobs within their work area teams. Improvements in quality, on-time delivery, cost, and productivity were reported in both cases. Workers were involved in both design and implementation of new work systems, although the scope and intensity of their involvement varied from one site to another. Union representatives were not always involved at the early stages. Their involvement was later formalized through the recommendations of a Joint Taskforce on Workplace Reorganization. While such redesign of work was still not common in the industry by early 1995, this was clearly a growing trend within Bell Canada. It is also likely that other telephone companies will follow suit, although it is difficult to predict the rate of diffusion of such innovations.

Quality and Other Process Improvement Programs

All the companies reported a variety of quality and process improvement programs. The stated goal of these programs ranged from better awareness of customer needs to streamlining internal processes for better quality of service and reduction of costs. Although hard data were not available to assess the impact of these efforts, some consequences for human resources and employment relations can be generalized.

In all cases, these programs began with a training initiative. Thus, they have resulted in more investment in training especially in such "soft" skills as problem solving, teamwork, and interpersonal skills to improve communication. At three companies, MTS, AGT, and SaskTel, the efforts involved the union in a variety of ways. For example, MTS and the CEP formed a joint steering committee with decision-making powers provided there was a consensus. The committee developed two programs for workers on the shop floor: a half-day quality orientation program and a one-day workshop on quality improvement skills. There were "work simplification" teams on the shop floor that engaged in improving work processes. The committee has also developed a new job called "quality advisor" who helps teams learn various quality-related skills and apply them to problems. By late 1994, more than 50 percent of the workforce had taken the one-day quality training and all workers had gone through the half-day program.

At AGT, there was extensive implementation of quality improvement groups under the name of process development and improvement teams (PDI) for both operators and craft workers. These groups were involved in identifying problems in the production process and problem solving around those issues. The form these teams took varied. Some groups were formed by taking people off their regular jobs for a period of up to three months, so that they could work full-time on major process change projects (i.e., where they think such improvement is both necessary and feasible). Usually, these processes affected several aspects of AGT's operations, and thus involved workers from multiple departments.

Other groups formed through impromptu meetings, and were concerned more with process improvements in specific work areas. A rough estimate suggested that workers spent up to four hours per week in such informal groups; the primary purpose of these efforts was to streamline operations or to simplify existing procedures. One estimate put the number of both operators and craft workers involved in quality improvement teams at 15 to 20 percent. The major impetus to the introduction of PDI was the need to follow a TQM-type path, which was announced in 1985. Roughly 50 to 60 percent of workers who participated in quality improvement teams had received some form of training. AGT made an effort to give workers full-time training even if for a short period so that they could earn a trainer certificate.

Another program was a company-wide suggestion system called Improve, which requires all employees to come up with suggestions to improve the quality of working life; the program also involves a point-based incentive system.

Initially, there was very little involvement by the union, but by 1991, it became more involved, and with the 1994 agreement, involvement was expected to increase even more. The union became formally involved when AGT management and the union decided to create a joint program. Both the program and relations with the union survived a difficult period of layoffs in the early 1990s.

SaskTel formed a Process Reengineering Team, composed of employees from all parts of the organization with different expertise and skills. This initiative was introduced in early 1994 through a memorandum of agreement. There were some growing pains with the reengineering effort, primarily because many of its decisions potentially involved changes that are accompanied by the elimination of jobs. Since most of the team members were also members of the bargaining unit participating on a voluntary basis, decisions involving the elimination of jobs met with some resistance from these participants. At one point, the union considered opting out of the memorandum of agreement, but then decided to remain part of it.

Joint Union-Management Initiatives

Another trend in the 1980s and the 1990s was to move toward joint regulation of many activities that were traditionally the exclusive domain of managerial decision making. Table 4.8 shows a list of joint committees reported by the six companies in our sample. Almost all of them were formed in the 1980s or the 1990s. Some of these were written into the collective agreement, others were established simply by a letter of understanding, yet others operated through unwritten agreements. Some of the areas of operation included traditional topics such as health and safety, job evaluation, and subcontracting. Another set included newer areas of joint regulation: training, workplace reorganization, equity issues, and technological change. In a perceptible new trend, these committees ac-

TABLE 4.8. List of joint committees

	Year established	In collective agreement	Role
Joint Evaluation Committee			
MTS		No	Advisory (operators only)
Training & Development Committee			
BCTel	1993	Yes	Decision making & advisory
SaskTel	1994	Yes	Decision making & advisory
Technical Change Committee			
BCTel	1977	Yes	Decision making
MTS	1991	Yes	Advisory (operators only)
Employment Equity Committee			
MTS	1986–88	No	Advisory (operators only)
SaskTel	1982	Yes	Decision making & advisory
Pay Equity Committee			
MTS	1986–89	No	
Health & Safety Committee			
AGT Ltd.	1989	No	Decision making & advisory
Other			
Joint Conference—NB Tel	1970	Yes	Advisory
Journey of Operator Services—MTS			
Job Evaluation—BCTel	1992	Yes	Advisory
Trial Change—MTS			
Craft Classification Program—MTS			
Workplace Reorganization—Bell	1994	No	Decision making & advisory
Disability Income Plan—SaskTel	1981	Yes	Decision making & advisory

quired more decision-making powers in contrast to the advisory role that traditional labor-management committees have played.

The trend toward joint regulation was building on some historical strengths in employment relations in the industry even as it faced numerous challenges to sustain the momentum achieved in the 1980s and early 1990s. The years of monopoly regulation made employment relations in the industry a little less antagonistic than in many other industries. The organizational culture in many firms was essentially one of benevolent paternalism. For some companies the transition from benevolent paternalism to joint regulation was relatively smooth. For others, it was very difficult. The increase in competition following deregulation squeezed the profit margins at all telephone companies. This made it difficult for the companies to be as generous to their employees as in the past. Since the parties at Bell Canada had moved the furthest in this direction, we provide a brief description of developments in their joint efforts.

Organizational Responses at Bell Canada

The first union at Bell Canada was the CTEA which was formed as an independent, although their operators' unit soon broke away. During the 1975 to 1980 period the Communication and Electrical Workers of Canada (CWC) successfully raided two locals covering operators and technicians, respectively (Verma and Weiler 1992:417–18). Clerical and sales employees continued to be represented by the Canadian Telephone Employees' Association. In the early 1990s, the CWC merged with the Canadian Paperworkers' Union and the Energy and Chemical Workers' Union to form the Communications, Energy, and Paperworkers Union (CEP).

During the 1980s, collective bargaining between Bell Canada and the CEP centered largely on the core monetary issues of wages and benefits, the introduction of technological change, and the role of part-time work (Verma and Weiler 1992). Bell Canada and the CWC also began to develop employee involvement and employee training and development initiatives; Bell currently spends around 4 percent of the value of its payroll on training (Verma and Weiler 1992; Bell Canada 1994). The company participates with both its unions, the CEP and the CTEA, in two separate Common Interest Forums (CIFs) (Verma 1995). The forums were created to share information and to consult on a wide range of subjects at a senior level.

Recent labor relations developments between Bell Canada and the CEP represent a broad-based effort at cooperation and shared decision making. The two sides are involved in cooperative approaches formally, through collective bargaining, Common Interest Forums, and joint labor-management committees described earlier. By 1990, the CWC (now the CEP) had taken a major step toward employee involvement programs with the formulation of a formal statement on work reorganization that sets out guidelines for undertaking workplace employee involvement initiatives. During the 1990 collective bargaining round, Bell Canada and the CWC signed a letter of intent to constitute a joint union-management consultative committee on work reorganization (Verma and Weiler 1992:430–31). The collective agreement achieved in 1991 gave rise to a joint union-management task force on workplace reorganization that ultimately engaged in a broad examination of the firm, including aspects of technology, firm competitiveness, organizational culture, the union-management relationship, and human resource development (Bell Canada 1993). The various elements of the proposed initiatives between Bell Canada and the CEP constitute a formal strategy for change that is aimed at building on past successes in a stepwise manner. Several key elements of the recommendations and conclusions of the task force included (Bell Canada 1993; Chaykowski 1995):

- Developing a "customer first" workplace model based on joint union-management workplace teams combined with joint union-management resource and support teams;
- Creating senior joint union-management "steering" and "working" committees to undertake strategic planning and oversee the implementation of programs, respectively;
- Establishing training and education initiatives that are jointly planned and delivered by management and the union and that concentrate on training for workplace teams;
- Committing to employment security issues;
- Developing an alliance between the management and union where Interest-Based Negotiations are adopted and a comprehensive set of joint union-management activities are developed at all levels of the organization;
- Providing the required resources (human and financial) to support the various initiatives;
- Emphasizing a total quality program with direct union involvement;
- Developing complete and universal access to information.

In their collective agreement negotiated in 1994, the parties agreed to form a senior level Steering Committee and two Working Committees to begin the task of work reorganization and process improvement. In the first phase, forty-one teams were formed and given extensive training. The company also created the positions of a trainer and a facilitator to train and coach the teams. The trainers and facilitators were drawn from both the union and company ranks. Thus, the overall regulation of the entire process was fully shared by the union and the management. Plans in early 1995 called for gradual expansion of the team system.

Also in 1994, Bell Canada formed a similar joint task force on workplace reorganization with its other union, the CTEA. This task force recommended a similar governance structure of a joint steering committee to oversee workplace reorganization efforts (Verma 1995). By late 1995, at the time of this writing, the parties had concluded negotiations of a new three-year collective agreement which contained, among other things, an agreement to implement most of the recommendations of the joint task force.

Under the new contract, the parties agreed to create a WPR Joint Working Committee reporting to the Common Interest Forum (CIF). The committee is to be responsible for implementing workplace reorganization policies developed within the CIF. The company the union also agreed to create a cadre of trainers and facilitators to ensure that workplace reorganization is achieved through employee involvement and that it leads to more interesting jobs as well as improvements in quality and productivity.

Until 1994, the company was organized into two geographic operating units: Bell Ontario and Bell Quebec. The company announced a major internal reorganization in late 1994 after a CRTC decision to deregulate local telephone services. The new organization divides the company into two business units: local services and competitive services that include long distance operations and other services in which Bell Canada faces competition.

By early 1995, competitive pressures had put a big squeeze on company profits in the long distance market. As the company looked for ways to restore its profitability, the company announced that it was ready to begin workforce reductions of 10,000 employees (roughly 25% of the core employment) over the next three years (Bourette 1995). These cuts were to be spread as follows: 1,700 in 1995, 4,300 in 1996, and 4,000 in 1997 (Surtees 1995b). Even though the precise method of reductions was not known at the time, it was virtually certain that the firm would cut its employment rolls well beyond the normal rate of attrition through retirements, quits, and other voluntary leavers. The implication was that Bell might have to take recourse to involuntary layoffs for the first time in its 115-year history. In interviews conducted for this research, senior managers maintained that the firm would do its very best to avoid involuntary layoffs. Despite these assurances, it was likely that many employees remained apprehensive about their employment prospects over the next three years.

By March 1995, at the time of this writing, the cooperative approaches developing at Bell Canada were at a formative stage of development. The establishment of joint committees with decision-making powers and access to financial and information resources to develop the new initiatives were central to the cooperative approach. Yet the mounting pressures to reduce employment levels appeared to severely test the cooperative approach. As the competitive pressures on Bell Canada mount, the company would be increasingly forced either to reaffirm its past practice of supporting employment security and working coopera-tively with the union or to abandon the old system in favor of a more traditional approach to employment reductions through layoffs and to an "arms-length" relationship with its major unions.

Conclusions

The Canadian telecommunications industry provides an excellent labora-tory for examining an industrial relation system undergoing change in response to changes in technology, regulation, and the increasing global-ization of markets in general. Each of these changes in the environment present threats to the old order as well as opportunities for creating new products and services for an ever-larger market.

Deregulation in Canada followed a pattern similar to that in the United States with a time lag. There were major differences in the 1980s and the early 1990s between the two countries. Deregulation of the long distance market in the United States preceded Canadian deregulation by seven years. In general, this was true of deregulation of most other ser-vices. However, by 1995 when the CRTC opened hearings on direct com-petition between the cable and telephone industries, the regulatory gap had closed considerably. Another important difference is that Canadian firms were so small in size that there was no mandatory separation of local and long distance providers comparable to the AT&T divestiture in the United States. The largest Canadian telephone provider, Bell Canada, did reorganize itself into local and competitive (i.e., long distance) ser-vices but there was no indication that these two parts may become sepa-rate corporate entities.

Employment relations in the industry were characterized in general by a high degree of employment security typified by Bell Canada which had no layoffs till early 1995 in its 115-year history. This system was clearly a product of the regulated monopoly regime that existed from the turn of the century until 1991. Since 1991, most Canadian telephone firms have reduced employment mostly through voluntary separation, early re-tirement, and normal attrition. In the second half of the 1990s, it is likely that the pace of downsizing in the former monopolies will increase. This is bound to create tensions in the employment relationship.

Collective bargaining has been relatively free of strikes compared to many other industries. During the long period of regulated monopolies, several firms developed joint working arrangements and common interest forums with their unions. In the 1980s and the 1990s, the number of joint labor-management committees with decision-making powers increased across several companies. This suggests that there is a good foundation on which future initiatives in labor-management alliance can be built.

At the workplace, most companies have undertaken a series of measures to simplify work, enrich jobs, and increase skills and employee involvement. The number of job classifications have been reduced particularly among field service technicians. For others, jobs have been more broadly defined by adding new duties. Both of these developments have increased the emphasis on training. The quantity of training appears to have increased and there is more "soft skills" training than ever before. Some firms have introduced a variety of teams: task or project teams, work area teams, and ongoing quality improvement or problem-solving teams.

In an earlier study of Canadian industrial relations, it was suggested that many companies and unions go through a "crisis" stage before strategic bargaining or strategic alliances develop between the parties (Chaykowski and Verma 1992: 450–53). The telephone industry may follow this path, although the evidence in this chapter suggests that there is an opportunity for many telephone companies to skip the "crisis" stage. Firms such as Bell Canada can potentially make adjustments while they are still profitable and without destroying their relationship with their unions and their employees. In order to achieve this transition both the company and the union will have to put a high priority on joint problem solving. There is a real danger that many joint approaches will unravel when the pressure on firms to downsize increases. As posited by Kochan, Katz, and McKersie (1984), these are some of the strategic choices the parties face in 1995. Whether they choose the traditional path of involuntary layoffs and arms-length dealings or the unconventional path of employment security within a strategic labor-management alliance remains to be seen.

PART 2

Labor-Mediated Restructuring

Chapter 5

Germany

Owen Darbishire

As the world's third largest telecommunications company (after AT&T and NTT), and largest cable television company, Deutsche Telekom continues to enjoy nearly unhindered monopoly status in Germany.[1] Simultaneously, Telekom has been a late starter in adjusting to the potential of new technology, and it has been slow to improve its poor (and expensive) services, or to develop a customer orientation. Nevertheless, the ongoing (but distinct) processes of privatization in Germany, and voice and network deregulation led by the European Union (EU), are driving a revised corporate strategy. Termed "Focus '98" this strategy entails divisionalization, decentralization, rationalization, and substantial work reorganization. This strategic reorientation emphasizes a stronger customer orientation, tariff reform, greater internationalization, and the development of network- and application-related value added services.

A central argument of this chapter, however, is that this strategic reorientation is characterized by mutuality. That is, new technology and impending commercial pressures are reacting with strong, highly centralized, employee representation and worker rights to force Telekom to seek a mutually acceptable strategic path. An important theme in the following analysis is, therefore, stability and consensus. However, "mu-

1. I thank Jeff Keefe, Harry Katz, and Serafina Negrelli for comments on an earlier draft.

tuality" implies more than a simple compromise of interests. Rather, the case of Deutsche Telekom illustrates a critical comparative distinction: The causal relationship between business strategy and industrial relations is not one-dimensional, but instead reciprocal. While human resource and industrial relations practices are being significantly impacted by the revised strategic choices, existing institutions are likewise impacting on the strategic path chosen, and the pace of change.

Both the process and the outcomes of the adjustment thus reflect a constrained strategic choice, though a choice that is, in fact, facilitated by the minimal current regulatory, financial market, or immediate commercial pressures. Although the resultant (bargained) strategy entails increased flexibility, it is the form of that flexibility that is most strongly affected. Institutions are directing Telekom to attempt to maintain a high-trust, cooperative adjustment strategy, building on the technical skills of its workforce. Nevertheless, while the outcome reflects worker influence and constraints imposed by existing institutional structures, and although there is a consequent emphasis on a revenue-enhancing, up-market strategy, the studied process of change has been slow in delivering performance and service improvements for customers. Indeed, it is argued that the same institutionalization of stakeholder interests that influences business strategy also constrains the adjustment process. The result is an incremental adjustment, rather than more fundamental innovation and experimentation in work organization. Such incrementalism has slowed the pace of change, though leaving the potential for more successful implementation.

The first section of this chapter analyses the slow development of Telekom as an independent company (separate from both political control and the postal service and post-bank), and the limited nature of deregulation and competition. It is argued that the institutionalization of the position of stakeholders created a quasi-corporatist entity, though the absence of market and political incentives to move beyond an emphasis on the infrastructure has limited Telekom's commercial performance and the level of service provision. Nevertheless, the extensive cable TV and integrated digital services networks (ISDN) provide the potential for an up-market strategy. The second section examines the transition away from a centralized, functional, work organization being initiated by technological change. There is an increasing emphasis on market segments (achieved through corporate reorganization), customer service, and the flexibility of (previously rigid) employment structures. Although these remain complicated by the civil service status of half the workforce, the emphasis on a high level of training, technical competence, and responsible autonomy has remained. The third section discusses Telekom's strategy of using subsidiaries to increase flexibility of employment, though without undermining employment conditions, while the strains over employment adjustment are becoming increasingly prevalent as Telekom aims to eliminate at least 60,000 jobs by the year 2000. The Deutsche Postgewerkschaft (DPG) union is adamantly opposed to the scale of this reduction. The bargaining structure and changing pattern of employee representation, together with the union's policies and the implications of incrementalism, are analysed in the last section.

The Environmental Context

Structure of Telekom

Deutsche Telekom was transferred to private-sector status (as an *Aktiengesellschaft*) on 1 January 1995—an event that marked the end of a long political process, rather than a shift in the market context within which Telekom operates. The intense debate (and indeed strife) surrounding the so-called Post Reform II remarkably concerned only ownership structure,[2] and did not itself directly address any further liberalization of the German telecommunications market. Telekom thus continues to operate as an essentially monopoly telecommunications supplier, with 39.2 million connections and a turnover of DM64 billion in 1994, while with 23.2 million households served by cable television, and with 14.6 million subscribers by the end of 1994, Telekom also has a de facto cable TV monopoly.

As throughout much of Europe, the German telecommunications services industry has historically been publicly owned and integrated into one company along with the postal service and post-bank. Originally consolidated in the Reichspost, in 1950 it was incorporated in the Basic Law. Operating under the constitutional requirement to provide an infrastructural service, the monolithic Deutsche Bundespost was an administrative section of the federal Ministry of Posts and Telecommunications, and functioned largely as a "parapublic institution" inside Germany's "semi-sovereign state" (Katzenstein 1987). That is, in addition to the requirements of the Basic Law, the government, unions, and equipment manufacturers were well represented in the policy-making process, insti-

2. The transfer of Telekom (with *Postdienst* and *Postbank*) to *Aktiengesellschaft* status is not an actual privatization, since the first tranche of shares will not be sold until mid-1996, and the government will retain a majority shareholding until at least 1999. Nevertheless, for ease, the term privatization is used.

tutionalizing a quasi-corporatist structure, partly through the role of the Postal Administration Council (Postverwaltungsrat). Policy initiatives and important managerial decisions consequently became the product of informal tripartite negotiations between the minister of Posts and Telecommunications, the DPG, and the principal equipment suppliers (Morgan and Webber 1986; Schmidt 1991; Darbishire 1995).

The quasi-corporatist structure of the Bundespost institutionalized the interests of employees beyond the norm achieved through codetermination rights. This helped to make the DPG one of the most powerful unions in Germany, enhance employee rights, and increase the emphasis given to the telecommunications industry as an infrastructural service provider. Similarly, together with the institutionalized influence of equipment manufacturers, the shift toward commercialism was slowed.

Nevertheless, Telekom has undergone two recent, fundamental changes in its organizational structure. Post Reform I in 1989 separated the Deutsche Bundespost (DBP) into its three constituent parts (telecommunications, postal services, and banking), and established each as an independent operational unit administratively separate from the ministry of Posts and Telecommunications. It thereby separated operational and regulatory decision making, though substantial political involvement remained, with the ministers of Posts, Finance, and the Interior in particular retaining competence in their respective jurisdictions. Furthermore, the requirement of Article 87 of the Basic Law that the Deutsche Bundespost be operated as a "federal administrative body with its own administrative structure," and in accordance with the general economic, financial, and social policies of the government, remained. Some greater independence in entrepreneurial functions was granted with the commercial objectives of each company defined such that revenue covered costs, and an "appropriate" level of profit be made. Nevertheless, cross-subsidization within the DBP companies continued (essentially from Telekom), and Article 87 of the Basic Law, "which effectively stands against a primarily profit-oriented supply" (Schmidt 1993: 4), ensured the retention of a basic infrastructural obligation and focus.[3] Indeed, the demands of unification were only to reemphasize this. Management strategy thus remained "not directed towards commercial success but solely towards the completion of their legal duties, whilst taking into consideration the need of the economy" (Witte 1966).[4] While Post Reform I increased its independence, Telekom continued to operate in a politically determined

3. For further details see Darbishire 1995, Büchner 1993, and Schmidt 1991, 1993.
4. Quoted in Büchner 1993: 279.

environment, with substantial political interference on central strategic, operational, structural, tariff, investment, and human resource-industrial relations decisions. With investments of DM23.1 billion in 1994 (the equivalent of 25% of all manufacturing and process investment in Germany, including mining) the incentive for political interference in a federal administration is well illustrated.

Post Reform II "privatizing" Telekom on 1 January 1995 is perceived by Telekom as bringing freedom from political control and bureaucracy; easing the financial constraints by reducing payments to the government, politically determined investment levels, and subsidies to the other DBP companies; and allowing Telekom to raise capital outside tight federal budgets. This access to extra capital is of particular importance in allowing Telekom to engage in international joint ventures, from which it had been (partly) constrained by its constitutional mandate.[5] Telekom also sought privatization with the central objective (though not one easily realized) of bringing greater freedom in human resource management, employment adjustment, and bargaining.

The transfer of Telekom to *Aktiengesellschaft* status has put political decision making at a further remove, with a holding organization (Bundesanstalt Post) managing the government's shares, while not having managerial competence. Nevertheless, political influence will not disappear: The government will remain the majority shareholder until at least 1999; it will continue to influence tariff structures, senior appointments (including those to the Supervisory Board), and critical management decisions; and over 50 percent of the employees remain *Beamte* (civil servants) on "permanent loan" to Telekom, with their employment conditions still determined by parliamentary legislation.[6]

Competition and Regulation

Telekom has enjoyed a very sheltered regulatory structure, which is currently concerned with ensuring that Telekom has the opportunity to adjust to forthcoming competition, develop into a dominant international telecommunications company, and safeguard employment oppor-

5. The constraint of the Basic Law on Telekom's globalization strategy was such that it focused either on infrastructural investments (as with Ameritech in forming the Magyar Com Group in Hungry), or limited the extent of data services offered (as in its joint venture with France Télécom). The agreement to purchase 20% of Sprint with France Télécom in June 1994 would have been of questionable legality without privatization.

6. The resignation of Helmut Ricke as chairman in December 1994 followed complaints about the persistence of political intervention and bureaucracy, and controversial political appointments to the Supervisory Board.

tunities. For the government, liberalization and competition remain secondary objectives to promoting the position of the national champion, with the extent of deregulation being almost fully driven by the European Union (EU) Commission. This reflects the politically high-profile issue that telecommunications deregulation has consistently been in Germany. Thus, the absence of a direct link between privatization and deregulation in Post Reform II constituted more than simply the need for a political consensus in the decision to change the ownership structure—a consensus demanded by the need for a two-thirds majority to alter the Basic Law. Rather, the government's initial objective of restricting reform to enable Telekom to develop new services, and thereby smoothing the adjustment process for stakeholders, has only given way to a strategy of more rapid liberalization where delay appears detrimental, and where EU pressure has been greatest. Hence, the October 1995 decision to allow alternative networks to carry liberalized telecoms services from 1 July 1996, and the March 1995 decision to allow unlimited licenses for network competition from 1998, were a response to potential barriers to Telekom's global objectives—EU Commission objections to the Atlas joint venture with France Télécom, and U.S. objections to the proposed purchase of 20 percent of Sprint, both of which the Kohl government publicly supported.[7] Simultaneously, the government has resisted pressure within both the EU and Germany to divest Telekom of its near-monopoly cable TV network, thereby enhancing its domestic strength, and the potential for new product development and a multimedia strategy.

The government's policies have, therefore, slowed deregulation, which is driven by the EU. Post Reform I in 1989 opened all telecommunications services except voice to competition. Since 1 July 1990 all terminal equipment has also been open to competition, while in 1993 corporate networks were permitted to transmit voice for closed user groups, in addition to data. However, Telekom retains its network and voice monopolies—which constitutes 90 percent of revenue from service provision. Competition over value-added network services (VANS) does occur, though this has been slow to develop both because of regulatory restrictions with the conditions of use of leased lines (which remain in the Tele-

7. The October 1995 decision followed explicit "quid pro quo" negotiations in Brussels, between telecommunications minister Wolfgang Bötsch, Deutsche Telekom CEO Ron Sommer, their French counterparts François Fillon and Michel Bon, and EU Competition Commissioner Karel van Miert. The detailed agreement, including restructuring of domestic markets, succeeded in securing Commission support for the Atlas and Phoenix joint ventures.

kom monopoly), and the cost of those lines—between 3 and 10 times international prices.[8]

Furthermore, Telekom has retained a near monopoly (an estimated 90%) in the data services market—though in 1994 the Bundeskartelamt (monopoly commission) found it had achieved this through illegal cross-subsidies of DM1.9 billion between 1989 and 1994, enabling it to operate at 46 percent below costs in 1992, and 25 percent below in early 1994. Its share of other deregulated markets is less, with Mannesmann Mobilfunk now having over 50 percent of the high-growth digital mobile market.

The strategically advantageous regulatory structure is highlighted by Telekom's near monopoly (90–95%) of the cable TV network. Although in most locations this is physically separate from the telephone network, both are operated and maintained by a single set of field technicians. Now that Telekom is beginning to break the bounds of its traditional orientation, it is seeking to integrate both networks and develop corresponding high-technology multimedia competitive strategies. This strategy is most clearly illustrated in Telekom's massive upgrading of the east German network, where it has installed fiber optic cable to the home (FTTH). The appointment of the head of Sony Europe, Ron Sommer, as the new CEO of Telekom in March 1995 to replace Helmut Ricke (who resigned over frustration with government intervention in managerial decision making) likewise highlights both global and multimedia ambitions.

Telekom's strategic intent to focus on multimedia strategy, and to dominate the development of digital TV in Germany, is illustrated by multimedia trials in Baden-Württemberg, Bavaria, and Berlin; by joint ventures to develop new Windows-based multimedia products with Microsoft and Intel, announced in 1994; by becoming the biggest shareholder in the Astra satellite operations; and by the attempt to established a joint venture in April 1994 with Bertelsmann and the Kirch Group to manage and distribute interactive TV, pay-per-view, video, and specialist telecommunications services (before hitting an EU competition hurdle). Thus, insofar as there is an asymmetry of regulation, in Germany it currently stands as the reverse of many other countries (such as Britain) where the dominant telecommunications company is excluded from the cable TV market, but smaller competitors compete in both markets. Fur-

8. An INTUG (International Telecom Users Group) survey found prices 3 times those of the U.K. (quoted in EIU, *Business Europe,* 28 March 1994), while FDR (1994) found prices to be up to 10 times higher than the average in the OECD.

thermore, it has been European Union competition regulations, rather than German ones, that are limiting the extent of Telekom's strategic ambitions.

In addition to this "asymmetrical" strategic advantage, Telekom has not experienced significant incentive price regulation. Rather, the pricing structure has been the result of an essentially political negotiation between Telekom and the Ministry for Posts and Telecommunications—itself strongly influenced by the high revenue the government has collected from Telekom (an average of DM6.4 billion per annum between 1990 and 1994 in Ablieferung and Finanzausgleich payments), the weak financial position of Telekom,[9] and the desire to maintain the cross-subsidization of local calls by long distance and international ones. In sharp contrast to companies such as BT, therefore, there has been no recent history of significant (regulator-induced) price reductions, in spite of the high level of prices for telecoms services in Germany. The Tariff Concept '96 price reform program was brought forward to mid-1995 in the face of imminent competition, though it covers price reductions only between 1996 and 1998, and was itself the result of a political bargain in 1993-94. This pattern reflects the belief within the government that an "aggressive regulation" of prices (with regulatory determined price reductions in the absence of competitive pressures) is not in the longer-term interests of Telekom. The tariff structure has thus been ultimately a facilitator of reform, not an instigator of it.

Performance of Telekom

In spite of the strategic opportunities that Telekom enjoys thanks to having the world's most extensive ISDN and cable TV networks, in addition to its telephone network, it has been slow to utilize new technology and develop new services. Although digitalization began in 1985, by 1994 only about 30 percent of the overall network was digital (FDR 1994), due not only to the infrastructural investment focus in east Germany, but also to political constraints in the structure of Telekom's organization. Thus, for example, switching and telephone services were long organizationally separated from transmission operations at both board and operational levels—a politically determined structure that suited a technological orientation in an analog environment, but inhibited the effective planning of a digital network or gaining economies of scope in a digital environment (Pospischil 1993). As such, it reinforced the empha-

---

9. In 1994 Telekom had a ratio of capital and reserves as a proportion of total assets of only 20.7%.

sis, which persisted at least until 1992, on optimizing the use of existing analog technology, rather than on digitalization. Telekom's refocused strategy has, however, led it twice to radically update its original plan to complete the digitalization of the network by 2006, with a new target set late in 1994 of full digitalization by 1997.

The comparatively slow rate of digitalization has occurred in spite of investing substantially more than other telecommunications companies,[10] while its performance has been low, and high investment levels have not been reflected in superior technological features providing a flexible range of innovative customer-oriented services. Network structures and operating procedures have also not been adjusted to realize performance gains where new transmission and switching technologies have been introduced (Gerpott and Pospischil 1993), or where an extensive ISDN has been established. Low levels of service (including, for example, the underdevelopment of data transmission and absence of itemized billing), high prices (with basic calls approximately 20 percent above the OECD average, and leased lines up to ten times higher), long waiting lists, and high fault rates (FDR 1994, DTI 1994), have been compounded by the basic absence of integrated computer systems to provide enhanced customer service—illustrated by the failure to have a computerized customer records system before the end of 1993. In contrast to AT&T, the RBOCs, and BT, therefore, Telekom has enjoyed far greater strategic, operational, and social stability, though a notably worse economic performance.

This poor performance, and the failure to utilize new technology, reflects more the absence of political and market incentives than a Luddite approach by stakeholders. While all stakeholders (including the federal government and states, trade unions, equipment suppliers, and consumers) were well represented, both before and after Post Reform I (Schmidt 1991), they have not historically displayed opposition to new technology. Indeed, Telekom's technical competence, and particularly that of its workforce, has consistently been extremely high. Nevertheless, prior to Post Reform II, the stakeholders did utilize the quasi-corporatist structures to form a passive coalition against any fundamental shift in the strategic orientation (or organization) of the industry—yet just such a fundamental shift is implied by the digitalization of the industry. The absence of a dominant reformist business cohort in Germany had re-

10. The high levels of investment partly reflect the high prices paid, in a politically determined relationship, to equipment suppliers, such as Siemans. Switch prices, for example, have been 4.5 times the international price, fiber 2.79 times, and average equipment prices 2.32 times (DTI 1994).

sulted in only moderate reform of the strongly institutionalized position of existing stakeholders—an institutionalization secured within the constitutional position of the Deutsche Bundespost as a public-sector administration with an essentially nonprofit infrastructural obligation. This contrasts with the United States and United Kingdom. In the United Kingdom ties to manufacturers are weaker, while in the United States although AT&T and GTE had their own equipment suppliers, external manufacturing firms sought entry into this highly lucrative market. Together with the relatively greater importance of service industries, this helped promote the emergence of a reformist (deregulatory) business cohort driving (judicially or politically) liberalization. The strong political interest in Telekom (given its investment and employment levels, and financial contributions) also reduced the incentive to deregulate the market or otherwise produce regulatory incentives to improve commercial performance. Indeed, the political imperative on the basic infrastructure was illustrated by the planned DM60 billion investment to develop the east German network into the most advanced in the world between 1990 and 1997—a plan that was, by mid-1995, marginally ahead of schedule.

Quasi-corporatism, resulting from the institutionalization of all stakeholder interests, did therefore limit the extent of deregulation, and the pressures for a service (rather than infrastructural) orientation. The consequent insulation Telekom has enjoyed, together with political constraints on Telekom's organization, help to explain the poor performance record. Nevertheless, as the evidence of the process of Telekom's more recent restructuring (discussed in the following sections) illustrates, three additional factors are especially important. First, the extreme centralization of managerial decision making has inhibited local flexibility, experimentation with alternative work systems, and adequate localized cost control. Second, the potentially radical implications of new technology on required skill-sets and employment levels has led the works councils and union to be extremely cautious of reorganizations. Third, and relatedly, employee representatives have used their strongly institutionalized voice to participate in highly detailed negotiations on new work organization. These negotiations have been characterised principally by caution and centralization. In combination, the centralization, caution, and detailed negotiations of change have produced only slow, incremental performance adjustment.

Organization of Work

The organization of work in Telekom has reflected its political and infrastructural orientation, being highly centralized, regulated, and functional, though not such that it could be defined as Tayloristic or Fordist. Furthermore, although there were sharp lines of demarcation between individual jobs, skill sets were broad (particularly among technicians), supervision both in the field and internally has been low, and there has traditionally been little separation between conception and execution of tasks. Workers have been flexible despite defined job structures, there has been minimal formal or informal job control, and the practical level of discretion on the job was high.

Centralized, Functional Regulation

Both before and after Post Reform I the extensive central regulation, minimal decentralized managerial autonomy, and the single-digit specification of employment levels for branch offices resulted in a commonality of work structures throughout Telekom. However, an important distinction between the regulation of the process of work and job procedures has meant that local discretion on work organization has been present for first line managers and field operating procedures.

Centralized regulations have principally concerned the process of work, specifying work flows and the tasks of both managers and workers within that process—typically on very functional lines. Indeed, in 1994 there were approximately 900 regulations concerned with the everyday flow of work in network operations alone. There has, however, been far greater flexibility in the job procedure. High levels of training have been a primary method for ensuring commonality of job methods, and while periodically updated, extensively detailed procedures for clearing faults, installing telephones, conducting routine switch maintenance, or interacting with distribution controls have not been a feature of Telekom. This has given greater flexibility to clerical workers, first-line managers, and technicians in particular. Indeed, this flexibility has been reinforced by the absence of monitoring capabilities (either through close managerial supervision or detailed performance statistics), leaving much technical work (whether in the field or in remote exchanges) as highly autonomous. In this respect, workers have been given high trust and responsibility.

This technical responsibility and autonomy has been reinforced by a characteristic of much work undertaken in the analog environment—the coexistence of control and execution in maintenance work. The regular preventive manual monitoring of analog equipment left significant control with the technicians in exchanges and on external switches, and they also enjoyed autonomy in the execution of this work. Nevertheless, as will be argued below, it is a feature of the digital environment (though by no means exclusive to Telekom) that control over tasks and their execution is now being increasingly separated, causing a fundamental change in working practices.

The commonality of work processes has been reinforced by the centralized determination of work systems, such as computer systems which were functionally organized, leading to a multiplicity of (national) systems for customer orders, or service, or billing by each product type. This structure has been reflected, in particular, in the internal (or office-based) organization of work with the functional separation of such tasks as reception, testing, resource control, and dispatch, while in customer sales and service there were product specialists. The scope of responsibility has thus been low.

The localized organization of Telekom led, however, to an informal networking structure. The combination of the absence of integrated computer systems, sequential work organization, and (for example, in the area of customer service) the proximity of workers, led to informal interactions to ensure the smooth flow of work. Indeed, the use of index cards to record customer details until the end of 1993 reinforced this networking structure, which aimed to effectively prioritize work, make optimal use of resources, and dispatch work to appropriate field technicians—namely, those with the skills appropriate to the fault initially diagnosed. This networking structure consisted, in essence, of the exchange of information through interpersonal interaction. Even though it necessitated an (informal) understanding of different job functions, it did not involve either any job rotation or cross-skilling. Rather, it represented an *ad hoc* response to the need to manage the flow of work through a highly complex system that was organized functionally, and that frequently had difficulties in prioritizing work, or allocating it most effectively. Thus, networking represented an informal and supplemental work structure, whose operation reduced the practical individualization of work, through the creation of informal groups and teamwork, which helped promote different occupational community identities. It depended on the local, or decentralized, organization of both control centers and exchanges, since local centers possess relatively high personal knowledge of the work requirements and "their" field technicians.

This networking structure was most common in areas of basic service, and was less frequent where advanced services involving detailed network planning, construction, or sophisticated products were concerned. This reflected the traditional spatial organization, frequency of use, and the depth of specialization, of these advanced services. Although the "paper flow" was more extensive here, some networking structures did exist.

Field technicians (those who construct, repair, and maintain the network and exchanges) were less directly affected by this internal functional organization. Local telecommunications offices have been organized (prior to the current Telekom Kontakt reorganization) on a "patch" (local geographical area) structure of between 70,000 and 200,000 lines, rather than a customer-focused one. Within local exchanges work has been largely autonomous, with little direction and significant flexibility in conducting everyday tasks of maintenance on analog systems. Flexibility in the field was somewhat less, with residential repair and installation work both more high volume and reactive, and technicians typically distributed a "3-job" work order by dispatch (and 9 to 15 jobs per day). Although training has been both broad and extensive, there was some functional specialization—such as between provision (by a *Monteur*) and repair (by a *Service Techniker*), or, in spite of the similarity of the tasks, between these, the service of public telephones, and the maintenance of the cable TV network. Indeed, this reflected the inclusion of separate dispatch organizations in the internal functional organization, which in turn impacted on the organizational structure of the field force.

This form of functional work organization led to the "furthering" (or referral) of many jobs to other technicians, even where the additional tasks were well within the competence of the technician. That is, with limited ability to detect the precise location of faults remotely, a technician could easily discover that the cause lay outside the formal job function, requiring the job be "furthered" to the responsible technician even if the identified fault was not complex. However, prior to the divisionalization of Telekom from April 1994, technicians could work on both residential and business lines, which prevented excessively narrow job requirements. Meanwhile, technicians working on larger business systems and switches were generally more skilled specialists, and worked either individually or in pairs on specialized equipment with higher value and lower volume work, often by specialist product type.

Supervision of field technicians has traditionally been low, with the first-line field manager *(Gruppe Leiter Servicemonteur)* acting principally as a "team leader" for groups of fifteen field technicians who worked independently. Typically 80 percent of the field manager's working day is office-based, "servicing" the technicians through administrative functions (the lack of computerized support systems has left the field manager with responsibility for much logistic support, coordinating leave and training schedules, and some secondary level dispatch and resource control). Active "field time" has been more supportive than supervisory or disciplinary, with a focus more on quality than productivity levels.

The collection and analysis of performance data for each field technician has increased, particularly with the introduction of personal computers for the processing of this data since 1991. However, this productivity data (which consists of basic performance measures such as provisions or clears per day) has not been systematically used, and no formal performance appraisal system exists. Nevertheless, the introduction of a performance-related pay system *(Leistungszulagen)* in 1990 for *Beamte* (extended to all workers in 1992) has led to some increase in the application of performance measurement, though limited by its manner of operation.

Neither branch offices *(Niederlassungen)* nor regions *(Direktion)* have operated as cost or profit centers, and as a public authority there has been (at best) an apparent half-hearted approach to measuring costs (with an absence of internal accounting mechanisms). That is, the national full-cost accounting was unable to "be used either to illustrate the dependence of costs on performance levels nor provide information about costs at local levels" (Büchner 1993: 280). While on the one hand this has produced a lack of accountability, it has also increased the potential flexibility for local managers. Nevertheless, the strict hierarchy within Telekom (which has extended as far as central purchase of stationery) has been operated among management in practice. There is surprisingly little evidence of variation among branch offices, other than those connected with the different regional makeup. That is, in light of the lack of local performance measurement systems, the adherence to central regulations has been unusual. There is no distinction (common in British Telecom) between "said policy" and "done policy," and it is widely estimated within Telekom that the degree of centralization amounts to 95 percent of important decision making in practice, even though allowing greater flexibility in theory.

Employment Structures and Flexibility

One of the most notable effects of Telekom's public-sector status has been the three categories of employee—*Beamte* (civil servants), *Angestellte* (white collar employees), and *Arbeiter* (manual workers). The division between these employment categories does not depend on occupational area or function, but rather primarily on the method of recruitment into Telekom. Thus, with 1994 employment split 51 percent *Beamte,* 20 percent *Angestellte,* and 29 percent *Arbeiter,* it is usual to have both *Beamte* and *Arbeiter/Angestellte* working side by side on the same tasks.[11] *Beamte*, however, have no bargaining rights, have their pay and working conditions determined through the Federal Remuneration Act (Bundesbesoldungsgestetz), and cannot undertake industrial action. Nevertheless, they retain their status for life, have substantial employment security from the day of their appointment, and from the age of twenty-seven cannot be dismissed except for very serious disciplinary offences. The legal determination of the employment of *Beamte* also includes training, the structure of career progression, and their functional and geographic mobility. Indeed, the extreme external rigidity is compensated by (at least theoretically) a substantial degree of internal mobility.

Beamte have no "job control" rights, and with the reorganization of work can be reassigned to other jobs within their employment category, or to different geographic areas. Nevertheless, the advantage of reassignment is countered in that they must be offered a job that has a similar status (including job skills and sophistication), and where there is a "reasonable expectation" for them to move.[12] This limits the degree to which new technology can be used to deskill work. As Telekom's human resource strategy is shifting to emphasize the likelihood of layoffs and the necessity for a *Dopplte-Mobilität* (double mobility of jobs and location), the status of *Beamte* is of contrasting benefits—the high internal flexibility being countered by the near-absolute external rigidity. However, *Arbeiter* and *Angestellte* also have substantial job protection in Telekom, with de facto employment security once they reach the age of forty with fifteen years of service, as the result of the 1972 Protection Against Rationalization contract negotiated in the public sector. The practical limitation on Telekom to reassign *Beamte* comes not with regulations applying to them, but rather from the DPG negotiating the application of agreements made for *Arbeiter* and *Angestellte* to *Beamte*.

Greater limitations do, however, exist with respect to the structure of the internal labor market for *Beamte*. The port of entry into the civil service is highly dependent upon formal training, skills, and qualifications. These formal conditions are heavily regulated by the government, and determine within which of four *Laufbahn,* or career ladders, a civil servant is employed. *Beamte* progress through subdivisions with a career ladder, but since each is founded on different formal qualification and

11. Historically a distinction was such that tasks involving the exercise of sovereign power were exclusive to *Beamte*. This principle has, however, now largely fallen by the wayside.

12. The exception is that they may be transferred to a lower status job for a period of up to 3 years.

education levels progress from one career ladder to another is severely restricted. The government also legislates the wage structure for *Beamte,* based on the principle of "alimentation," which determines that salary is essentially not related to performance, but to the post occupied (and thus the career ladder), the pay grade, and the length of service *(Dienstalters- tufen)*—a principle designed to ensure that wages cannot be excessively influenced by political decisions (Büchner 1993). In the context of a pri- vate-sector company, however, the essential separation of pay from per- formance (especially when combined with statutory or contractual employment security) imposes substantial restrictions on Telekom's abil- ity to increase productivity through the intensification of the pace of work.

Post Reform I did, however, add some flexibility of deployment of per- sonnel within career ladders, and also promotion between ladders, by easing the previously rigid ratios of employment in each career step (par- ticularly with respect to specialist fields). This created greater promo- tional (and thus motivational) opportunities, while also allowing a shift in promotion policy from one based on seniority to one with greater discretion, increasingly emphasizing performance—a grading flexibility that has been used by local management to motivate performance, with some pressure for work intensification.

A second unique change to the rigid regulations governing *Beamte* was the introduction of the Postleistungszulagen in 1989. This established performance-related pay initially for *Beamte* alone, again reflecting the government's recognition of the difficulty of motivating *Beamte* given their employment security and progression through their career ladder as they accrue seniority. Since the "alimentation" principle precludes mak- ing any portion of normal *Beamte* pay contingent on performance, the bonus represents a supplementary payment (such that pay then exceeds that of the rest of the civil service). Payments are restricted to 25 percent of employees in any department, with a total budget of up to 2 percent of expenditure on personnel, are paid monthly, and are based on a four- step ranking. Payments are also dependent on the workers' employment classification. The significance of the payment is indicated in that they can amount to as much as DM2,760 per annum for A3 classification workers, or DM14,760 for B3 classification workers (the variable pay- ments could thus reach as much as 15% of the basic wage).

The structure of the Postleistungszulagen is designed to force managers to differentiate between workers, rank performance levels, and thus use these payments competitively. To achieve this objective it is decentralized in its operation, with practical decision-making power delegated to the workers' (or managers') immediate superior. Telekom's intent has been to use the Postleistungszulagen as a tool of decentralized management, to force local managers to increase contact with "their" workers, and thus to improve effective management as well as the performance of workers. Thus, a senior manager reported that "it is intended to be a tool for local business managers to reach business goals and so to help in management-by-objectives" now being introduced. This goal reflects the belief within Telekom that a principal weakness is in decentralized management capabilities, rather than foremost the productivity performance of technicians or clerical workers.

It follows from the managerial goal that the Postleistungszulagen is fundamentally an individually based system of payment for performance, which does not allow for team-based bonuses. Indeed, together with the absence of specified or objective criteria as to its operation, and the lack of any role for either the union or the works council (though they do receive monthly information), this forms the basis of the DPG's opposition to the program. Thus, both the DPG and works councils argue that this system will create competition between workers, undermine cooperative (and "team") work, and increase the authority of local managers. In spite of their concerns, in 1992 the DPG and Telekom extended it to *Arbeiter* and *Angestellte*. The purely "supplementary" nature of the payments led to membership pressure for its extension, though the DPG was unable to negotiate more transparency or objectivity.

Ironically, however, there is currently no evidence that the consequences feared by the DPG and works council have occurred. Local managers, members of the works council, and union stewards report that care is being taken not to create local antagonism in a period of substantial transition by using the performance-related pay system to shift power to management. In addition, a number of "informal" instructions have been issued by the *Generaldirektion* to local managers emphasizing that the fundamental reorganizations occurring require that a cooperative spirit be maintained wherever possible. Furthermore, the lack of objective criteria and the uncertainty surrounding the awarding of bonuses actually limits worker competition. Works councils also report that the secrecy surrounding the practical operation of the scheme has reduced both its effectiveness and any adverse effects on the workforce.

Two additional forms of bonus payment exist within Telekom—a flexible one-time payment is given to employees for specific contributions to performance or productivity, and a non-individually-based "Workplace Premium" is paid to compensate for adverse (or "hard") employment conditions (including high-pressure work such as telephone sales, customer service contact points, and new computer software configuration). Nevertheless, Telekom is most concerned to expand performance pay systems for senior managers, again reflecting their desire to move to a management-by-objectives approach, and their belief that this is where their principal weakness lies as they try to increasingly decentralize managerial decision making. Currently performance pay based on objectives is permitted for only about fifty senior managers, though it is utilized more fully in subsidiaries, and extending its use post-privatization is a key Telekom goal.

Training Structures

Although customer orientation, the availability of services, the utilization of computer systems and database management, and cost levels within Telekom indicate a low level of performance, the workforce enjoys extensive (and in comparative terms enviable) apprenticeship and further vocational training, and is highly skilled and technically competent. Determined in the first instance for *Beamte,* and extended to *Arbeiter* and *Angestellte,* the structure of training throughout the Deutsche Bundespost is subject to tight legal regulations, with the curriculum governed by the federal government, states, and social partners. Indeed, prior to 1990 training programs had to be ratified by the Interior Minister (which amounted to considerably more than a mere formality), and although Post Reform I yielded additional flexibility, ratification by the minister of Posts and Telecommunications is still required. Furthermore, changes to the apprenticeship programs for *Arbeiter* and *Angestellte* (though not *Beamte*) are subject to codetermination.

Apprenticeship training *(Ausbildung)* for technicians lasts for three or three and a half years of formal schooling, covering both theoretical and practical issues. Typically undertaken at one of the multiplicity of DBP institutions—which include two Fachhochschule (technical colleges), and over 100 vocational training offices—up to 70 percent of this training is generic, prerequisite training for all *Beamte,* and 30 percent specific to the demands of Telekom. The emphasis is thus clearly on general, rather than company-specific, human-capital development. Although training structures for *Arbeiter* and *Angestellte* exhibit greater specificity and flexibility, they also contain a high general component. Similarly, formal training for operators is high—normally three months long, compared with one or two weeks in the United States and United Kingdom—again with much of this generic to a range of clerical functions. The use of temporary operators in Telekom is also low, at approximately 5 percent, though it is expected to increase significantly. The DBP has also operated its own training institutions for both engineers and management, though Telekom recognizes its continuing weakness in the sphere of marketing, sales, and business administration skills.

Beginning in 1987, the emphasis has shifted somewhat to greater use of on-the-job vocational training, though less with a strategy of cost reduction than of enhancing effectiveness, flexibility, and quality. This is illustrated by a new training program introduced for customer service representatives *(Kaufmann/Kauffrau für Bürokommunikation)* introduced in 1992–93, which intersperses 40 percent formal and 60 percent closely supervised on-the-job training. Further vocational training *(Fortbildung)* for technicians within Telekom is also extensive, averaging three or four days per employee each year. Again, however, the emphasis is on technical, rather than commercial or consumer service, skills. Although Telekom is increasingly intent on introducing greater flexibility and commercial skills into programs, their strategy is not to deemphasize training. Given the legal determination of *Beamte* training, and codetermination rights for *Arbeiter* and *Angestellte,* this would be problematic, and indeed Telekom has extended the west German structure to the east. One notable problem, however, has concerned the structure of career ladders for *Beamte.* Because the possession of formal qualifications bears an intimate relationship to job assignment, the traditional emphasis on seniority in access to "promotional training" has limited both overall worker mobility, and the mobility of employees from one career ladder to another.

Corporate Reorganization

The status as a public administration necessitated that Telekom be organized with a three-tier structure—below the *Generaldirektion* were 23 *Direktionen,* and 123 *Ämte* or *Niederlassungen,* subject to extensive hierarchical and centralized regulations. The lack of local autonomy has been identified within Telekom as the principal deficit with the old organizational structure, manifested in poor cost control, comparatively low productivity, and insufficient attention to quality.

Consequently, a fundamental restructuring of the corporate organization—Telekom Kontakt—was initiated at the *Generaldirektion* level in 1993, and extended to 16 pilot regions in April 1994. Telekom Kontakt's objective is to reorganize the company into three divisions (to manage the network, business customers, and residential customers respectively), while decentralizing managerial competence, establishing cost and profit centers, and setting performance objectives against which branch offices are to be managed. The principal goal is to drive productivity up, while simultaneously ensuring high quality by redefining market segments to meet differentiated customer demand. However, cost control is also a central objective, and through transfer pricing Telekom Kontakt aims to institutionalize a conflict over internal costs, driving these down.

Through a decentralization Telekom Kontakt seeks to separate long-run strategic decisions, and short-run operational plans (these having previously been centralized and united). Competence is thus being shifted to branch offices *(Niederlassungen)*, which are to become the location of decision making, with significantly increased autonomy and flexibility. A divisionalization and decentralization is planned for sales, marketing, pricing, finance, controlling, and service organization, as well as network strategy, access line planning, trunk lines, and network services. The decentralization of such tasks, together with the specialization of the divisions, means that the principal direct effects of Telekom Kontakt are within middle management.

Telekom is thus pushing for a more proactive management style, while simultaneously granting new flexibility in personnel deployment, work organization, and both staffing ratios and numbers at the branch office level (though branch office managers do not expect such flexibility for three or four years in practice). Indeed, this shift is being supplemented by a "KQM" programme,[13] introduced during 1993, which likewise aims to significantly reduce the extent of regulations, while increasing internal measurement (and publication) of performance levels. What these changes do not establish, however, is what this new managerial style will be.

Nevertheless, two central characteristics of this reorganization are the pace it is being conducted, and the involvement of worker representatives. Pilot offices were begun in April 1994, and completion of the reorganization is not due until late 1996. The slow pace of change largely reflects the total absence of decentralized information and management systems required by the reorganization—not expected to be completed even for pilot regions until late 1995 or 1996. In addition, however, this pace of change reflects the centralized and consultative manner of institutionalizing this reorganization. Project teams developing the Telekom Kontakt concept have included members of the works council and union at every stage. Indeed, the strongest illustration of the influence of the union has concerned the contrasting notions of the optimal decentralized branch office structure.

One model envisaged *Niederlassungen* specialized according to the di-

13. Kunden Qualität Management, or Customer Quality Management, a derivation of a TQM program.

vision (network, business, or residential), with workers being account-able to different managers dependent upon their division; the alternative was that there should be a general regional office supplying the full range of services on a localized basis, with managerial structures separated only at the *Direktionen* level. That is, the contrasting models were for a strict divisional structure, and a "patch working" geographical structure. Tele-kom strongly favored the former (perceiving that this would lead to greater customer focus, while allowing for more flexibility according to the different divisional requirements), while the DPG promoted the latter (preferring geographically smaller branch offices, opposing the potential differentiation where workers in the same location have separate local managers, and being concerned that the new organizational structure would not be compatible with the union structure or preferred works council structure).[14] The DPG's influence is illustrated by Telekom simul-taneously testing both models, with established criteria concerning how the success of each should be judged. Although there was a bias in favor of the model preferred by management (which was finally adopted in July 1995, in spite of having performed marginally worse owing to the greater transition required) the process demonstrates the institutionalized strength of the union, while also indicating that the form and structure of decentralization and proactive management is not independent of em-ployee representatives.

Work Restructuring

The customer facing divisions are also involved in the Telekom Service 2000 program to reorganize the workforce (rather than managerial struc-tures) along a divisional basis. This is primarily a response to the digitali-zation of the network, the development of ISDN, and the realization that Telekom's functional organization inhibited a customer orientation. It consists, in the first place, of a concentration, consolidation, and ratio-nalization of such tasks as customer reception, diagnostics and dispatch, operator services, and network maintenance. The objective is to halve the number of departments, to reduce the customer facing workforce of 40,000 by 11,000 and to improve services to customers. To achieve this, TS2000 integrates tasks across functional boundaries. Additional work reorganization is occurring in the network division. The implications of

14. Although the former organizational structure is currently more "in favor" with international telecommunications companies (and the ubiquitous international manage-ment consultants), neither is obviously operationally superior. Thus, for example, BT is currently in the process of shifting its divisionalized structure to a patch-focused organiza-tion—an event which occurred after Telekom began its pilots.

these changes are not, however, uniform for all workers within each division, or across divisions.

The TS2000 reorganization has been characterized by a high degree of centralization and a relatively slow pace of change since its original conception in 1983–85. The original plan reflected Telekom's functional organization, and prior to 1990 pilot regions focused on improving efficiency within the existing structure. A strategic reorientation to increase the customer focus in 1990–91 laid the basis for the more extensive reform underway in earnest since 1992.[15] The extent of the centralization is, however, demonstrated by nearly 900 pages of TS2000 regulations, including the continued specification of single-digit employment levels. The degree of centralization and studied, slow reorganization reflects the continued impact of public-sector status, while the detailed program of reform has also been subject to intensive consultation and agreement with the central works council.

For office-based workers, TS2000 has its most immediate impact through the introduction of integrated computer systems (particularly the "ITS" system). This is leading to the concentration of much customer service, control, and dispatch work, and the replacement of a "paper flow" job process with computerized information flows. With index cards of customer data having been transferred to computer at the end of 1993, the computerized flow of job details between reception, diagnostics, control, and dispatch is significantly increasing the individualization of work. That is, preexisting informal networking structures are being removed (even where there is no change to office layout) because of the changed nature of the information flow. The opportunity for informal networking is reduced; there has been a reduction in interpersonal communication and an increase in the isolation of work. This effect is directly related to the computer system having initially been introduced into the existing functional work organization, and it is removing the benefit of having at least an informal understanding of different job tasks. Simultaneously, the rationalization and "concentration" of operational units is removing elements of local knowledge that facilitated the earlier networking structure.

Nevertheless, this shift represents an intermediate step in the reengineering. As Telekom further integrates its computer systems between

15. It is noteworthy that although both Telekom Service 2000 and Telekom Kontakt are premised on a divisionalized customer focus, they are organizationally separate. In particular, TS2000 predates Telekom Kontakt. The introduction of new (customer focused) working practices for employees, as implied by TS2000, does not require a divisional management structure, even though synergy exists.

1994 and 1996, tasks are due to be broadened such that there is "one face to the customer" service. That is, in at least 70 percent of cases it is planned to integrate reception, diagnostic, and control functions, while also initiating an automated dispatch system, and the initiation of the closing/billing procedures (which are also currently based on a "paper flow" system). With two departments—sales and service—and a single dispatch function, TS2000 implies a broadening of job tasks internally. This task integration (common in many other telecommunications companies) facilitates a reorganization of field technicians' work.

By integrating dispatch for both installation and repair, TS2000 facilitates the creation of a new, multiskilled employment group—the *Servicemonteur*. Thus, in 1994 the tasks of the *Service Techniker* (provision) and *Monteur* (repair) were merged, broadening the job and creating additional flexibility in the deployment of labor. Formal job processes have also been eased to give the technician flexibility to undertake "extra" jobs for customers, without the traditional public administration bureaucracy. These changes were promoted by the DPG, who were motivated by the desire to extend task breadth for technicians, rather than exercise job control, and simultaneously to upgrade the less skilled *Monteur* employment category and pay. For Telekom, this also facilitated synergy and flexibility in the field.

Work reorganization for field technicians has not, however, been a simple case of task broadening. Two factors counter this: First, prior to divisionalization service technicians could undertake work within both small businesses and residencies (the exception being specialist business equipment), a task variety that has now been eliminated—though this should not be exaggerated. Second, and more important, has been a conflicting (and complex) change owing to the introduction of new technology which has mechanized many skilled tasks, while also necessitating a working knowledge of a broader range of equipment.

The deskilling effect of new technology can be seen most clearly with new switches—whether they be business switches, or in exchanges. Diagnostic work is increasingly possible remotely, while manual intervention for either repair or preventative maintenance is being progressively removed. The strategy of remote monitoring is designed to improve response time and service quality, while also reducing the costs of having technicians undertake direct diagnostic work. In doing so, this strategy is leading to the increasing concentration of work in so-called *Betriebszentral,* a concentration that is expanding the (software) skill sets and investigative techniques required at this level. Where faults are present, a technician replaced a "card" (or microprocessor circuit) that is (remotely) identified as faulty. Skills are somewhat polarized, while separating control and execution of maintenance. Skilled monitoring work is now completed remotely, and the maintenance technician is then directed (and controlled) in the execution of the repair. With control and execution no longer united in the field technician there is a significant loss of autonomy and discretion in the field, which combines with the narrowing of tasks.

Nevertheless, the skills required of field technicians undertaking repair and maintenance of switches are being complicated by the proliferation of technology. Technicians in the networks division require competence in both digital and analog systems, while technicians in the business division face an increasing array of technology, for which they must possess at least the latent skills, should the initial (remote) diagnosis be incorrect. They are also becoming skilled in broader ranges of tasks, creating a potential dichotomy between latent and regularly utilized skill sets. This complexity is also present, though in a less stark form, for other field technicians. The increasing sophistication of the monitoring of cable pressurization, for example, significantly helps technicians to identify the location of leaks, reducing many of the skills previously used, as does the replacement of plug-in telephones, rather than ones that need wiring and repair. Nevertheless, the use of both copper and optic fiber creates additional variety of work, which has prevented a simple deskilling.

Meanwhile, new technology has led to the potentially increased monitoring of workers' performance levels. This monitoring has not, however, been utilized in any significant manner in Telekom for three reasons. First, as a monopoly Telekom has been largely insulated from those financial pressures promoting a speed-up strategy to improve performance. This was reinforced by being a public administration. Second, the basic exclusion of performance as a criteria by which *Beamte* can be judged reduces the potential of a speed-up strategy. There is currently no evidence that *Beamte* are less productive as a result, though the effective constraint on how Telekom seeks to motivate them encourages a strategy of high trust, especially among field technicians, where the daily mobility of the workers has long been characterized by a high degree of autonomy, individuality, and responsibility. Third, even insofar as Telekom does seek to intensify the pace of work, use of computer monitoring is significantly constrained by both public law and agreement with the DPG.

The DPG has been concerned by the introduction of new decentralized management systems, such as the DELKOS decentralized cost control system, and the DASPO personnel data and management system, which have the potential for increased workforce measurement. The central works council has utilized its codetermination rights concerning the introduction of technology capable of monitoring workers' behavior to ensure that such systems have been accompanied by *Dienstvereinbarungen* (agreements between the company and central works council) which limit the use of this data to achieve such an intensification of work. Beyond this, however, German data protection laws, and in particular the workplace data protection law, also restrict the use of computerized data to measure the performance of the work group, and generally prohibits its disaggregated use to monitor individual performance. Thus, where information on worker performance is directly recorded by computer its use is limited to assessing the work group. Again, while these factors do not determine Telekom's human resource strategy, the limitations imposed on alternative strategies helps to promote trust and a "responsible autonomy" approach.

There is, correspondingly, no evidence that new work organization is shifting in a manner to reduce the traditional "high discretion" system. Currently the managerial focus has been on the introduction of new systems and decentralized capabilities, rather than addressing additional work methods. Thus, although the high discretion system has thus far not evidently been restricted, neither is there evidence of innovative extensions to this system with examples of high performance work systems among customer service representatives or field technicians. Indeed, neither Telekom nor the DPG have clear strategies in this regard, though the DPG's strength and codetermination rights, and the status of employees, mitigates in favor of a continuation of the responsible autonomy approach.

Employment Rigidity and New Opportunities

Public-sector employment regulations are highly centralized, bureaucratic, formal, and orientated toward the completion of "sovereign tasks" rather than customer service. To circumvent these, Telekom has formed subsidiary companies to acquire additional flexibility, while its inability to adjust employment numbers was a principal rationale behind the desire for privatization.

Subsidiaries and Subcontracting

Subsidiary companies have been created with the strategic objective of increasing the flexibility of the use of human resources. Wholly-owned subsidiaries operating in Germany include DeTeMobile (mobile telephone, employing 4,000 at the end of 1994), DeTeSystem (management of corporate accounts; 600 employees), DeTeCSM (computer services; 240 employees), DeTeMedian (publications including white and yellow pages; 335 employees), DeTeBau (network planning and construction; 350 employees), DFKG (developing engineering and installation performance of network; 645 employees), DeTeBerkom (research and development of digital network systems and services; 50 employees). In addition, the decision to establish Multimedia Services GmbH was taken in December 1994, and from January 1995 the Atlas joint venture with France Télécom was planned to employ 3,000.

In spite of the substantial employment in these subsidiaries, Telekom's strategy must be contrasted with strategies aiming to directly reduce labor costs or create a two-tier employment structure. Telekom's strategy aims to remove the "chains" binding Telekom to the public sector, to escape government employment regulations (particularly concerning *Beamte*), and to avoid governmental financial and organizational constraints (such as having a three-tier organizational structure). The constraints on Telekom to reduce employment levels have, however, impelled it to use subsidiaries as an alternative employment outlet for core salaried staff,[16] though with more flexible employment conditions. An average 75 percent of employees in subsidiaries have voluntarily transferred to them.[17] Recruitment external to Telekom has been concentrated in skill sets such as sales, marketing, finance, and business management, where Telekom is internally weakest. The voluntary nature of the transfer means that if Telekom is to increase the flexibility of employees, it has to offer working conditions that are viewed by the workers as at least as good as those within Telekom itself. Thus, there is an effective constraint on the form of flexibility Telekom can seek, while necessitating higher compensation.

The introduction of closer connections with the labor market therefore aim at giving Telekom flexibility to pay higher wages (a flexibility absent with *Beamte* pay regulations), and include greater performance-related pay, with incentive structures centered on Telekom's management-by-ob-

16. The principal exception is DeTeBau, created in 1992 to undertake construction work in east Germany, and extended to west Germany in March 1993. Most employees were recruited from outside Telekom, with the aim of acquiring cheaper workers in the "free" labor market. DeTeCSM is also exceptional in that it was purchased from the Treuhandanstalt.

17. No *Beamte* are employed in subsidiaries. To voluntarily transfer to a subsidiary they must therefore take a temporary "holiday" from their *Beamte* status *(Beurlaub)*. If they decide to remain within the subsidiary beyond five years they lose their *Beamte* status, although up to that time they retain the right to return to being *Beamte*, and to transfer back into the core employment of Telekom.

jectives drive. The subsidiaries also make far greater use of individual contracts, are not being bound by *Laufbahn* (career ladder) regulations, and have greater flexibility (both weekly and over the year) in the use of (the lower) contracted hours.[18] Extensive use of *Betriebsvereinbarungen* (company agreements made with the subsidiary's works council, rather than a more rigid framework being negotiated with the union) are used for working time and many other details of working conditions. Although a framework agreement establishes common subsidiary pay groupings, actual pay levels are differentiated in each subsidiary. The DPG has also had to create separate contracts for the subsidiaries.

The subsidiaries do not threaten the institutional position of the DPG, since Telekom has conceded the obligation of all subsidiaries to bargain with the DPG. Nevertheless, bargaining is fragmented and decentralized, there is a reduction of direct union control, and the union admits to the subsidiaries having a "significantly lower" rate of unionization, which could affect the ability of the DPG to influence the details of the *Betriebsvereinbarungen*. Primarily, the subsidiaries indicate the desire for increased flexibility without lowering employment conditions. Telekom is likely to continue to expand the use of subsidiaries, creating further differentiation of working conditions, while the DPG's focus on the subsidiaries is also motivated by Telekom's use of the subsidiaries to experiment on conditions for the whole company, particularly with respect to establishing new wage group structures, and working time practices.[19]

As a public sector administration, Telekom has historically been required to use private subcontractors for 25 percent of its work. Much of this has been concentrated in lower skilled construction work (such as cabling or installation), though more highly skilled work, including the construction of new exchanges and installation of switches, has also traditionally been completed by external equipment suppliers, such as Siemens. Ironically, however, privatization and technological change are being associated with a reduction in the use of private subcontractors. As technology is displacing labor, the employment security enjoyed by the core workforce has meant that subcontractor use has been progressively lessened, implying a decreased emphasis on a dual labor market. The political constraint of displacing work undertaken by small companies has, furthermore, been eased by unification: The use of turn-key construction projects in east Germany (i.e., the multiple use of private con-

18. Contracted hours are 38 rather than 38.5, and although the form of compensation shows greater flexibility, actual pay levels are higher than within Telekom.

19. In this respect, however, Telekom will remain constrained by the existence of *Beamte* regulations which cannot be changed or circumvented within the core of the company.

tractors to build defined sections of the local network) has provided an alternative employment opportunity within Telekom for subcontracting work otherwise displaced in the west. Although the use of subcontractors has always been high, the political determination of this use (rather than it being the result of a strategy of externalization based on either cost or flexibility) has prevented it from becoming highly contentious, and in light of strong employment security the traditional extent of subcontracting will prove a positive benefit to Telekom in the process of employment adjustment. That is, reliance on the secondary labor market is being reduced not to respond to a cyclical burden, but rather a structural one.

Employment Stability and Reduction

The most notable feature of Telekom's employment record, in comparison to countries such as the United Kingdom and United States, is that there has been an upward trend over the past decade (Table 5.1). This trend is, however, less dramatic than is first apparent, owing to the effects of unification: In 1993 an average of 44,100 employees were employed in east Germany, and 187,100 in west Germany—reflecting a moderate employment reduction in the west, achieved through attrition, the transfer of workers to subsidiaries, and an average of over 4,000 "wessies" (west Germans) working in the east on "partnership" programs.

Despite the relative employment stability, technological changes (particularly digitalization) and rationalizations are substantially reducing staffing requirements. Consequently, and like other telcos, Telekom has begun a program of large scale employment reduction: In March 1995

TABLE 5.1. Employment

Year	Full time equivalents
1984	191,911
1985	196,306
1986	199,116
1987	202,524
1988	205,401
1989	206,156
1990	212,205
1991	225,279
1992	230,058
1993	231,344
1994	225,435

Source: Eurostrategies (1990) and company data. These figures exclude junior staff in training (of which there were 14,150 in 1994, though they are not guaranteed subsequent employment).

the goal of eliminating 30,000 jobs was officially doubled to 60,000 by the year 2000, with initial reductions being concentrated in the west given the continued efforts to construct the basic infrastructure in the east. Although successfully managing this reduction is a top priority for management, Telekom faces significant constraints, not least since maintaining employment security for all employees is the primary strategic objective of the powerful DPG, their opposition to unrestrained employment reduction is fundamental, and their threat of industrial action real.

The works councils' and DPG's position is strengthened by legal restrictions on collective redundancies in Germany. Although the Protection Against Dismissals Act (Kuñdigungsschutz) allows redundancies for economic reasons such as the introduction of new technology and rationalizations, the works councils must be provided with full information about why and how company plans are leading to layoffs and possible alternative plans, while management must also reach a "compromise of interests" on how their plans are to be carried out. Furthermore, codetermination exists in the development of a "social plan" (selecting those whose jobs are eliminated, and including compensation and retraining programs). In the case of Telekom, however, these legal provisions of codetermination are less a prohibition against dismissal than a procedural hindrance that can increase the union bargaining position.

Nevertheless, the ability of Telekom management to reduce staffing levels is constrained significantly beyond the normal German legal limitations by additional worker's employment rights—both the legal rights of *Beamte,* and the contractual rights of *Arbeiter* and *Angestellte* over the age of forty with fifteen years of service, to employment security. Indeed, these constraints were themselves exacerbated by political forces while Telekom was a public administration.

The weakness of the labor market made large-scale redundancies from a public administration politically unacceptable, while fiscal constraints at both federal and *Länder* levels have led to pressure to increase the working time of *Beamte* (such as in Bavaria) and hold back their wages, and not supplement the (publicly resented) employment security of *Beamte* through lucrative voluntary early retirement schemes. The political ramifications perceived by the Minister of the Interior have been such that, in the words of a senior manager, "they won't even let us talk about it," though Telekom (privately) pushed strongly for this flexibility. Thus, the interdependence of Telekom's *Beamte* on other civil servants has been of crucial importance in determining its adjustment possibilities. The perceived unavoidability of employment reductions and the need to remove this constraint was a foremost human resource consideration in privatization. Although the privatization act does not alter the employment security of workers,[20] it does permit voluntary retirement for *Beamte* at the age of fifty-five or sixty depending on career level, while similar (and additional) schemes can be negotiated for *Arbeiter* and *Angestellte*. Telekom's age structure limits the effectiveness of early retirement, since only 5.5 percent of employees are over fifty-five, and 12.2 percent over fifty. Indeed, 64.2 percent of Telekom employees are forty and under. Nevertheless, privatization has removed a substantial political barrier to employment reduction.

The constraints employment security and DPG strategy impose on Telekom are having significant effects on both human resource and corporate strategies. Telekom is curtailing recruitment (in 1995 employing only 600 of 5,700 apprentices, while offering DM15,000 per apprentice to companies offering them employment); actively retraining workers for new nontechnical, commercial, customer orientated posts; encouraging workers to transfer to part-time status; and continuing to staff subsidiaries primarily through the transfer of employees. Given that early retirement and increased part-time status are expected to reduce employment by no more than 10,000 jobs, Telekom's strategy (strongly and actively promoted by the DPG) is to seek new employment opportunities, and concentrate on revenue per employee as the basic performance measure, not lines per employee. Indeed, an objective of DM80 billion (or DM470,000 per employee) has been set, indicating the nature of Telekom's underlying strategy. That is, although Telekom has a high cost base (resulting partially from its employment of *Beamte*, but also from its high level of debt, and the high cost of its network) institutionalized industrial relations constraints are diverting it from a simple cost reduction strategy, and are promoting a revenue enhancement strategy. The impact of industrial relations on business strategy is in turn facilitated by the favorable regulatory environment, and the absence of countervailing financial market pressures. Employment and cost reductions remain critical, though not the principal focus of Telekom.

Joint ventures, such as those utilizing Telekom's ISDN and cable TV networks for multimedia services, are being supplemented by others with

20. Telekom wanted privatization to include a cancellation of all existing contracts, such that they could then be renegotiated. Without this there is a de facto protection against a weakening of the contract even if Telekom were to cancel it, since under German labor law its provisions would continue to apply until the negotiation of a new agreement. Telekom was unsuccessful in this goal. Indeed, the political pressure exerted by the DPG, together with warning strikes, led to the extension of the contractual employment security provisions enjoyed by *Arbeiter* and *Angestellte* (of no layoffs after age 40 with 15 years service) to eastern Germany.

such companies as Compaq, Cannon, Fabis, and IBM. New schemes generally seek to utilize the ubiquitous presence of Telekom's technicians to provide on-site service, in addition to remote hardware refurbishment. Telekom's corporate strategy is thus that as other companies outsource activities, it can then increase the services (such as third-party maintenance) offered. The DPG is not only constraining employment reduction by Telekom, but developing new employment strategies, such as with extensive proposals concerning the use of operators as their employment numbers are reduced. Indeed, by mid-1995 the DPG had presented Telekom with in excess of fifty proposals for generating new business to enhance employment security—proposals taken seriously by the company. It is noteworthy, however, that the DPG and central works councils do not believe that a multimedia strategy will safeguard long-term employment within Telekom (van Haaren and Hensche 1995), which adds to their concern about the appropriate strategic adjustment path for Telekom.

For the DPG, the extensive nature of rationalizations brought about by digitalization increases their power with respect to short-term employment protection. The rights of the works councils with respect to the introduction of new technology and rationalizations, the regrading of employees, transfers, and appointments requires that Telekom work cooperatively with the union. Indeed, between June 1993 and March 1994 the DPG negotiated a unique contract in light of the 11,000 posts being eliminated by the TS2000 reorganization, which clearly illustrated both the DPG's strategy and power. This contract guaranteed all workers employment security, while also specifying compensation for those required to travel longer, or otherwise affected by the TS2000 rationalization plan. In late 1994 the DPG was able to extend this, in negotiations over the Focus '98 strategy (which includes the Telekom Kontakt reorganization), to all workers, thereby guaranteeing comprehensive employment security until the end of June 1996.

In November 1995 Telekom finally reached an agreement on downsizing with the DPG. The core of the agreement was the combination of a very generous early retirement program with voluntary redundancy bonuses of between DM80–100,000 for any worker with at least two years service. Furthermore, and in spite of the fact that technology is the principal source of downsizing, the agreement seeks to protect all workers displaced by the digitalization of the network by requiring that they must be offered an alternative job. There will be no involuntary redundancies until at least 1998.

Although Telekom has devised this very attractive package, dilemmas remain. First, and critically, many operational areas where employment reductions are anticipated (especially amongst technicians) are overwhelmingly dominated by *Beamte*. However, voluntary redundancy packages are primarily directed to *Arbeiter* and *Angestellte*, who comprise only half the workforce (and indeed less in west Germany, where some 62 percent of employees are *Beamte*, there being almost none in east Germany). Political constraints remain with respect to *Beamte* receiving offers, and while they can renounce their *Beamte* status, they then lose their lifetime employment security in a volatile labor market. Second, layoffs among younger workers (who do not yet have contractual employment security and for whom the redundancy offer is most generous) would impact upon those who frequently possess skill sets applicable to newer digital technology. Third, the DPG remains a powerful influence, determined to protect employees even at the expense of a slower deployment of new technology or rationalizations. The costs of a potential conflict are so substantial that Telekom must utilize all strategies to redeploy labor productively and cooperatively. Thus, although substantial downsizing is now taking place, it is the search for cooperative solutions, and emphasis on revenue generation, that characterizes Telekom's adjustment strategy—whether ultimately successful or not.

Employee Representation and Incrementalism

Employee representation in Telekom is strong and highly institutionalized, with a 90 percent unionization rate among employees (management and nonmanagement), and works councils that are dominated by the DPG (which holds some 92% of seats).[21] The strength of the DPG has been reinforced by its unusual structure in Germany as a largely single-company union, with membership confined to the three Deutsche Bundespost companies. This facilitates the DPG focusing more closely on Telekom, and having a closer interaction with the works councils. Both the DPG's and the works councils' position was reinforced by Telekom's public-sector status, and the constitutional requirement that it include "social considerations" as part of its goals.

Unions, Works Councils, and Bargaining

The two voices of employee representation, unions and works councils, have extremely close institutional ties inside Telekom, while the cen-

21. The DPG represents some 80% of employees, and is clearly the dominant union. In addition, however, the Deutsche Postverband and the Chrisliche Gewerkschaft Post represent Telekom employees.

tral works council's practice of information and consultation has long exceeded that legislatively determined. The duality of Telekom's employment structure has, however, had a significant effect on the framework of employee representation—through the absence of collective bargaining rights for *Beamte,* and the impact of public sector status on the structure of bargaining for *Arbeiter* and *Angestellte.* The pre- and post-privatization works council structures also exhibit important differences.[22]

Post Reform I in 1989 resulted in a change in bargaining competence, such that the Management Board of Telekom obtained the right to conclude independent collective agreements with the DPG, in place of the Minister of Posts and Telecommunications. In practice, however, this right was constrained prior to privatization by the Minister of the Interior's right to approve pay *(Lohntarifvertrag)* or working condition *(Manteltarifvertrag)* agreements insofar as they are of "fundamental importance" to the rest of the public sector—a linkage that was held to be ever present. Thus, Telekom's negotiations have been conducted in parallel with the those of the whole public sector (in a *Tarifgemeinschaft öffentliche Dienst*). Since these negotiations are led by ÖTV, the public-sector union, both Telekom and the DPG were significantly constrained in their ability to establish their own bargaining agendas. Furthermore, wages set in these negotiations, or through the Federal Remuneration Act for *Beamte,* were not taken out of competition, since Telekom is not competing for labor with those in the more administratively orientated, labor-intensive, low-technology public sector. This has led to overpayment for certain skill sets, and recruitment difficulties for others, and though some flexibility existed (for example, through the grading of technical jobs specific to Telekom,[23] and through negotiations which apply to specific conditions at Telekom, such as the TS2000 and Focus '98 reorganizations) it was limited.

Significant changes to this bargaining structure are underway: Privatization removed Telekom from the public sector negotiations for *Arbeiter* and *Angestellte,* separated bargaining between the three DBP companies, and with the expansion in the use of subsidiary companies is leading to a greater fragmentation of bargaining, which the DPG is seeking to minimize. During the privatization debate, the DPG pushed to ensure that bargaining would subsequently be conducted for the three Deutsche Bundespost companies together through the newly established holding

22. For more details, see Darbishire 1995.
23. Thus, for example, Telekom has two more wage groups than the rest of the public sector.

company, given its long-standing goal to maintain uniformity of conditions within these three companies. Although this will apply for working conditions *(Manteltarifverträge)* it will not for wages, so that pay bargaining will be at the company level, rather than throughout the DBP. However, with *Beamte* continuing to have their wages and conditions set by parliament (which is in turn closely linked to the results of the ÖTV-led public-sector negotiations) there will be a complication to the wage structure.[24]

Indeed, although the DPG strongly opposed privatization, it argued that if it was to occur *Beamte* should be given collective bargaining rights—a long-standing goal, which they were unable to realise. More generally, the DPG's opposition to privatization was founded in their fear that it would not only threaten their significant institutional position, strength, and influence, but would also threaten employment security, lead to deteriorating employment conditions, and reduce the emphasis on the infrastructure and universal service. Thus, although they accepted the need to grant greater managerial independence from political influence, they wanted this to occur within the confines of a public-sector body *("Anstalt des öffentlichen Rechts")*.

The extent of political pressure mounted by the DPG (including 30 days of industrial action involving 100,000 DPG members in May-June 1994) illustrated the strength of this opposition to privatization. Although it did not achieve its ultimate aim, the DPG was successful in strengthening its institutionalized position by securing the duty of the Deutsche Bundespost companies and any subsidiaries to bargain with the DPG, it obtained equal employee representation on the Supervisory Board, established a staff committee (headed by a workers' representative) responsible for the personnel matters of the Management Board, ensured the continuation of all existing contracts and "social institutions and services" run by the DBP, committed the DBP companies to apply equal conditions to all new workers (preventing a two-tier employment structure as has occurred in the Bundesbahn), extended contract conditions (including employment security at the age of 40 with 15 years of service) to *Arbeiter* and *Angestellte* in eastern Germany, and set a limit for the equalization of wages in eastern and western Germany as paralleling the public sector.

24. The extension of these public-sector negotiations to *Beamte* is usual, though not necessary. Thus, for example, in 1984 and 1994 the government did not extend the pay increase to *Beamte* owing to budgetary pressures, while in 1993 there was a delayed implementation (of 1 May, rather than 1 January).

Privatization has also changed the basis of the works council structure from the Bundespersonalvertretungsgesetz (Federal Staff Representation Act) to the Betriebsverfassungsgesetz (Works Constitution Act). Although both acts provide essentially the same codetermination, consultation, and information rights, the change leads most fundamentally to a shift from a three-tier, hierarchical, and centralized structure, to a two-tier, nonhierarchical, decentralized structure (Darbishire 1995). As such, it is challenging the union to increase the coordination not only between the central works council and workplace works councils, but also between the workplace works councils themselves—there being no automatic coordination in the decentralized private-sector works council structure. The difficulties for the union are being compounded by the divisionalization of the company, which Telekom has demanded should in turn lead to a divisionalization of the works council structure.

The response of the DPG to this fragmentation is threefold: First, it has utilized its institutionalized strength to promote both a different organizational structure and works council structure. Significantly this included negotiating, during the privatization debate, an extension of the three-tier works council structure until June 1997, and an increase in the number of works councilors released from work duties—which are nearly twice as high in the public sector. Second, the DPG is building new coordinating structures between works councils, utilizing its (almost unique) contractual provision assuring the institutionalization of union stewards *(Vertrauensleute),* enabling them to hold meetings, elections, and other activities on company facilities. Third, the DPG is maintaining its traditional degree of central control, which minimizes the use of company agreements made with the works council, preferring the greater legal protection contained in union contracts (such that there are only five recent examples of important company level agreements, covering DASPO, DELKOS, working time, representation structures in the newly divisionalized company, and transfers between divisions when employment reductions are occurring). The company-focused structure of the DPG facilitates this strategy, and in light of the potential increase in fragmentation of the new works council structure, the DPG is intent on retaining this higher than normal degree of centralization (Darbishire 1995).

Beyond this coordinating role, the DPG has prioritized its strategic goals until 1998 as securing job prospects through "competence, concepts, and initiatives" of the DPG. That is, ensuring employment security in response to the Focus '98 program of organizational changes, to secure improvements in working conditions, and to use its influence to produce (with Telekom) the development of new revenue-enhancing services and products. The DPG (and correspondingly the works councils) are thus a central (and powerful) force driving Telekom management to adopt a strategy based on revenue generation, not cost reduction, while it will continue to seek to secure further agreements on the model of the TS2000 and Focus '98 contracts guaranteeing employment security during the duration of customer oriented work reorganization and rationalization. Indeed, for the DPG the goal of employment security precedes that of a rapid technological or commercial transition.

Incrementalism Reconsidered

A central feature of Telekom's adjustment path has, as argued earlier, been that of building on existing skills and organizational structures, while simultaneously undertaking considered, closely negotiated, and cautious reform. By balancing the diverging interests of management and employees, existing institutional arrangements, which confer significant substantive and procedural rights on workers' representatives, have significantly influenced the strategy Telekom has adopted. The evidence is thus clearly consistent with what Kathleen Thelen (1991) identifies as "negotiated adjustment" and Peter Katzenstein (1989) as "institutional adaptation." Both Katzenstein and Thelen identify this process as an important source of economic advantage. Changes occur in business strategy and work organization, though the requirement to bargain this change leads to more incremental, progressive, and considered change. There is a reduction in risk and uncertainty, while a consensual approach to implementing change promotes its acceptance and effectiveness.

Incrementalism is clearly evident within Telekom's reorganization. However, an important element of German incrementalism is clarified through Telekom, namely that its success in helping firms adapt to changing market circumstances is founded on the ability to make minor, but progressive, adjustments to existing strategy and work organization. New technology is accepted and implemented because it threatens neither the institutionalization of workers' representation, nor the basic interests of workers (particularly skilled workers). Indeed, in traditional manufacturing industries, where skilled workers also dominate the union decision-making process, bargained changes in work organization have typically built incrementally upon existing craft skills and craft work organization.

For Telekom, however, a more fundamental break is occurring in strategy, and the organization of work, with an adaptation from a bureaucratic, public service, technologically focused company, to being commercially and consumer driven, and with a shift from a universal service requirement (characterized by mass production of simple dial tone) to a significantly differentiated market. Similarly this strategic reorientation, and the nature of the new technology in telecommunications, implies a radical reevaluation of previous craft skills (that German unions have long protected) and functional organizational barriers. The careful and highly detailed process of negotiation of work organization and corporate structure, together with the corresponding implications for Telekom's business strategy, has not challenged the preexisting balance between workers and business. Nevertheless, the process of incrementalism has limited the extent of innovation in Telekom, and the speed of the transformation to a service orientation. Similarly, by avoiding challenging existing skills, Telekom has been slow to develop new (particularly commercial) skills, to exploit digital technology, or to move rapidly to a service orientation.

Similarly, the centralized process through which new work organization has been negotiated has retarded the development of local competencies, either in management or works councils. Instead, negotiations occur between competing models of work organization or organizational structure. This does not prevent carefully coordinated, centrally directed experiments (as with Telekom Kontakt, and Telekom Service 2000), though it has both slowed and reduced the potential for innovative localized experimentation, and the progressive development of alternative work systems, such as self-directed teams that have been experimented with in America and Britain. Although Telekom is thus aiming to decentralize, centralized structures and competencies have yet to be fundamentally challenged. While this deficit does not simply explain Telekom's poor performance record, it has retarded steps to improve it.

Conclusion

There is little doubt that a radical transformation of the operating environment and strategic orientation of Telekom is underway. The direction of Telekom's new strategy has been heavily influenced by the extent of employment restrictions, union and employee influence, and the absence of external regulatory constraints. Indeed, the strength of existing industrial relations institutions has evidently influenced corporate strategy. This underlines the characteristic of mutuality in Telekom—a bargained change that accepts the institutionalized position of stakeholders, and that is striving to achieve a mutually acceptable path within the constraints the stakeholders' positions impose. Mutuality thus reflects far more than a compromise of interests. More important, it involves constraints on managerial strategic choices, which illustrate that strong institutions of worker representation are critical to understanding not simply employee relations strategies, but also business strategies.

Employment adjustment, and the use of both subsidiaries and subcontracting, show that Telekom's path is neither one of tactical adjustment centering on short-term cost cutting nor a price-centered strategy focusing on work intensification. Rather, the strategic goal is directed as utilizing the potential of new technology to generate new revenue and competitive opportunities over the longer term. The combination of strong employee rights and union influence is thus driving the "up-market" strategy developing high quality multimedia services. That is, the strategy aims not only at providing advanced services in the high-value business market, but also in the lower value residential market that could otherwise become a price sensitive "commodity" market subject to work intensification and deskilling once competition develops.

Nevertheless, despite this "up-market" strategy, Telekom remains a late developer where the process of change is subject to extensive consultation, but service levels are low, and change excessively centralized and slow. The slow pace of reform is not simply a result of emphasizing the need for careful adjustment to avoid a detrimental impact on workforce morale, or to promote skills development to ensure that labor can be used as a "strategic asset" for the longer term benefit. Rather, it also reflects the absence of decentralized capabilities, an inability to have local experimentation, the impact of the public sector, and the need for consensus in the reform process. Indeed, Telekom is only now beginning to make fundamental changes to its work structure, and their high quality strategy thus far still emphasizes the "product" as much as customer focused service. Although the institutionalized worker voice has promoted the choice of an up-market strategy, the incrementalism inherent in decision-making structures has also constrained the speed and innovativeness of that change.

The difficulties in the reorganizations are illustrated by Telekom Kontakt, TS2000, and adjusting employment levels. On the one hand Telekom benefits by the ability to learn from the reengineering experiences of other telecommunications companies. However, the excessive centralization inherent in operating as a public-sector administration, the high degree of regulation, and the infrastructural orientation have resulted in a deficit in managerial capabilities more than in workforce skills. The challenge for the company and the union is to develop new structures that decentralize capabilities and competence, enhance performance and customer orientation, while simultaneously securing the institutionalized position of each stakeholder. It is this difficulty that is leading both sides to regulate very carefully how the reforms occur, ironically resulting in highly centralized and detailed regulations designed to decentralize competence. Thus, for example, debate surrounding the Telekom Kontakt program is concerned less with the need for decentralization than the form of that decentralization—with the DPG concerned about the institutionalization of its influence and the potential to manage diversity in a divisionalized company structure.

This does not, however, imply that the DPG, the works councils, or Telekom are motivated by the desire to inhibit change, but rather to influence the impact, form, and pace of that change. Consequently, the reform process is characterized by the active development and promotion of strategic choices not only by the company, but also by employee representatives. That is, both are taking proactive stances in the reorganization, and are bargaining over what is to be adopted, even within the context of a mutual agreement that the required approach is an upmarket one. Even though this approach has thus far demonstrated limitations, it retains a potentially significant advantage—successful, embedded implementation of new work organization. An important trade-off between speed and innovativeness on the one hand, and implementation on the other, could be demonstrated in this case.

Furthermore, the potential for the continued strength of both parties and performance adjustment is present. Thus far, although the union position has remained strongly institutionalized, and employees have retained good working conditions and employment security, the lingering effect of other stakeholders (in particular the government and equipment suppliers) has adversely impacted on Telekom's financial and operational performance, with poor service for consumers. The realization of higher quality service in both network capability and work organization, while retaining the imperative of mutuality, is the central (or decentralized) challenge for Telekom. The beneficial regulatory framework indicates the potential for success, though fundamental adjustment is still necessary.

Chapter 6

Japan

Keisuke Nakamura and Shin'o Hiraki

In April 1985 all legally approved monopolies in all fields of the telecommunications industry in Japan were abolished.[1] Accordingly, Nippon Telegraph and Telephone Public Corporation (NTTPC), which had monopolized domestic telecommunication services, was privatized as Nippon Telegraph and Telephone Corporation (NTT). This was done without breaking the company up into separate long distance and regional service companies. At the same time, Kokusai Denshin Denwa Co., Ltd. (KDD) was also exposed to competition in the field of international telecommunications services.

Since privatization, the work practices at NTT have drastically changed from rigid and legalistic ones to practices that are flexible and thereby more typically Japanese. This transformation seems to have proceeded smoothly without any serious conflicts, although a massive reduction in employment has occurred. It is our view that this transformation

1. Our research has been supported by the Japan Institute of Labor in many aspects including financial support. We would like to express our appreciation to Akira Takanashi (General Director of Research, the Japan Institute of Labor), to Atsushi Yashiro (Researcher, the Japan Institute of Labor), and to Michio Nitta (Professor, Social Institute of Science, University of Tokyo) for their invaluable advice and support. We would like to thank Kumiko Ogino (staff of the Japan Institute of Labor) for her devoted research assistance. Finally, we would like to express our gratitude to all the managers, unionists, and employees at NTT who kindly participated in interviews.

has been brought about partly by the strategic choice of the trade union. In the past an arms'-length relationship prevailed between the union that represented employees at NTTPC and NTTPC management, and the union had been reluctant to participate in managerial decision making. Since the late 1970s, however, the union at NTTPC gradually changed its strategy so as to participate actively in managerial decision making in order to ensure employment security for union members and to improve their working conditions in the midst of a radically changing environment. The Japanese Telecommunication Workers Union (JTWU), which represents almost 100 percent of the eligible employees including assistant section managers in NTT, has maintained a cooperative relationship with management at NTT, and in the process the union has greatly influenced the changes in work practices occurring at NTT.

The first section of this chapter describes the evolution of the telecommunications industry in Japan, with a particular focus on NTT. Then we describe the union's commitment to the reform of NTTPC before privatization. The third section describes the transformation of work practices at NTT and analyzes the role played by union policies. This chapter is based on extensive field work in the Industrial Relations Department of NTT and the JTWU headquarters, at a central network center in the Long Distance Communications Department of NTT and the respective union branch office, and at a branch office of the Regional Communications Department and its respective union branch office.

Public Policy and Economic Environment

The objectives of the reform of NTTPC were to enhance development of the telecommunications market and to reduce customer charges. Improving the business performance of both NTT and KDD was another important goal.

As indicated by Table 6.1, new entrants have joined many sectors of the telecommunications services industry since 1985. As of 1994 there were 111 Type I carriers and 1,995 Type II carriers. The Type I and Type II classifications were introduced in the Telecommunication Business Law enacted at the time of the reform. Type I carriers are companies which offer telecommunications services over their own networks and facilities; these firms are subject to regulation by the Ministry of Posts and Telecommunications (MPT) which regulates quite a few aspects of business activity. Telecommunications service providers other than Type I carriers are defined as Type II carriers, which in practice provide services over networks and facilities leased from Type I carriers. The regulatory envi-

TABLE 6.1. Number of Telecommunication carriers

	1985	1986	1987	1988	1989	1990	1991	1992	1993	1994
Type I Carriers										
Domestic										
NTT	1	1	1	1	1	1	1	1	1	1
Long distance	3	3	3	3	3	3	3	3	3	3
Regional	—	3	4	4	7	7	7	8	10	11
Satellite	2	2	2	2	2	2	3	3	2	2
Mobile telephones[a]	—	—	3	5	13	16	17	26	36	60
Paging	—	2	18	26	33	36	36	36	31	31
Overseas										
KDD	1	1	1	1	1	1	1	1	1	1
New entrants	—	—	2	2	2	2	2	2	2	2
Type II Carriers										
Special	9	10	18	25	28	31	36	36	39	44
			(10)[b]	(12)	(15)	(19)	(24)	(25)	(27)	(31)
General	200	338	512	668	813	912	1,000	1,143	1,550	2,107

Source: Ministry of Posts and Telecommunications, 1991, 1994, 1995a, 1995b.

[a]The figure for carriers for domestic mobile telephones after 1992 includes NTT Docomo and its regional subsidiaries, which offer mobile services. Carriers for mobile telephones include carriers for marine telephones, simple on-shore mobile telephones, and digital data transmissions.

[b]Figures in (parentheses) for Special Type II carriers are the number for Type II carriers for overseas services.

ronment facing Type II carriers is far less restrictive than that facing Type I carriers.

The total sales of domestic and international services by Type I carriers rose from ¥5,145.7 billion (U.S. $51 billion) in 1985 to ¥7,327.8 billion (U.S. $73 billion) in 1993, for an average annual increase of 4.52 percent. Table 6.2 shows the sales of major telecommunication services from 1987 to 1993. These figures demonstrate that sales grew for all types of service and that growth rates varied considerably, with mobile phones experiencing the highest growth followed by leased line services and paging, while growth in conventional telephone services was considerably lower. As a result, sales of telephone services declined from 89.9 percent to 72.0 percent of total sales. On the whole these figures indicate that market growth and the introduction of new products, which were the objectives of reform, have occurred.

How was the second objective—price reduction as a consequence of competition—attained? Table 6.3 shows the considerable decline that has occurred since 1985 in the cost of a standard long distance telephone call placed with either NTT or other Type I carriers (new common carriers; NCCs). Although not included in the table, other charges including those for leased lines and mobile communications also dropped during this period. The figures in this table also illustrate the price differences that exist between NTT and NCCs, a topic discussed later in this chapter.

Evidence regarding the degree to which the third objective—improving management efficiency—was achieved is provided in Figure 6.1, which traces productivity growth at NTT. The rate of change in NTT's total factor productivity was far greater in the post-reform period (1983–1991) than it was in the previous period (1977–1982). Labor productivity recorded particularly dramatic improvement after 1983 (Oniki, Oum, and Stevenson 1993; Ito and Imagawa 1993).[2]

One structural characteristic of Japan's telecommunication services industry is that a relatively large number of companies offer domestic services, and these companies specialize in one type of service or operate in one particular region (Matsuura 1994). As indicated by Table 6.1, there are many companies active in long distance, regional, satellite, and mobile telecommunications markets. Markets for ordinary and mobile telecommunications are subdivided by regions. NTT is an exceptional carrier in that it provides numerous categories of service including long

2. "Total Factor Productivity" means, in brief, an index indicating the comprehensive efficiency of input of labor, capital, and raw materials (Oniki, Oum, and Stevenson 1993: 174–78).

TABLE 6.2. Sales of major telecommunication services (in hundred million Yen)

	1987	1988	1989	1991	1992	1993	Growth	Share	
							(%)	1987	1993
Telephone	42,025	45,995	47,436	49,400	49,687	50,387	11.9	83.9	72.0
Leased lines	3,016	3,578	3,990	4,644	6,299	5,263	74.5	5.6	7.5
Mobile telephone	530	844	1,356	3,397	4,665	6,080	1047.2	1.0	8.7
Paging	944	1,073	1,160	1,506	1,788	2,184	131.4	1.8	3.1

Source: Ministry of Posts and Telecommunications, 1991, 1994, and 1995a.
Note: Leased line service includes general leased lines, high-speed digital leased lines, image transfer services, video relay services, etc.

TABLE 6.3. Charge for a standard long distance telephone call (three minutes, daytime, between Tokyo and Osaka, in yen)

	1985	1986	1987	1988	1989	1990	1991	1992	1993	1994
NTT	400	400	400	360	330	280	240	200	180	180
NCC	—	—	—	300	280	240	200	180	170	170

Source: Ministry of Posts and Telecommunications, 1993 and 1994.

FIGURE 6.1. Productivity Growth at NTT (in percentages)

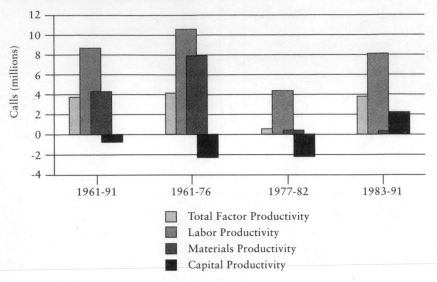

Source: Oniki, Oum, and Stevenson 1993: 181.

distance, regional, and satellite telecommunications. No carrier provides both domestic and international services; the "NTT Law" prohibits NTT from offering international services and the "KDD Law" prohibits KDD from offering domestic services.

Despite the presence of a large number of companies in the market, NTT remains the dominant player, as indicated by the numbers in Table 6.4. The trend since 1987, however, has been a steady decline in NTT's market share for all types of services. Even in the market for domestic telephone services, NTT is losing market share for long distance calls due to competition from NCCs although NTT does still dominate regional

TABLE 6.4. NTT's market share of major telecommunication services as a percentage of sales (in yen)

	1987	1988	1989	1990	1991	1992	1993
Telephones	99.7	98.5	96.9	95.3	93.5	92.1	89.9
Leased Lines	97.9	96.9	93.2	89.0	86.4	86.0	83.9
Mobile Telephones	100.0	99.5	89.1	71.3	64.2	63.1	63.7
Paging	98.8	88.0	77.7	70.8	67.7	65.5	64.5

Source: Ministry of Posts and Telecommunications, 1991, 1994, and 1995a.
Note: Figure after 1992 includes those for NTT Docomo and its regional subsidiaries which were separated.

telephone service (see Figure 6.2).[3] In the market for international telecommunications services, there are two new carriers other than KDD.
KDD has still dominated the market as shown by the fact that it has a
70.5 percent share of international telephone services in 1993, but its
market share has been falling off from the complete monopoly it held in
1988 (Ministry of Posts and Telecommunications, 1995a).

Regulation

A number of laws govern the business activities of Type I carriers. The
Telecommunication Business Law controls entry into and withdrawal
from the market in order to control overall supply and demand relations.
Toward this end the law stipulates that a company intending to enter
the market must apply for approval by the MPT for each category of
telecommunications service it intends to provide, such as long distance
or regional telecommunications. Companies wishing to withdraw from
the market must also seek the minister's approval.

The "NTT Law" controls the business activities of NTT. Article 1 of
the NTT Law defines NTT as a corporation that performs domestic telecommunications business, and prohibits the company from offering international services or manufacturing telecommunications equipment.

FIGURE 6.2. Market share for long distance calls

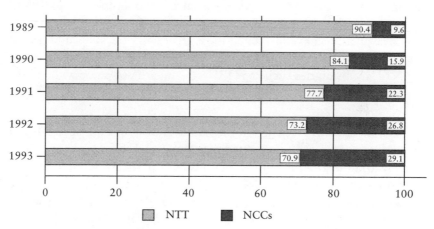

Source: NTT 1993, and Ministry of Posts and Telecommunications 1995b.
Note: Market share (percentage) in terms of the number of telephone calls.

3. Only one enterprise other than NTT is active in regional telephone service. It served
528 companies as of 1993 (*Joho Tsushin Sogo Kenkyusho* 1994: 208).

Article 2 of the NTT Law obliges the company to offer universal service, and to conduct research and development on telecommunications technology and to diffuse the results of these activities.

Furthermore, NTT's charges are regulated. Paragraph 1 of Article 31 of the Telecommunication Business Law obliges carriers to obtain MPT approval for service conditions including charges. This provision on charges has been the most controversial among the various regulations imposed on the telecommunications industry.

Before NTT was privatized, prices for long distance calls were set far above cost, with the surplus used to subsidize regional services, which were priced below cost. This practice is known as internal cross-subsidization and it was continued after NTTPC was privatized (Nagai 1994). NTT has been requesting price rebalancing but the MPT has in nearly all cases refused these requests. NTT's internal cross-subsidization has helped NCCs compete in offering long distance calls and other services, and the price differential between NTT and NCCs (maintained intentionally by government policy) has protected the NCCs. Thus NTT is in a difficult situation because it has not been permitted to rebalance long distance and connection charges and is obliged to supply universal service. The company was permitted to collect access charges for the first time in 1994, but the government refused NTT's request to charge for the installment and maintenance of local telephone lines (Kojo 1994). Thus the problem of price rebalancing remains unsolved. These policy-driven regulations have facilitated the market entry of NCCs and helped them to increase their market shares.[4] Furthermore, most NCCs excluding NTT's subsidiaries such as NTT Docomo, are not unionized.

Technology

As Table 6.5 shows, in Japan the numbers of both high-speed digital leased line services and integrated digital network services have grown steadily and the growth of the latter has been particularly rapid. NTT's long distance switches were 94 percent digital, and local switches were 72 percent digital, as of the end of fiscal 1993.[5] NTT's aims at achieving 98 percent digitalization of long distance switches and 76 percent digitalization of local switches by the end of fiscal 1994, with the remainder being electronic switches. Digitalization of local switches is expected to

4. Regulations imposed by the MPT are reportedly aimed at further rationalization of NTT (Nagai 1994).
5. NTT 1994.

TABLE 6.5. Numbers of digital service subscribers

	High-speed digital leased line services	ISDN services
1985	640	—
1986	2,231	—
1987	5,002	—
1988	6,454	1,198
1989	8,559	6,754
1990	11,283	27,873
1991	15,075	85,890
1992	20,012	159,920
1993	26,438	239,431

Source: Ministry of Posts and Telecommunications, 1991, 1994, and 1995a.

be completed during fiscal 1997.[6] As of the end of fiscal 1993 there were 94,400 kilometers of optical fiber trunk line and 15,281 kilometers of optical fiber local line in Japan; the network backbone has been entirely optical fiber cable since 1985.[7] Compared with NTT's total 1,240,000 kilometers of line, installation of optical fiber cable is still limited and in the local line has just begun.

Union Commitment to the Reform of NTTPC

As discussed in more detail later, the work practices at NTT have changed drastically since the company was privatized. In this transformation process, JTWU policies regarding participation in managerial decisions have radically changed, which has contributed to the successful reform of NTTPC and to the transformation of work practices without any serious conflicts. Below we discuss the JTWU's strategies on the reform of NTTPC and its policies from the latter 1970s to immediately before privatization in 1985.

The Union's Search for Participation in Management

The "Memorandum about consultations on business plans" of 30 November 1957 stipulated that prior consultation had to be held at both central and regional levels regarding plans for facilities and staff assignments. The following indicates the attitude the JTWU had toward this prior consultation requirement.

6. Minutes of collective bargaining meeting. "Facility operations in the digital era." (13 March 1991) in JTWU 1991.
7. NTT 1994.

"Consultations about planning do not imply JTWU participation in NTTPC management, nor do they imply setting up a labor-management council. The agreement on prior consultation was concluded as a measure to resist rationalization, as were the existing collective agreements on working conditions and on limiting job transfers." (JTWU 1979: 862).

The JTWU viewed the prior consultation system as simply a measure for avoiding employment insecurity or the deterioration of working conditions as a result of rationalization, but nothing more was desired. The union at that time did not seek a means of participating in managerial decisions. Though the union's voice within the prior consultation system over time gradually became stronger, the union held to its basic strategy of avoiding involvement in managerial decisions.[8] However, during consultations on the Sixth Five-Year Plan which was to be implemented in fiscal 1978 there was a change in the nature of JTWU policies.

"In previous struggles against rationalization we decided our policies by analyzing the character of business plans and their influence on all JTWU members and telephone users, after the plans had been revealed. However, regarding the Sixth Five-Year Plan, we began our discussions and examinations as part of the struggle against the post-fifth plan before the sixth plan had been revealed in any detail and while management was still considering the contents of the plan" (JTWU 1992a: 599).

In the fall of 1977 NTTPC management released the Sixth Plan, presenting it to the union on October 27. Union discussions on the plan had begun in June 1976. Union meetings for discussing countermeasures to the plan were held in the telephone operation, maintenance, and sales and marketing divisions, and the union had independently prepared a counter-plan. The concept behind this action was expressed thus: "We create our own policies, and take the initiative from management" (JTWU 1992a: 600).

Included in the union's fourth long-term policy statement adopted in 1979 was the policy that the union should intervene in the process of formulating industrial policy and business plans, should attempt to participate in the decision-making process, and should set up regular opportunities for discussions on business plans and policies between labor and management before management finalized them (JTWU 1992a: 860–63).

8. In 1970 negotiations over the Revised Seven-Year Plan, JTWU drew the following statement out of NTTPC: "We fully understand what JTWU is insisting: that implementing plans and measures before a labor-management agreement has been reached about them will inevitably cause disputes. It will also result in violating the essence of basic agreements. We will positively try not to implement plans and measures one-sidedly in the absence of a labor-management agreement upon them" (JTWU 1990: 720).

In the late 1970s the JTWU adopted a strategy supporting participation in managerial decisions. The following conditions influenced the JTWU's change in its strategy. Two goals that had remained in existence since the company was founded had almost been accomplished, one being elimination of the backlog of telephone installations and the other being completion of a dial telephone network. It appeared that in the future rather than endlessly expanding the telephone network, most work would consist of operations and maintenance, and developing new services such as data transmission. The economic environment surrounding the company was beginning to change drastically and becoming unstable, which in turn was expected to have negative effects on NTTPC's employees. Under these circumstances the JTWU independently decided to create countermeasures and to attempt to participate in the management of the company in order to ensure union members' employment and improve their working conditions.

Changes in Union Policy Regarding Rationalization

While the JTWU was searching for a way to participate in managerial decisions, it also changed its policy for rationalization. The JTWU did not oppose the company's rationalization plans which were proposed one after another by management in the years before privatization, but the union was skeptical of the effectiveness and the rapid pace of change. The union criticized management's plan for modifying the Third Five-Year Plan in 1965, describing the plan as monopolistic and neglectful of public convenience, as evidenced by management's unnecessary installation plan which, it claimed, did not correspond to the nation's standard of living. The union also claimed that the plan for a dial telephone network would do nothing for the public (JTWU 1982: 655). Also, in its third long-term policy statement adopted in 1975, the JTWU said it would deal with business plans under the assumption that the public has no desire for further improved convenience (JTWU 1990: 872).

In the late 1970s, this policy also changed. The union's fourth long-term policy statement, issued in 1979, stated that in the future it would positively seek to enhance the company's services and business based on the concept that the company would not be able to secure stable and guaranteed employment without improving its services (JTWU 1992a: 861). Moreover, during negotiations in 1982, the JTWU proposed to management that during an era in which the telegraph and telephone were giving way to other modes of information exchange there must be serious discussion on how the telecommunications business, which would play a critical role in the emerging information society, should be created, and how its infrastructure should be built (JTWU 1992b: 606).

Thus, facing environmental changes that threatened union members' employment security, the JTWU decided to seek participation in management and came to have a say in the company's business strategies. Along with this active participation in managerial decisions, the JTWU started to develop its own perspective on the regulatory reform of NTTPC.

The Reform of NTTPC and the Union's Policy

The JTWU started discussing the reform of NTTPC and the telephone system in 1980. At that point both labor and management at NTTPC came to the realization that on their own they lacked the capacity to solve the problems facing the company. Of particular concern to both the labor and management of NTTPC was the restrictions that existed on wage determination. Wages at NTTPC were determined in the following manner (Tishima 1982). The JTWU had the right to organize and negotiate over wages and employment conditions, but had no right to strike.[9] Management was constrained by having to accept annual budgets passed by the Diet, so its freedom to set wages was restricted. Thus both labor and management were unable to act as fully independent negotiating parties. Wage discussions were mediated by the Public Corporation and National Enterprise Labor Relations Commission, and if necessary, were settled through arbitration. The government had the greatest influence over annual wage increases.

In order to get rid of such constraints, in March 1981 the JTWU announced its support for democratic management of NTTPC, self-reliance, fairness in customer charges, and reform of the budgetary system based on the slogan of "disclosure, decentralization of authority, and participation" (JTWU 1992b: 143–49). It should be noted that the JTWU did not favor either privatization or the breakup of NTTPC, nor did it favor the introduction of free competition into the telecommunications market. The union only supported reform of the rigid bureaucratic system within NTTPC with the continuation of NTTPC as a public corporation.

On 16 March 1980 the government established the Second Committee on Administrative Reform to examine proposals for fundamental reforms that would provide simple and efficient administration. One topic

9. Article 17 of the Public Corporation and National Enterprise Labour Relations Law withheld the right to strike from employees and unions of public corporations and national enterprises. However, the JTWU frequently went on "illegal strikes" during *shunto* (the "spring wage offensive").

discussed by the committee was reform of NTTPC. The committee's third report concerned the telecommunications industry and was presented to the prime minister on 30 July 1982. This report included a draft outlining NTTPC reform including privatization, recommended that competition be introduced into the telecommunications market, and suggested that NTTPC's data transmission services division become a separate company. In response to this report, NTTPC reform was promoted full-scale and the company was privatized in 1985. The following describes how the JTWU reacted to the company's privatization and how the union came to participate in the management of the company.

First, the JTWU prepared its own detailed plans for the reform of NTTPC, and revealed a strong commitment to reform efforts. The union's plans were articulated in the "Basic demands and policies regarding telecommunications in the future" (October 26 1981) and in "The plan for telecommunication business in the future" (March 4 1982).

Then, the JTWU continued discussions with management and the two sides finally formed a common vision of the company's future. These discussions were frequent after 1983, when preparation of the reform legislation began. Labor-management agreement was achieved except over the issue of whether corporate ownership of the new NTT would be public or private.[10] Finally, at executive negotiations on 20 January 1984, both sides came to agreement on important issues such as: no breakup of the company; corporate autonomy regarding decisions on wages, investment, and capital planning; deregulation with the exception of essential services; and the granting to the union of the right to strike (JTWU 1992b: 990-91).

However, both labor and management had to find ways to solidify their new cooperative relationship and each had to overcome strong internal opposition to their common vision of reform. Both labor and management were surrounded by others holding different opinions. The MPT, responsible for supervising NTTPC, was at first opposed to reform of the company.[11] When the ministry later agreed to the reforms it re-

10. There are witnesses to the convergence of labor and management views. Ryutaro Hashimoto, the LDP Diet member who was in charge of NTTPC reform at the time, recognized labor-management agreement on basic factors (JTWU 1993: 896). JTWU General Secretary Komori also stated that the opinions of labor and management were almost entirely in agreement except on the form of ownership (Komori 1988: 86).

11. The director of the MPT bureau responsible for NTTPC at the time expressed his opposition to reform, stating that "there are many ways in which the public corporation system can be rationalized. Changing the form of ownership seems too radical a measure if other methods of rationalization have not been attempted" (*Mainichi Shinbun News*, 8 December 1981).

quested greater supervisory authority by asking that items such as business plans, financial plans, plans for income and expenses, the appointment and dismissal of directors, incidental business, investment, and other important matters be subject to MPT approval (JTWU 1992b: 1001). Within the Liberal Democratic party (LDP), which was promoting general administrative reform, there was opposition to the reform of NTTPC (NTT 1986: 630).[12] There was also dissent among NTTPC executives.[13] Those in favor of reform, centered around the JTWU and President Hisashi Shinto (of NTTPC), had no choice other than to band together to overcome those opposing reform of the company.

The JTWU exercised some political influence in the Diet deliberations over the privatization bill. The union traditionally had thrown all its political support behind the Japan Socialist Part (JSP), and as of the end of 1983, there were nine JSP members in the House of Representatives and two in the House of Councilors with whom the union had particularly deep relationships. With the cooperation of these legislators, in November 1982 the JTWU set up a meeting involving Diet members from five opposition parties (including the JSP) to discuss telecommunications reforms. According to reminiscences by the promoter of the meeting, the purpose of this meeting was to convince these opposition parties to work against the breakup of NTTPC (JTWU 1988: 217). Powerful members of the LDP were eventually influenced by those who attended the meeting.[14]

Finally, in 1985, the NTTPC reform bill passed. As mentioned before, the bill includes privatization and free entrance to the market, policies which the JTWU had strongly opposed. However, NTTPC was not broken

12. Mr. Hashimoto said he had to behave as if he were not a member of the LDP, and was placed in the position of relying on the alliance of the JTWU and opposition parties (Komori 1988: 834). General Secretary Komori recalled that Diet members who were former MPT officials strongly opposed the reform (JTWU 1988: 894).

13. There is no valid first-hand information regarding this point, but Mr. Hashimoto has been quoted as saying that NTTPC executives (with the exception of President Shinto) resisted the privatization (Komori 1988: 83). Chairman Takashi Shiga of the Posts and Communications Committee of the House of Representatives, stated that top executives of NTTPC were against privatization (JTWU 1988: 842). Hitoshi Kojima, General Manager of the Industrial Relations Department of NTTPC at the time, said that obviously there were people inside the company who were against privatization but did not speak out. It was NTTPC retirees who openly expressed their opposition (JTWU 1988: 891). These comments indicate that there were NTTPC executives opposed to privatization, but apparently the nature of their opposition differed from that of JTWU (which was also against privatization) since General Secretary Komori said that the activities of executives opposed to privatization were extremely unfavorable for JTWU activities (JTWU 1988: 892). The aim of these executives was to preserve the status quo of NTTPC.

14. These included Mr. Hashimoto, Mr. Shiga, Secretary General Rokusuke Tanaka, and Minister of Posts and Telecommunications Takakazu Okuda.

up, and moreover many other reforms supported by the union were in the bill including: no MPT intervention in collective bargaining over working conditions such as wages and no system of official approval on planning for income, expenses, and capital; the exclusion of incidental business (e.g., sales of telephones) from mandatory MPT approval; MPT approval required only for charges constituting major sources of income and almost complete freedom to set charges in markets where competition is present; and a promise to review the restriction on the union's right to strike with the aim of eliminating the restriction in three years (JTWU 1988: 504–6, 590–94). These modifications and additions were gained in spite of strong opposition because the JTWU worked hard with a pro-reform group within NTTPC management to promote their reform plans and the union exerted its political influence.

Summary of the JTWU's Position toward Regulatory Changes

In the late 1970s, the JTWU began to seek greater participation in managerial decisions and changed its policy regarding corporate rationalization. The environmental pressures facing NTTPC helped push this switch in union policy. The JTWU worried about its members' employment security and their working conditions, which depend on the company's future. At the same time, the JTWU began to discuss the need to reform the rigid and bureaucratic systems within NTTPC and also sought to add greater independence to the company's wage determination system.

The administrative reform which included changes in NTTPC led the JTWU to support further policy changes. The union went on to issue its own reform plans and engaged in discussions with management which eventually led to an agreement. The union was actively involved in the formation of the legislative reform bill and won significant modifications and additions to the bill, even though some of the things the union opposed, such as privatization and free competition were included in the bill. The form of the new NTT was heavily influenced by the JTWU and the pro-reform managers of NTTPC. For the JTWU, the reform process was a way to participate deeply in the management of NTT.

Changes in the Work Practices

The heavy roles that both the JTWU and management played in the reform of NTTPC led them to the view that labor and management had to share responsibility for the new company and its employees. This idea was expressed in a basic agreement reached between NTT and the

JTWU. The basic agreement concerning industrial relations concluded on 1 April 1985 between NTT and JTWU was a significant departure from the industrial relations and human resource management practices that had been in force in the formerly public NTT. Paragraph 1 of the basic agreement states that both labor and management should do their best to enrich jobs, to establish a wage system which corresponds with the quality and quantity of labor, and to achieve the objective of developing the company's business. Paragraph 3 stipulates the establishment of a prior consultation system to discuss the various business issues that affect employment and working conditions, as well as basic managerial policies. Paragraph 4 confirms that there will be employment security.

Employment

One issue that has been confronting NTT and the JTWU is employment reduction.[15] Table 6.6 shows that the firm's work force declined from more than 304,000 in 1985 to 215,600 in 1993. The employment adjustment was carried out without dismissals, by transferring employees to affiliated companies (about 16,700 as of 1992 excluding those who changed employer) and by attrition. Employees retire upon reaching the mandatory age limit, through early retirement schemes, or voluntary retirement plans. The early retirement schemes at NTT apply to employees that are forty-five years old or over with ten years of service or more who are willing to retire or quit. Without these schemes, those employees would have had to resign for personal reasons and receive reduced retirement allowances. In its voluntary retirement plans, NTT proposes the elimination of a certain number of employees at a particular time, and

TABLE 6.6. Number of NTT employees (thousands)

	1985	1986	1987	1988	1989	1990	1991	1992	1993
Total	304.0	297.6	291.1	276.6	266.0	257.6	249.9	232.2	215.6
Transferred	0.6	1.1	0.9	1.3	1.9	1.8	2.3	6.8	8.3
Retired	13.9	9.3	9.0	17.5	11.6	9.6	8.4	13.9	9.7
Hired	4.9	4.0	3.4	4.3	2.9	3.0	3.0	3.0	1.4

Source: NTT 1993, and 1994.
Note: The 1988 figure for Retired includes 6,800 workers who moved to NTT Data Telecommunications, which was separated from NTT as an independent company. Among those hired in 1988 were 1,100 former employees of Japan National Railways who moved to NTT. The 1992 and 1993 figure for retired employees includes those who moved to the newly separated NTT Mobile Communications and those moved to a building maintenance company.

15. The third report of the Committee on Administrative Reform urged extreme staff rationalization. The MPT directed NTT to promote thorough rationalization beginning five years after privatization.

then recruits voluntary retirees. The applicants are paid an expanded retirement allowance and usually an additional lump sum payment.

Efforts to avoid dismissals are not new to labor and management at NTT (or NTTPC). Since 30 November 1957 (well before privatization) there was a labor-management understanding that employees would not be sacked for the purpose of rationalization, but the market environment has changed immensely since then. The telecommunications industry grew very rapidly from the 1950s through the 1970s while NTTPC held a domestic monopoly which precluded the need for employment reduc-tions. Since privatization, work force reduction has been imperative to meet the increased competition that has come from NCCs.

One way of avoiding dismissals, which NTT has used only since privatization, is the transfer of employees to affiliated companies. Workers transferred to affiliated companies are classified among three categories. Type A transferees work at a different company while performing work for NTT and remain employees of NTT. Type B transferees have an employment relationship with the company to which they transferred and perform work for that company while remaining employees of NTT. Type C transferees resign from NTT and establish an employment relationship with a new employer, but are schedules to be rehired by NTT in the future. Below are some rules governing employee transfers at NTT.

(1) Before the transfer is performed management presents to the union a transfer plan which includes the destinations and the purposes of transfers and the number of employees involved. Management explains to the union if there will be Type A transferees, and holds consultation meetings with the union if there will be Type B and C transferees.

(2) The desires, adaptability, needs, family circumstances, and experience of individual employees are considered comprehensively when selecting transferees.

(3) The company holds a seminar for those expected to be transferred, which lasts about one week, to provide an opportunity for them to learn about business activities in their new employment situation and to acquire basic knowledge they will need at their new jobs.

(4) The length of time transferees are employed by other companies is added to their length of service when seniority-oriented pay and retirement allowances are calculated at NTT.

(5) The working conditions of Type A transferees are based on NTT rules. The new employers' rules for newly-hired workers apply to

Type B and C transferees, though a wage level equal to that which they received prior to the transfer is assured. Employees transferred to NTT Data Telecommunications or NTT Mobile Communications, which were separated from the parent company after privatization, resign from NTT and conclude new employment relationships with these companies. Work conditions (including pay) equivalent to their previous working conditions are assured.

Another method frequently used for employment adjustment is reassignment, sometimes accompanied by a change of occupational category. On 1 December 1955 an agreement concerning reassignment was concluded at NTTPC. Employees were often involved in reassignments before the privatization of NTTPC, due to the introduction of automation equipment and organizational restructuring, but as indicated by the figures in Table 6.7, the volume of transferred employees increased markedly before and after privatization. The numbers of employees moved between regions has also increased, and moves between job categories have became more common (for instance, from a maintenance or information service section to a sales section). The rules concerning reassignment have not changed a great deal since 1955 and resemble those for transfers to another organization.

A voluntary retirement plan was adopted from 1993 through 1994 as a new method to cope with work force reductions. The target was to eliminate 10,000 workers between the ages of forty and fifty-seven who had worked for the company for ten years or more. Applications for voluntary retirement were to be collected three times: December 1993,

TABLE 6.7. Employee reassignments

	1953–1957	1958–1962	1963–1967	1968–1972	1973–1975	1985–1989
Total	8,827	25,189	35,844	28,352	11,674	82,600
Annual average	1,785	5,038	7,169	5,670	3,891	18,520
Percentage of total work force reassigned each year	1.4	2.7	3.1	2.1	1.3	6.5

Source: Figures for total number of reassigned from 1953 to 1975 were obtained from NTTPC 1977, part two, p. 393; figures for total work force were obtained from NTTPC 1978, appendix, p. 100; figures for the total number reassigned from 1985 to 1989 were obtained from NTT internal data; and figures for total work force for 1985 to 1989 were obtained from NTT 1993.

Note: Only total numbers reassigned are available for 1953 to 1957 and 1958 to 1962. The total number of employees was divided by the annual average to obtain the percentage of employees reassigned.

and June and December 1994. An expanded retirement allowance and a lump sum payment equivalent to twelve months' salary (nine months' salary for June and December 1994 applicants) were to be paid to those agreeing to retire voluntarily. The number of applicants totaled 9,900.[16]

Employment security, which is articulated in the basic agreement, has been maintained, as there have been no involuntary dismissals at NTT. In order to maintain employment security while reducing the work force, various measures other than dismissal have been utilized, as is the case with most large private firms in Japan. As a result, NTT's total work force is dramatically smaller and its composition has changed. Table 6.8 shows that considerably fewer people are working in NTT service departments such as telegraph, directory services/operator assistance, and maintenance; also, the proportion of NTT employees working in the telegraph and directory services/operator assistance departments has fallen sharply. In contrast, the number of employees working in the sales/marketing departments has increased by 46 percent and these workers now make up one third of the company's total work force.

Wages

After privatization, the JTWU was awarded the right to strike and management was freed from budgetary restrictions imposed by the MPT. Wage increases at NTT have come to be determined through bargaining between truly independent negotiating parties. Before privatization the Public Corporation and National Enterprise Labor Relations Commission presented arbitration awards which granted very similar annual wage increases to the employees of three public corporations and five government enterprises (including NTTPC and Japan National Railways).

TABLE 6.8. Work force allocation at NTT (% of all NTT employees)

	1985	1991	Change between 1985 and 1991
Total	100.0	100.0	− 17.8
Telecommunications	3.2	1.3	− 66.0
Directory/connection services	13.7	8.9	− 46.8
Sales/marketing	19.8	35.1	45.8
Maintenance	33.8	29.6	− 27.9
Other	29.5	25.1	− 30.1

Source: Figures for 1985 from Management and Coordination Agency 1990: 51; figures for 1991 from NTT unpublished internal data.

16. *Tsushin Kogyo Shinbun News* (23 May 1994), and unpublished NTT data.

This created considerable problems for the employees and the union at NTTPC, since the company was experiencing extraordinary growth but the outcome of NTTPC wage negotiations was low wage raises due to the poor business performance of other public corporations. The JTWU strongly advocated a scheme for independent wag negotiation and settlement, and made every effort to have such a system implemented. Owing to privatization, NTT labor and management became able to determine wage raises without previous constraints and the company's employees gained relatively large wage increases. When the average scheduled wage for all industries is indexed at 100, in 1984 the wage level of NTTPC was 90.8 while in 1992 the wage level of NTT was 105.4.[17] Below we describe the traditional and new wage systems used at NTT (and NTTPC).

The wage system that existed prior to the privatization of NTTPC was established in 1968 (Honda 1977; JTWU 1978: 449–69; JTWU 1982: 1410–6; NTTPC 1977: 487–95). The basic wage was calculated by adding accumulated annual wage increases and a variety of other wage supplements to the employee's starting wage, which itself was primarily determined by an individual's academic achievement.

The pre-privatization NTT wage system (at NTTPC) can be characterized as follows:

(1) It was a seniority-based wage system in that wages increased with no direct relation to duties but rather as a function of length of service. (2) The wage differential among occupations was substantially compressed.[18] Merit ratings played no part in determining wages and differences in job ability among employees was not reflected in wages at all. The JTWU refused to allow a merit rating system before privatization. In June 1966, management introduced merit rating to summer bonus payments as compensation for reconsidering mass disciplinary punishment. The union at first accepted but soon opposed even this limited use of merit ratings (JTWU 1982: 623–24, 1025–27) and won complete abolition of this practice in 1972 (JTWU 1990: 813–14, 1076). (3) Wages did differ between a general employee and an employee promoted to the rank of assistant section manager, even if both these employees were the same age, and had the same length of service and academic achievement. As the number of managerial posts, including

17. JTWU data, and unpublished data from the Ministry of Labor's *Wage Census*. Scheduled wages are compared using the Paasche method controlling for age and length of service.

18. Interview with Mr. S, a member of the JTWU's staff.

assistant section manager, became limited due to the imposition of budgetary restrictions on NTTPC, promotion to assistant section manager (or to other managerial positions) became an important source of competition and wage variation between employees. Since employees up to the assistant section managers were union members, this process intensified competition among union members which caused problems for the union.

Under the wage system used by NTT since its privatization in 1987, basic wages consist of a combination of age and ability-based components.[19] All workers receive age-based wage increases. A personnel ranking system based on job ability recently has been introduced and this system provides the basis for ability-based wage payments. The job ability that management expects each employee to exhibit is analyzed and classified according to job cluster and rank. Each employee's rank is based on a merit rating. The job cluster and merit ranking is a central pillar of NTT's human resource management system as it affects decisions on pay, training, and promotion.

The job clusters at NTT are divided into eight job ability groups that include four major groups: the general group, the planning group, the specialist group, and the sales and marketing group. The general group includes the core duties in areas such as engineering, sales, operations, construction, and office work. General workers belong to this group. Workers who acquire planning and management responsibilities are promoted to the planning group. Lower-level managers such as group leaders, assistant section managers, and deputy section managers are in the planning group. The specialist group is for workers with sophisticated abilities in a particular field, while the sales and marketing group includes personnel involved in sales and marketing activities who have the ability or potential to perform at high levels. There are five ranks within the general group, three ranks in the planning group, five ranks in the specialist group, and seven ranks in the sales and marketing group.

The following is a brief description of the promotion system used either for moves within a job group or for moves from one job group to another. Most NTT employees join the company after graduation and start at Rank V (for high school graduates) or Rank IV (for college graduates) in the general group, and climb the ladder of promotion in that group. Individuals who demonstrate above average abilities rise

19. The description of NTT's current wage determination method is based on NTT-JTWU 1994 and in NTT 1992.

smoothly through promotions to one of the higher three groups (planning, specialist, and sales and marketing) depending on their particular expertise. These individuals are then eligible for further promotion within the group. The promotion criteria and procedures are as follows: (1) There is an automatic promotion system within the general group. Regardless of the results of merit evaluations, workers are promoted almost automatically after spending the maximum time of three to seven years in each rank. Promotion from Rank I of the general group to a higher group as well as promotion within a higher job group is not automatic. (2) Annual merit evaluations that assess ability and performance cumulatively affect the speed of promotion. The performance of employees in the general, specialist, and planning groups is evaluated with respect to three criteria—speed, accuracy, and creativity—while sales performance is the only criteria for evaluating the performance of those in the sales and marketing group. The evaluation is normally performed primarily by the employee's section manager and secondarily by his or her department manager.

It is noteworthy that promotion in the personnel ranking system does not necessarily require movement to a higher managerial post. One of the features of this promotion system is that promotion in principle is not constrained by the number of managerial posts. Employees are promoted in the personnel ranking system based on their performance and ability, whether or not there is a vacancy in a higher managerial post. As a matter of course, there is some relationship between promotion in rank and that in post, as commonly some of the employees promoted to a particular rank are assigned to a particular managerial post.

The ability-based wage component is calculated using the ranking system. This wage component consists of the starting wage, determined according to academic career, plus annual wage increases determined according to job group rank and other factors. Annual wage increases vary depending on rank and are higher for those at higher ranks in a given job group or in a higher job group. There are various allowances in addition to the basic wage payment. The following allowances relate to functional rank, managerial position, and performance: the rank allowance, the responsibility allowance, and the telecommunications equipment sales allowance.

The key points of comparison between the current wage system and the wage system that existed at NTT prior to the company's privatization are: (1) Wages increase with length of service under the current system, as was true for the previous system. In this sense the wage system is still seniority-oriented. (2) Merit ratings play an indirect and crucial part in determining the wage under the current system, while there was no merit ratings in the previous system. The influence of merit ratings is indirect because the results of merit rating do not directly determine the amount of the annual increase in the ability-based wage component. Rather, the merit rating affects an individual's rank, which in turn influences the size of the wage increase the individual receives. Merit ratings are crucial because they permit wages to differ across employees, even across general employees. There are sizable differences in the annual wage increases received by employees with high ratings and those with low ratings. The JTWU, which had strongly opposed any merit ratings before privatization, changed its policy after the privatization of NTTPC. When the merit rating system was introduced to wage decisions, the JTWU stated that the rating system would improve worker motivation and stimulate the company's business since wages would rise in accordance with improvements in employees' abilities. The union also said the new system would prevent the development of excessive wage differences between those in managerial and nonmanagerial positions, as had occurred under the old system (JTWU 1986a: 224–25; JTWU 1986b: 88–91). (3) In principle, the new system encourages employees to improve their job ability and performance and puts them into competition in improving individual job ability, while the old system put employees into competition for managerial posts. The employees who improve their ability and are promoted to a higher rank in a higher group get a higher wage increase, even if they are not assigned to a higher managerial post, or are not promoted in post. Thus, the current system is free of the problems caused when there is a limited number of new managerial positions.

However, the new wage system has some potential problems. Under the new personnel ranking system, the new wage system has the possibility to increase labor costs unreasonably. There is no limit in the new system on the number of employees assigned to a particular rank. Furthermore, employees who demonstrate improvements in their abilities expect to be promoted and to receive a higher wage under the new system, even though there may not be an adequate number of jobs suitable for employees with improved abilities. Without suitable jobs, workers would have to be assigned to jobs with low difficulty while being highly paid. The result would be an increase in unit labor costs. The more workers improve their abilities and are promoted to higher ranks, the more likely will be this mismatch in worker skills and job difficulty. In order to limit the development of this overqualification, the number of employees assigned to a particular rank could be limited, which would discourage employees from improving their abilities. Thus there is no harmless way to avoid overqualification in the new ability-based wage system.

In summary, in terms of wage determination the reforms introduced after the privatization of NTTPC brought independent collective bargaining, a higher wage level, merit ratings, and competition in improving individual job ability. These changes have been supported by changes in union policies.

Skill Formation

This section of the chapter describes off-the-job-training (Off-JT), which contributes heavily to skill development at NTT. The company's public predecessor emphasized education and training and this policy has not changed since privatization.

NTT's Off-JT can be broadly divided into three types of courses: for different management levels, for skill improvement, and for self-development. Courses for different management levels are conducted for new employees and for each level of managerial positions. Skill improvement courses consist of education and training which suit the individual worker's level of skill, training for new technology or new services, and education to assist in obtaining qualifications. Participants in these types of courses are selected by the company, but employees can attend self-development courses at their own discretion while the company helps them with the financing. The self-development courses include correspondence courses, outside seminars, enrollment at a domestic or foreign college, and study at NTT's own Expert College. Those who wish to study at the Expert College or another college are screened by the company.

The Expert College system was introduced in 1987. To cope with rapid technological innovation, relatively young workers with two years or more experience are selected to acquire advanced knowledge or technology skills. There were 17 such courses taught in fiscal 1994. Below are brief descriptions of a few of these courses.[20]

(1) A switch engineering course teaches about the systems and structures of digital switches; troubleshooting; programming; design and construction; networking; and related knowledge.

(2) A cable engineering course teaches about cable-related technologies, cable design, construction, and maintenance; countermeasures for technical problems; negotiating with people outside

20. NTT, undated.

NTT; general troubleshooting; safety issues; and related knowledge.

(3) A course on sales and marketing teaches about basic technologies; product information; sales skills; strategies for making proposals based on corporate and market analyses; and related knowledge.

Managers have a great deal of responsibility for determining who will take which course among those offered by NTT's extensive Off-JT system. The company introduced a skills inventory program in 1990 by which the skills of individual workers are tracked. Skill description forms are distributed among workers in June or July every year and each worker enters his or her levels of skill. Employees evaluate themselves according to the work content items listed on the form and submit the completed forms to managers. In some cases the employee's supervisor (a section manager) may offer advice. Using the completed form, the section manager talks with the employee to formulate a career plan and drafts a personalized training plan. NTT's education policy is that there should be an accurate understanding of the individual worker's ability to perform his or her duties, and the worker should be educated toward acquiring the level of skill required for his or her job. Section managers are responsible for overseeing the process.

The new training and education system is valued by NTT employees.[21] A branch employee responsible for labor relations commented that "The number of workers to experience a particular sort of training used to be set by an upper organization like the head office. The desires of the particular establishment were neglected. One consequence was that sometimes the establishments just sent off workers who could spare the time. Training was seen as a kind of holiday. Today, though, the requirements of the establishment are taken into account when training courses are planned. And workers with career plans suited for particular training programs are deliberately identified. But a new problem has come up during this period of personnel adjustment, in that potential trainees must sometimes cancel their plans at the last minute because they are too busy to attend a course."

As for the training system, two main changes were made to provide more efficient Off-JT. One change was the introduction of new training programs where young workers are expected to acquire high technologi-

21. Interview with member of the industrial relations department of NTT's Tokyo branch office of the Regional Communications Sector.

cal knowledge and problem solving skills such as Expert College courses. The other key change was the skills inventory system.

Work Organization

A key concept for NTT's work organization since privatization has been "multiple duties." This means such things as that sales staff should perform simple repairs or sell a wide variety of products; switch operators should do maintenance while monitoring and operating their equipment; and information services staff should do database preparation, marketing, and monitoring and statistical work such as traffic surveys and analyses in addition to providing directory assistance services. The basic idea is to transform the rigid work organization of the preceding public corporation into a flexible organization suitable for a private company. This transformation has been supported and facilitated by changes in union policies.

Formerly, the JTWU did not support flexible policies regarding work organization. Management introduced "Management by Objectives" (also known as the "ZD Movement") in the mid-1960s. The union's 1968 policy statement claimed that Management by Objectives aimed at motivating workers, by making them work at management's discretion, and that it was a human resource management policy intended to achieve rationalization. Upon recognizing "management's actual goals," the JTWU vowed to end Management by Objectives through discussions among union members and negotiations at workplaces (JTWU 1978: 862). In 1972 the JTWU requested suspension of report meetings on work improvement which had been part of the Management by Objectives program.[22] The union built its counterargument by stating that the meetings would thoroughly and individually manage workers and intensify their work; that the meetings would change the content of work and directly affect various aspects of working conditions; and that the meetings were implemented by ignoring the union and pretending that changes in work content were made voluntarily by the workers despite the fact that they were actually initiated by management (JTWU 1990: 267–68).

However, in the late 1970s when the JTWU's policies regarding participation in managerial decisions were changing, the policies regarding work organization were also changing. The JTWU's third long-term policy statement of 1975 said that the union would secure humane job con-

---

22. These "report meetings for work improvement" apparently resembled QC circle meetings.

tent by changing the combinations and processes of tasks, inspecting and analyzing labor mechanisms, and discussing and reviewing employees' labor from the workers' perspective (JTWU 1990: 876–77). At a general meeting in 1977 the union proclaimed that the contents and methods of current jobs should be analyzed and avoid the isolation of workers (JTWU 1992a: 326).

Below is described how work organization has been changing in information services, customer services, and engineering.

Information Services. Since the privatization of NTTPC, reform of the telephone sector, including connection and information services, was a significant issue for both labor and management. JTWU policies for 1986 state that "by utilizing the skills of union members working in the manual-operation divisions, and while considering current traffic trends, we are willing to discuss expanding the business scope of the divisions toward a comprehensive information sector based on the concept of making a work place which is desirable for the workers" (JTWU 1986: 222). When the personnel ranking system was introduced, the ranking of conventional telephone operators became an issue between labor and management. Eventually they came to receive treatment similar to that accorded other technical staff and sales staff, which meant that work practices in the telephone sector had to be restructured (JTWU 1987: 145–46). The matter was discussed within the union and there were repeated negotiations with management. An agreement was reached in April 1994.[23] Under the new agreement, the information services division consists of personnel performing directory services, connection services, operator-assisted VAN services, database preparation, marketing, consulting, and auditing and handling statistics.

Since directory services and connection work have been significantly simplified and standardized, most tasks can be performed by part-time workers from affiliated companies. NTT employees have been transferred to the affiliated company to instruct the part-timers, and they perform telephone directory services and handle claims from users as one part of their career development formation. Operator-assisted VANs are services which provide information concerning hotels and restaurants, and other types of information, on demand. Database preparation entails updating subscriber data to incorporate changes while rectifying errors. Marketing includes collecting information about events, registering customers for information services, and planning new services. Consulting tasks include proposing modifications of names registered in NTT's data-

23. JTWU 1993c and JTWU 1993a.

base (telephone directory) and identifying duplicate listings. Auditing and statistical work includes performing surveys and analyses for directory services and operator-assisted VAN traffic as well as collecting and evaluating statistical information.

It is expected that employees in the information services sector gradually will be promoted from their current positions as providers of directory assistance and customer information services into jobs associated with database and traffic management.

Customer Services. Since the privatization of NTTPC the content of sales jobs at the branch offices has been enlarged so as to widen the range of services handled by a worker. Now it is common for workers to take care of whole work processes including the arrangements associated with equipment installation.

Tasks performed at branch office customer service desks include taking orders in person and by phone for NTT services and equipment (including new subscriptions and relocations, telephone transfer and discount services); answering inquiries about NTT services such as toll-free numbers and ISDN, and products and services provided by NTT affiliates such as mobile telephones; and forwarding messages to the appropriate division or affiliated company. Reception desks are a key point of customer contact and are expected to serve customers as a window into the entire organization.

Orders for telephone services and other NTT products are handled in the following manner. Upon receiving a phone call from a customer wishing to order a new subscription, the receptionist asks the name and address of the caller and uses a computer to check whether there is a cable to the desired location and to verify that local facilities have the capacity to handle the service. If there is no problem with regard to these items, the receptionist accepts the order and provides the customer with a new telephone number, and then sends a bill for the installation work. After the charge is paid by the customer and confirmed, an appointment for the installation work is made with the customer. In determining the date this work is to be done, the receptionist checks the branch's installation schedule and arranges the installation to suit the customer's convenience. Usually the work is completed within three days after the order is received. The work schedule is sent to another section with a service order (SO) slip bearing the customer's name, address, and telephone number. This completes the order process.

Normally the above series of tasks for a particular order is performed by a single receptionist and is not distributed among several workers. Orders are handled on a one-to-one basis between the customer and the receptionist. Basic skill requirements for the customer service job are: a knowledge of NTT-related products; ability to decide whether to transfer the order to another division; ability to understand the status of the section's pending installation work; and sufficient care to avoid potential problems such as an unwanted change in a registered name.

Engineering. The engineering divisions perform technical tasks to meet orders taken by receptionists for new phone line subscriptions, relocation, and other NTT services (these tasks are collectively referred to as "SO work"). The divisions also resolve problems described by customers and maintain facilities such as switches and cables. SO work done outside NTT facilities is subcontracted for, and in 1989 subcontractors performed 69.7 percent of the quantity and 73.6 percent of the value of all SO work at NTT's twenty-six branches nationwide (Management and Coordination Agency 1990: 117–18). According to recent information compiled by the JTWU, about 85 percent of SO work is performed by NTT-affiliated construction companies (JTWU 1993b: 56).[24]

Switch maintenance technicians working at NTT facilities locate the sources of problems and resolve the problems after being alerted by a customer complaint or a self-monitoring system in a switch. The causes of such problems are either defective parts inside a switch, or software or data input errors. If a part is defective a parts package will be replaced. Each branch office stocks about 8,000 such packages. If the source of the problem is software the technician will contact NTT's software development center in the event of a systems error, while data errors are corrected on the spot. Self-generated switch error messages do not reveal the type or location of the problem in detail. This information is specified by the repair technicians who consult reference materials and use the switch's diagnostic system. Experienced technicians are able to track down the source of a problem much faster than those with little experience. Other important tasks performed by these workers include revising and managing customer data files and preventive maintenance schedules for switches. One branch we visited now has twenty-four switch maintenance technicians, of whom four have spent two years in the software development division. The relation between switch maintenance technicians and the software development division has received high priority recently, and experience in the software development division is now considered a normal part of a switch maintenance technician's career path.

24. It is unclear whether 85% refers to the number of jobs or their value.

Corporate Governance

This section describes how workers or the union participate in managerial decisions at NTT. As discussed in previous sections, the JTWU started seeking participation in managerial decisions in the late 1970s and deepened its involvement in managerial issues during the process of NTTPC's reform. These efforts eventually led to a collective agreement concluded at the time of privatization which helped to promote a new relationship between labor and management at NTT.

As mentioned before, paragraph 3 of the basic agreement on industrial relations (concluded on 1 April 1985) states that the union will participate in corporate management. Another agreement (concluded the same day) concerns the design of a labor-management consultation scheme. The latter document states that NTT labor and management shall discuss important management issues such as business planning and work force reduction, aiming for sound development of the company's business. In addition to the central council whose members are drawn from the JTWU headquarters and the NTT head office, branch-level councils have been organized on a geographical basis by dividing the nation into eleven blocks. In these councils labor and management discuss important management issues which are subject to the authority of the branch directors. Joint labor-management conferences at the prefecture level were started in November 1985. Labor-management meetings at the workshop level were first held in October the following year.

Quite a few years before the privatization of NTTPC, the JTWU was involved in consultations with management on matters related to plans for facilities, personnel assignments, and the introduction of new technology. Consultation also occurred at the prefecture level. The labor-management consultation scheme formed after privatization extends the previous system. But differences are evident when the old and new systems are compared.

First, the purposes of consultation are different. The former agreement stated that the public corporation was responsible for planning the expansion as well as the provision of telegraph and telephone networks. Because implementing the plans affected employment and other working conditions both directly and indirectly, the contents of the plans were to be presented to the union in advance so as to prevent any potential friction accompanying implementation of the plans.[25] The agreement stated that though the public corporation was responsible for planning and im-

25. From "Memorandum on Consultation on Business Plan."

plementation, prior consultation with the union should be held in order to avoid conflict.

The objectives of the current consultation scheme do not refer to these two points. The agreement on the scheme states that consultation provides an opportunity for both labor and management to discuss business matters for the purpose of sound development of the company's business. It appears that under the current consultation scheme both management and union play a major role in planning and implementing business plans and that prior consultation is held not only to avoid conflicts but also to discuss business matters. Second, the agenda of consultation has evolved. Before privatization consultation concerned facility plans or the introduction of new technology which might affect employment and working conditions. Today labor-management councils discuss a wide range of important management matters including basic policies.[26]

Third, labor-management conferences are now held even at the branch level. In addition to union participation via the labor-management consultation process there are two other significant types of participation underway at NTT. One involves the appointment of a former JTWU chairman as a corporate auditor, which occurred at the general shareholders' meeting in 1985 immediately after privatization.[27] Also in 1992 one of the four regular auditor positions was occupied by a former JTWU general secretary. Another type of worker participation is that provided by the employee share ownership plan. After the government (which, holding about two-thirds of all shares, is the largest shareholder), the employee share ownership society is NTT's second largest shareholder with 152,222 shares or 0.98 percent of the total outstanding shares.[28]

Conclusion

The restructuring of the Japanese telecommunications services industry has been successful so far in terms of business performance. Three objectives, that is, development of the telecommunications market, a reduction in customer charges, and improvements in the business effectiveness of

26. Ibid.

27. Japanese commercial law obliges corporations to be audited by corporate auditors. Corporate auditors monitor the jobs executed by directors in terms of accounting and other aspects. They are obliged to check the bills and documents presented to a general meeting of stockholders by the directors and to report to the meeting if there is violation in the management of business against law and the certificate of incorporation. The certificate of incorporation of NTT stipulates that it has three corporate auditors.

28. NTT 1994.

former monopolies, have been achieved. In terms of industrial relations the restructuring also has been successful in that there have been no serious industrial disputes. The restructuring of NTT (NTTPC) has played a major role in the restructuring of the entire telecommunications services industry.

It is our view that the successful reform of NTT has been assisted by two key changes that occurred in the policies of the JTWU. These key policy changes involved the JTWU's efforts to become more fully involved in managerial decisions and the JTWU's revised policies toward corporate rationalization. During the process through which NTTPC was restructured, the JTWU worked hard to maintain a cooperative relationship with the company's management. These changes in JTWU policy were in part as a result of the union's recognition of the economic pressures that affected the telecommunications industry. The turbulent economic environment led the JTWU in the late 1970s to worry about the company's future and the employment security and working conditions of the union's members. The administrative reform that affected the NTTPC also spurred the JTWU to reassess its policies. As a result, the JTWU has come to participate successfully in the management of NTT and to share responsibility for the company and its employees.

The transformation in the JTWU's strategy was accompanied by a number of changes in work practices and these changes in work practices in turn helped reinforce the union's new strategy. Supported by changes in the JTWU's policies, the work practices at NTT (NTTPC) have been transformed in the following manner:

(1) Employment. NTT is trying to provide as much employment security as possible. It utilizes reassignments and transfers to affiliated companies more frequently now to cope with work force fluctuations. Even when employment reductions are desired, dismissals are avoided by soliciting voluntary retirements or through enhanced early retirement benefits, both of which are new practices at NTT.

(2) Wages. A seniority orientation continues in NTT's wage system, but the merit rating system that was previously strongly opposed by the JTWU before privatization is now supported by the union and plays an important role in wage determination. Under the new wage system employees are encouraged to develop their ability to perform their duties and wages now reflect differences in individual ability. Front-line managers play an important role in performing merit ratings in this system.

(3) Training. To improve employee abilities, schemes to provide more efficient Off-JT have been implemented. One such example is the skills inventory system within which front-line managers play very important roles. In addition, training programs such as the Expert College through which young workers are expected to acquire high technological knowledge and problem-solving skills are available.

(4) Work organization. A Key concept for NTT's work organization since privatization has been "multiple duties." The basic idea is to transform the rigid work organization of the preceding public corporation into a flexible organization suitable for a private company. This transformation has been supported by changes in JTWU policies.

(5) Corporate Governance. Worker participation in management has progressed through activities such as the establishment of a labor-management consultation scheme, the appointment of former labor representative as auditors, and the employee share ownership plan.

These practices are not unique to NTT; they are typical of leading private-sector companies in Japan. In this sense, the work practices at NTT have changed from a rigid and legalistic style to a flexible style that is typical of Japanese private-sector companies.

Although the reform of NTT generally has been successful so far, there are some problems looming. One problem involves the potential breakup of NTT which the council of the MPT has been discussing. A recommendation on this issue will be announced in 1996. Both management and the union at NTT strongly oppose the breakup of NTT, but some members of the Liberal-Democratic Party favor a breakup to stimulate greater competition in the telecommunications industry. If a breakup occurs, labor and management at NTT will be forced to transform again.

Another key problem confronting NTT concerns the competition NTT faces from new common carriers, competition that is getting fiercer and fiercer. Since, as mentioned before, most of the NCCs (excluding NTT's subsidiaries) are not unionized, JTWU and NTT now face for the first time competition from nonunion firms. It is not clear if employees at NTT will be able to continue to enjoy improved working conditions in the face of such competition.

A third key problem facing NTT relates to the aging of the company's work force. The average age of employees at NTT has increased substantially over the last ten years and is now slightly above forty years old.

This aging of the work force has produced two kinds of problems—an increase in training costs and large increases in unit wage costs. Generally speaking, the older a worker gets, the more difficult it is for him or her to adapt to technological innovation. To cope with the rapid technological innovation occurring in the provision of telecommunications services in the midst of work force aging, training expenditures will have to increase substantially. Training is also likely to increase due to the fact that under the new wage system employees are asking for more training in order to improve their job abilities and receive higher wages. If employees succeed in improving their ability, they have to be paid according to their improved ability under the new wage system, whether there are suitable jobs for them or not. When the number of the employees with improved ability grows to the point that it exceeds the number of appropriate jobs, unit labor costs will be pushed upward. The aging that is occurring in NTT's work force could accelerate this problem.

Chapter 7

Norway

Sidsel K. Solbraekke

Deregulation, new technology, the development of competitive markets, and greater demand for service have changed market conditions in the Norwegian telecommunications industry in recent years. The aim of this chapter is to answer the following questions: To what extent and through which policies has competition increased in the Norwegian telecommunications industry? What factors have changed the market situation of Telenor (the main telecommunications company in Norway)? Is Telenor in real competition with other telecommunications companies? What are the changes that have been made in the organizational structure of Telenor and how have these changes affected employees? What conflicts, if any, have accompanied the changes?

The first section of this chapter describes the organizational restructuring that led up to the creation of Telenor. Then we examine the effects of economic changes on the working situation of the different groups of employees within Telenor. Here we consider the consequences that regulatory and business strategies have had for the different groups of employees. The effects of the changes are seen in an analysis of work practices: workplace governance, work organization, skill formation and training, compensation, employment security, and staffing arrangements. The analysis focuses on the effects of restructuring on the following occupations: telephone operators, field service technicians, customer service representatives, engineers, technicians, and middle managers. This chapter draws heavily upon the results of an employee survey carried out throughout Telenor and on intensive interviews conducted with a number of Telenor employees.[1]

The Transformation of Telenor into a State-Owned Limited Company

The dominant provider of telecommunications services in Norway is Telenor.[2] Before 1 November 1994, Telenor (then called Norwegian Telecom) was a state-run enterprise under the direction of the Ministry of Communications. The ministry made final decisions concerning corporate reorganizations, price reductions, and most other key managerial decisions, taking into consideration regional policy, especially in the area of job distribution. However, the ministry had only a limited role in the day-to-day running of Telenor.

In 1992 Telenor was, for the first time, given parliamentary authority to establish limited companies, to buy shares in other companies, and to transfer activities within certain limits defined in the national budget. This legislation introduced mixed ownership to the telecom industry in Norway. As a result of these changes, Telenor in recent years has gained even wider authority and a freer standing than other state-owned organizations in Norway.

On 1 January 1993, the most comprehensive organizational change in the history of Norwegian telecommunications was made, and Telenor was established in accordance with new lines of authority. Local "Tele-areas," small, largely autonomous profit centers serving regional needs, were closed as part of this reorganization.

In November 1994, Telenor was transformed into a limited company after the government concluded that this would be in the best interests of

1. From 3 February to 30 April 1994, a survey of 5,450 employees in the organization was conducted. All employees in three of the seven regions in the country received a questionnaire, and the response rate was 62 percent. The regions which were chosen differ in terms of infrastructure, population density, means of subsistence, and customer base. Intensive interviews of 49 employees were arranged in the same period. Twenty-seven of the interviewees were managers at different levels. Fieldwork, informal conversations, Telenor's employment statistics, and extensive written material, including the entire decision-making process prior to the reorganization, constitute an essential part of the data which form the basis of this chapter. In addition the author conducted two research projects in Norwegian Telecom in 1990 and 1991.

2. The name Telenor is used throughout this chapter to describe the large telecommunications company which was referred to as Norwegian Telecom before 1994. The official name of Telenor is Telenor AS.

customers, employees, and the company itself. As a state-owned limited company, Telenor is now free from formal state budgetary procedures and long-term government planning.

The two biggest employee organizations, which together represent some 14,500 employees, strongly opposed the government's decision, arguing that a crucial political crossroads had been reached in which traditionally accepted social values were at stake. A two-hour political strike was held in order to demonstrate union opposition. However, the plans were implemented and an integrated enterprise with a single profile and coordinated market operations was established.

A clear line is drawn between areas where Telenor has a monopoly and areas where it has to compete in the market. Telenor is now organized into seven business sectors, each controlling its own business units, as shown in Figure 7.1. The new group structure was designed to present a consistent face to customers and to provide a tidy organizational structure.

Telenor has two roles. It continues to have social responsibilities as a state-owned limited company and it is now also a market participant. As one of the largest companies in Norway, even in the face of the changes that have occurred in its ownership restructuring, Telenor is still seen as having a responsibility to contribute to the creation of national wealth and to carry out other social responsibilities. Telenor is also required to offer the same basic telecommunications on the same terms nationwide (Telenor 1995).

As a market participant, the company also is responsible for gaining sufficient competitive advantage, and adequate profitability. Telenor's market role has become increasingly pronounced in recent years and the political signals have been unambiguous—Make a profit!

Telenor is rated, in terms of income, as the country's eighth largest company (Økonomisk Rapport 1992:11). As of December 1994, Telenor had 15,200 employees (including 13,795 full-time jobs).[3] Compared to international companies, Telenor is a small organization. However, it does have strong international standing in the fields of network technology, satellite communication, and mobile telephony.

Early investment in technological innovation has made Norway a leading nation in the field of telecommunication infrastructure. Digitalization

3. It is difficult to compare the number of employees before and after the 1993 organizational changes. If the subcompanies such as Telenor Mobile, Telenor Plus, and TBK are included then Telenor had a total of 18,469 employees as of December 1994. Before 1993 many of these employees were employed in the core company of Norwegian Telecom.

FIGURE 7.1. Telenor Organization as of 1 January 1995

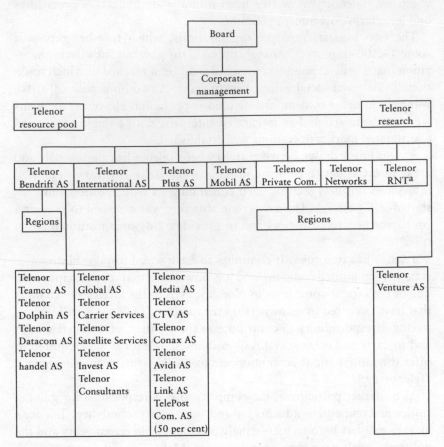

a Regulated Network Services

of the telecommunications network began in earnest in 1987. The degree of digitalization reached 60 percent in 1993, and by 1998 the network will be almost entirely digitalized. Accessibility in the network was 98.3 percent in 1993.

An analysis of the level of telecommunications infrastructure among twenty-three countries in the world put Norway in the third position in 1990 (Stanislawski 1993).[4] Only the United States and Sweden reached a higher level. The growth of subscriptions per inhabitant in Norway has been particularly rapid since 1980, as shown in Table 7.1.

4. The items that make up the Infrastructure Index in the analysis are: (1) main lines

TABLE 7.1. Telephone subscriptions per 100 inhabitants, 1980–1993

1980	29.3
1981	31.6
1982	34.5
1983	37.6
1984	40.0
1985	42.3
1986	44.6
1987	46.4
1988	47.8
1989	48.9
1990	50.2
1991	51.4
1992	52.8
1993	54.0

Source: Telenor Employment Statistics.

Regulatory Changes Defining the Nature of Competition

Until 14 June 1990, when the Norwegian government decided to introduce competition in mobile telephony in Norway, the state and Telenor had a monopoly in the telecommunications market. Competition was extended further on 1 January 1993 when all data transmissions were opened to free competition and resale of unused capacity on leased lines was permitted.

Telenor does still have a high degree of monopoly power in the Norwegian telecommunications market. Telenor has the exclusive right to build and operate public telecommunications networks, including the supply of leased lines, unless stipulated otherwise in accordance with the Norwegian Telecommunications Act. Furthermore, only Telenor and other specially licensed telecommunication operators may offer and deliver public two-way real-time voice services, either alone or in conjunction with other telecommunication and telex services. All other telecommunication services can be offered and delivered by other service suppliers in competition with Telenor.

The conditions for connection to Telenor's network and reserved services are the same for all parties (Annual Report 1993). To ensure that these conditions are met, general regulations covering open telecommuni-

per 100 population, (2) national traffic per head, (3) international traffic per head, (4) payphones per 1,000 population, (5) waiting time for main line (months), (6) revenue per employee, (7) mobile subscribers per 1000 population, (8) percentage of main lines connected to digital exchange, and (9) network quality.

cations networks and network services were introduced by the government on 1 January 1993.

Part of the rationale for the regulatory changes described above is Norway's efforts to comply with European agreements that are pushing for a more open international telecommunications market. The European Economic Area (EEA) agreement makes the European Union (EU) Open Network Provision (ONP) binding in Norway. The EU's ONP requirements are set by EU Council directives and recommendations. Similar directives for speech telephony and other services are expected in the future. The EU Council Resolution of 16 June 1993 calls for the abolition of exclusive rights to voice services no later than 1 January 1998 (Gemini Consulting 1992:13).

The general EU legislation governing public purchasing entered into force 1 January 1994. At the same time the public sector, including Telenor, was made subject to Norwegian regulations corresponding to the EU directives on the purchase of civil engineering services. The EEA rules governing public purchases will also have an impact on Telenor as a supplier, since the agreement allows companies to compete for deliveries to the public sector in all EEA countries. The EEA legislation forbids partnerships and other arrangements which may hinder competition, and thus cause higher prices. Partnerships proposals can still be submitted to the European Commission for evaluation on a case-by-case basis (Annual Report 1993).

The net effect of all of the regulatory changes that have occurred in Norway is that some telecommunications services remain regulated while others are open to free competition. Telenor offers services in both fields. The conditions for connection to Telenor's network and regulated services are required (by law) to be the same for all competing service operators whether they are one of Telenor's subcompanies or competitors.

Market-Related Changes That Result from Technological Innovations

Technological innovations, especially during the last decade, have given impetus to the development of competitive markets and the creation of cheaper and more varied telecommunications services in Norway as elsewhere. In this and other ways technological advances have radically affected both national and international telecommunications networks. The telephone and the telegraph used to be the most important means of communication. Today bits and bytes are the very basis of the competition, and the boundaries between speech, text, and video communications are gradually being erased. In the long run data, speech, and video suppliers will operate in the same market.

At the beginning of 1994, eighteen foreign telecommunication companies were registered as having activities in, or directed at, Norway.[5] Eight of these companies were not active in Norway at the beginning of 1992. All of the new entrants are larger than Telenor. They have a larger home market and a stronger capital base (Annual Report 1993).

Telenor also increasingly faces competition from domestic competitors. But because Telenor retains a monopoly in the telephony market, domestic contractors first have challenged Telenor in the provision of catalog services, cable television, mobile telephony, paging, mobile data, and value-added services in general. The possibilities in the new digitalized network and satellite communication enable both the domestic contractors and Norwegian companies to offer and use total bypass services, and in that way avoid using the fixed network, which is the foundation of Telenor's present profitability. Rival firms have already entered the private market through sale of services for mobile telephones and cable television.

In 1993 the telephony market was responsible for 72.6 percent of all of Telenor's profits. Telenor will certainly be facing increased competition in the corporate market, but the company currently has a sound market position because nearly all Norwegian businesses and government institutions are already its customer.

In 1993 telecommunication traffic to and from Norway increased by 7 percent to a total value of NOK 2.3 billion. Telenor International (TI) has continually worked to establish bilateral agreements with the new network operators on exchange of traffic. To strengthen its international infrastructure, TI entered into a number of agreements concerning capacity on sea and land cables outside Norway. Intensive negotiations led to Telenor's signing of an agreement of cooperation with British Telecom in April 1994. Telenor had for the first time in its history a strategic alliance partner. The agreement gives Telenor's corporate customers direct access to British Telecom's global network and services (NTI UpDate 1994 2).

Price Reductions as a Competitive Advantage

Telenor will increasingly use prices as a competitive tool in a steadily more competitive market. Overall prices of telecommunications services were reduced significantly in 1993 and 1994 and price reductions continue in 1995. Prices of telecommunications services were reduced by 30 percent between 1989 and 1994, while consumer prices during the same period increased by 15 percent. This amounts to a cost reduction for

5. The most important companies are: Telia, Sweden; PTT Telecom, Nederland; Swiss PTT Telecom; AT&T; Telephonica, Spain; France Telecom; Deutsche Bundespost; Sprint, U.S.A.; MCI, U.S.A.; British Telecom; Amritech, U.S.A.; and Singapore Telecom. The last two together own 50 percent of NetCom, a Norwegian company which offers mobile telephony in competition with Telenor Mobile AS.

Norwegian businesses and firms in 1993 of approximately NOK 500 million. For the first time ever Telenor was able to offer large customers a bonus scheme, based on a three-year contract, which gives savings of up to 16 percent on telephone calls. Norwegian telephone costs for Norwegian business subscribers in 1994 were the lowest in Western Europe (NTI UpDate 1994:2).

The Consumer Revolution

The market liberalization of telecommunications services in the 1990s opened up new alternatives for customers. They no longer accept a quality of service in which they have to put up with being on a waiting list for a private telephone or where complaints are dealt with slowly. Furthermore, corporate customers prefer to negotiate about a wide range of product services and prices, which until recently was unheard of. Despite reduced exports, high unemployment, and low economic growth in Norway in the early 1990s, there has been an increased demand for telecommunications services. The number of subscribers and telephone traffic have increased substantially.

For Telenor, adaptation to service production is seen as important in meeting the needs of its customers, who to an increasing extent are now able to choose among several alternatives in the telecommunications market. Open competition can be an advantage to everybody, especially to consumers or customers (Hernes 1978:29). In 1998 the last bastion of the telecommunications monopoly will fall. Then there will be full competition in every telecommunication area, with the customer exercising sizable influence.

The next sections of this chapter analyze the changes in work practices that have been spurred by the changes occurring in Telenor's market, regulatory, and technological context. The effects of and the controversies surrounding the changes will be discussed. Telenor's reputation as a secure, predictable, and caring employer will be evaluated. My research has focused on employees in Telenor's basic organization, as well as the telephone operators, who belong to the separate financial unit TeleService.

Workplace Governance and Participation in the Reorganization Process

The Framework of Laws and Agreements

Employment relations in Norway take place in a social-democratic context.[6] The position of Norwegian workers, represented by powerful

---

6. See Sivesind et al. (1995), who argue for using the concept of employment relations instead of industrial relations in analyzing Norwegian working life. This work also gives a more detailed presentation of the Norwegian social-democratic context.

political parties and unions and protected by a framework of laws and agreements, is strong. Ragnvald Kalleberg (1993) refers to "the privileged position of labor" when describing the period between 1945 and the 1980s. This framework is built into the structures of Norwegian firms by employee representation on governing boards, by the existence of work-environment committees, and through other institutionalized cooperation based on agreements between central employer and employee organizations (Kalleberg 1993:3).

The types of governance processes which are practiced within Telenor are similar to those found in other Norwegian companies. Cooperation is largely based on two binding documents—the Main Agreement between the Norwegian Federation of Trade Unions (LO) and the Confederation of Norwegian Business and Trade (NHO), and the Work Environment Act. The Company Act gives employees representation on management boards.

Until Telenor became a limited company, the State Employee Act ensured union participation in the recruitment process. Negotiations on special wage agreements and working conditions (e.g., working hours and age of retirement) were conducted according to the terms of the State Employment Disputes Act. When Telenor became a limited company, one of the most important processes was a reformulation of its employer-employee agreements. During the first months of 1995 a completely new contract, replacing the State Employee Act, was signed after lengthy negotiations.

The general aim of the Work Environment Act is to contribute to improvements in the workplace, both physical and psychosocial. The machinery for implementing the act is decentralized and local, and employees are able to participate in and influence all kinds of organizational development, such as the introduction of new technology. Consequently, the act may be characterized as not only a strategy aiming at better health and safety in the workplace, but also as a participatory, democratic reform (Kalleberg 1993:4). In Telenor the Work Environment Committee and workers' representatives are given the power to improve the working environment, especially with regard to problems of noise or ergonomics.

Employment Relations in Practice

Telenor's employee organizations are regarded as a normal part of the governance structure. The employer's duty to inform and the employees' right to have discussions and negotiations are institutionalized. Nearly 95 percent of all employees in the basic organization of Telenor are members of an employees' organization, but their active interest is generally very limited (Solbraekke 1993, 1995).

Workers are represented by four employee organizations: (1) The Telecommunication Workers' Union (TD) has members in both the public and private sector and is affiliated with the Norwegian Federation of Trade Unions, which has strong ties to the Labor party (Det Norske Arbeiderpartiet). Most field service technicians and network technicians belong to this union, but some managers are also members. TD organizes both men and women, but males dominate the membership and committees. (2) The National Association of Telecommunication Workers (KTTL) has been affiliated with the Confederation of Unions, a politically independent alternative to the Norwegian Federation of Trade Unions, since 1977. Most members in KTTL are telephone operators, customer service representatives, or staff personnel, and they are mostly women. TD and KTTL represent together some 14,500 employees in Telenor. (3) Engineers with a three-year education are members of the Norwegian Society of Engineers (NITO), an independent association for engineers in both the public and private sectors. In Telenor, NITO represents 1,500 employees, and although this association has members of both sexes, it is male-dominated. (4) Chartered Engineers are members of Telenor's Society of Chartered Engineers, an independent branch of the Norwegian Society of Chartered Engineers. Both men and women (about 650 at Telenor) are chartered engineers and have a four-year engineering education.

As well as participating in formal organs, the elected representatives participate in a number of ad hoc groups. Work groups, project groups, and various committees not only have the task of implementing decisions, but also have a role in shaping the organization's development, especially in the early stage of strategy formulation.

In the past, when Telenor recruited managers, it was seen as an advantage if they had gained experience as an elected representative of an employee organization. Only a few years ago it was quite common for high-ranking middle managers also to be union representatives. Thus, managers have often been sitting on both sides of the negotiating table. It is no longer possible for individuals to play such a double role because managers are no longer allowed to be union representatives. If a union representative is promoted to a managerial position, he or she must give up the position as a union representative.

Governance Policy and Participation in Practice: Changes and Consequences

The 1993 reorganization of Telenor was a typical one-step transfer, where everything took place simultaneously. Commenting on the problems commonly encountered in this sort of critical transfer phase, where one moves into the unknown, Philip Herbst states: "At this stage in the development it will be of significance that all parties involved have attained agreement on which direction to go, and have gained sufficient trust in each other" (Herbst 1977: 23). Thus, employees' participation in the planning process is of fundamental importance in determining the success of a reorganization. It is vitally important that changes are perceived as legitimate. Whether or not future large-scale organizational changes at Telenor win legitimacy is therefore dependent on what influence employees expect they will have on the result.

Low participation in the planning process of a reorganization can lead to other problems as well. One of them is that low participation prevents middle managers from adding their experience to the decision-making process, despite their close contact with customers and production (Mintzberg 1990: 26). Middle managers are the nerve centers of their organizational units (Mintzberg 1989: 17). One of their responsibilities is to inform subordinates about changes which are to be implemented.

The reorganization process at Telenor illustrates how the problems mentioned above can surface. When Telenor's middle managers were not involved in the important reorganization processes, information always came to them second hand and was therefore filtered. Consequently, these managers could not give good enough arguments and explanations for decisions that were made. Their subordinates distrusted them for withholding information, and managerial authority was lost (Solbrackke 1995).

Robert Merton states that fundamental considerations such as technical effectiveness and profitability are important, but decision makers also have to be conscious of the organization's culture, traditions, history, and value systems (Merton 1976: 85). At Telenor there was limited sensitivity to such concerns. The most recent planning phase at Telenor was carried out in accordance with formal agreements, but the elected representatives were reduced to being mere players in the different networks. Employee organizations have had the right to express their opinions on changing strategies. However, compared to earlier years when the company was less cost-conscious, it is clear that the bargaining power of the employee organizations has been reduced.

At Telenor now there is serious discussion of the possibility of comprehensive and systematic cost cutting and layoffs. Yet, the employee organizations' proposals, recommendations, and demands were not given serious consideration by Telenor's corporate management. Neither the elected representatives, nor indeed a great majority of the managers, have had any discernible influence on the strategies of market-oriented change (Solbraekke 1995).

The changes that have recently occurred at Telenor have therefore very little legitimacy among employees, especially those concerning organization structure, transformation to a limited company, compensation arrangements and, last but not least, cost cutting through staff reduction. Consequently Telenor has experienced a lot of turbulence and opposition. A major part of the work force experiences the reorganization process as a breach of trust (Solbraekke 1995). This sense of employee distrust comes through in the field interviews conducted with employees from a wide range of sites and occupations.

At the same time, objective indicators of such employee mistrust are difficult to find. It may be significant that customer surveys after 1 March 1993 showed less customer satisfaction than earlier. During 1994, however, customer satisfaction attained the same level as before the 1993 reorganization.

In public organization almost 140 years old, with a strong organizational culture, one cannot isolate the ongoing events from the history that has shaped employees' expectations and the structure of work. The system of internal education, the routines for appointments and promotion, and the wage and industrial relation system all influence the ongoing events at Telenor. I will go on to give a more detailed description of the changes that have affected employees, focusing particularly on changes to their day-to-day working lives.

Work Organization: Skill Formation, New Technology, and Centralization

Until a few years ago, when Telenor began externally recruiting some employees with special qualifications in the fields of marketing, sales, and accounting, most of its staff started to work for the company right after they had completed their secondary or upper secondary school education. In the postwar period Telenor developed a complete education program for every purpose in the organization. Central in Telenor's competence development program has been the idea of giving each employee a training relevant to his or her individual interests, abilities, and career plans. Such training should also be consonant with Telenor's needs. A main goal of this personnel strategy was to offer employees education and development opportunities which would enhance their possibilities of advancement within the organization and enable them to compete with external applicants. Internal education has in only a few cases provided employees with formal qualifications that gave them better opportunities with other companies.

In spite of extensive support and encouragement to take further education at university or college, it is mostly managers, or staff who already have some higher education, who have made use of the offer. As shown in Table 7.2 the level of formal education has therefore been low in Telenor.

As a consequence of the recent market orientation process, Telenor's education program has changed, both ideologically and in practice. When new workers are recruited today, they have to be both broadly skilled and qualified to do the particular tasks linked to the position. Internal education now focuses on small, specially constructed courses, organized to train employees in areas such as new technology, customer service, project work, financial planning, and management.

Telephone Operators

Telenor's telephone operators help customers with national and international directory enquiries, and provide long distance calls, telephone meetings, the Norway direct service (a reverse-charge service for callers from abroad), a personal seeking service, a waking service, and different telegraph services. In 1992 these services were radically centralized, and today it is only the national directory enquiries service that has not been centralized in Oslo. This service was organized into 18 centers throughout the country as a part of governmental regional employment policy until a March 1995 reorganization plan. Seven of these groups will be shut down during 1995 as a final step toward complete centralization.

In the course of 1992, new technology was installed that enabled telephone operators to execute all of the above-mentioned services (with the exception of national and international directory enquiries and telegraph services) from one computer. After the introduction of new technology it is not far-fetched to describe the working situation of the telephone oper-

TABLE 7.2. Education levels in Telenor, percentage of the workforce

	1990	1994
Level 2—7–9 years	9.3	8.7
Level 3—10 years	29.6	24.6
Level 4—11–12 years	38.0	37.9
Level 5—13–14 years	7.9	10.6
Level 6—15–16 years	10.9	12.1
Level 7—17–18 years	4.2	5.1
Ph.D.—19–20 years	0.1	0.2

Source: Telenor Employment Statistics.
Note: Norwegian standard classification of education from the Central Bureau of Statistics is used.

ators as a modern version of Taylorism. Taylor's ideas are built into the computer systems, and the computer itself has taken over many managerial responsibilities. The machine organizes the work, the executioner carries out the work and is instructed to do so in the most efficient way.[7] Moreover, work is subject to physical surveillance by managers who at any time have complete control over who is in their seats, who is eating, who is having a ten-minute break, who is in the lavatory, who is using the telephone for a private call, or who is having a chat with their neighbor. Statistics which show the average response time, the number of answered calls, and the number of lost calls give at any time information on the relationship between resource use and income.

In Norway employees generally work a 37.5 hour week. The telephone operators work both days and nights and their weekly hours were not changed after service centralization. However, their work schedule has been transformed. Earlier they were on duty either morning, afternoon, or night. Today they are on duty at all hours, in a number of arrangements whose main goal is to tackle customer peaks. The early shift is often divided in two, where the operators have to work from seven in the morning to eleven o'clock, and then be off duty until three o'clock in afternoon. They will then be on duty until seven o'clock in the evening. For those who live an hour or more from work this is an untenable working situation. Night duty can often start at seven o'clock in the evening and finish at two A.M. For those who do not have a car, it is necessary to take a taxi to get home because there is no public transport at night.

The telephone operators are probably the group of employees in Telenor who have had the lowest formal competence and lowest status. Few employees in these groups have formal education above level 2 or level 3.[8] Over the years many of the telephone operators have become highly skilled linguists. Language courses and language grants for study abroad have been the most important ways in which the company has raised their level of competence. It is not unusual that operators handling long distance calls and international directory enquiries speak three to four foreign languages fluently. In 1992 all telephone operators underwent extensive training programs in the use of new computer systems and customer service.

Telephone operator services became an independent financial unit, TeleService, in 1992. As a result they went from being accepted as un-

---

7. See Solbraekke (1993: chaps. 6 and 8) for a more complete discussion of the telephone operators' computer system and the influence it has had on their working situation.
8. See Table 7.2 for information about education levels in Telenor.

profitable services to having to face hard demands of profitability, demands they could not meet without raising national directory enquiry charges. After extensive discussions with the Government, Telenor was allowed, for the first time, to raise the charges for this service to a level more reflective of costs. With a turnover in 1993 of NOK 247 million, the national directory enquiry service covered its own expenses.

Customer Service Representatives

Usually customer service representatives have a 37.5 hour week and fixed working hours. This occupational group belongs primarily to the Personal Communication Division, even if some are found in the Network Business Division.[9]

Prior to Telenor's reorganization in 1993, a completely new customer service concept was developed and the customer services were split up into numerous areas of responsibility—order reception, finishing process, reclamation, fault complaint service, and line register. The customer service concept was founded on the following principles: (1) The customer shall be met by a united Telenor. (2) Through training the customer service representatives shall be able to service a wide and flexible front-line aimed at the customer. (3) Peak-period delays are to be avoided.

All customer service personnel received new computer terminals which are linked to all computer systems that are being used. Earlier at least three different terminals had to be used by the same person in order to execute the task, in addition to significant manual labour (Karstensen 1994). The customer service representatives are responsible for the line register, hence they also serve field service technicians directly via terminals where orders are written daily. The objective is to develop closer cooperation between the two groups of employees.

Through the customer concept the customer service representatives will get better knowledge of the different working tasks in the total process of which they are a part. In spite of the fact that they have to execute more tasks, their autonomy is not increased. On the contrary, because they can today handle all tasks from one computer they face demands by management to reduce response time. Like the telephone operator, they

9. The Network Business Division was, until the organizational changes made in January 1995, responsible for Norwegian Telecom's activities in the corporate market. The Network Business Division accounted for approximately 33% of Norwegian Telecom's annual sales in 1993. The Personal Communications Division develops and supplies telecommunications services to private customers over the fixed network. Its activities gradually have expanded into entertainment and multimedia and information services although ordinary telephone services still dominate the division's business.

are today subject to physical surveillance by supervisors who can more easily control their movements. Information on the number of answered calls, lost calls, and so forth completes the control over their working situation which is no less "Tayloristic" than the work of telephone operators.

While the changes described above have made the job of customer service representative less attractive, since 1993 improving the customer service representative's job has become a top priority with Telenor because of their frequent contact with customers. As part of the new customer service concept, they are all to receive certification. The customer service representatives will clearly enjoy higher general status in the organization as a result of the extensive training program they will go through, before taking their exams and receiving the title of customer consultant. In addition to general training in all customer service functions, they will receive quality training as sales representatives. The training program is separated into three main modules, representing three training levels. In order to keep their jobs, representatives will have to pass at least the first level. Whether this training will counteract the negative effects described above remains to be seen.

Field Service Technicians

Traditionally field service technicians have had freedom in Telenor. They have to a great extent been able to plan their own day as long as the customers have had their faults repaired and telephones installed in a reasonable time. A basic working week is 37.5 hours. To ensure that repairs are carried out if special problems arise, there is a voluntary overtime arrangement. The field service technicians belong primarily to the Personal Communication Division.

The work of field service technicians traditionally was divided into three clearly defined areas—installation, fault repair, and construction the telephone network. The field service technicians were specialized in one of these areas. Today all field service technicians must execute tasks in all three areas. The work force is to be directed to where it is needed most, and stricter norms for precision of delivery have been implemented.

A new arrangement whereby technicians begin their working day at the customer's site rather than clocking on first at the joint base is to be implemented nationally. Today this is only fully practiced in Oslo. This gives about two extra effective working hours per day. However, unless distance makes it impossible, the field technician will have lunch at the base with his or her colleagues, and at the same time receive the next day's work schedule. Some years ago two field service technicians always worked together on the same job. Today, this is seldom the case, apart from larger jobs. The field service technicians have therefore become more isolated from their colleagues than before, and the job's social dimension will suffer when new arrangements are implemented nationwide.

Field service technicians usually have no formal education above level 2 or 3.[10] The special field service technician training course, which has been the foundation of the internal education program, is no longer given and the last internal apprenticeship certificates were awarded in 1992. Since then, workers without an internal apprenticeship certificate have been offered an officially approved course. Many take advantage of this offer because this qualification gives them better opportunities in the external labor market. This change in the internal education of the field service technician does not affect their opportunity for taking training courses in fields such as the new technology of digital exchanges or computing. Applicants for future field technician positions will have to possess a formal educational qualification in computer technology.

Self-managed work groups have never been established in Telenor, although team organization earlier has been tried out among field service technicians in Oslo. The team organization was a result of a local management strategy when Oslo represented a local Tele-area. However, these teams were shut down during the reorganization because structuring of the Personal Communication Division should be the same in all parts of the country. This is a clear illustration of the highly centralized management-by-objectives policy the company has embraced.

Engineers and Technicians

This group of employees is very heterogeneous both in terms of education and work tasks. In the basic organization most of these workers belong to the Network Division, but some still have their jobs in the Personal Communication Division or in the Network Business Division.[11] These employees are the first affected by the reorganization process through the changes in the organizational structure. Through the divisionalization and centralization of many functions, the local decision-making centers were shut down. For many of the engineers and technicians, positioned in the local Tele-areas, this meant that their services

10. See Table 7.2 for information about education levels in Telenor.
11. The Network Division is the operator of the fixed network and has overall responsibility for Telenor's joint product platform. The Network Division's primary tasks are to build, plan, and operate the network, but it also assists in product development.

were no longer required. To avoid moving they had to apply for new positions, that is, management positions. Engineers and technicians have traditionally had a significant level of freedom and flexibility in their work.

These are the occupational groups in Telenor who have the highest formal education, even though many of them started as field service technicians or telegraph operators. The oldest of the technicians have taken their higher technological education inside Telenor, the so-called Higher Course, while others have taken college courses with economic support from Telenor. The technological staff have always been a powerful group. The company has focused on technology rather than the customer. Work on developing customer understanding in technical fields has therefore intensified recently. Technological developments will make the older technical knowledge superfluous, and without competence in data processing systems or digital exchanges a lot of the older technicians will face an insecure future.

Middle Managers

All management positions were internally advertised during the 1993 reorganization at Telenor and all managers in Telenor were reappointed. Due to staff reductions and the restructuring of several central functions, all positions received a high number of applications. Traditionally, employees had moved into management positions by seniority. Yet, in recent years criteria such as personal proficiency and formal qualifications have been more decisive. The regional management themselves decided on the practice to be followed in the appointing process, and in many situations it seems as though they have taken care of their own interests by maintaining the social network of which they already are a part, a common phenomenon according to Mark Granovetter (1985: 75). But occasionally regional management did an enormous amount of work to appoint managers with qualifications best suited to a market-oriented organization, that is, managers who take care of and develop the company's human resources, without losing sight of track of the main objective of good financial results. The employee organizations' representatives had no influence in the appointing process, which traditionally have been area of union influence in Telenor.

It is very rare to find a middle manager who has not climbed Telenor's organizational ladder. Many of them have been through the company's internal education programs, usually starting in a telephone operator, telegraph operator, or field service technician training program. Even at the top management level, the majority have their field service technician certificate or telephone operator qualification. For example, a former executive personnel manager began as a telephone operator. After a number of years of internal education and a period in which she led the National Association of Telecommunication Workers, she ended up as personnel manager for nearly 20,000 employees. Most managers in Telenor are men with technological education which they have acquired while they were employees of the organization. In addition, most managers have participated in one or more of the internal management training programs.

In connection with the introduction of the customer service concept, a separate training program for the customer service managers has been developed. The program will offer formal training in marketing, market research, and project work. All customer service managers will have to complete the training program. During 1994, two extensive management training programs were held. One of them was aimed at new managers who had limited experience of personnel or financial responsibilities, while the other was for top managers. This was a joint offer, in which managers from both small and large units participated. In addition, a two-year trainee program for younger potential managers with at least two years of experience started in August 1994. These candidates, in the 25 to 30 age group, have to have a degree with excellent grades. The great effort put into management training is grounded on the need for responsible, independent, and flexible managers with a high competence in both financial and human resources.

All middle managers have generally faced harder demands to achieve results than ever before. Without exception, managers state that the most significant difference in the new organization is the focusing on results, the stricter reporting routines, and the increased involvement in day-to-day operations (Solbraekke 1995). There is no longer the liberty to lean back in their chairs with folded arms.

Work Organization and Education Policy: Changes and Consequences

The result of the century-old recruitment and education policy is that the company's personnel have a relatively low level of formal education. The extensive internal training Telenor has carried out has made the organization predictable and conservative, but has also developed loyal and dependent employees (Solbraekke 1995). Their acquired knowledge is hardly transferable to business outside Telenor, and personnel turnover has been extraordinarily low. There has been little infusion of new blood and this has particularly affected recruitment to management positions.

The changes in educational and training policy are founded on the following principles: (1) Extreme importance is attached to customer treatment. (2) There is no recruiting of workers who do not have a formal qualification directly relevant to the position to be filled. (3) An organization in a competitive market derives general advantage from a work force with a high formal education. (4) Extensive management training of all Telenor's managers is an important feature of organizational development.

For Telenor's employees the new market orientation is most apparent through increased insecurity, centralization of the different services, new technology, and increased work pressure because of staff reductions. Those who experience the greatest increased work pressure are most troubled about work during their leisure time and have most trouble sleeping. Thirty-five percent of employees report they go to work when they are ill because they fear negative consequences (Solbraekke 1995). The fact that absence due to illness dropped from 5.9 percent in 1991 to 5.1 percent in 1993, does not necessarily give a correct picture of the situation—it might just as well illustrate an increased fear of losing one's job. However, during 1994, emphasis is being placed on health, environment, and safety in the organization as an important part of the internal control and a total quality ideology. Staff satisfaction surveys are meant to be a central tool in this work.

Flexible and efficient use of the organization's human resources will be developed in the future and, consequently, each employee is going to have to execute more tasks than before. Statistics which at any time give information about response time and customer service time will make it possible to compare different groups of telephone operators and customer service representatives to show which group is the most efficient so as to learn from their example. The Personal Communication Division also introduced systematic market studies in 1993, in which private customers were asked about their satisfaction or dissatisfaction with telecom services. The 1993 studies showed that Telenor is doing a good job in a number of areas, but there is room for improvement in others, such as the handling of complaints about telephone bills.

In the service industry it is important to establish successful cooperation between the customer and the supplier, and human resources are a vitally important factor of production (Normann 1991). Training and other personnel development therefore have strategic importance. However, the extraordinary emphasis put on customer service is problematic.

Firstly, a fully developed customer service concept implies work force reductions because the new technology leads to dramatic rationalization, and employees feel insecure about their future in the company. This is a fact of life for both managers and customer service representatives.

Secondly, in spite of the fact that the Work Environment Act emphasizes central union participation in the introduction of new technology, the development of the customer service concept was a process managed from the top. Neither the employees who meet the customers face to face nor union representatives had any influence. Lack of information before the concept's introduction has led to a loss of morale and suspicion. Consequently, employees have focused more on their own insecurity than on satisfying the customer, and the willingness of managers to do their best in fully implementing the concept has varied (Solbraekke 1995).

Forms of Compensation

A well-established tradition in Scandinavian countries has been a union policy of wage equalization, or wage solidarity. Organized labor in Norway has generally advocated a lowering of wage differentials between white and blue collar sectors as well as within the sectors themselves. This policy should be seen in the context of the relatively strong egalitarian tradition in Norwegian society (Gustavsen and Hunnius 1981: 23).

Because Telenor until recently has been a government institution, wages have followed the Public Wage Scale. This wage scale, which is for all public employees, is based on the Main Agreement of Tariffs, between the State, the Federation of State Employees, and the Norwegian Union of Teachers. Agreements are usually signed for a period of two years. The Main Agreement of Tariffs consists of wage tables, wage scales, and general agreements. There are also other regulations in the form of wage adjustments, wage norms, regulation of certain incitements, pension conditions, and so forth.

The government introduced a new wage policy in 1991 which gave state-run companies a greater opportunity to establish independent and flexible wage policies. Since 1991 the state has, as a part of the wage agreement, offered a certain amount of money to the state-run companies which is to be distributed through local wage negotiations. In 1993 this represented 0.4 percent of all public-sector wage increases (TD-bladet 1993:7).

One of the features of a local wage policy is the use of alternative wage scales. There are five different wage scales—the basic scale, the alternative scale, and three direct wage level placements. A direct wage level placement, as opposed to the wage scales, is a fixed wage level based on the job, and this component of the wage never increases. Telenor has made extensive use of alternative wage scales for all positions, and local wage agreements have become a central plank of personnel policy. Telenor had from 1991 a higher percentage (36 percent) of direct wage level placement than what is usual for the state (30 percent). There is no automatic wage advancement in these positions.

In wage negotiations, pay offers made by state-run companies are dependent on central government decisions. However, Telenor has been the exception to this rule, contributing to local wage agreements with its own funds. In 1991 this represented NOK 4.2 million and in 1994 NOK 9 million (at the 1993 exchange rate 7.1 NOK equalled one U.S. dollar). Telenor's freedom to define its own priorities has in this area been larger than is usual for state-run companies. Telenor management intends to use the company's greater economic freedom to adapt its wage policy to the market.

There is not a big gap between those with high wages and those with low wages in Telenor. On 1 May 1993, NOK 421,757 was the highest yearly salary among managing directors, and there was hardly any employee who earned less than NOK 155,825. Some individuals, such as the corporate managing director, however, had additional bonuses. The average monthly wage in the corporate management and staff divisions is NOK 22,656. In comparison, the average monthly wage in certain financial units is NOK 17,001. These financial units primarily consist of telephone operators, where both ordinary wages and fixed and variable bonuses, such as night and weekend remuneration, are included in the calculations.

Wage Policy as a Part of the Market Orientation Policy

The average rise in wages during the period October 1992 to June 1993 was 3.5 percent. The most generous increases have been made in connection with the new positions that were established as a result of reorganization. Employees who have been appointed to new positions, about 11 percent of the workforce or 1,800 employees, have in the same period had an average wage increase of 10.5 percent. The others, that is to say about 14,700 employees who remained in their own positions, had an average increase of 2.5 percent. The highest wage increases were given to the managers appointed to new positions. They had an average increase of 11.6 percent, compared to managers who continued in their old positions, who had an average increase of 3.5 percent.

The tendency is the same in all occupation groups; the newly appointed are those who have received the highest salary increases. In contrast to the previous practice where collective negotiations set the terms and conditions of employment for all employees at all levels, pay progression is now based on individual performance appraisal and personal contracts. Official policy stipulates that all employees can experience performance appraisals. However, only managers and a few highly skilled employees actually undergo performance appraisal at Telenor. In these cases, performance appraisal is typically used to meet market pressures and to provide extra pay increases.

Pay is based on achieved results, problem solving, decision-making expertise, and service quality performance. It is not unusual that individual managers within a management team, for example district managers within a region, have different salaries, according to education, experience, and results. This breaks with Telenor's tradition of basing salaries on title, position, and seniority.

Since the early seventies, one of the slogans of the Norwegian feminist movement has been "equal pay for equal work." In spite of union policy on wage equalization and wage solidarity and the work of the feminist movement, the wage statistics shown in Table 7.3 make it clear that in all occupations, men get more money than women in the same position. This is also the case in occupations where there are a majority of women. But the difference is largest in traditionally male jobs such as field service technicians, technicians, and engineers. In recent years there has been a tendency for this "wage gender gap" to narrow.

Wage Policy: Changes and Consequences

An important strategy in market orientation has been that of establishing a less rigid wage system. Earlier it was only seniority and category of position that counted in determining wages. Today, highly educated employees and managers have individual paysetting determined by personal qualifications and they also have possibilities for well-paid jobs in competing companies. Other groups' wages are arrived at through collective bargaining. However, even employees who are appointed anew in the groups affected by collective bargaining can now get individual paysetting based on individual ability and qualifications.

Employees who were appointed to new positions during the recent reorganization have experienced a higher relative increase in wages. Those

TABLE 7.3. Average monthly wage in NOK in relation to gender

	1989		1990		1991		1992	
	Female	Male	Female	Male	Female	Male	Female	Male
TO/CSR	12,009	12,184	12,912	13,292	13,776	13,989	14,055	14,291
FST	10,997	11,986	12,684	13,641	13,741	14,555	14,014	14,637
T	12,752	44,995	13,731	16,065	14,701	17,192	15,048	17,103
E	15,804	16,798	17,108	17,785	18,620	19,013	19,042	19,296
Ch.E	17,245	19,713	18,456	20,843	19,007	22,019	19,796	22,272
MM	21,574	21,851	21,967	22,412	23,065	23,536	23,645	24,191

Source: Telenor Employment Statistics.

Note: Averaged wage includes all the additional bonuses, e.g., night, weekend, and afternoon bonuses.

TO = Telephone operators.

CSR = Customer service representatives.

FST = Field service technicians.

T = Technicians with internal course or education level 4 or 5.

E = Engineers with education level 6.

Ch.E = Engineers with education level 7.

MM = Middle managers: averaged wage includes top and two lower middle manager grades (technical and office managers).

who kept their old positions kept their wage level, and hence, in terms of pay, have been left far behind. Among employees with the same seniority and same type of position, there is now a salary gap which may be as high as NOK 5,000 a month. This new state of affairs has made for an uneasy internal working environment.

The internal job market in Telenor is large, and mobility between different positions has increased considerably after reorganization especially because of the new wage opportunities. In 1992 and 1993 it was not unusual for employees with highly sought-after skills to change jobs three or four times in order to increase their wage level. There was no time to develop and consolidate the groups that were affected by this mobility, and therefore, additional advancement for such workers was frozen for six months in the autumn of 1993.

In a context where wage solidarity has been a basic norm, it is quite natural that the new wage policy led to great dissatisfaction among employees who have not been able to exert any influence on their own wage levels. New criteria for wage-determination will certainly not be accepted either by union representatives or the average employee, as long as personal assessment is a central part of these criteria.

The new wage policy which is outlined above is an example of an area in which the unions have lost influence in Telenor. Nevertheless, the calculation and determination of wages seems steadily to move in the direction of more flexibility. In spite of the fact that wage policy in Norway is still ideologically based, the market would seem to be winning greater acceptance as a wage determinant (Sivesind et al. 1995).

Employment Security and Staffing Arrangements

Telenor is one of several government institutions that traditionally have offered young people internal education and a high level of job security. Aud Korbøl (1977) emphasizes that this job security was valid nationwide. Earlier research has shown that young people have applied for work in Telenor because it was considered a safe and secure place of work, a perception which is one of the main conditions for loyalty toward the institution (Falck 1978). The organization has always offered membership in the public pension fund, an arrangement which also provided financial security in old age.

Telephone automation in the 1970s was the first sign of the changing times. Thousands of women's jobs disappeared when the small exchanges in Norway were shut down. Technological development has since the 1970s influenced the staffing situation, but it was not until 1989 that a new staffing policy was applied. Until then, management power in

Telenor was connected to how many employees one was responsible for. Consequently, no managers wanted to compare the number of functions which were to be performed with the number of employees. Manual routines continued in spite of technological innovations that could have replaced them.

Early in 1990 a project called GANT (Gain of New Technology) was carried out. GANT's main purpose was to compare functions and staff, and the project was seen as a preparation for the reorganization's planning phase, which started in early 1991. At that time there were many part-time workers in the organization. In connection with the GANT process it had been decided to limit the possibility of being a part-time worker, and such employees were offered full-time jobs where vacancies occurred.

As shown in Table 7.4 staff reductions started in 1989 at Telenor. Recruitment stoppage and natural redundancies were, however, sufficient to meet the first demands of staff reduction. With the 1993 reorganization of Telenor, jobs and job prospects which earlier had been secure and predictable were now no longer so. All employees state that insecurity as a result of change is the hardest thing to cope with in Telenor's market orientation process. An employee survey finds that 65 percent (of 2525 employees) did not feel secure about their jobs in Telenor. (Solbraekke 1995).

TABLE 7.4. Male and female employment at Telenor, 1983–1994

	Total	Male	Female
1983	21,786	12,734	9,052
1984	21,222	12,495	8,727
1985	21,306	12,471	8,835
1986	22,964	12,906	9,159
1987	22,686	13,128	9,558
1988*	20,483	11,556	8,927
1989	19,790	11,010	8,489
1990	18,794	10,798	7,996
1991	18,159	10,526	7,633
1992	17,717	10,315	7,402
1993	16,167	9,658	6,509
1994	15,568	9,349	6,219

Source: Telenor Employment Statistics.
Note: In 1988 the first sub-company TBK was separated from the base organization. Reductions in 1988 reflect this. As of December 12, 1988, 2159 persons were employed in TBK. In 1993 and 1994 the competitive business were separated into sub-companies, and in 1993 these companies employed 2683 additional employees.
Employee numbers refer to employment as of December 31 each year, except 1 September, 1994.

During the period of 1 March 1993 to 31 December 1995, a staff reduction of 4,200 employees took place. In September 1995, Telenor announced another corporate reorganization which would bring greater centralization in the technical, economic, and personnel office areas. As a result of this centralization about 420 staff employees will have to move to new jobs either inside or outside the firm, or be transferred to the Telenor resource pool described in the next section. Telenor also announced that by 1998 another 2,000 employees would have to find jobs outside Telenor.

How will Telenor solve the problem of overmanning? The reduction program which until recently has been based on recruitment stoppage and natural redundancies inside each section, has so far proved to be insufficient and inappropriate. New steps being adopted to respond to the problem of overmanning are discussed in the next section.

Telenor's Resource Pool

The first of March 1993 marked the start of what is perhaps the largest employment experiment in Norwegian business and industry in recent times. At this time approximately 2,500 employees were transferred to Telenor's Resource Pool (to be referred to as TNM, Televerkets Nye Muligheter). In TNM males and females are represented in almost the same proportion as in the basic organization. Men have therefore since the beginning been in a majority.

The purpose of the TNM division is to find alternative jobs for employees through retraining, new business development, and temporary services in a transitory stage. From April to December 1993, 873 people left TNM. Many of these accepted offers of early retirement. At the end of 1993, TNM had 2,281 employees. Six hundred left TNM during 1994, and the personnel turnover in the division was 36 percent that year. The goal for TNM is to find new work for employees in or outside Telenor (Arbeidsmiljø 1994: 8).

Despite the enormous task of employing so many people outside Telenor's ordinary operations, nearly 90 percent of TNM's employees have been employed the whole time, with the exception of the first few months. In the program, around 700 persons are on study programs. In addition, many have taken shorter, skill-building courses especially designed for the division. Temporary and contract assignments for the rest of Telenor were important activities in 1993. This proved to be of great benefit during the start up of the new organization because the reduction of the employees in Telenor had occurred at too fast a rate. In some instances Telenor had to hire personnel from TNM back to their old positions. This created great dissatisfaction among those affected.

It is mainly employees from administration, support functions, telephone operators, customer service representatives, and field service technicians that have been transferred to TNM, but other occupation groups are also affected, both managers and technicians. All of these occupational groups face severe staff reductions in the coming period.

Alarm Service

A considerable number of business concepts were tested, primarily in the growth areas of travel, environment, safety, transport, and communications. One particularly interesting project is the Trygghetssentralen, an emergency alarm system for elderly and handicapped who live in their own homes. Telenor has purchased Oslo Trygghetssentral and used the concept to establish several switchboards throughout the country. Resource Pool employees are being trained as auxiliary nurses to work for the alarm service. On 24 May 1993, a 24-hour switchboard in Bergen was opened. By the end of the year, the necessary preparations had been completed to offer parts of the service in other areas of the country.

Is TNM an Alternative to Real Work?

Apart from those who have applied for management positions in TNM, or are in further education, employees do not see TNM as an alternative to real work. They consider TNM to be merely a waiting room for unemployment (Solbraekke 1995). The idea of creating new business activities has proved to be unsuccessful. Because of the new staff policy, there could be reasons for believing that the employees would want to leave Telenor and apply for jobs elsewhere. This is not the case. In spite of the fact that the corporate management have decided to close down TNM at the end of 1997, only a third of its employees have plans to search for work outside the organization during the next twelve months.

For those who have spent their entire working life in the organization, there are no external alternatives. They want to stay with Telenor. Telenor has become a part of their identity, and the large staff reductions are considered as a personal betrayal (Solbraekke 1995). They are approaching the edge of the cliff with their hands folded, so to speak.

Early Retirements

An important part of the staff reduction strategies was the offer of early retirement to all employees age sixty or over. Many employees have accepted this offer, which has been valid from 1993 and, provisionally, until the end of 1995. Although early retirement is voluntary, some feel pressured to accept in order to make way for younger employees.

This pension scheme is not covered by the pension provided by the Norwegian Public Service Pension Fund. The costs of early retirement will be met by Telenor. Early retirement pension payments total 66 percent of the employee's pay upon retirement plus a supplement equal to one-quarter of the basic pension amount. This financial compensation means that all will receive a pension equivalent to the one they had received if they had worked to the age of sixty-seven. Staff who accept this offer will not lose their pension entitlements.

Employment Security and Staff Policy: Changes and Consequences

If we are to analyze Telenor's strategy, we have to look at the wider social context. At the time Telenor started the reorganization process, the government would never have allowed it to lay off thousands of employees. The decision as to who had to go to TNM and who could stay in the basic organization was based on age and seniority. The principle of seniority has been strictly followed when reducing staff. Those with least seniority had to go first. This principle has a very strong position in Norway. Through a revision in 1982 of the Main Contract between the Norwegian Federation of Trade Unions and the Confederation of Norwegian Business and Trade the seniority clause was made legally binding. Section 9-e states that in the case of dismissals caused by downsizing or organizational change, seniority shall under equal conditions be applied. No other principle besides seniority is explicitly mentioned in the Main Contract, although the formulation "under equal conditions" must be handled with discretion (Engelstad 1994: 6).

Fredrik Engelstad (1990: 331) draws attention to three reasons why the seniority principle is so firmly established in Norway and elsewhere: (1) Seniority is an objective feature and can be defined. (2) Seniority has no implicit assertion that somebody is less competent and less valuable than others in the organization. (3) Seniority is easy to use.

Telenor's experiences show, however, that the practice of the principle is not without complications, both because "under equal conditions" is subject to interpretation and because seniority is not always easy to calculate. A lot of employees had been a few years in the sub-company TBK, and those years did not count in the calculation of seniority in the basic organization, in spite of the fact that they were encouraged to follow

TBK in 1988.[12] In addition, the reductions did not solely take place in the regions, but in the smaller districts within each region. The reductions were made by a certain percentage in each district and were not based on the total number of employees in the region. This resulted in long-serving employees being transferred to TNM because average seniority in their district was high. This variation brought protests.

The result is a spread of seniority in TNM ranging from one to forty-nine years. About 30 percent have under ten years, and the average is seventeen years. A lot of employees in TNM have spent their whole working life in Telenor. It was the personnel offices in the different regions throughout the country, and their staff officers, who calculated seniority. However, it is possible that managers are able to get rid of employees who are not wanted because of their age, health, or other personal characteristics.

Bitterness and the feeling of being treated unfairly has led to about 265 requests to Telenor's Appeal Body to review the decision which had them transferred to TNM. About ten employees have won their appeals and got their old jobs back. The union representatives have not had any influence on the process which transferred employees to TNM.

The last date for transferring employees to TNM will be 31 December 1996. TNM will be disbanded in 1997. For employees who are transferred to TNM in 1996, there will be a focus on specific, short-term measures. All study applications which are granted from autumn 1994 will be linked to final compensation or voluntary redundancy. Those affected will receive one year's salary, but in special cases Telenor can grant up to two year's wages.

A consequence of the downsizing is a general lack of trust between the employer and employees. Security as a part of the working contract, especially knowing that one's job will be there tomorrow, in a reasonable recognizable setting, is associated with higher flexibility and lower resistance to change. "Insecurity with respect to some basic continuities in the system can produce ritualistic conformity and fear of change—change as a threat, rather than change as opportunity," states Rosabeth Moss Kanter (1990: 85). Telenor employees no longer feel secure. The company's policy must be one of clarifying new norms and values in working relationships in such a way that they can be accepted and understood

12. The subcompany, Norwegian Telecom Business Communication (TBK) was established on 1 January 1988, as a limited company wholly owned by Norwegian Telecom. TBK's main activity has been to meet demands for equipment for the largest customers. The company has built a complete and countrywide sales and service organization, including services involving speech, data, and picture communication.

both by employer and employee. Especially in a situation of competition where Telenor is dependent on a workforce with high flexibility, willing to provide creative and conscientious customer service, it is therefore of great importance to make perfectly clear the conditions of further redundancies as soon as possible. Telenor has no time to waste.

Conclusion

Because of its traditional monopoly situation, Telenor never previously needed to give special priority to market, customers, or service. A strictly bureaucratic organization, based on models from large-scale industry characterized the company. The focus was on technology rather than organizational structure, customers, and service.

Telenor's main challenge today is to adapt to the changes accompanying the transfer from product orientation to market orientation. It has lost its monopoly and its customers have a greater level of awareness as far as service is concerned. Telenor now must compete with both international telecommunication companies, which have targeted the Norwegian market, and domestic suppliers of telecommunication services.

The first major step toward market orientation was completed in 1993–94, and this involved the largest reorganization of Telenor. Telenor's changing strategies are concentrated on two main areas, customer focusing and rationalization. Telenor has undergone a centralization of its functions involving an amount of staff reduction that is huge in Norwegian terms, and for the employees the new market orientation is most apparent through increased insecurity and increased work pressure because of staff reductions. Training and other personnel development have strategic importance, and another important strategy has been that of establishing a less rigid wage system.

Neither the unions nor a great majority of the managers had any significant influence in reorganization decisions, and the corporate management must pay the price in lost legitimacy. It is clear that the bargaining power of the employee organizations has been reduced.

As a part of the new market orientation Telenor became a state-owned limited company and altered both its corporate strategies and its structure. Change is likely to continue. During autumn 1995 the clearly defined boundaries between the regions was removed in the organizational structure, and greater centralized control was given to the divisions.

Telenor has always been regarded as a secure and predictable employer, both because the organization has been a part of the state administration and because of its staff policy. Today, in contrast, there is a new reality and nothing is predictable any longer. The basic values and norms of working life have changed.

For the majority of employees the changes in basic values and norms are viewed as a breach of trust. Confidence has to be restored between employer and employee before Telenor can fully realise the potential of a skilled and motivated work force. In the future Telenor must not be so myopic as to limit its priorities to advanced exchanges and efficient signaling systems. Telenor is people at work, facing the double challenge of new working practices and new human relationships.

Chapter 8

Italy

Serafino Negrelli

In SIP, the state-owned company that has long held a monopoly in the provision of telecommunications services in Italy, changes in managerial structures, technology, and the organization of work were the focus of several collective agreements and joint consultations reached between management and trade unions in the 1980s. A transformation process has been oriented toward improving the quality of service in SIP (now Telecom Italia) while retraining existing personnel, recruiting individuals with specialized skills, and eliminating many obsolete professional positions. This transformation has been taking place in an incremental manner free of major confrontations between labor and management.

Management has sought to change work organization so as to increase the flexibility of jobs, working hours, and wages, and to expand an array of training and retraining activities. All this is being accomplished through a participative model of industrial relations involving the disclosure of information, consultation, and labor-management committees. This participative approach will be tested in the future under pressures for downsizing and cost reduction, although the latter pressures are likely to be less severe in Italy than they have been in the United States and the United Kingdom. However, efforts to make the industrial relations system less bureaucratic are likely to remain strong. Before examining the changes that have been occurring in work practices in the Italian telecommunications services industry, this chapter describes the environmental context that has helped shape these changes.

The Historical, Economic, and Institutional Context

Historical Background of Telecommunications Services

In 1881 the Italian state issued the first licenses for telephone service and the first two telephone exchanges came into operation. But for many decades, the diffusion of telephone services was limited by the relative lack of state regulation (whether for private or state-owned enterprises), by Italy's late industrial development, and by low national income. To avoid a monopolistic situation, in 1925 the national territory was divided into five zones, with five private autonomous business companies (Stipel, Telve, Timo, Tert, Set) providing telephone services. The state enterprise for telephone services (ASST) was then created to control and supervise these five companies.

A new public enterprise, STET (Società Torinese Esercizi Telefonici), was later created by IRI (Institute for Industrial Reconstruction) to reincorporate a major part of the Italian telephone sector. IRI purchased the majority of shares of SIP (Società Idroelettrica Piemonte), the telephone company. Steady development of a national telephone network continued without interruption until the 1950s.

The old government concessions to the telephone companies ended in 1957 and they had to be renewed. The new laws favored the public STET and ASST. STET then purchased the majority of shares of all the private telephone concessionaires and a "National Regulation Plan for Telephone Service" was then approved. Between 1962 and 1964, SIP incorporated the five previous concessionaires providing telephone services and became a state monopoly provider of telephone services throughout Italy. The national territory was divided into the five zones in which the previous five telephone companies had operated.

Many problems arose after this incorporation including problems associated with the creation of one centralized general management. In the face of these problems the global reorganization of the company was postponed until the 1980s. The number of telephone subscribers rose from 4.2 million in 1964 to 13.5 million in 1978. But different managerial systems and cultures in the five zones produced a low level of coordination. The four levels of management (top management, zones, regions, and local agencies) within SIP had similar difficulties: bureaucratic relationships within and across levels; duplicated tasks and responsibilities;

wasteful human resource practices; and fragmented organizational structure. Recognition of these problems led to a major reorganization of SIP.

Reorganization, Decentralization, and Managerial Autonomy at SIP in the 1980s

The reorganization of SIP which occurred in the 1980s was forced by many factors: technological innovation (from electromechanical to electronic equipment); the need for more coordinated structures; more complex and integrated services; and pressures from unions. The latter arose during the renewal of the National Collective Agreement in 1980 when labor and management agreed for the need for a strong reorganization of SIP, with the decentralization of collective bargaining to the regional level and the abolition of the five zones.

The top executives of SIP then launched a decentralization of activities and operational responsibilities.[1] The old geographical divisions, corresponding to different entrepreneurial and technical cultures, were abolished between 1981 and 1983 and only three managerial levels (central, regional and local agency) were retained (Gabrielli and Canu 1993).

The goals of the reorganization were defined as: a focus on new markets and new services; the acceleration of technological innovation; and the improvement of the overall performance of the system. The directions of changes were mainly two. Horizontally, seven areas of activities were defined with the following duties and responsibilities: strategic planning; external relationships; purchasing; market; network; personnel; and administration. The network area was considered "the only point of global responsibility (technical and economical) for the equipment." The market area was considered the only interface with customers and was divided into large users, users' systems, the overall public, and public telephones.

A vertical separation was made in the duties and goals assigned to the three new managerial levels (general management, regional management, and local agency management). Managerial tasks were decentralized with "a method of management and responsibility." This decentralization led to an enlargement of the tasks assigned to the regional level ("autonomous entrepreneur and profit-making centers") and agency levels ("sales center, and not only technical-commercial assistance"). This de-

1. On this evolution, see the Italian case in Gabrielli and Canu 1993; Negrelli and Treu 1993; Butera 1985; and Boldizzoni 1989. Dr. Ruggero Parrotto, Director of the Industrial Relations' Research Office at Telecom Italia, also greatly assisted my efforts to understand recent developments at Telecom Italia.

centralization also required changes in work organization away from the traditional fragmented, bureaucratic, and repetitive jobs and toward enlarged and enriched jobs that give workers greater autonomy and responsibility.

This reorganization was the subject of consultations between trade unions and management. These consultations included extensive information disclosure, and informal bilateral commissions were created to deal with questions of employee mobility at the different territorial levels and of possible overemployment. In 1981 and 1982 there were many meetings about these questions between STET-SIP, the three union confederations with membership in the telecommunications industry Confederazione Generale Italiana del Lavoro (CGIL), Confederazione Italiana Sindicati Lavoratori (CISL), and Unione Italiana del Lavoro (UIL), and Federazione Italiana Telecomunicazioni (FLT) (the then-coordinated union of telecommunications workers). A 1982 collective agreement established the general plan for the transition inside SIP from zones to regions; the division of tasks and procedures of collective bargaining between national and regional levels; and tools to solve redundancy and/ or lack of personnel (including incentives for resignations, early retirements, and worker transfers). In the new agreement the regional levels were given responsibility for managing the reorganization process within SIP. Management retained authority for final decisions concerning reorganization policies; but management and union together discussed and bargained about the effects of the reorganizations on work organization, job classifications, and working conditions.

The new bilateral commissions included representatives of technical and personnel management and union representatives. These commissions examined, debated, and eventually reached agreements about many problems (including hours of work, worker transfers, and changes in work organization). The commissions also laid the groundwork for the industry-wide collective bargaining which followed.

In November 1984, after many meetings of the bilateral commissions, and a national strike, a new national "category" agreement was signed. It was very innovative in areas such as labor-management relations, training, wages, working hours, and work organization. Collective bargaining was extended to all levels of SIP down to regional levels; information disclosure processes were set at the three managerial levels (central, regional, and agency); joint consultation bodies were established; and procedures for verifying compliance with the agreement were created. Regarding work organization, management and the unions reached agreement concerning the need to improve the professional qualifications of workers based on the criteria of job enrichment, job rotation, and increased horizontal mobility in different sectors. As for training, the parties agreed that there will be 1.1 million hours of training provided each year to technical workers; 200,000 hours of training to white collar workers; and 48,000 hours of training to managerial staff. With regard to wages, important collective agreements were reached concerning incentives for sales staff, and in particular, concerning the criteria for these incentives and new pay procedures for the three types of sales staff. Working hours on an annual basis were reduced by 28 hours in 1985 and by 36 hours in 1986.

Undoubtedly, the unions' success in achieving many of their goals in these negotiations was due to the favorable market conditions facing SIP at the time, particularly the relatively high degree of market protection still afforded to SIP. Favorable market conditions also help explain the delays that occurred in the reorganization of regional levels, the slow transition to autonomous profit-making centers within SIP, and the slow progress made in changing local agencies into sales centers.

But other important managerial objectives were being accomplished and these should not be forgotten, such as higher labor productivity. Value added per employee, for example, rose from 100 million lire in 1985 to 130 million lire in 1989, and the number of subscribers per employee also went up over the same period from 225 to 255. Service quality, which has become SIP's major objective in order to compete in the market for new services, also improved.

Toward Privatization: The Shift from SIP to Telecom Italia

In the early 1990s, a new organizational structure developed at SIP, in part in response to the reorganizations begun in 1983, and in part as a reaction to analogous initiatives underway in other European telecommunications companies. The changes included a shift away from a hierarchical, functional structure (with a Central Board of General Direction, 16 Regional Directions, and 101 Local Agencies) and to a multidivisional structure. The managerial objectives of the SIP restructuring in the 1990s were to differentiate the organizational structure so as to bring the structure in line with emerging business specializations; to control technological innovation and development; to achieve organizational rationalization; to place a new emphasis on quality; to reinforce the corporate control systems; and to increase attention to international activities (ISTUD 1993).

In 1992 a new law reorganized STET (the IRI financial company overseeing SIP and other telecommunications companies) through the creation of Telecom Italia. Telecom Italia started on August 1994 through the merger of five separate state-owned companies: SIP, Italcable (Continental Telephone Services), Telespazio (providing satellite telecommunications services), Iritel (a formerly state owned enterprise providing public telephone services), and SIRM (providing telecommunications at sea).[2]

During the last three years these five companies have been fully integrated into the one national company that provides basic telephone and other telecommunications services. In Telecom Italia there are now six business divisions:

The Private Customers Division, responsible for managing and developing telecommunications of diffuse and residential customers, with standard services and products. There are 18 regional subdivisions and a variety of branch offices.

The Business Customers Division, for specialized telecommunications services offered to large Italian national and multinational companies. This division has 10 territorial subdivisions (including offices in Rome and Milan).

The International Services Division, responsible for international services and joint ventures. This division is divided into specific customer segments and cooperates with the Business Customers Division (multinational companies). There are nine world area subdivisions each with marketing functions and relationships with local carriers; and four area subdivisions of Tele Media International responsible for foreign sales in the United Kingdom, United States, Hong Kong, and Argentina.

The Mobile Telephone Division, in charge of marketing, maintaining, and servicing mobile telecommunications for all categories of customers. This division includes seven area subdivisions responsible for territorial maintenance of the network and three area subdivisions in charge of territorial sales.

The Network Division, responsible for the technological strategies and development of the global network infrastructure. This division includes ten territorial subdivisions responsible for coordinating and maintaining local equipment.

The Internal Services Division, oriented to purchasing functions, logistic problems, buildings, and general services. This division includes ten territorial area subdivisions (Telecom Italia 1995).

2. The Berlusconi government nominated new top management for STET, Telecom Italia, and IRI.

Within Telecom Italia there are ten centralized staff functions including internal auditing, statutory bodies' secretary, personnel and organization, administration, external relations, strategic control and planning, operations control and planning, information technologies, legal and general affairs, and quality. Yet, Telecom Italia's corporate structure is very lean with the primary tasks of managerial and strategic control. Many specific staff functions have been decentralized to the divisions. This has brought a shift in power to the new business divisions and away from the traditional territorial levels.

The infrastructure of Telecom Italia was constructed through the merger of the networks of SIP, Italcable, Iritel, and Telespazio, and through a unification of the marketing and technical functions of the five original companies. The network division is the only supplier for both internal and external customers. The most important external customer is likely to be the independent private company that provides mobile telephones and services large enterprises.[3]

These organizational changes are being driven by the pressure on Telecom Italia to adapt to turbulent markets and rapid technological change in the international telecommunications services sector. The new organizational structures aim at creating a specific business focus within each division and providing improvements in economic efficiency and quality by changing the corporate culture.

Within Telecom Italia a decentralizing drift that followed the creation of the six divisions has been counterbalanced by centralizing tendencies that include the strengthening of corporate control over technological developments, human resources, quality, information technology, and control systems. As for the personnel function, the newly created regional territorial structures act as a counterbalance to other centralizing tendencies. The strengthening of horizontal structures and reductions in hierarchical levels have been encouraged throughout Telecom Italia in an effort to favor autonomy and improve the decision-making process.

Work Organization and Functional Flexibility

The Trade-off Between Employment Security and Functional Flexibility

The trade unions at SIP and more recently at Telecom Italia, like their counterparts in other continental European countries, have primarily

---

3. Note that the creation of such a second independent company is required by the European Union.

been concerned with the quantity and quality of employment. The union has had some success in its efforts to affect employment-related issues. For example, the industry-wide agreement in 1984 established that management and the union had to discuss each year at a national "forecasting meeting" data (presented by general management) on managerial programs, technological innovations, maintenance criteria, subcontracting, health and safety issues, the professional qualification of workers, forecasts of occupational changes, training and retraining programs, and the mobility of workers. SIP's renouncement of any numerical flexibility (i.e., layoffs) as a result of automation, institutional changes, or the decentralization of company organizational structures, has helped to moderate trade unions' fears and to make the unions and workers more receptive to functional flexibility.

A 1992 union-management agreement provided for 1,500 early retirements and 1,000 workers' transfers. These steps were taken as part of corporate efforts to increase the share of professional employees while avoiding the need for collective dismissals. Labor-management relations were improved through the fact that, prior to these agreements, management at the national level presented to the unions preliminary proposals, while at the regional level management and unions bargained on how to implement the agreements including discussions over the timing of worker transfers and the employment conditions workers faced in the jobs they were transferred into. These consultations and bargaining activities were accompanied by extensive information disclosure.

Since the 1980s, changes in work organization, often linked to the introduction of new technologies, have been the subject of several labor-management agreements and joint consultations between management and trade unions at different levels. These changes have focused on making job classifications more flexible and productivity "multiskilling" (Negrelli and Treu 1994).

In the proposals presented by unions during discussions surrounding the renewal of the 1984 industrywide Collective Agreement 1984, the unions asked for "new models" of work organization based on improvements in service quality and productivity; occupational stability and development, with specific attention to women; full utilization of workers' abilities in suitable jobs; improvements in working conditions; and a decentralization of responsibilities.

As the general manager of personnel, Antonio Zappi, pointed out, "in the field of work organization and with reference to the results of the bilateral commission, the role of unions was essential. We think that technological development, the necessary qualification of technical assistance, and the implementation of the new models of work organization are pushing toward more joint consultation and verifying the correlated job classifications." The union also supported these joint discussions. A justification for these changes in human resource policies at Telecom Italia was found in the view that "competencies are more important than skills," and that "to know what to be" is now more important than "to know what to do" (Armaroli 1994).

Internal job mobility was another subject in the bilateral commissions and the informal negotiations that expanded at Telecom Italia. An example is provided by the territorial mobility of the staff that followed the earlier mentioned shift from zones to regional divisions at SIP (Negrelli 1985). After the national agreement in 1983 the unions and management carried out a joint examination of worker transfers. The union gave its consent to these transfers with the conditions that the union receive: (1) information about the process of mobility (which workers were being chosen for transfers and why); (2) information about investments, employment, and training trends; and (3) financial incentives for early retirements and resignations that were included in the program. After deliberations and the exchange of extensive information an agreement was reached in April 1984 concerning the transfer of 780 clerical workers (Negrelli 1985).

Flexibility in working hours has emerged as another key human resource issue in recent years. At Telecom Italia the work week as of January 1993 was fixed at 38.2 hours and these hours are normally distributed over five working days. Certain personnel categories (such as computer operators and installation workers) work in shifts and work different hours, which depend strictly on the nature of their individual tasks. Alongside the basic time schedule there are a variety of shift schedules in use including basic shift hours, staggered shifts, and alternating shifts. Flexible hours are also resorted to in certain conditions, whereby the beginning or end of the working day can be shifted by one hour, and the rest of the hours adjusted accordingly.[4]

The Organization of Work

The 1992 SIP Collective Labor Agreement mentions the need for improvements in work organization. On the one hand, there is some move-

4. Work carried out outside normal working hours is considered overtime, and is reimbursed at the hourly salary rate, the cost-of-living allowance, the monthly rate of the yearly bonus, plus the following increases: daytime, weekdays (25%); nighttime weekdays (55%) daytime weekends (50%); and nighttime weekends (80%).

ment toward broad skills, job enrichment, and a non-Tayloristic organization of work. On the other hand, these movements appear less frequently in technical and manual jobs. The new fully electronic technological systems being introduced now involve extensive indirect supervision and technical controls. These supervisory and control systems have led in some cases to more narrow and Tayloristic work.

Conforming to the Italian legal workforce classification system, Telecom Italia personnel are in four main categories: managers, cadres (a new category of professional and managerial staff introduced by Law No. 190 in 1985), white collar, and blue collar workers.[5] A separate job category also exists for telephone operators (only night switchboard operators are included in this category) although this last category is being phased out. A separate collective agreement concerns the classification of managerial positions and the procedures used to evaluate managers.

Personnel is broken down further into ten levels on a classification scale structured by the Italian Collective Labor Agreement. Level 1 is the highest, and above it lie jobs in upper management, while levels 3, 2, and 1 together form the so-called cadre which covers, as defined by contract regulations, those workers who "explicate functions involving responsibility and control of organizational units of particular complexity, wide margins of independence and individual judgement . . . in other words, being considered in possession of appropriate knowledge and competence . . . and perform functions of strategic interest for the company which are of a highly specialized nature."

There was strong growth in the number of white collar and clerical workers in the last decade as a result of changing duties, and the higher skills required by technological innovations. There was a corresponding reduction in manual labor while some jobs, such as switchboard operators, have been extended to include white collar job elements.

Employee Involvement in Workplace Decisions

Technological innovation in telecommunications services was particularly great in the 1980s. This trend is likely to continue through the

5. The Law No. 190 of 1985 amended Article 2095 of the Civil Code by adding the cadre category of employee to the three existing categories of blue collar workers, white collar workers and managers. The law was approved after pressures from large groups of technical, specialist, and managerial employees opposed to the egalitarian policies pursued by union confederations in the 1970s. The 1985 law defines cadre as employees who rank between managers and white collar workers and who perform functions of "considerable importance to the development and implementation of the company's objectives." But determining a specific definition of cadre category is left to collective bargaining.

1990s until telephone exchanges and networks all are digitalized. This process has been particularly acute in maintenance and installation jobs. In contrast, the substitution of fiber optic cable for traditional copper cable has led to increases in subcontracting and supplier work. This has reduced demand for the previously relatively highly skilled copper cable installers.

There have also been extensive changes in the organization of work in the marketing area (user services, sales, and subscriber installations) and in the network area (exchanges and transmission lines). Many of these changes have been linked to the introduction of new technologies and have been the subject of several agreements and consultations between management and trade unions at a variety of levels (Butera 1985).

In recent years Telecom Italia has focused much attention on human resource issues. Management stated their interest in strategies that would improve employee participation including:

flexible management of the organizational set-up, which needs to be more efficient and market oriented;

strong personnel motivation and involvement, in order to develop a company culture aimed at satisfying market needs;

the pursuit of personnel policies aimed at instilling entrepreneur and decision-making capacity, especially in management and cadre;

the creation of internal and external communication policies focused on "global quality";

pursuit of policies aimed at gaining union consent and agreement on company strategies through increased worker and union involvement in decision making.

Teamwork and employee participation in reorganizing firm structures are emerging from managerial initiatives such as "Progetto Territorio" (Territorial Project), "Gruppi di Miglioramento" (Improvement Teams), "Progetto Qualità Totale" (Total Quality Project) and "Cortesia e professionalita del Personale dei Servizi in Decade 1" (Courtesy and Pleasant Manners in Telephonic Services) (Gabrielli 1993). The latter project covers about 13,000 staff with 250 million person-contacts per year, and therefore strongly influences the customer's perception of the company's service (Gabrielli and Canu 1993).

The Territorial Project is based on monitoring teams aimed at designing training and communication for adapting managerial skills to changing environments. Higher internal flexibility on tasks and more interactions between functions and divisions resulted from this initiative along with the implementation of a total quality management program.

Management claims that the changes in work organization initiated in the 1980s and 1990s encountered substantial union resistance. At the same time management is generally satisfied with the progress made which they attribute to the success of the new participative model of industrial relations. Unions in turn complain that their consent was principally asked with regard to the effects of management decisions after those decisions were already made and they (the unions) were not adequately consulted before changes happened (Negrelli 1985).

Skill Formation and Development

Training for Blue Collar and White Collar Workers

Changes in work organization and strategic HRM led to changes in training at Telecom Italia. There was a shift toward more continuous training, learning by doing, computer-aided teaching methods, and self learning. These programs affected more than 60 percent of employees.

The training system is supporting the diffusion of new organization models and a new corporate culture. Training is divided into general training schemes, adaptation-to-role schemes, and development interventions. The first area covers basic training courses aimed at orienting new employees (technicians and office workers) and also includes job preparation courses, designed to provide the know-how required in the various job areas. This training is supplemented by "on-the-job-training". In the past, this type of training was provided primarily to network and marketing employees (both were primarily male). In the last three years the training programs have been redesigned in an effort to generate a new sensitivity to customers and to improve communication across professional categories without losing track of distinct competencies.

The adaptation-to-role schemes are aimed at providing the theoretical and practical knowledge that enables individuals to update their skills and organizational roles. The objective of these programs is not to change the jobs (for example, the same individual who performed cable maintenance in the past will continue to do so in the future), but rather the focus is on changing the way jobs are done so as to make them more responsive to customer needs. Giving attention to external and internal customers and developing a marketing culture are now the key objectives of this type of training. Finally, development interventions support employees who are moving to higher skilled jobs or to a different organizational and functional task.

The central role of training within Telecom Italia's human resource management and development system is demonstrated by the fact that five million hours per year of training took place over the period of 1987–92. It is important to underline that the emphasis put on training and retraining processes is closely related to Telecom Italia's strategy to avoid the collective dismissals appearing among British and U.S. telecommunications companies, and the mass layoffs appearing in a number of other Italian companies. The training initiatives at Telecom Italia were launched after union agreements (at the centralized level), a very important difference from the case of Fiat at Melfi, where unions were not involved in the development of that company's new extended (two-year) training program for new hires.

In collective labor agreements at SIP, and more recently at Telecom Italia, union and management jointly established the main training policies, the internal distribution of the training system, and the allocation of training to nonmanagerial personnel. For example, for SIP the 1992 Collective Labor Agreement outlined the specific training institution of "On-the-Job Permanent Training." The agreement states, "Regarding this type of training, there will be training and communicative initiatives to give more elements of knowledge to the employees about the strategies, goals, and specific programs of the company." This cooperative approach to training has been extended by the fact that one of the four joint consultation bodies of the new "participative area" of Telecom Italia focuses on training.

Management Training and Cadre Policies

The traditional distinction that existed between human resource management and industrial relations at SIP and Telecom Italia is blurring, as shown by the recent management and union discussions on the legal recognition of the cadre ("quadri") category. This category of employees emerged for the first time in the 1988 Collective Labor Agreement. In the mid-1980s the government had requested formal recognition of the cadre category in collective bargaining. Furthermore, this type of job was growing in the company due to technological and market developments. In addition, higher professional staff in the company were asking for more specific attention and responses from the company concerning human resource issues among the cadres.

The 1988 Collective Labor Agreement recognized the cadre category at the top of the job classification scale among managerial and professional employees. But the agreement did not provide a separate collective bargaining agreement for cadre. The cadres are covered by collective bargaining agreements signed by the national unions of telecommunications, just like other employees. The Collective Agreement did introduce a wide cadre area, including those falling into levels 2 and 3 on the job scale. Cadres also are covered by specific regulations concerning flexible working hours, limited overtime, traveling expenses, and special wage payments.

The 1988 agreement also included detailed language describing differences in expectations, skills, experience, and motivation between those cadre who coordinate other personnel (head or executive cadres) and those cadre (of increasing number in the company) who perform mainly specialized functions. The latter typically possess expert knowledge in areas such as technical systems or sales. The 1988 agreement also provides that the company could implement special programs targeted on meeting the needs of the cadres. The mention of special targeted programs represents an important evolution in union and company strategies. This language legitimizes the growing "non-negotiated" managerial efforts to respond to the wide variety of career paths appearing within the company.[6]

After the signing of the 1988 Collective Labor Agreement the company also modified the management and development policies that address executive and professional cadre staff. Policies to respond to individual expectations and create "personalized" management and training were then set out in a special document known as the "Cadres Project." The Cadres Project is defined in the 1989 document as "an integrated, flexible system of management operations aimed at recognition of the role performed by cadres within the company and at exploiting the individual professional and motivational differences typical to each cadre." It goes on to specify the policies and management tools adopted by the company in regard to these personnel. Special attention is given to performance evaluation, considered the basic tool for analyzing and checking results achieved from a program.

The company made large investments in executive and professional training. A special program of "Internal Communication" was developed in 1989 revolving around a training project known as the "Agency Project." The aim was to diffuse communication and interfunctional problem resolution skills among agency executives, while at the same time creating the conditions required to maintain these skills.

Compensation: Wage Structure and Wage Policies

The overall cost of labor (including pay, obligatory contributions, severance pay fund contributions, and other costs) at SIP decreased from 40

---

6. For more details about cadre policies see SIP 1992.

percent of total company revenues, in 1981, to 28 percent in 1989 (Gabrielli and Canu 1993). This decline resulted from a number of trends including a stabilization in wage growth during the period 1984–87 in response to governmental control of inflation. Since 1989, labor costs have risen more substantially in part as a result of the company's investment programs and resulting employment growth.

The biggest increases in labor costs occurred in the years immediately following the renewals of the Collective Labor Agreements (10.6% in 1985 and 10.2% in 1989, the latter was less than the average increase of 12.1% experienced in Italian industry). Voluntary retirement (early pension) schemes provided by legislation and/or collective bargaining form a significant component of labor costs.

Telecom Italia's wage structure is determined by collective bargaining, automatic elements, and unilateral company elements.

Collective bargaining determines professional salary (according to skill levels), which consists of a basic wage, plus a professional pay element for the cadre category, and an annual bonus; and the productivity bonus, which varies according to a scheme that takes into account the differing contributions toward overall productivity from employee groups). The last interconfederal agreement of 23 July 1993 between Confindustria and the union confederations (CGIL, CISL, and UIL) and the government established that only two levels of collective bargaining on wages are allowed: at the industrywide level for increases in the basic salary of all employees and at the decentralized company or territory level for increases related to productivity improvement. This agreement confirmed the abolition of COLA.

The automatic elements are a cost-of-living allowance and seniority payments. The cost-of-living allowance is a variable element provided by Italian law, which partially covers losses in earning due to inflation. In 1991 a law was passed that eliminated COLA allowances for subsequent inflation. At Telecom Italia the contribution from COLA allowances for inflation prior to 1991 represents 40 percent of the total wage. Seniority payments are 5 percent of the basic wage for every two years of service up to a maximum of fourteen increments; the latter has been reduced to seven for new hirings since July 1992.

The unilateral company elements include a merit bonus scheme managed directly by the company, to adjust for increasing contributions made to the company by highly qualified employees (cadres and managers) which takes into account the labor market and considers differences in job performance and levels.

Wages are still largely determined by automatic elements. Management has tried to gain more discretion and flexibility in pay setting and pushed the following changes in the collective contract renewals of 1988 and 1992 to serve these ends: larger salary differences in recognition of skill levels; wider application of productivity bonuses; limited standard salary elements that provide wage compression; and reductions in the role of seniority in collective agreements.

The Telecom Italia Productivity Bonus

The flexible part of Telecom Italia wages is 3 or 4 percent of contractual pay, a high level by Italian standards. This percentage is related to the company's productivity and the productivity of specific work groups as indicated by their job tasks, quality, and efficiency. Table 8.1 lists the average productivity bonus from 1988 to 1993.

The productivity bonus was introduced at SIP in 1986, was formally adopted in the Collective Wage Contract of 1988, and was increased in 1990–92. It is a variable system of payment, linked to productivity for a given year to the extent that the various employee groups contribute to this productivity. The system makes reference to ten functional sectors common to each of the 101 peripheral offices or agencies.

The productivity bonus resulted from extensive consultations between management and the trade unions and the development of the productivity bonus coincided with reductions in automatic pay based on seniority. The company aims in the future to modify the productivity bonus so it takes into account external quality as perceived by customers.

At Telecom Italia a separate incentive system rewards sales personnel. This system includes specific objectives (sales, production mix, development of new products) and provides on average 24 percent of the pay received by the sales staff.

Recent Changes in the Pay Structure

The real earnings of SIP employees on average rose substantially between 1980 and 1992. Workers at level 7 (32,957 employees, 38% of the total workforce), starting the period with fourteen years seniority, received over this period a 13 percent real wage increase. Workers at

TABLE 8.1. Operating productivity and productivity bonus as a percentage of contractual pay

1988	1989	1990	1991	1992	1993
3.90	6.07	3.50	3.89	4.09	3.09

Source: Unpublished data from Telecom Italia.

level 1 (1,406 employees, 1.6% of the total workforce) received a 28 percent real wage increase. These pay increases can be compared to the increases experienced in productivity over the same period which have been steady and substantial. Productivity increased at a 3.5 percent annual rate over the period 1980–92 at SIP. In 1980 there were 178 telephone subscribers per employee, while in 1992 there are 271 subscribers, an increase of more than 50 percent.

The 1992 Collective Labor Agreement provides for a scale of 100 to 240 in minimum wages, a scale of 100 to 370 related to total wages increases, and a scale of 100 to 977 (388,000 lire yearly for level 10; and 3,792,000 lire for level 1) in a productivity bonus (Vittiglio 1993). The Collective Labor Agreement in 1992 responded to equity concerns by raising the pay of highly skilled personnel (by raising their scale from 100 to 220 to a range of 100 to 240). This and other recent efforts to raise differentials and increase individual pay variation have helped make internal equity issues the most significant pay issue inside the firm.

From 1980 to 1993 the importance of the productivity bonus and the professional wage rose and the contribution of cost-of-living allowances and the seniority pay component declined. The distribution of the major pay components for level 1 and level 7 employees in 1980 and 1993 is reported in figure 8.1.

Employment Security and Staffing Arrangements

Employment stability or, at least, the terms and scale of employment adjustments, has been the major preoccupation of both trade unions and workers in the telecommunications sector. Technological changes and market pressures raised employees' fears of job loss. Yet, in fact, total staff grew at SIP (and its successor) from 73,217 in 1980 to 87,960 in 1993 (see Table 8.2). Only after 1992 did worker quits exceed new hires.

The need to improve quality of service promoted the search for more qualified personnel and led to increases in the number of managers in recent years (see Table 8.3). There have also been dramatic reductions in the number of certain personnel such as telephone operators.

From the early 1980s changes in the size and composition of the staff have been facilitated by planned workforce reductions (early retirements and subsidized voluntary resignations) and the hiring of young diploma holders and graduates. This resulted in increases in the number of high school and university graduates and declines in the share of blue collar workers (the less-than-high-school-degree category) as shown in Figure 8.2.

FIGURE 8.1. Contractual wages structure

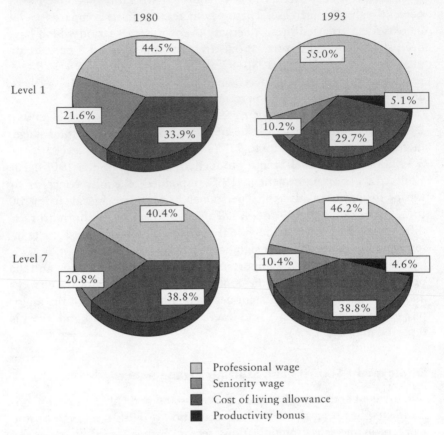

TABLE 8.2. Personnel trends

	1988	1989	1990	1991	1992	1993	1994
Male	67.559	69.453	70.982	72.507	72.464	71.671	76.671
Female	14.721	15.787	16.388	16.968	16.829	16.289	18.715
Total	82.280	85.240	87.370	89.475	89.293	87.960	
Telecom Italia						101.338	95.713

The average age and seniority of employees has fallen in recent years as a result of these changes. The average age of white collar employees was 41 to 50 years in 1988 and 31 to 40 years in 1993; while the average seniority of these employees was 15 to 20 years in 1988 and 11 to 15 years in 1993. The average age of managerial employees did not change (41 to 50 years) nor did average seniority (it is still more than 20 years).

TABLE 8.3. Staff categories, 1988–1994

	1988	1989	1990	1991	1992	1993	1994
Management							
Male	773	778	6.349	6.603	6.902	6.940	8.018
Female	6	6	377	476	544	562	794
Total	779	784	6.079	7.079	7.446	7.502	8.812
Blue collar							
Male	37.111	34.691	28.715	27.583	18.852	18.152	17.463
Female	1.299	950	292	270	111	103	196
Total	38.410	35.641	29.007	27.853	18.963	18.255	17.659
White collar							
Male	29.675	33.984	35.919	38.321	46.710	46.579	51.617
Female	13.416	14.831	15.719	16.222	16.174	15.624	17.715
Total	43.091	48.815	51.638	54.543	62.884	62.884	69.332

FIGURE 8.2. Staff education degree

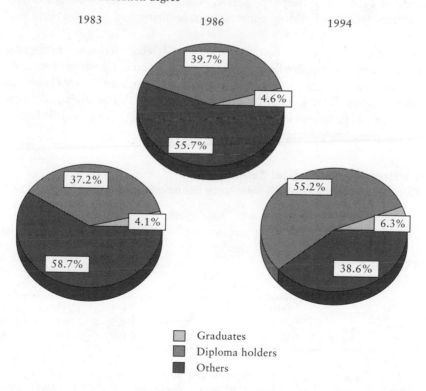

1983   1986   1994

Graduates
Diploma holders
Others

The average age of blue collar workers declined from 31 to 40 years to 41 to 50 years and the average seniority of these employees rose from 11 to 15 years to 15 to 20 years.

Female employment rose from 17.9 percent of total staff in 1988 to 18.5 percent of staff in 1993 (this was exactly the level set in the trade union agreements). Part-time employment increased from 3.9 percent of the total workforce in 1988 to 4.2 percent in 1994 (see Table 8.4).[7] Part-time employment is concentrated among female employees (women are 77.4% of all part-time workers) and low skilled employees.

SIP management became more attentive to manpower planning problems in recent years. Voluntary redundancies and resignations and employee transfers were extensively bargained with trade unions. The firms adopted a plan, "Europe Plan" (1988–92), which set out to avoid hiring people in those departments that had short-term needs but were likely to face long-term cutbacks. The strategic orientation of SIP manpower planning has always focused on keeping internally within the company the core business of telephone service while subcontracting other complementary (such as building construction, security, and cleaning) and seasonal activities.

The merger of the five companies to form Telecom Italia will bring new manpower planning challenges. But, as a management document recently pointed out, the fact that existing employment levels are relatively low as compared to other European companies, and the company's good performance in productivity and service quality could make controlled manpower planning possible throughout the 1990s.

Participative Industrial Relations and Complementary Human Resource Management

The trade unions that represent employees in all of the European telecommunications companies are strong with substantial membership

TABLE 8.4. Part-time staff

	1988	1989	1990	1991	1992	1993	1994
Male	719	699	741	944	938	1.212	1.308
Female	2.517	2.679	2.877	3.319	3.225	2.994	2.770
Total	3.236	3.378	3.618	4.263	4.163	4.206	4.078

7. Note that this put part-time employment at Telecom Italia much below the rates at Dutch PTT Telecom (near 20%) and the rates at France Telecom and the Germany DBP Telekom (both near 10%) (Visser and Besselaar 1993; Lyon-Caen 1993; Büchner 1993).

across white and blue collar employee ranks. In addition, these unions generally have cooperative relationships with the managements of their respective companies. Telecom Italia (and formerly SIP) fits this pattern. Trade unions at Telecom Italia represent about 60 percent of all employees although union membership has decreased in the last ten years by approximately 4 percent.

A large proportion of the union members (over 85 percent) belongs to specialist unions affiliated to one of the three main Italian Federations of Trade Unions, CGIL (General Federation of Italian Trade Unions, basically excommunist but with a socialist minority), CISL (Italian Federation of Trade Unions, of Catholic and Christian-Democrat inspiration), and UIL (Italian Labor Union, of lay-socialist background). These union federations are organized both vertically (in product and service categories) and horizontally (territorial).

Among telephone workers at Telecom Italia, the telecommunications workers union of Federazione Italiana Lavoratori Poste e Telecomunicazioni (FILPT)-CGIL retains the majority, even though it experienced a significant loss in membership in the 1980s (from 22,095 in 1984 to 20,784 in 1990). In contrast, both Sindicato Italiano Lavoratori Telecomunicazioni (SILTE)-CISL and Unione Italiana Lavoratori (UILTE)-UIL grew over the 1980s, respectively from 14,053 to 16,107 and from 7,826 to 9,761.

Recently, there has also been a reawakening of professional associations among cadres. Two professional associations operate at Telecom Italia, the Italian National Cadres Organization (Coordinamento Nazionale Quadri), a branch of Italquadri with most of its members in manufacturing, and Unionquadri, operating in many service industries. The two associations have approximately 2,000 members.

The current industrial relations system does not provide for any negotiation between the company and these associations; to the latter the system assigns the role of advisor to the company regarding matters concerning the overall management of cadre personnel. Current relations between Telecom Italia and these professional associations are in fact based on dialogue, exchanges of opinions, and information. These relations are naturally more intense during the start of negotiations with the trade union federations FILPT, SILTE, and UILTE (at the moment recognized by the associations as their sole bargaining agent) for the renewal of the collective labor contract. Tense moments have also surfaced recently during the planning of the Cadres Project.

The overall cooperative tenor of labor-management relations at Telecom Italia has been encouraged by the fact that union delegates from the company are key actors at both centralized and decentralized negotiation levels. This has led to the development of a problem-solving focus in collective bargaining rather than to the rigid codification of regulations, which occurs in many other industrial sectors.

Collective Bargaining and Participative Industrial Relations

The institutional environment in Italy did not encourage participative industrial relations. But Telecom Italia has tried to follow the lead set by the "IRI Protocol" which recognized the unions' right to participate in managerial discussions and also created bilateral consultation committees. The IRI Protocol was signed in 1984 after almost two years of negotiations between the IRI group and the three major trade union confederations, CGIL, CISL, and UIL. It was renewed and clarified in July 1986. In general, the agreement recognized both the need for economic and corporate restructuring and the positive contribution employees could make to the restructuring process. The agreement promotes a cooperative and participatory problem-solving approach to labor-management relations.

Participation is encouraged in the IRI protocol via "Joint Consultative Committees" at various levels. The tasks of these committees are (1) investigation of strategic options for industrial restructuring and relevant industrial relations policies; (2) union evaluation of managerial proposals and formal, but nonbinding input into these matters; (3) monitoring of the implementation of restructuring; and (4) discussion of proposals on work organization, industrial relations, and the labor market.

The protocol also establishes a procedure for consultation between IRI and the CGIL-CISL-UIL confederation to enable the unions to learn about corporate policies, with meetings either weekly or at the request of one of the parties. Finally, a considerable part of the protocol is devoted to procedures for preventing and resolving collective conflict that may arise at the company level (very low in the case of SIP and Telecom Italia in the last decade) and procedures for settling individual and group disputes.

Joint consultation bodies have been difficult to establish at the IRI group as well as at Telecom Italia. Consultations have worked to date primarily only on an informal basis and on occasion when focused on specific critical problems, such as worker mobility, the reorganization of work, or productivity issues.

At Telecom Italia collective bargaining takes place at two levels, nationally on all matters typically contained in a collective contract, and regionally on matters delegated by "framework" language in a national contract such as working hours or new work organization experiments. Both labor and management at times complain that this structure is too rigid. For example, trade unions lament the lack of a decentralized level for negotiations where information rights are desired but remain ineffective. Meanwhile, local management still considers the negotiating power delegated to them from the center of the corporation to be limited (Negrelli 1985).

The system of union information rights is based on three methods of communications: (1) Technological issues are discussed in an annual meeting. Management presents to trade unions the main results of the previous year and the plan for the next year. (2) Periodical reports are made on service quality. These reports provide trends in different quality indicators and the parties jointly discuss critical issues. (3) Specific information related to significant organizational and technological changes and the broad evolution of telecommunications is reported as necessary.

The 1992 Collective Labor Agreement introduced a new "participative area" of industrial relations in addition to the previous two areas of information and negotiation. In management's opinion this participative area will be an important tool in the management-union relationship because it implies communication and taking part in the objectives and strategies of the enterprise, and therefore higher involvement and responsibility regarding company results.

The new participative area of industrial relations is concretely based on four bilateral commissions. The commission on total quality is oriented toward understanding the basic philosophy of quality programs and interventions that can improve technical systems and managerial processes and initiatives to diffuse culture and focus organizational behaviors on service quality. The purpose of the commission on training is to support cultural change and adaptation to new skills through joint examination of the returns to ongoing training initiatives and joint elaboration of specific relevant projects. This commission is working only at the national level. The objectives of the commission for equal opportunities for men and women are activities of research, studies of positive experiences, and removal of obstacles that make equal treatment for men and women difficult. The purpose of the commission on health and safety is to create knowledge of environmental problems and to support corporate prevention activities and respect the physical and mental well-being of workers. This commission established a specific training initiative for union representatives.

The four joint commissions work at national and regional levels (except for the training commission which works only at the national level).

Each commission has three company representatives and three union representatives. The commissions aim to promote discussions and consultations but do not aim at collective bargaining.

It is difficult to evaluate the outcomes of the new joint bodies. Only the joint commission on equal treatment for men and women did not work well due to the lack of active union involvement and interest. In 1993 and 1994, the commissions on work environment and total quality were more active. In particular, the latter had many meetings at regional levels concerning technological changes, technical assistance, and problems within installation and maintenance of corporate offices. These commissions have found it difficult to negotiate collective agreements on key topics and have confronted increasingly antagonistic industrial relations at local levels in the company.

The negotiation of the 1992 Collective Labor Agreement also did not proceed smoothly. The negotiation involved five months of bargaining and it was affected by the government's general abolition of the "scala mobile" (COLA). The majority of Telecom Italia workers initially voted against the agreement and it was approved only after subsequent modifications.

Industrial Relations and Internal Relations

Employment relations at Telecom Italia involve both collective bargaining and what the company refers to as "internal relations." The latter refers to the direct relationship (usually of an individual nature) that exists between management and employees. Management's main goal in internal relations is to reconcile employees' individual expectations with the achievement of the firm's economic objectives. In fact, internal relations are in large part complementary to the system of collective bargaining. In management's opinion, "through the direct relationship with the workers the company is in search of a transparent dialogue with the employee who is stimulated to increase his or her proactive role in the service process. So, the bargaining system and internal relations will be used as complementary tools to attain effectively the company aims." Collective bargaining and internal relations concerns overlap, for example, in the development of policies regarding productivity bonuses, information disclosure, and the management of cadres.

Conclusion

For a long time in Italy, monopolies had predominated in the telecommunications sector and these monopolies had been considered as a suitable provider of a public service that was offered at a uniform price to all customers. This arrangement was altered during the 1980s in the face of a trend in Europe toward deregulation, privatization, and market liberalization. Recent telecommunications restructuring has been driven by the view prevalent in many European countries and in many initiatives of the European Economic Community (EEC) that the telecommunications sector forms the basis of the future service economy.

Even in the face of a deregulation trend it is still the case that the telecommunications service sectors in all EEC countries retain a high degree of monopoly in the areas of network infrastructures and basic telephone services. These developments in telecommunications are typical in the European model of capitalism (Albert 1991). Some observers had forecast that continental Europe would more quickly emulate the fast and extensive deregulation occurring in Britain, but this has not turned out to be the case. In moving more slowly toward privatization and market liberalization in the telecommunications sector, continental Europe has avoided the antagonistic labor-management relationship that developed in Britain, particularly during the Thatcher government (Negrelli and Treu 1993).

When Telecom Italia was partially privatized in 1994, it became the largest Italian company in terms of total sales (with sales of almost 29 trillion lire [$18 billion U.S.] per year). Controlled by STET (with 55% share ownership) and with foreign ownership of 25 percent of its shares, Telecom Italia is now entering into a more complicated stage of privatization.

Throughout Europe a decentralization of the organizational structure of telecommunications companies has been proceeding and Telecom Italia fits within this pattern. The company has been adopting flatter managerial structures and closer ties (with fewer intervening layers of management) have also surfaced between Telecom Italia, STET, and IRI. Telecom Italia is now the sixth largest telecommunications company in the world in terms of annual sales (behind NTT, AT&T, Deutsche Telekom, France Telecom, and BT). Furthermore, in recent years Telecom Italia has earned high after-tax profits (1.4 trillion lire in 1992, at SIP).

Telecom Italia does face a number of challenges as it moves toward even further privatization and internationalization. With the creation of Telecom Italia through the merger of the five previously separated state-owned companies, employment in the unified company stood at 101,338 (15% more than in the old SIP). While the number of subscribers per employee is still higher at Telecom Italia than in most of its counterpart European competitors, Telecom Italia's international telephone-call prices are among the highest in the world. Therefore, there is likely to be pressure on Telecom Italia to downsize in the future. How to accomplish any reductions in employment in a nontraumatic manner likely will be a critical issue.

Further corporate restructuring also may occur. There is some talk about a possible future merger between STET and Telecom Italia. The development of the second private company of cellular telephones and the separation of Telecom Italia's division of mobile telephone into an autonomous company are also future possibilities.

There is also some discussion about the possibility of making Telecom Italia into a public company based on more diffused shareholders; or selling large blocks of the company's shares to a few core corporate clients such as Pirelli (which makes telephone cables as well as tires), Alcatel, or other companies. This sort of corporate restructuring would have severe consequences on employment relations at Telecom Italia.

Two key employment relations issues at Telecom Italia are how to maintain a "virtuous trade-off" between stability, flexibility, and productivity and how to make the labor relations system less bureaucratic. As for the first issue, this chapter has shown that a participative approach has great potential to drive changes in employment arrangements, work organization, compensation, and skill development. It is hard to see, however, how a virtuous trade-off could be sustained if large downsizings occur in the future at Telecom Italia.

Reducing the bureaucratic tendency within internal relations at Telecom Italia is a more difficult problem. A participative approach might disconnect unions from their base as the interests of union leaders at central levels of the union diverge from local union interests. A participative union has to work to avoid becoming bureaucratic and too oriented toward company needs. The workers' vote against the first draft of the 1992 Collective Labor Agreement is a worrisome indicator that internal problems may be surfacing within the unions that represent employees at Telecom Italia.

Management has contributed to these problems. Management's ambiguous view of the union appears in the words they use to describe employment relations, "Our employment relations system and the unions are the ways to make personnel responsible for company goals." Yet, if a participative approach is oriented only toward serving management's interest, then severe problems are inevitable. The current rigid framework that maintains a separation between information exchange, negotiation, and participation is also not productive.

Unions have been asking for more joint consultation before decisions are made about new technology or changes in work organization. And they are interested in being involved in codetermination through the activities of bilateral commissions, in particular, through activities concerning total quality and training. But management fears union opportunism particularly at more decentralized levels of the collective bargaining system. So, management has not aggressively pursued a more dynamic collective bargaining process and has been timid in their expanded labor participation.

The stated objective of Telecom Italia is to make employment relations more adaptive to total quality, productivity initiatives, and managerial goals. In the past, unions and management limited their bargaining processes primarily to interactions occurring at the national level, without facing protests from the periphery. But technological innovations, changing managerial structures and strategies, and intensified competition are requiring deeper participation by employers and unions and more expansive collective and individual bargaining. How to bring about a controlled decentralization of employment relations, a stronger integration of industrial relations and human resource management, and a deepening of participative processes are the challenges labor and management face at Telecom Italia.

PART 3

State-Led Growth and Modernization

Chapter 9

Mexico

Enrique de la Garza and Fernando Herrera
(with Germán Sanchez, Joel Oropeza, José Cruz Guzman,
and Alejandro Espinosa)

Labor relations in the company that has traditionally had a monopoly in the provision of telephone services in Mexico, Teléfonos de México (Telmex), have followed a path that differs from the typical Mexican pattern. Both before and after its 1990 privatization, Telmex has viewed the labor union that represents its employees, Sindicato de Telefonistas de la República Mexicana (STRM), as its partner in determining important aspects of technological change, labor relations, and the organization of work. This chapter explains the factors that helped create the uncommon "bilateral" relationship between Telmex and STRM. This partner relationship contrasts sharply with the more typical authoritarianism found in Mexico's system of industrial relations and the breakdown of collective labor contracts that has occurred in many Mexican firms since the early 1980s.

Our explanation of the Telmex-STRM partnership emphasizes the following factors: (1) the changes that occurred in government regulation of telecommunications including the privatization of Telmex and the opening up of telephone services to competition; (2) Telmex's modernization policies involving the introduction of new technologies, new forms of work organization, internal labor flexibility, and the establishment of incentives for productivity and quality; (3) the shift in the STRM's strategy toward modernization and productivity; and (4) the Mexican national government's new corporatist policy promoting the opening of markets, globalization, and labor-management partnerships of the Telmex-STRM style.

The Deregulation of Telephone Services in Mexico

Until 1988, the provision of telecommunications services in Mexico was monopolized by Telmex and the Dirección General de Telecomunicaciones (DGT), the General Office of Telecommunications. The DGT was under the jurisdiction of the Secretaría de Comunicaciones y Transporte (SCT), the Department of Communications and Transportation.

The DGT was in charge of the transmission of television, data, and telegraphic signals as well as international telegraph service, telex, videotel, voice, teleinformatics, facsimile, telephotography, radio maritime services, and telereservations. This office also managed the federal microwave network, the national land station network, the telegraphic network, telex services, mobile services, satellite transmissions, and rural telephone networks.

Also under the SCT's jurisdiction was the General Office of Concessions and Licenses for Telecommunications that regulated telecommunications-related concessions, licenses, authorizations, and standards. The SCT provided regulation but did not direct investment or other managerial decisions. Telmex generated more than 95 percent of all its sales income in the telecommunications sector (Sánchez 1993).

The national government owned 60 percent of the shares of Telmex, with the other 40 percent owned either by telecommunications suppliers or individuals who bought shares of the company on the stock exchange. Telmex's top executive was appointed by the government, but the company had a lot of autonomy in its managerial decisions and operated much like a private company.

SCT's policy until the beginning of the 1980s was to maintain Telmex's monopoly. However, the appearance of new technologies in the 1980s provided the opportunity for redefining basic telecommunication concepts and restructuring this sector. In 1990, the SCT issued new regulations for telecommunications after having created Telecom, which is responsible for managing telecommunications services, the networks previously under the DGT's jurisdiction, and the satellite network and land stations.

In the new regulatory structure the SCT has the authority to grant all concessions (operating rights) in telecommunications; the national government retains a monopoly over the system of satellites and land stations; the prices for telecommunications services must be approved by the SCT; and long distance services will not be opened up to competition until 1996 (*Official Journal of the Federation*, 29 October 1990).[1]

After these regulations were issued, the Telmex concession was adjusted. Among the most important points of this adjustment are the commitments it acquires: the expansion of services at an annual rate of 12 percent during the period from 1990 to 1994, the establishment of telecommunications in all towns with a population of more than 500 inhabitants, the installation of public telephones to achieve a rate of two for every thousand inhabitants by 1994, a reduction in the waiting time for new services, and an increase in the quality of services to reach the level of international standards (*Official Journal of the Federation*, 10 December 1990).

In exchange for these commitments, the SCT established in the concession that Telmex may request authorization to provide the services of mobile radiotelephone, value-added services, and distribution of television signals; to manufacture telecommunication, computer, and electronic equipment through its subsidiaries (in addition to basic services); and to sell all types of terminal equipment.

A set of basic telecommunications service prices were established that are indexed to increases in the national consumer price index. However, as of 1997, telecommunications service prices must decrease to take account of an automatic productivity adjustment factor. This price structure was modified in 1989 and prices have since been increasing in an effort to eliminate subsidies across telecommunications services. In summary, the new regulations limit the national government's direct participation in the telecommunications sector but maintain governmental control through limits on new concessions and through price controls. Although an oligopolistic structure has been maintained in most parts of the telecommunications services sector, in some cases, such as cellular telephone services, competition has intensified greatly in recent years.[2]

Four companies were issued concessions for cellular telephone services. Table 9.1 shows the rapid growth that has been occurring in this segment and how competition has developed. In some regions of Mexico

1. A new telecommunications law adopted in June 1995 provides that the national government can grant concessions involving telecommunications communications by satellite and public networks, but foreign investments in these new concessions cannot exceed 49% of the capital of each enterprise, except concessions involving cellular telephone services.

2. Information on the extent of competition in services such as mobile radio services, specialized radiocommunication, cable television (which has 114 concessions with 90 companies), and value-added services, is more limited.

TABLE 9.1. Cellular telephone service in Mexico

Year	Total subscribers
1989	1,150
1990	65,800
1991	175,350
1991	175,350
1992[a]	278,646
1993[b]	300,000
1995[b]	745,000

[a]up to the month of August.
[b]*Iusacell: Cellular,* May 1992, page 17.
Carlos Salina de Gortari, 1992, *Fourth Presidential Report,* Mexico City.
Department of Communications and Transportation, 1992, *Report Document,* Mexico City.

a battle has developed between Telcel (Dipsa-Telmex), which acquired 207,462 users by 1994, and Iusacell leading to economic losses for both companies as a result of subscription campaigns (Vérut 1993).

Privatization

On 17 September 1989, President Salinas de Gortari announced that Telmex would be disincorporated from the national government. He claimed that the government did not have enough financial resources for necessary expansion and modernization of the company during the period 1989 to 1994 (equivalent to ten billion U.S. dollars).

The president announced a resolution that included six conditions for privatizing Telmex: (1) That the national government's ultimate control over telecommunications in Mexico be guaranteed. The government's role will be to regulate and supervise the sector, thus guaranteeing the diversification and efficiency of services as well as Telmex's financial balance. (2) That public telephone services be radically improved, with objectives established for repairs and for the installation of telephone booths and long distance telephone services. (3) That the rights of workers be guaranteed, in accordance with collective labor contracts and that the workers participate in the new ownership structure of Telmex. (4) That telephone services be expanded with the objectives of annual growth of 12 percent; the installation of four million lines in the 1990–1994 period; an increase in telephone density from five to ten lines per hundred inhabitants; and an investment of 25 billion pesos (equivalent at the time to ten billion U.S. dollars) of which 70 percent would be financed with domestic economic resources. (5) That scientific and technological research be continued in telecommunications services. (6) That

Telmex remain under Mexican control by maintaining a majority of shares in the hands of Mexicans. Foreign investment may not exceed 49 percent of the capital, and individually, no foreign shareholder can own more than 10 percent of the shares. The profitability of Telmex would depend on the company's productivity (Solis 1992). After a long process, Telmex was sold to a conglomerate headed by the Carso Group. The Carso Group owns 5.2 percent of Telmex's shares. Other owners of large blocs of Telmex's shares and partners with the Carso Group (and the respective fraction of Telmex stock that they own) are France Cable and Radio (5%), a subsidiary of France Telecom, Southwestern Bell (5%), a U.S. regional Bell operating telephone company, and other Mexican associates to the Carso Group (5.2%).

The Carso Group is able to exercise control of Telmex because the current shareholder structure includes three types of shares. Type A (19.6%) shares have free subscription (any individual can own the shares) and the share owners have voting rights in corporate decisions. Type AA (20.4%) shares were sold to the Carso Group and its partners and have voting rights. Type L (60%) shares with free subscription do not have voting rights. This share distribution gave the Carso Group and its partners 51 percent of the shares with voting rights. In addition, 4.4 percent of the shares (type A shares with voting rights) were sold to the STRM, but since Mexican law stipulates that one must have at least 10 percent of the shares in order to have the right to be represented on the firm's board of directors, the union was denied participation on Telmex's governing board.

According to information provided by the new management, there is a "natural" division in the firm's internal organization: the Carso Group specializes in legal, social, and real estate matters; Southwestern Bell is in charge of commercial matters, mobile telephone service, and the publication of directories; and France Cable & Radio concentrates on the modernization of the network and the satellite system.

Effectively then, since 1990 Telmex has been a private company controlled by Mexican capital (the Carso Group). Telmex has twenty subsidiaries that function generally as subcontractor (supplier) companies to Telmex and other telephone companies. As of March 1994, Telmex employed a total of 62,828 workers. Of these, 45,901 were members of the STRM which also represented 8,376 workers in six of Telmex's subsidiaries. In addition, another 5,829 workers in Telmex's other subsidiaries were members of the Confederación de Trabajadores de México (Confederation of Mexican Workers, or CTM). Telmex also contracts with some of its subcontractors to fill temporary jobs. The number of workers used in these temporary jobs fluctuates, but union sources estimate the number to be around 10,000. There is one STRM-Telmex collective contract covering unionized Telmex employees throughout Mexico.

Telmex still has a monopoly in the provision of basic telephone services including both local and long distance services. Since its privatization, Telmex has been trying to maintain a high growth rate and a high degree of modernization in order to achieve international competitiveness, especially in long distance services, which will be opened to competitors in 1996.

In recent years, the number of telephones, telephone lines, and long distance calls handled by Telmex has increased considerably. However, the personnel employed by Telmex has remained stable primarily due to the high rate of growth in labor productivity at Telmex (shown in Table 9.2). The growth in labor productivity occurring at Telmex in recent years has been a consequence of a high level of investment (number of lines), growth in the national economy (increases in the number of long distance calls), technological changes, and constant employment.

In the last four years Telmex's income and profits increased by 82.5 percent and 81.7 percent respectively. Profits have been enhanced by increases in the prices for telephone service. Meanwhile, Telmex's income has shifted from being based on long distance services (as it was in the 1980s) to local services (as shown in Table 9.3). Income from local services include installations, measured services, and basic rental charges. Income generated by long distance calls declined as a share of total income in the 1990s due to a sharp rise in local call income caused by the introduction of measured service.

New services, which are included in the "other" category in Table 9.3, are still very limited despite the fact that, according to some internal projections, they were expected to reach a level of more than 15 percent by this time period. However, the change in revenue sources is very clear—an increase in local and national service provision.

Table 9.4 shows that wages and related personnel costs have been a

TABLE 9.2. Productivity at Telmex

Year	Worker/1000 lines	Long distance calls/worker
1990	9.6	23.5
1991	8.5	27.1
1992	7.5	33.0
1993	6.6	36.7

Source: Figures were calculated from data from a Telmex work report.

TABLE 9.3. Telmex: Composition of income (%)

Year	National long distance	International	Local	Other
1987	29.6	54.0	14.7	1.8
1988	29.9	47.4	21.0	1.7
1989	33.5	42.9	20.9	2.7
1990	36.8	28.9	32.3	2.0
1991	38.0	23.8	36.0	2.2
1992	36.5	22.0	39.8	1.7
1993	33.7	19.7	42.8	3.8

Source: Figures calculated from Telmex, *Annual Report* (from several years).

TABLE 9.4. Wage costs as percentage of Telmex's total expenditures

	1990	1991	1992	1993
Wages and related personnel costs/total expenditures	37.8	36.9	39.8	39.3

Source: Figures were calculated from Telmex, *Annual Report* (from several years).

stable share of Telmex's total expenditures during the 1990s. This stability occurred even in the face of the changes made to pay procedures, which are discussed in a later section of this chapter.

Modernization at Telmex

From 1979 on Telmex has been engaged in a technological modernization drive. The factors leading to Telmex's decision to modernize were the following: (1) It was structurally impossible to respond rapidly to the increasing demand for telephone services which was caused in large part by population growth. This was reflected in the fact that as of 1979, 1.5 million applications for telephone services were not being met. (2) Productivity was stagnant at the company. The equipment in use had reached its maximum level of productivity by 1976 with yearly growth rates of 12 to 14 percent. The annual rate of productivity growth decreased after that period. From 1982 to 1986, productivity grew at annual growth rates between 5 percent and 6 percent. (3) There were technical problems caused by the electromechanical (analog) switchboard equipment. There were increasingly frequent equipment failures as a result of progressive wear and tear and difficulties in finding spare parts. (4) Within a context of obsolete equipment, there was an excessive dependence on workers for maintaining equipment and providing services. This gave the workers a very advantageous position in relation to the company, providing them with a high degree of control over the work process and bargaining leverage. (5) The STRM was using workers' bargaining leverage to obtain more extensive control over the work process. (6) The San Juan and Victoria stations were destroyed in Mexico City's 1985 earthquakes. (7) The tendencies toward globalization and the opening of markets were bringing greater competition for Telmex (Lara 1992).

Face with this situation, the company developed three strategic plans for modernization. The first was the Programa Inmediato de Mejoramiento del Servicio (Immediate Program for Service Improvement or PIMES), created for the purpose of increasing the quality of service. Specific improvements were to include increasing the number of lines per hundred inhabitants (density), new management plans, reforms in the management of subsidiaries, and innovative financing policies. The second plan involved a change in labor relations and labor "culture." It was clear that improvements were needed in services and responsiveness to customers. A transformation in human resource management and labor relations was necessary. The company's public image was also to be improved. The plan for modernization and diversification dealt with quality improvement, diversification, and provision of new services, the introduction and development of new technologies, and the international development of the company (Solis 1992).

Telmex signed contracts for supplying digital stations with the Indetel and Teleindustria Ericsson companies to purchase their S-12 and AXE systems. It is important to note that these companies committed themselves to producing much of this equipment in Mexico (Sánchez 1993).

Major technological changes then appeared at Telmex in switching, involving the rapid transition toward electronic stations and the digital system; and in transmission, the use of satellites, optic fiber, and cellular telephones (see Table 9.5).

According to Telmex plans, by the year 2000 there will be 30 million telephones, 80 percent digitalization of local facilities, 100 percent digitalization of long distance facilities, 15 million lines and 75,000 workers—which will imply an increase in productivity of almost 100 percent in comparison with 1985, in terms of telephones and lines per worker (Telmex 1994).

Technological changes produced the following capabilities at Telmex as of 1993:

Lines in service: 7,620,880
Digitalization of telephone facilities: 65 percent
Telmex cellular telephones (Telcel): 195,409 users

TABLE 9.5. Characteristics of Telmex exchanges (1992)

| | Local exchanges | | Tandem exchanges | | Toll exchanges | |
	Number	% of capacity	Number	% of capacity	Number	% of capacity
Electromechanical switches	19	0.8%	—	—	—	—
Crossbar switches	766	41.0%	2	4%	71	17%
Semielectronic switches	24	1.0%	—	—	4	7%
Digital switches	1,611	57.2%	69	96%	81	76%
	2,420	100%	71	100%	156	100%

Source: Telmex, Internal Report, 1992.

Optic fiber: 8701 kilometers

Operator-assisted traffic: 100 percent digitalized

No more electromechanical stations (1994)

Submarine Cable, Columbus II, made of optic fiber, used to connect America with Europe

New services were opened: 800 (free call) service; telephone card charge; virtual private networks; universal numbers; personal numbers.

Telmex's modernization plan for 1994 includes:

Investment: US$ 2 billion, 300 million pesos

Stations: 1,520,000 new lines

Optic fiber: 9,600 kilometers (new)

Another element of Telmex's modernization has been management reorganization including the creation of two corporate directorates. The first includes four sections: finance and administration; corporate development; human resources and labor relations; and another directorate in charge of the operation of telecommunications services. The latter includes: long distance, telephone development (including developing new services and providing them to large users), and local services (divided into three regional subdirectorates: Northern, Metropolitan, and Southern).

Changes in Labor Relations at Telmex and Labor Union Strategy

Labor unions in Mexico typically have sought to protect jobs, wages, benefits, and working conditions, and to negotiate with the national government over economic and social policies that affect labor. In exchange, the national government received political support from the labor unions.

During the last ten years, the Mexican economy has been opened to the international market and the national government reduced its intervention in the economy and limited public spending to only the poorest sectors in the economy. In this new context, the possibilities for labor unions to influence economic and social policy through interactions with the national government were reduced. This weakened the corporatist pact that had previously prevailed between labor unions and the state. Under these conditions the restructuring of large companies stimulated a process that greatly affected labor relations and the contents of collective contracts. Over the last ten years there has been a strong movement toward labor deregulation and a substantial decrease in the negotiating power of most Mexican labor unions (De la Garza 1993).

The Telmex case, however, contrasts sharply with the pattern of labor deregulation and union weakness that typified most sectors of the Mexican economy in recent years. In Telmex, a bilateral agreement was initiated between management and labor. Unlike most other Mexican labor unions, the STRM has played a major role in shaping events at Telmex and in the process has created a novel labor-management partnership. The three basic changes that occurred in labor relations at Telmex are: a transformation in the collective labor contract, productivity agreements, and joint commissions involving company and union representatives. A central theme in these processes was a shift in the union's focus to issues related to productivity and service quality (Vasquez 1988).

Several factors influenced the strategy of the STRM with regard to Telmex's modernization. First, although the labor union at Telmex is corporatist, it has always maintained high levels of internal democracy, even to the extent that it has some very influential leftist opposition factions (Torres 1990). A second factor was the pressure exerted by high-level technicians working at the central Telmex stations. These technicians were (and continue to be) politically involved and well educated. Third, a group of outside advisors (high-level specialists) hired on a permanent basis by the executive committee of the STRM have been key players in the development of the union leadership's proposals. And finally, the leadership of the STRM, during the era of labor union decline (the mid-1980s), analyzed international experiences and recognized the need to change strategies in the face of new economic, political, and productive conditions (De la Garza 1990).

The STRM's initiatives at Telmex included the following. In 1986, the labor union won Clause 193 of the collective labor contract and proposed a "quality model" to the company. The principles of the quality model (agreed to by the company) were: (1) The company recognized the labor union's right to participate in the modernization projects, digitalization, and the implementation of new services. (2) The labor union also obtained the right to be informed about modernization projects. (3) A joint commission on new technology was formed which, among other attributes, would have access to information concerning company projects and their impact on training, work conditions, and labor relations. (4) A joint modernization commission was created, which would be in charge of defining the technical and operational implications of the modernization projects and would analyze their implications for labor. (5) The company agreed to develop jointly with the union a broad-based training program. (6) It was decided that a joint commission would analyze the impacts of modernization on job safety and health conditions. (7) It was also decided that there would be no reduction of personnel due to the company's modernization (Xelhuantzi 1989).

One of the first effects of contract clause 193 came through the creation of the Immediate Program for Service Improvement (PIMES) in 1987. This was a plan negotiated with the labor union to improve services. It represented the formal beginning of the labor union's co-responsibility in achieving quality. In that same year, within the framework of Telmex's Eighth Meeting for Corporative Planning, the strategic planning directors' plans for "structural change" were discussed with the union. It became clear at this point in time that Telmex's plans for expansion, diversification of its services, and modernization would require significant changes in labor relations. While the negotiation of contract clause 193 and the union's involvement in the development of the quality model signaled a new turn in labor-management relations, in 1989 the spirit of bilateralism deteriorated due to macroeconomic pressures. In many industrial sectors in Mexico in 1989 national governmental labor policies led to changes in collective contracts which reduced labor union involvement in technological and organizational matters. Following this trend toward increased unilateral managerial control of labor relations, the collective labor contract at Telmex was modified in the following manner in 1989: (1) Labor union intervention in the introduction of new technology was eliminated from clause 193, and the company effectively dissolved the joint commission on new technologies. All that remained from this initiative was the company's commitment to inform the labor union whenever training for workers became necessary. (2) Internal worker mobility, prohibited under the previous contract, and broad job descriptions were established. (3) The only joint commission continuing to operate was the one concerned with personnel training. (4) The fifty-seven existing departmental agreements (which regulated in detail the work of each of the company's departments) were eliminated and replaced with simplified and broader job descriptions (De la Garza 1989).

The key factors that led management to push for a more flexible labor contract in 1989 were the national government's decision to privatize Telmex and pressure exerted by the company's future owners to modify the labor contract even before the sale. This sort of pre-privatization labor contract modification had occurred in airline companies and in the iron and steel industry.

When Telmex was privatized, the STRM won clause 195 in the 1990 labor contract. That clause reshaped the quality model agreed upon in 1988 and partially restored the bilateralism the union had lost in 1989. However, bilateralism was not immediately returned to its former level as the only major bilateral initiative involved the creation of a joint national commission for quality and productivity.

The national government then again changed its industrial relations policy. The government proposed that instead of having weak unions, a new type of labor union would be created—one that would make proposals concerning productivity and quality and be involved in the creation of a new more positive labor culture. The national government at this point recommended that industry throughout Mexico follow the approach being proposed by the STRM—an approach that was different from the old corporatism favored by the CTM. The national government exerted substantial influence over Telmex management who fully identified with the government's neoliberal economic policies. The principal shareholders of Telmex are the type of business people created through neoliberal policies—those who have acquired important companies that were previously government-owned. With the national government's encouragement, the STRM has since been able to benefit from three agreements that focused on productivity and quality improvements at Telmex (Ortiz 1993).

The most important of these agreements is the "Agreement on quality, productivity, and training for the integral modernization of Teléfonos de México" signed in November 1990. With the signing of this agreement, a new horizon was opened up in labor relations. That agreement established the following: the right of workers to participate in making proposals concerning the company's modernization and workers' right to be rewarded for any additional work effort; the commitment that both the company and labor union will jointly design a program to increase productivity and quality; joint determination of administrative and operational modernization processes; the promotion of a new labor culture based on negotiation and mutual benefit; and approval of the quality model. In addition, it called for the establishment of training programs with the purpose of encouraging creative capacities; the encouragement of teamwork and efforts to improve work conditions; the creation of a joint commission in charge of defining productivity criteria and measures; and the commitment of the company to train management in total quality.

Although it defined some essential elements for the creation of a bilateral modernization project, this agreement primarily focused on establishing only basic guidelines. In March 1992, with the signing of the "General Permanent Program of Incentives for Productivity," more detailed modernization plans were specified. The March 1992 agreement was the first concrete product of the Joint Commission for Productivity which had the task of defining productivity criteria and measures. The 1992 Permanent General Program established: that the company will determine the maximum annual amounts to be paid out in productivity enhancing incentives (in 1993 the amount was 324.65 million new pesos); the areas in Telmex where incentives would be implemented (commercial, external plant, commutator, and traffic); and physical productivity objectives for each area. For example, in the external plant area, the objective is line repairs to be achieved per day. In the traffic area, the objective is that operators answer calls in less than ten seconds. In the commercial area, the objective is to prepare internal duty orders without error. In the switching area, the objective concerns damage control and repairs. In addition, the Permanent General Program included two types of pay incentives (monthly and yearly); and stated that 50 percent of the monthly pay incentives will be paid when 90 percent of the objectives are achieved and the total amount will be paid when 100 percent of the objectives are accomplished; that the annual pay incentive will be paid if all the objectives in the labor area are met; that 85 percent of the total incentives are to be paid monthly while 15 percent will be paid on an annual basis. The pay incentives are to be calculated on the basis of performance in each work area, and joint work unit (analysis) groups will be established with the participation of unionized supervisors and chiefs in order to carry out follow-up monitoring and adjustment of the incentive system. The functions of the analysis groups are to design plans and methods to improve productivity, and to conduct evaluations and make proposals regarding productivity improvement methods. Unionized workers and managers participate in these groups.

The other important aspect of the new bilateral labor relations at Telmex is the many new joint commissions (formal entities that design programs in different areas). Some of these have existed a long time, others were restructured after being eliminated in the 1990 contract revision, and still others have been created as a result of the new productivity-related negotiations. There are six commissions.

The Joint Commission for Productivity and Quality has existed since 1987 and has been the forum for the discussions that led to the Telmex quality model. The 1990 contract modifications interrupted the operation of this joint commission for over a year, but since 1992 the commission has recovered the important responsibility for designing training courses that promote the quality model. This commission also is in charge of negotiations surrounding productivity-related agreements, in particular, this commission establishes productivity objectives and the indicators used to measure productivity.

The Joint Commission on Modernization is now the most important commission (although its functions overlap with those of other commissions). It supervises the negotiations that deal with quality and productivity incentives. This commission includes the qualification and new technology program; the labor conditions program; the culture and relief program; the specialties qualification program; and the permanent program for improving services.

The Joint Commission on New Technology was created in 1987. This commission lost its importance with the 1990 contract modifications. At present its functions have been reduced to receiving information whenever new training is required due to the introduction of new technology. The Training Commission was created in 1986. This commission designs training courses. The Health and Safety Commission was created in 1987. Finally, there is a Commission of Medical Studies.

The breadth of the productivity agreements affecting telephone services and the progress made in implementing those agreements propelled Telmex into the status of the most highly-developed case of bilaterally negotiated work restructuring in Mexico. Telmex is frequently cited in governmental and internal union discussions as a model productivity improvement process.

Impact on Internal Labor Markets and Human Resources

The restructuring of Telmex has not involved employment reductions. On the contrary, employment has remained stable since 1988 (see Tables

9.6 and 9.7). Factors that have contributed to this stability are: the company's growth; the labor union's offer of flexibility and quality in exchange for pay incentives and the company's efforts to avoid cutbacks in personnel; and management's acceptance of the labor union as its legitimate counterpart in confronting productivity problems. Six main human resource adjustments have occurred at Telmex since the late 1980s. There are no firings but rather personnel are frequently relocated or reassigned. Job positions and categories have been consolidated. Despite the Telmex modernization, gender segmentation by job type is still substantial. There is greater flexibility in the contract that deals with either external or internal personnel adjustments. Wages increasingly depend on individual and departmental performance. Job qualifications have been steadily raised.

Employment

Although total employment at Telmex has been stable in recent years, there have been many relocations and early retirements. Many of the relocations have involved employees in the general services department, operators, installers, and PBX and telephone equipment maintenance

TABLE 9.6. Telephone services and employees at Telmex, 1976–1993

Year	Telephone apparatus in service (thousands)	Telephone lines (thousands)	International distance conference (thousands)	National long distance conference (thousands)	Employees
1976	3,309	1,850.6	23.3	197.3	22,078
1977	3,712	2,077.1	24.3	220.0	23,403
1978	4,140	2,307.1	29.6	268.5	24,870
1979	4,543	2,498.8	38.1	222.1	26,006
1980	5,013	2,720.5	47.3	402.4	27,568
1981	5,533	2,969.8	56.7	461.2	29,566
1982	5,975	3,163.1	55.4	510.3	31,385
1983	6,378	3,318.0	52.0	520.5	32,509
1984	6,796	3,458.0	55.6	563.8	34,663
1985	7,325	3,705.0	60.8	608.4	37,487
1986	7,735	3,927.0	69.6	665.2	40,662
1987	8,176	4,092.8	78.9	724.7	44,700
1988	8,653	4,381.4	103.6	768.6	49,995
1989	9,558	4,847.2	141.5	860.6	49,203
1990	10,323	5,355.0	169.0	951.0	49,912
1991	11,072	6,025.0	210.0	1,068.0	49,488
1992	11,126	6,875.0	248.0	1,204.0	49,893
1993		7,621.0	387.5	1,403.0	48,771

Source: Telmex, *Annual Report* (several years).

TABLE 9.7. Types of employees at Telmex (without subsidiaries), 1985–1994

Year	Total	Unionized	Chiefs and supervisors	Operators
1985	37487	32452	5035	11509
1986	40662	35045	5617	12444
1987	44700	38036	6614	12699
1988	49995	42663	7332	13421
1989	49203	41621	7682	NA
1990	49912	42100	7812	NA
1991	49488	NA	NA	NA
1992	48937	41722	7215	NA
1993	NA	NA	NA	NA
1994*	NA	45901	NA	10584

Sources:
a) Telmex, Report to Shareholders' Assembly (various years).
b) Telmex, Census, October 1992.
c) Solís (1992).
d) Telmex, Wage Scale, 1994.
*March

staff. For example, when ongoing relocations are completed, 50 percent of the operators will have been relocated. Meanwhile, employment growth has been occurring in external plant, commercial, customer services, exchange, and long distance.

Consolidation of Jobs and Job Categories

Prior to recent restructuring, complex regulations at Telmex specified jobs and job categories. These regulations emerged as a consequence of a long series of confrontations and negotiations from 1976 to 1989. The regulations were contained in fifty-seven departmental agreements, which in practice functioned as collective subcontracts. These contracts specified 585 labor categories. With the 1989 productivity agreements, these agreements and the associated regulations disappeared and a smaller number of job specializations (24) and job profiles (125) were defined.

Segmentation by Gender

Although women represent 42.4 percent of the workforce at Telmex, there is sharp gender-based job segmentation.[3] As can be seen in Table 9.8, thirteen job specialties (or departments) are staffed only by men, and three job specialties (or departments) are filled only by women. These two groups of specialties include the vast majority of Telmex personnel.

3. The average age of the wage earners is 34 years.

TABLE 9.8. Workers by specialty or department at Telmex, 1994

Specialty	Number of employees	Gender
Central maintenance	3,023	mixed
Long distance maintenance	1,076	male
Energy	321	male
Projects engineering	375	male
Lines central	129	male
Long distance building	210	male
Long distance lines maintenance	539	male
Storage	821	male
Marketing	3,888	mixed
Administration	3,942	mixed
Repair of equipment	842	male
Technicians	259	mixed
Day care center	154	female
Specialties of the Secretary General	11	mixed
Finances	334	mixed
Drivers	155	male
Automotive	138	male
Files	9	mixed
Exterior plant	13,493	male
Supervision and construction, ext. plant	200	male
Networks and construction	505	male
International traffic	2,153	female
National traffic	8,431	female
Total	41,192	

Source: Wage scale for 1994 and conversations with Telmex workers.

As reported in Table 9.9, 18,804 workers are concentrated in the specialties in the first group (only men) and 10,738 workers are in the second group (only women). Only the remaining 28.3 percent of the unionized personnel (11,650 workers) are distributed in categories which include both men and women.

Recruitment norms at Telmex

Telmex and the STRM have established three documents that provide rules governing entry into and movements within Telmex's internal labor

TABLE 9.9. Segmentation by gender at Telmex, 1994

Number of categories	Workers
Only women: 3	10,738
Only men: 13	18,840
Mixed: 6	11,650

Source: Telmex, Internal Report, 1994.

market. These documents include: (1) the Contrato Colectivo de Trabajo or CCT (collective labor contract); (2) the Reglamento Intero de Trabajo or RIT (internal labor regulations), and (3) the Perfiles de Puesto or PP (job profiles) for each department.

Chapter 11 of the collective labor contract (CCT) stipulates that individuals hired into Telmex must already be members of the STRM, have the necessary abilities for the job, and be tested by examination. Clause 15 of the CCT requires the company to inform the union and workers of any vacancies—permanent or temporary—so that the union can propose candidates to occupy those positions. This clause also describes how to fill a new position or vacancies created by promotion, resignation, dismissal, death, or retirement.

The internal labor regulations (in chapter 1 of the CCT) also establish the requirements that applicants must satisfy in order to join the company. The requirements mentioned in the collective labor contract are in addition to those included in the job profiles. The departmental agreements had served as "small" collective labor contracts in each department. The April 1989 negotiation carried out between the company and union replaced the departmental agreements with "job profiles." The job profiles established more specific job requirements and promoted what at the time was referred to as an expansion of "labor flexibility" at Telmex. The net effect of the introduction of job profiles was consolidation of job and wage categories.

Chapter 2 of the CCT allows for admission examinations for joining (or rejoining) the company. It also specifies the knowledge required for workers in each of the following departments: national and international traffic, commercial offices, claims and repairs, long distance lines, networks, and mechanical workshop. Article 3 of the CCT allows the company to require a medical examination of job applicants.

The new job profiles perform the following functions. They provide the 125 categories for the 24 job specialties; they outline in detail the principal functions and activities expected of personnel; they establish the conditions under which work must be carried out; and they describe the training and other procedures that enable promotion to a higher category. A common characteristic in these job profiles is mention of the importance of labor flexibility.

The regulations described above are much broader than previous Telmex policies in that they regulate assignments, promotion, and retirement, and it is noteworthy that they do so in a bilateral manner.

Pay Procedures

The three components of pay at Telmex are wages, extra wages, and productivity incentives. The first two of these components and the respective labor contract clause defining each are described in Tables 9.10 and 9.11.

The productivity incentives mentioned in earlier sections of this chapter provide extra compensation that averages between 30 percent and 43 percent of workers' base salary whenever the productivity goals in each labor area are achieved. Telephone workers' wages are generally much higher than the minimum wage in Mexico (equal to about U.S. $100 per month), especially if the productivity incentives are included. Examples of Telmex worker base wages are listed in Table 9.12.

Despite the novel system and size of wage incentives now used at Telmex, national government economic policies led to significant declines in real earnings in recent years as reported in Table 9.13. However, these declines were less severe than the declines experienced by most workers in other sectors in Mexico.[4] In part, the declines in real earnings at Telmex result from the fact that the productivity incentives merely replace what was previously paid as overtime payments.

Training

Since the early 1990s, both management and the union at Telmex have recognized the increasing importance of training and the advantages of joint regulation of training. As of 1993, Telmex workers on average were receiving eleven days of training per year. Telmex's training effort thus

TABLE 9.10. Direct wages at Telmex

Wages	Concept	Form of calculation
Clause 103	Based on daily wages	The weekly wage is calculated on the basis of the seven days of the week
Clause 104	Aid for paying housing rent	Telmex provides $5,926.39 per year[a]
Clause 105	Aid for transportation expenditures	Telmex provides $1,769.03 per year[a]
Clause 108	Overtime	The daily wage is multiplied by six work-days, and the result is divided among the number of hours corresponding to the daytime, mixed, and nighttime shifts. The quotient is divided by two, thus providing a type of overtime payment.

[a]New pesos for all unionized workers. Each new peso equals one U.S. dollar.
Note: The base salary depends exclusively on each worker's job category.

4. Note, the minimum wage in Mexico fell by 22.3% in real terms between 1990 and 1993 due to high inflation.

TABLE 9.11. Extra wages at Telmex

Extra wages	Concept	Extra payment
Clause 113	For driving a car, truck or motorcycle on the job (except those employed as drivers)	$2,307.14 per year for driving a car, truck or motorcycle. $387.96 for driving a bicycle
	Incentives for not having an accident	Funded from a company-wide fund of $50 million per year (except for those employed as drivers)
	For those who are not payers but handle money for payments	$1,000 per year
	When traffic personnel handle matters of the Commercial Department	They receive an extra amount in relation to the number of local telephone lines
	For using English	15% of the daily wage
Clause 114	For commissions	For wage earners who also receive commissions, the total gained during the last three months will be averaged, to obtain the daily wage
Clause 15	To operators making long distance calls	15% of the daily wage
Clause 16	For porters and watchmen	20% over the base wage for performing cleaning work

Note: Each new peso equals one U.S. dollar.

TABLE 9.12. Base wages at Telmex for various worker categories

Category	Monthly wage (in U.S. dollars)
Highest level technicians (maintenance stations)	800
Engineer assistant (engineering and design)	857
Foreman assistant (long distance construction)	800
Warehouse commissioned (warehouses)	600
Commercial assistant	700
Operator	620
Average base salary for unionized workers	670

Note: These figures do not include extra wages or incentives. These figures were those before the devaluation of the peso in November 1994.

TABLE 9.13. Index of the average real wages of Telmex workers

Year	1990	1991	1992	1993
Index	100	85	90.9	92.1

Source: Our own calculations based on Telmex reports.

was higher than the training that was occurring at Southwestern Bell (Telmex's U.S. partner) which provided ten days of training per year, or France Télécom which offered only six days of training per year. Intelmex was created through joint discussions at Telmex to oversee training. It provides workers with seventy-nine programs on new technology including the impacts of digitalization on operators and optic fiber networks and the impacts of digital technology on communication and transmission-related work. Telmex's training programs include jointly run courses aimed at sensitizing workers regarding improved quality and productivity, teamwork, customer needs, and the new labor culture.

Conclusions

Mexico's monopolistic telephone service company was privatized in 1990, and in 1996, the long distance services will be opened to competition. The expanding cellular telephone system has always been open to competition in Mexico. This opening of the market has exerted pressure on Telmex to accelerate its modernization, to create new services, and to improve its quality and productivity.

Significant technological changes driven by efforts to improve and expand communications services were implemented in Mexico during the last decade. By 1993, 65 percent of telephone facilities were digitalized, there was rapid development of an optic fiber system, and the use of telecommunications satellites was expanding markedly.

While these transformations were taking place, labor relations were being substantially modified in three ways. First, labor flexibility was increased through the consolidation of jobs and the increased functions assigned to each job category. Furthermore, the new emphasis on quality and internal mobility led to heightened labor flexibility. Second, the union at Telmex gained an increased role through the negotiation of productivity agreements which establish that the union can participate in measuring productivity, diagnosing the factors that hinder productivity, designing training programs, and improving work conditions. A new type of labor relations has thus been born, characterized by flexibility and, at the same time, bilateral negotiation between management and the union.

The union's involvement in the development of the plans guiding Telmex's modernization prevented that modernization from causing the dismissal of workers. Instead, there has been an ambitious plan to retrain and relocate workers.

Third, wage payments have been made less rigid and are now generally semi-flexible. There are incentives for achieving productivity and quality goals that provide significant extra compensation. This has permitted the real wages of telephone workers to diminish less than wages in other sectors of the Mexican economy.

The fact that Telmex has become a model for bilateral labor relations, which is unlike the path followed by the country's other companies, cannot be explained simply by structural factors, given that other companies in similar conditions have opted for different strategies. Without a doubt the regulatory changes affecting Telmex provided the context for and a spur to changes in labor relations. Mexico's telecommunications services sector is now more open, although it is not entirely deregulated, and pressure for further opening in the market for telecommunications services could challenge Telmex. Faced by these pressures, including the need to offer new services, Telmex proposed over ten years ago to make changes first in technology, then in organization, and finally in labor relations.

In the mid-1980s, when technological modernization had already begun at Telmex, the labor union and its strong position were viewed in business policies as an obstacle to be overcome in order to increase productivity. In the end it was a switch in labor union strategy that convinced Telmex management to begin a process of bilateral negotiation, a policy extended by the new owners of Telmex in 1990. The bilateralism adopted at Telmex contrasts sharply with the deregulation-authoritarian path followed by the majority of Mexico's businesses. The switch in union strategy that drove the process was itself precipitated by the union leadership's recognition of the economic pressures confronting Telmex, by the presence of an intellectualized opposition within the union, by the advice provided by a group of high-level specialists in the union, and by the fact that the union was relatively democratic. The fact that Telmex was not in the midst of a financial crisis, but rather was earning positive profits although it faced economic challenges, also helped the union push for bilateralism.

But the path to bilateralism was not an easy one. A year before the privatization of Telmex, the power and position of the union was severely weakened. Nevertheless, once the company was privatized, the labor union leadership's push for bilateralism helped convince the president of Mexico of the need to transform the state's traditional corporatist model of labor relations. As bilateralism developed at Telmex, the STRM and Telmex workers gained influence over employment conditions, in particular, through the negotiation of successive productivity agreements.

The STRM was thus converted into the leader of a new trend in Mexican labor unionism which contrasted with the corporatism of the CTM. A new federation, Federación de Sindicatos de Empresas de Bienes y Servicios or FESEBES (Labor Union Federation in Businesses Providing Goods and Services) has been formed and has inspired the leadership of the teachers' union, the public service workers' union, and the bank workers' union to favor bilateralism instead of corporatism.

Industrial relations in Mexico are, however, permanently contaminated by electoral politics and in 1993 the race for the country's presidency began, once again making the CTM the privileged counterpart from the government's point of view (the CTM has 5,000,000 members as opposed to FESEBES' 120,000 members). That same year the negotiations surrounding the North American Free Trade Agreement concluded and at the last minute, the Mexican president promised to index wages with productivity. The CTM, and not the telephone workers' union was asked to represent labors' interest in the negotiation of the specific index.

Mexico now finds itself once again submerged in a deep economic crisis. The national government's economic adjustment program has emphasized the need to balance the trade account and proposals for a new labor unionism have been abandoned. At the same time, pressure for a broader opening of the Mexican telecommunications services sector from the United States and other sources is building. The future for bilateral labor relations at Telmex is unclear. Nevertheless, the fate of this pioneering experiment in Mexican labor relations is worthy of future study.

Chapter 10

Korea

Young-bum Park

The telecommunications business in Korea is very highly regulated, as is the case in most countries. In addition, Korea Telecom, a government-owned enterprise, and its subsidiary companies dominate the industry and enjoy a monopoly in their primary markets. However, the future environment will be markedly different. Foreign companies as well as private Korean companies will be allowed to provide services in Korea's telecommunications industry in the coming years.

This chapter focuses on the industrial relations and human resource management practices of Korea Telecom, one of the five largest firms in Korea. Korea Telecom has a monopoly in Korea's general telecommunications business sector which includes telephone (domestic service only), telegram, information telecommunications, all kinds of integrated transmission services, and the setting-up of telephone circuits. In 1991, another company was permitted to provide overseas telephone services.

This chapter analyzes a set of core industrial relations and human resource management practices in Korea Telecom and the prospects for change in those practices. We also investigate the effects of developments in Korea's industrial relations since 1987 on Korea Telecom's practices.

The set of core industrial relations and human resource management practices that serve as the focal point of the analysis are: (1) changes in the organization of work, (2) new compensation schemes, (3) changing patterns of skill formation and training, (4) issues of job mobility and employment security, and (5) corporate governance issues. These practices will be analyzed using the framework guiding a comparative study of telecommunications services.[1]

The research was based on extensive interviews with senior and middle-level managers, supervisors, and union officials in Korea Telecom. Also, documents and publications produced by Korea Telecom were analyzed.[2]

Developments in Industrial Relations and the Labor Market

There have been major changes, legal reforms, and far-reaching developments in Korea since 1987 in the field of industrial relations. Most important was the explosive increase in labor disputes that occurred after the "Democratization Declaration" in 1987 which entailed 3,749, 1,873, and 1,616 strikes respectively in 1987, 1988, and 1989. Before 1987 trade unions in Korea did not independently represent workers' interests in the process that determined wages and working conditions. However, after mid-1987, the labor movement expanded greatly. For example, the number of organized establishments increased from 2,725 in July 1987 to 7,883 in December 1989 and total union membership increased from 1,000,000 to almost 2,000,000 during the same period. Nowadays, collective bargaining is used to fix the working conditions of many employees. As of December 1993, union membership in Korea amounted to 1,667,000 and the rate of unionization with respect to permanent workers in the nonagriculture sector was 17.2 percent. The rate of unionization seems to have reached a stable point (Korea Labor Institute 1993).

The Federation of Korean Trade Unions (FKTU) has been the only national union federation authorized by the labor law since the 1950s. The membership of the FKTU is officially said to cover most unions in Korea. However, official FKTU membership figures cover some unions, including the membership of the "Chunnodae," which have been trying to form another national organization, and some industrial federations which, in fact, are not affiliated with the FKTU and conduct independent activities. The recognition of non-FKTU affiliated unions has been one of

1. The framework is outlined in greater detail in Verma, Kochan, and Lansbury 1995.
2. Korea Telecom's annual performance reports for a number of years were particularly useful. Under the Government Investment Enterprise Regulation Act, Korea Telecom is subject to annual evaluation by the Public Enterprise Performance Evaluation Commission. For this evaluation, Korea Telecom publishes a very detailed annual business performance report.

the central issues within recent discussions concerning potential labor law revisions.

Union membership also rose rapidly after 1987 in those parts of the public sector where the trade union movement is legal.[3] Since June 1987, 151 new public enterprises have been organized, while only 32 public enterprises were unionized before June 1987. Union membership in the public sector was 296,000 as of December 1991, with the unionization rate being 92.3 percent (if only the workers who were allowed to join a union are considered), which is very high in comparison to the rest of Korea. In addition, the proportion of the public sector in total union membership is large: 16.4 percent as of December 1991 (Park 1993b).

The relatively high level of public-sector unionization in Korea can be explained mainly as the effect of the large plant size. Public-sector enterprises have generally more than 300 employees: three out of four Korean public and private-sector establishments with 300 or more employees are organized.

With Korea's system of industrial relations in a process of fundamental transformation since 1987, labor rights and laws have been a major political issue. It had been widely expected that shortly after the civil head of state took office in early 1993, the major labor laws would be amended by the National Assembly. However, in August 1993, the Korean government announced the postponement of labor law amendments, arguing that the debates surrounding these amendments would harm the Korean economy, which fell into a deep recession in 1993. Then in 1994, the president of Korea announced to top Korean business leaders that the labor laws would not be amended during his term since the country should not waste its resources in discussing such very controversial issues in a period of intense global economic competition.

This announcement greatly disappointed many trade union activists, particularly those in the "Chunnodae," a labor federation not recognized under the current legal framework.[4] There has been much interunion conflict in recent years and the postponement of amendments to the labor

3. In Korea, public servants, except for the employees of some government enterprises, do not have the legal right to join trade unions. However, where unionism is allowed in the public sector, the same labor rights, labor standards, and dispute resolution procedures prevail as those in the private sector.

4. "Chunnodae" is a national federation of trade unions which does not belong to the FKTU, the only recognized national union federation under the current legal framework. In Korea, multiple unions at the same work site are not allowed. For example, when a new union has the same objectives as an existing union, or is deemed to interfere with the normal operation of the existing union, the new union is not recognized as a legal trade union. See Park (1993c) for details.

laws is likely to prolong this conflict and make it difficult for cooperative action to take place between labor, management, and the government.

The objectives of the various public-sector trade unions, like those of other Korean labor unions, differ depending on whether the relevant union was organized before or after June 1987. Most trade unions established before 1987, including public enterprise unions, support the FKTU. On the other hand, many newly organized public-sector unions have different allegiances. Some of the new unions have formed industry or occupation-wide trade union federations that are not affiliated with the FKTU. The new trade unions in Korea to some extent reject business unionism and emphasize political action as well as the need for substantial improvements in workers' welfare, and generally support the Chunnodae. However, when actual union policies are considered, the political programs and ideological positions of the old and new unions do not differ as much as the rhetoric of the various unions would suggest.

Except for a short period following the 1987 "June 29 Democratization Declaration," the government has been involved in wage negotiations in the private sector. Annual wage increases have exceeded 10 percent since 1987. By introducing a "one-digit-policy," a "total wage system," and a "social accord between the FKTU and the Korea Employers' Federation," the government has been trying to influence wage increases in the private sector as well as in those parts of the public sector where collective bargaining has been taking place.[5] In this framework, hundreds of leading public and private establishments were advised to settle their wage negotiations within suggested wage increase guidelines. Many public enterprises were viewed as leading firms and expected to serve as role models for other firms.

However, the government's efforts to hold down wage increases have been problematic (in the public as well as the private sector), especially given the fact that trade unions are no longer passive actors. Wages on average rose 18.8, 17.7, 15.2, 12.2, and 12.7 percent, respectively, in 1990, 1991, 1992, 1993, and 1994. In the current environment, it appears that the government's wage restraint policy has limited effectiveness (Korea Labor Institute 1993). In 1995, the union representing

5. The one-digit policy and the total wage system were the government wage guidelines, respectively, in 1991 and 1992. Under the wage guidelines, private firms were asked to limit their wage increases to less than 10 percent. In 1993 and 1994, the government encouraged the FKTU and the Korea Employers' Federation to make an agreement on desirable wage increases for the country's development, which was called a "social accord." Then, this agreement was used as a government guideline for wage negotiations in 1993 and 1994.

employees at Korea Telecom led the opposition to the government's wage policy, which resulted in the imprisonment of the leaders of that union.

Since the mid-1980s the labor market in Korea has been near full employment despite the problems facing the Korean economy. Overall the growing service sector has been absorbing labor from the manufacturing sector.

Korea Telecom as a Government Invested Enterprise

Before 1981, telecommunications services in Korea were provided by a bureau of the Ministry of Postal Service whose employees were public servants. Telecommunications field operations were conducted by post offices, as in Germany. In 1981 Korea Telecom was established as a "Government Invested Enterprise" (GIE) and as such more than 49 percent of the equity was owned by the central government. The telecommunications industry was seen as a crucial part of the country's infrastructure and as a necessary ingredient for sustained economic development. Most of the employees who worked in the telecommunications bureau of the Ministry of Postal Service were transferred to the Korea Telecommunications Authority which was renamed Korea Telecom in 1990.[6]

With the amendments to the Trade Union Act approved in 1987, labor rights equal to those enjoyed in the private sector were extended to the employees of Korea Telecom. After this point the central government was no longer officially involved in labor relations at Korea Telecom.

However, the national government has in fact continued to play a critical role in labor relations at Korea Telecom. Some of the government's continuing involvement in Korea Telecom's labor relations followed from the Government Invested Enterprise Regulation Act (GIERA) which re-

6. The creation of Korea Telecom has been widely viewed as a successful endeavor. As an investment project of Korea's Fifth Five-year Economic and Social Development Plan from 1981 to 1986 Korea Telecom set out to construct a basic national telephone network (telephone lines and related equipment) and at a cost of 2 trillion won (U.S.$2.855 billion). From 1981 to 1986, the total number of telephone circuits increased by 140 percent to 8,903,000 with the addition of 6,143,000 circuits. This resulted in an increase in the diffusion of telephone services from 8.9 to 19 per 100 capita during the same period. Moreover, the electric rate (automation rate) of telephone network switches increased from 14.1% (88%) in 1981 to 65.3% (99.2%) in 1986. The quality of telecommunications service also improved substantially. The out-function time (time out of order per employee) of the telephone dropped from 120.68 minutes in 1981 to 28.28 minutes in 1986, and the completion rate for city calls increased from 58.3% to 76.4% during the same period.

quires that all major managerial decisions at GIEs, including those concerning personnel management, should be approved by the GIE's governing body. At Korea Telecom the governing board includes government officials from the Ministry of Postal Service and the Economic Planning Board. The number of workers in a particular grade as well as the total number of Korea Telecom's employees also must be approved by the governing board. Korea Telecom's budget is examined annually by the Ministry of Postal Service as well as the Economic Planning Board, and annual wage increments are determined in advance before wage bargaining begins. Therefore, despite the fact that Korea Telecom is a GIE, and is accordingly given some autonomy under the GIERA, the company still must follow the government's wage policy.

Furthermore, Korea Telecom is subject to an annual evaluation by the Government Invested Enterprise Performance Evaluation Commission (GIEPEC) explained in detail later. For the last few years, the GIEs' (including Korea Telecom's) adherence to government wage guidelines has been evaluated by the GIEPEC.

Finally, Korea Telecom employees have been subject to the emergency arbitration and/or compulsory mediation (in the case of severe strikes) required under the Trade Union Act, which regulates labor relations in industries that provide essential services (including gas, electricity, and hospitals).

External Environments and Industrial Relations/ Human Resource Management

Product Market

In Korea, telecommunications service businesses are classified into three categories; general, special, and added. The general telecommunications businesses include telephone, telegram, information telecommunications, integrated transmission services, and installation services. The special telecommunication businesses include mobile telecommunications, port telecommunications, and flight telecommunications. The added telecommunications businesses provide added services with rented telecommunications facilities. Foreign firms are not allowed to compete in the general telecommunications market.

Korea Telecom has a monopoly on all general telecommunications except overseas telephone services. Until recently the subsidiary companies of Korea Telecom also had monopolies in the special telecommunications business areas.

Since its establishment, Korea Telecom has expanded very rapidly, as

Table 10.1 shows. Korea Telecom's annual turnover and net profit in 1994 were 6.884 trillion won (U.S. $8.727 billion) and 637 billion won (U.S. $808 million), respectively. In 1983, Korea Telecom's annual turnover and net profit were 1.139 trillion won (U.S. $1.432 million) and 106 billion won (U.S. $133 million), respectively. The total number of telephone circuits increased from 3,491,000 in 1981 to 20,783,000 in 1994. The rapid growth of Korea Telecom has been attributed mainly to the shortages that prevailed in Korea's telecommunications sector until the mid-1980s and the fact that Korea Telecom has had monopolistic power in the market.

However, recently, Korea Telecom's privilege as a monopolistic public enterprise has faced a serious challenge as the Korean government has introduced more competition into the telecommunications sector by allowing private and foreign capital. In 1991, another company, Dacom, began to offer overseas telephone services. In 1993, Dacom's market share jumped to 25 percent. In 1994, Korea Telecom was forced to sell its 33.4 percent share of Dacom to the private sector under a government telecommunications sector rationalization plan. Before 1997, competition will be introduced in long distance telephone services, which is the most profitable business of Korea Telecom.

Until August 1993, Korea Mobile Telecom (KMT), a subsidiary company of Korea Telecom, was the sole mobile telecommunications service provider. In September 1993, an additional ten private companies began to offer communication pager services. In 1996, a second mobile telephone company will start operating. Korea Telecom is supposed to sell a 44.1 percent share of Korea Mobile Telecom's stock (out of the 64.01 percent share of KMT stock owned by Korea Telecom) to the private sector. Korea Telecom will be listed in the Korea Stock Exchange in 1995, which will put some additional financial pressures on the company.

Foreign investment in the Korean telecommunications services industry has been recently permitted and these investments are likely to grow in the future. Joint-venture companies were recently permitted to enter into the VAN market and many foreign telecommunications companies (including AT&T) already have, or are likely to open, business with a Korean counterpart. The national government has stated that as of 1997, the Korean telecommunications market, excepting the general telecommunications businesses, will be opened fully to foreign capital.

All this additional competition implies that Korea Telecom will face its most difficult challenge since its establishment as a public enterprise in 1981. Part of the challenge will come from the fact that along with additional competition, Korea Telecom will face fundamental modifications

TABLE 10.1. Selected labor productivity indicators in Korea Telecom

	1983	1984	1985	1986	1987	1988	1989	1990	1991	1992	1993	1994
Turnover (won in millions) (A)	1,139,070	1,385,514 (21.6)	1,591,506 (14.9)	1,889,509 (18.7)	2,264,970 (19.9)	2,650,076 (17.0)	3,089,875 (16.6)	3,761,166 (21.7)	4,569,547 (21.5)	5,152,154 (12.7)	6,032,657 (17.0)	6,994,653 (14.1)
Net Profit (won in millions) (B)	105,811	131,652 (24.4)	64,512 (−51.0)	233,634 (262.12)	244,822 (−4.8)	321,927 (31.5)	288,438 (−10.4)	316,977 (9.9)	475,641 (50.1)	619,373 (30.1)	482,856 (−22.0)	637,153 (31.2)
Wage & Welfare Cost (won in millions) (C)	319,689	374,377 (17.1)	411,934 (10.0)	447,275 (8.6)	545,789 (22.0)	740,749 (35.7)	875,384 (18.2)	972,381 (11.2)	1,151,987 (18.5)	1,208,336 (4.9)	1,332,539 (10.3)	1,771,258 (32.9)
Number of Employees (D)	40,078	41,449 (3.4)	43,112 (4.0)	46,585 (8.1)	49,284 (5.8)	50,859 (3.2)	52,531 (3.3)	54,183 (3.1)	56,163 (3.7)	58,301 (3.8)	59,802 (2.6)	59,906 (0.2)
A/D	28.42	33.43 (17.6)	36.92 (10.4)	40.56 (9.9)	45.96 (13.3)	52.11 (13.4)	58.82 (12.9)	69.42 (18.0)	81.36 (17.2)	88.37 (10.9)	100.88 (14.2)	114.92 (13.7)
B/D	2.64	3.18 (20.5)	1.50 (−52.8)	5.02 (234.7)	4.97 (−1.0)	6.33 (277.4)	5.49 (−13.3)	5.85 (6.6)	8.47 (44.8)	10.63 (25.5)	8.05 (−24.3)	10.64 (32.2)
C/D	7.98	9.03 (13.2)	9.55 (5.8)	9.60 (0.5)	11.07 (15.3)	14.56 (31.5)	16.66 (14.4)	17.95 (7.7)	20.51 (14.3)	20.74 (1.1)	22.28 (7.4)	23.59 (32.7)
Number of lines installed per employee	133.24	151.76 (13.9)	174.89 (15.2)	191.17 (9.3)	207.40 (8.5)	220.99 (6.6)	254.21 (15.0)	282.25 (11.0)	311.80 (10.5)	326.25 (4.6)	338.17 (3.7)	346.5 (2.5)
Number of subscribers per employee	104.29	134.98 (29.4)	133.71 (−0.9)	161.44 (20.7)	174.02 (8.4)	202.64 (15.8)	224.47 (10.8)	245.03 (9.2)	259.47 (5.9)	267.46 (3.1)	279.02 (4.3)	284.6 (10.6)
Overall economy (percentage)	11.0	8.7	9.2	8.2	10.1	15.5	21.1	18.8	17.7	15.2	12.2	12.7
Rate of wage change inflation rate (CPI)	3.4	2.3	2.5	2.8	3.0	7.1	5.7	8.6	9.3	6.2	4.8	6.2

Note: The numbers in parentheses are percentage rates of change.

in its relationship with the Korean government. Over a hundred government regulations concern Korea Telecom's business operations. Most importantly, service fees of Korea Telecom are still subject to the approval of the Economic Planning Board, which emphasizes the fees' impact on customer prices.

One might expect that the employees of Korea Telecom would enjoy extremely favorable wages and working conditions as a result of Korea Telecom's monopolistic advantages. However, this has not been the case, particularly after the company became subject to the government's wage restraint policy in 1990. Wages at Korea Telecom are on average lower than wages at Dacom or other major telecommunications companies. This disparity has had far-reaching effects on Korea Telecom's industrial relations and human resource management practices. These effects are analyzed in the following sections.

Labor Market

Korea Telecom had 59,906 employees in 1994. The number of Korea Telecom employees had increased from 40,000 in 1983, to 51,000 in 1988, and then to 56,000 in 1991. This employment growth followed from the expansion occurring in Korea Telecom's sales volumes and range of business activities.

Employment at Korea Telecom has been one of the most popular jobs for new university graduates in Korea, mainly because the telecommunications sector has been seen as one of the most promising industries for the next century and Korea Telecom had a monopoly position in the business. Since 1990, however, Korea Telecom has had some difficulty recruiting qualified manpower, particularly employees skilled in research and development activities since its wages are below those at competing companies. In 1993, for a new college graduate, Korea Mobile Telecom and Dacom paid 10 percent and 24 percent more than Korea Telecom, respectively. Longer service employees at Dacom earn even more when compared to their counterparts at Korea Telecom (Korea Telecom 1993).

New Technology

New technologies have produced major changes in human resource management practices at Korea Telecom. In the mid-1980s, for example, most of the telephone operators were displaced by new technology. However, Korea Telecom did not fire the operators. Instead, the telephone operators were offered training for other jobs including word-processor operators, and in their new positions were rated in the job classification code at the same level as telephone operators. A compulsory retirement age was imposed for the former operators that was much younger than in other occupations such as managerial jobs. A female worker brought this case to court by arguing that Korea Telecom discriminated against female workers since most of the operators were female. She won the case. The compulsory retirement age for an operator is now almost the same as that in the other occupations. The net effect of these decisions and of industrial relations policies was to make it unlikely that a worker displaced by new technology would be made redundant.

With the increasing pace of technological change in the telecommunications services industry, the pressure on companies to recruit qualified research personnel is greater than ever. As of 1994, research personnel constituted about 1.9 percent of all workers at Korea Telecom. Korea Telecom plans to increase this figure to 5 percent by 2001.

Also, Korea Telecom's research centers have become more flexible concerning their human resource management policies. In the near future, for example, the basic unit of work organization will be a team instead of the current department-based system in the research centers. The hierarchy will consist of director (or executive director) to senior manager to manager or chief to deputy chief to ordinary worker. As of October 1994, in various research centers, seventy-nine teams were organized on a experimental basis.

Business Strategy and Trade Union Policies

A separate trade union formed at Korea Telecom in 1982 right after the company was established as a public enterprise. Before that trade union members belonged to the Postal Service Trade Union. By the end of 1993, the Korea Telecom union had 50,000 members, which was a majority of the eligible employees. Under the current collective agreement, in general, all employees below the level of section head can join the union.

Collective bargaining concerning wages at Korea Telecom takes place annually. The collective agreement concerning other matters is valid for two years. Labor-management councils, established by the national Labor Management Council Act, meet quarterly. At the labor-management councils, labor and management at the workplace level discuss ways to improve productivity, promote employees' welfare, resolve workers' grievances, and plan worker-training programs.[7] However, any agreements reached by these councils cannot be enforced by the law.

7. Under the Labor and Management Council Act, workplaces with more than 49 employees must have a labor-management council. Labor-management councils existed in 14,762 enterprises or workplaces as of the end of 1990.

Until very recently, industrial relations at Korea Telecom were relatively stable as there were no strikes other than the labor disputes that occurred from 1987 to 1989. Many former officials of the Korea Telecom trade union work for the FKTU or the ruling Democratic Justice Party. Furthermore, the Korea Telecom union has adhered to the imposed government wage guideline since 1990.

In April 1994, however, a new group in the union won election to the major leadership positions in the union with the support of young Korea Telecom employees. In the last ten years, the number of employees at Korea Telecom has increased by about 50 percent. This has produced a relatively young workforce at Korea Telecom. As a result of the rapid employment growth, at least one third of the workers at Korea Telecom have never worked as government employees. The new union leaders have tried to gain greater independence from the influence of the national government as well as more democracy within the union. For example, the union recently changed its policy so that in the future the head of the union will be elected by a direct vote of the members. Also, the union withdrew from the Federation of Telecommunications Trade Unions which belonged to the FKTU. Since November 1994, the Korea Telecom union has not belonged to any union federation.

The management of Korea Telecom has found it difficult to work with the new union leadership. In the 1994 wage negotiation, the union won an 11 percent wage increase, in addition to automatic wage increments.[8]

In 1995, Korea Telecom's wage negotiations played a key role in the nationwide annual spring wage negotiations. Korea Telecom's union demanded that the government wage guidelines be lifted or ignored. The union also opposed the Korean government's telecommunications policies, particularly the government's plans to open the telecommunications market to foreign companies. A confrontation ensued between Korea Telecom's union and the Korean government which led to the arrest of some of the union's leaders as well as the replacement of the company president. As of July 1995, the management and union of Korea Telecom were negotiating the terms of the 1995 wage agreement. The union was bolstered by a strong vote of its members in support of industrial action. The likely outcome of these wage negotiations is difficult to predict.

Management has not allowed the trade union at Korea Telecom to be involved in major managerial decisions even after the 1987 labor disputes. In contrast, in many private-sector firms, the participation of trade unions in management prerogatives deepened after 1987.[9] For example,

8. Korea Telecom Trade Union, *Wage Offensive News,* 13 October 1994.
9. See Park and Lee 1995 and Park and Lee 1994 for examples.

the union at Korea Telecom was neither involved nor consulted during the planning of the company's response to the opening of the telecommunications market. Even in 1990, some union members were fired because they participated in demonstrations opposing the opening of Korea's telecommunications market to foreign companies. Until the new union officials were elected, the trade union was relatively passive and cooperative, and consequently, the management of the company as well as the government did not take the union seriously.

When Korea Telecom was transformed into a separate public enterprise in 1981 the trade union was offered few opportunities to participate in the planning process. However, most union members gained significantly higher wages as a result of this transformation. In 1982, the year after Korea Telecom's establishment, labor costs per employee increased by 60.2 percent.[10]

The election of a new more aggressive union leadership has changed this situation. In 1995, the union staged a sit-in demonstration for about two weeks in the most prestigious Buddhist temple while criticizing the government's telecommunications policies and the government's wage guidelines. The police eventually entered the temple to arrest the union's leaders, an unprecedented move (even in the midst of prolonged labor disputes in 1987 and 1988 the police did not enter temples). Strong public opposition to this action ensued and for this and other reasons the government as well as Korea Telecom's management will likely take more seriously the union's views in the future.

Core Industrial Relations/Human Resource Management Practices

Work Organization

Job responsibilities at Korea Telecom are defined on an individual basis except for field technicians in local offices and some research departments. Promotion is based on tenure and performance evaluation.

In Korea Telecom, jobs are classified into general, technical, manual, and research, as Table 10.2 shows. In the general job classification there are seven grades, while in the research job classification there are four grades. There are some subgrades in technical and manual jobs.

In the general job classification, most workers enter the company through an open competition and start at Grade IV (for university graduates) or Grade VI (for high school graduate). Aside from these two

10. See Y. Park 1993b for details.

TABLE 10.2. Grade structure of Korea Telecom

	Grade	Minimum qualifications for internal promotion
Executive Director		Some years of tenure as Director
Director		2 years of tenure as G1
General	G1 (Senior manager)	4 years of tenure as G2
	G2 (Manager)	4 years of tenure as G3 & qualification exam
	G3 (Chief)	3 years of tenure as G4
	G4 (Deputy chief)	university graduate or 2 years of tenure as G5
	G5	2 years of tenure as G6
	G6	—
	G7	—
Technician		—
Manual Laborer		—
Research	Senior Fellow (equivalent to Director or G1)	13 evaluation points
	Fellow (equivalent to G2)	8 evaluation points
	Research Associate I (equivalent to G3)	3 evaluations points
	Research Associate II (equivalent to G4)	—
	Technician (admin.) Technician (technology)	
	Fellow (equivalent to G2)	8 evaluation points
	Research Associate I (equivalent to G3)	3 evaluation points
	Research Associate II (equivalent to G4)	—
	Technician (admin.) Technician (technology)	

Note: Evaluation points depend on performance evaluation results, experience, certificates, and other factors.

grades, the other grades are usually filed through internal promotions. In the general job classification, the occupations are divided into eight groups: administration, telecommunications, industry, facility, telegraph delivery, operator, driver, and doorkeeper. These eight occupational groups are further classified into twenty-two subgroups. Once a worker is assigned to an occupational group, that worker is rarely transferred to another occupational group through his or her entire tenure in the company.

Internal promotions typically occur once a year. For Grade I and

Grade III to VI promotions, workers must first be nominated; the list of candidates is revealed before promotion review. The candidates outnumber the actual number of promotions by between three and five to one. To be eligible for a Grade II promotion a worker must pass a qualification exam. Performance in the company-offered training programs is also considered in promotion decisions. Internal promotion within the same occupational subgroup is also frequent. Performance evaluation by supervisors is a critical factor in all promotions. In practice, however, tenure matters most. Many workers quality the fairness and objectivity of supervisors' evaluations (Korea Telecom 1994: 2).

There is an automatic promotion system based on tenure, appropriately called the tenure promotion system, for promotions to Grades IV to VI of the general job classification and for movements across the technical job classification subgrades. For example, when a worker's tenure in Grade VII is longer than six years, he or she is automatically promoted to Grade VI. This system was introduced in 1989, and in that year, more than 3,000 workers were promoted through this system.

In all grades of the research job classification, outside hiring is done more often than in the general job classification. Since 1989, however, the research associates have been selected through an open competition. The criteria for internal promotions in the research classification differ from those in the general classification. Researchers are promoted by evaluation points. The evaluation points are based on job performance, experience, and degrees or certificates. This means that for promotion in research jobs, performance is more important than it is in promotions in the general job classification. Also, performance evaluation of employees in the research job classification is based on more objective criteria.

For the technical and manual job classifications, there is no requirement for educational attainment. Until recently, movements within the same occupational job classification did not involve promotions. The 1994 wage agreement provided that manual workers with more than five years of tenure could qualify for promotion to the technical job classification. However, there have been almost no such promotions into the technical job classification.

Employees are frustrated as promotion has come to be more difficult since the organization has not expanded as fast as in the past. For example, the average age of a Grade IV employee, the grade where college graduates are hired in to the firm, was 40.6 years old as of 1994, which means that many of these employees had stayed in the same grade for more than ten years. Korea Telecom is proposing to separate grades and positions as part of a new human resource system which would allow employees to be promoted without having to move to a higher position. However, this change might be opposed by the government on grounds that it serves merely to provide more promotion opportunities for the employees and will benefit Korea Telecom employees at the expense of the public who will face higher service charges.

Since 1984, the performance evaluations required under GIERA for all of Korea Telecom have been conducted by the Government Invested Enterprise Performance Evaluation Commission (GIEPEC). The results of the evaluations determine a very small portion of wage increases. Internal evaluation has also been conducted by GIEPEC. Since 1993, a very small portion of individual workers' wages has come to depend on these internal evaluations.

Work procedures and work rules are still very bureaucratic at Korea Telecom as Korea Telecom's former status as a government agency still influences the way work is done at the company. Most of the company's senior officials were government officials when the company was a government agency and their managerial style was shaped by that experience.

Higher management at Korea Telecom has been trying to increase organizational flexibility as well as entrepeneurialism within the company through various measures. One of the key efforts entailed the introduction of a "group-based" organization. The group-based organizational reform began in 1990 and was completed in 1994. Prior to this system, Korea Telecom was organized by function, which meant that virtually all tasks were controlled by the central office. Under the new group-based system, Korea Telecom now consists of various business groups and supporting centers, as seen in Figure 10.1. Each group or center has some autonomy. For example, they can change their organizational structure and transfer workers within the group. Each group can also select some of their workers. In the past, for example, the Data Communications Business Group and Long Distance Business Group were required to follow the same organization structure determined by the central office.

The company is also considering reforming its human resource management system in 1996. Under a proposed new system, job grade and position would be separated as mentioned above.[11] The occupational groups and subgroups will be reclassified with broader definitions. The

11. Under the current system, a worker in Grade I of the general job classification must always have the position of senior manager of a department. Under the new system, this worker can be promoted to a director grade without actually moving to a director position in a bureau (bureaus are larger than departments).

FIGURE 10.1. Organization of Korea Telecom

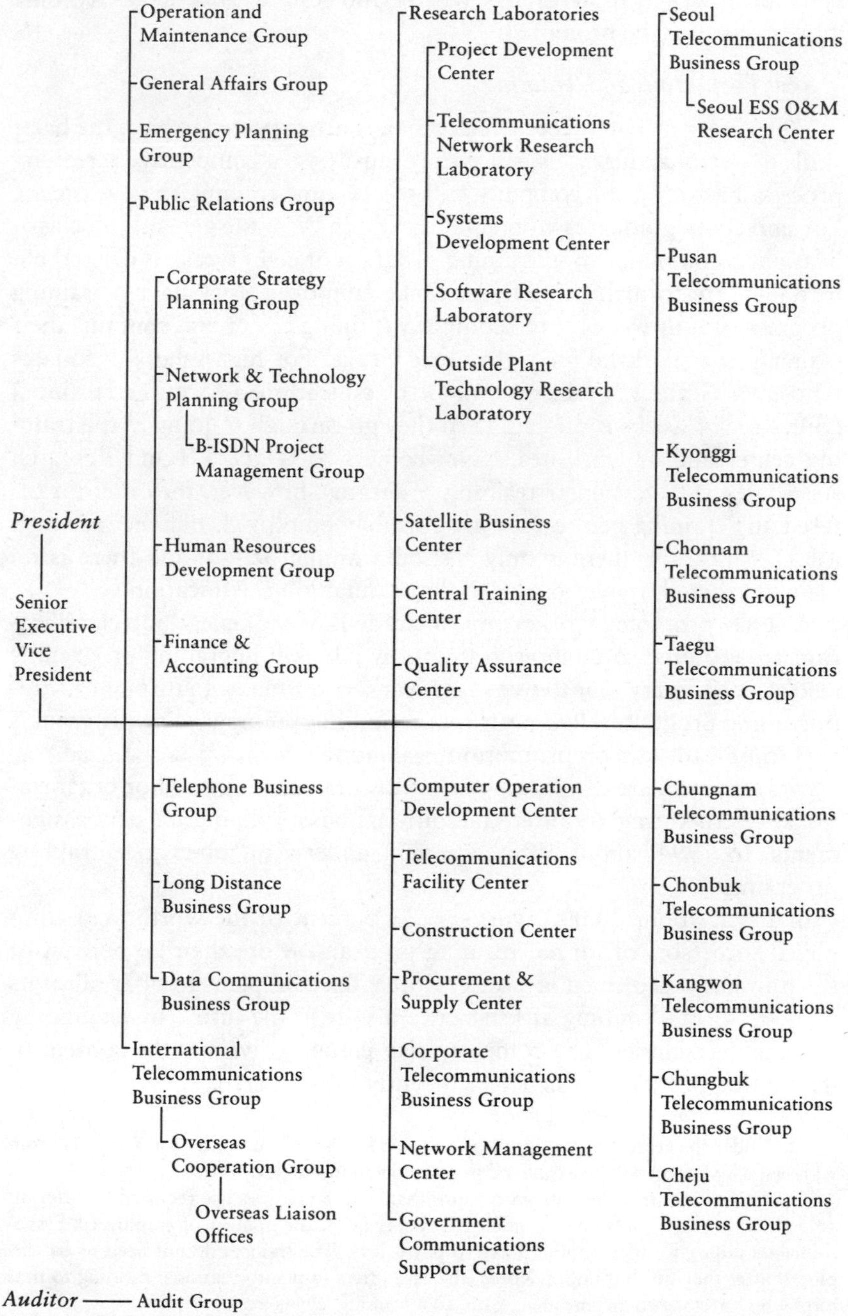

President

Senior
Executive
Vice
President

Auditor —— Audit Group

- Operation and Maintenance Group
- General Affairs Group
- Emergency Planning Group
- Public Relations Group
- Corporate Strategy Planning Group
- Network & Technology Planning Group
  - B-ISDN Project Management Group
- Human Resources Development Group
- Finance & Accounting Group
- Telephone Business Group
- Long Distance Business Group
- Data Communications Business Group
- International Telecommunications Business Group
  - Overseas Cooperation Group
    - Overseas Liaison Offices

- Research Laboratories
  - Project Development Center
  - Telecommunications Network Research Laboratory
  - Systems Development Center
  - Software Research Laboratory
  - Outside Plant Technology Research Laboratory
- Satellite Business Center
- Central Training Center
- Quality Assurance Center
- Computer Operation Development Center
- Telecommunications Facility Center
- Construction Center
- Procurement & Supply Center
- Corporate Telecommunications Business Group
- Network Management Center
- Government Communications Support Center

- Seoul Telecommunications Business Group
  - Seoul ESS O&M Research Center
- Pusan Telecommunications Business Group
- Kyonggi Telecommunications Business Group
- Chonnam Telecommunications Business Group
- Taegu Telecommunications Business Group
- Chungnam Telecommunications Business Group
- Chonbuk Telecommunications Business Group
- Kangwon Telecommunications Business Group
- Chungbuk Telecommunications Business Group
- Cheju Telecommunications Business Group

role of incentives will be increased in the proposed new compensation system. However, more grades will be introduced since it has become more difficult to be promoted.[12]

Skill Formation and Training

When workers enter Korea Telecom they are expected to have the basic skills to perform their jobs, since they must pass a competitive screening process. However, the company still offers some training to newcomers. For university graduates who enter as Grade IV in the general job classification, a communication training program of eight weeks is offered before they are formally employed. Once employed, they have a training program of four weeks at the company training center and continue their training at a worksite for eight more weeks. For high school graduates who enter Grade VI in the general job classification, a vocational training course of six weeks is offered, then they go through training at the training center and at worksites.[13] Newcomers to Grade VII and Research Associates II have similar training programs, however, they are not offered any training before they are formally employed. For the technical job classification, there is only a short training period; and there is no training offered to newcomers to the manual job classification.

A newly promoted workers up to Grade II of the general job classification are required to undergo training. A job skill upgrading program is also offered. Every four to five years workers normally go through a skill-upgrading program. Their performance in the skill-upgrading program is very important in their promotion evaluations.

Workers who are displaced by changes in technology and/or organizational restructuring are offered additional basic training for new assignments. In 1994, about 1,000 workers underwent job-change training programs.

In 1993, about 20,000 workers (33 percent of the workforce) completed some sort of formal training program. More than 90 percent of the training was offered in-house. Korea Telecom plans to offer all of its workers formal training at least once a year in the future by expanding its training facilities. The company also plans to diversify the content of its training programs which are currently job-centered.

12. Under the current system promotion provides the only incentive for Korea Telecom workers. This aspect will be explained in more detail in the next section.

13. In Korea, establishments with more than 149 employees are required to offer an amount of in-plant vocational training that depends on the number of employees. Establishments failing to offer training have to pay a levy. The trainees do not need to be employed after they finish training. Korea Telecom offers in-plant vocational training to new hires who have passed an entrance exam, so a training levy is avoided.

There are currently no systematic approaches to on-the-job training in Korea Telecom. In general, job rotation takes place within occupational subgroups. This is mainly due to the fact that the work is organized in a narrow, tightly circumscribed job-control fashion.

All newcomers to Grades IV and VI of the general job classification must work at local offices for their first year or two. Only those who are found to be capable (by evaluations) will be assigned to jobs at business groups or headquarters. This means that university graduates at the headquarters are the ones who have proven to be capable and to work hard by Korea Telecom's standards. This practice is consistent with the highly bureaucratic nature of Korea Telecom's job control procedures.

Compensation

In 1992, at Korea Telecom the yearly labor cost per permanent employee of 16,769,000 Korean won (U.S.$21,270) was 37 percent higher than the average wage of Korean workers working for establishments with more than 500 permanent employees (12,227,000 Korean won or U.S.$15,509). However, Korea Telecom's wages are lower than those of other companies in the telecommunications industry or other GIEs of about the same size, as discussed in a proceeding section of this chapter.

Wage increases at Korea Telecom were very modest relative to private enterprises from 1990 to 1993, a period when Korea Telecom was one of the leading firms in the government's wage constraint program. Wage increases (excluding the automatic annual wage increase which is about 2 to 3 percent) were 5.5 percent, 7.0 percent, 4.8 percent, and 3.0 percent, respectively, for 1990, 1991, 1992, and 1993. As a result, labor costs per employee rose 7.7 percent, 14.3 percent, 0.8 percent, and 7.5 percent over the same four years, as seen in Table 10.1. On the other hand, average labor cost increases in the private sector were 18.8 percent, 17.5 percent, 15.3 percent, and 12.2 percent over the same four years.

The employees of Korea Telecom were very unhappy with the government's wage policy since their productivity increases were much higher than their wage increases. Net profit per employee at Korea Telecom increased by 18.0 percent, 15.9 percent, 10.7 percent, and 12.1 percent, respectively, in 1990, 1991, 1992, and 1993. Net profits after tax were very substantial. For example, in 1993, net profits were 470 billion Korean won (U.S.$582 million).

However, with the election of new union leadership at Korea Telecom, the situation changed in 1994. Korea Telecom's labor cost per employee rose by 32.7 percent in 1994. The 1995 labor cost increase, although not resolved at the time of the writing of this chapter, is also likely to be very substantial.

At Korea Telecom, pay consists of a base payment and a bonus. The base payment consists of a "principal payment" (depending on the grade and tenure of an employee) and a job payment (depending on the grade of an employee). The proportion of the base payment to the total wage is about 50 percent. Across-the-board annual increases have been regularly made to principal payments. The annual bonus consists of a fixed portion, which is 300 percent of the monthly base payment and a monthly "telecommunications allowance," and an incentive no greater than 325 percent of the monthly base payment, which is determined after an evaluation of Korea Telecom's performance by GIEPEC.

While the bonus is supposed to vary depending on the evaluation made by the GIEPEC, in practice, it has not varied much over time. All GIEs, including Korea Telecom, have been provided a bonus equal to at least 300 percent of employees' base payment. Wage differentials between grades and occupations have decreased since the mid-1980s due to government policy and union pressure. An employee's starting grade depends on his or her educational attainment. However, after hiring, there are no pay differentials by education. This pay structure results in the determination of an employee's pay mostly by tenure and an employee's initial educational attainment (since the starting grade differs by educational attainment). Wage are only weakly related to individual, group, or company performance. Starting in 1995, Korea Telecom does plan to increase the performance-related portion of the research personnel's wages.

There is no discrimination in wages against female workers at Korea Telecom. However, in practice, female workers are disadvantaged in promotion. For example, the percentage of females with Grade III and above in the general job classification was only 3.3 percent in 1992.

Staffing Arrangements and Employment Security

Korea Telecom determines its own level of employment as well as the distribution of its employment among various grades and occupations. However, it must obtain approval from its governing board, the members of which include a government official from the Ministry of Postal Service and an official from the Economic Planning Board, before finalizing any major human resource management decisions. For example, Korea Telecom needs to obtain approval to increase the total number of workers, and the government is generally very reluctant to endorse an increase in the number of workers in public enterprises including Korea Telecom.

The result usually is that the level of employment and the distribution among grades and occupations at Korea Telecom (and at other public enterprises) is greatly influenced by the government.

Korea Telecom is also subject to many government regulations concerning the employment of selected groups. In principal, new recruitment should be done on an open competitive basis. For example, more than 90 percent of new hires at Korea Telecom in 1992 were selected through an open procedure. Government regulations require that at least 60 percent of new workers with Grade IV must be selected from universities which are not located in Seoul, the capital city of Korea. Korea Telecom also must employ handicapped people (274 workers as of 1993) to the level recommended by the relevant law. The company also must provide jobs for the offspring of the people who are publicly recognized for their contribution to Korea's development (3,048 workers as of 1993). In addition, Korea Telecom must provide jobs for other people recommended by public officials. For example, in 1989, it had to employ some of the people who worked for the 1988 Seoul Olympic Organizing Committee.

The selection of workers as well as the assignment of jobs are centrally managed inside Korea Telecom. Only a small portion of workers (who are low-ranked) can be selected by local offices with the advance approval of corporate headquarters. For example, in 1989, less than 5 percent of 1,433 new workers entered the company through a local office exam. Starting in 1990, each business group or center was given the power to transfer workers within a business group or center without the approval of the president of the company. Each year, the corporate headquarters of Korea Telecom reviews existing staff levels in all bureaus and local offices and reallocates redundant workers to areas facing labor shortages. In 1993, about one thousand workers were transferred to other posts through this process. Since 1993, only research departments have full autonomy from corporate headquarters to select new employees.

Employment security has not been a major issue at Korea Telecom given the steady growth that has occurred in employment at the company. This was true even when Korea Telecom was transformed from a government ministry to a public enterprise as employment reductions were not a part of this transformation. In the first five years after becoming a public enterprise the number of employees at Korea Telecom rose by about 30 percent. From 1984 to 1992, a total of about 8,000 workers were outmoded by new technology. However, most of these employees were not displaced from the company. Some of the redundant workers, including a number of former telephone operators, were retrained while others voluntarily left the company under an early retirement plan introduced in 1986.

The strong employment security found at Korea Telecom is typical of practices that have prevailed in most Korean firms over the last twenty years due to the strong economic growth that has occurred. The law and government policy have reinforced employment security. The Korean courts have permitted layoffs for business restructuring only if: (1) there are concrete needs; (2) there is little possibility of overcoming business difficulties except with the proposed measures; and (3) there are fair criteria for selecting the workers to be laid off (Yoon, Lee, and Kim 1990). The Ministry of Labor has imposed an additional impediment to layoffs by allowing layoffs for business restructuring only if without this measure the company would go bankrupt, or concerned workers cannot be transferred to other sections within the company because of unavoidable circumstances, or if the operation of that particular business is stopped.

With the expansion of union activities that has occurred since 1987, unions have become more involved in the preservation of employment security through the negotiation of protective clauses in collective agreements. The collective agreement at Korea Telecom reinforces employment stability by providing that: first, a worker cannot be assigned to another job within one year after a job is assigned to him or her except in special circumstances; and second, only in the case of a criminal offence or a decision of the discipline committee can a worker be discharged for disciplinary reasons.

There are also workers who have a secondary status at Korea Telecom. In 1993, the company employed 3,837 non-regular workers, which was about 10 percent of the workers in local offices. These non-regular workers do some simple manual jobs at the local offices. Under Korea Telecom's financial statement, they are not considered a part of Korea Telecom's workforce. Their work is considered subcontracted labor.

Firm Governance

The industrial relations policy of the central government has been the most important influence shaping Korea Telecom's industrial relations and human resource policies since the late 1980s. To some extent, Korea Telecom's interests have been disregarded by the government for the sake of lowering wage increases in the overall economy.

Until recently, the union at Korea Telecom did not independently represent workers' interests. Instead, the union was passive and highly cooperative, for example, in the way the union followed the government's wage policy. However, with the recent election of a new leadership, the union has become more active and more aggressive in defending members' interests. In 1994, the wage increase of Korea Telecom was far above the government's wage guideline. The minimum number of years required for automatic promotion was shortened, too. Promotion policies also were liberalized, for example, to allow workers in the manual job classification with five years of tenure to qualify for promotion to the technical job classification. The new union leadership also demanded to be consulted properly during the design and implementation of a new human resource management system.

In 1995, the union opposed the government's wage guidelines and telecommunications policies. As mentioned earlier, quite a few union officials were then arrested, and management and the union at Korea Telecom are still negotiating the terms of the 1995 wage agreement as of the writing of this chapter.

In most cases, the union as well as the human resource managerial staff have been virtually left out of the determination process of major strategic managerial decisions at Korea Telecom. For example, in making long-term managerial strategies, the role of the corporate human resource department is solely to forecast the number of workers needed.

The low regard in which corporate management at Korea Telecom held human resource issues developed from the strong demand the company faced for its services and the monopoly advantage the company held for many years in the marketplace. Yet, even though the competitive environment has changed, the top management of Korea Telecom is still more interested in the installation of facilities and the development of new technologies and services than in the more efficient use of Korea Telecom's human resource.[14]

With a new more militant union at Korea Telecom, however, in the future the management of the company and the government are likely to have to reassess their policies. The fact that the president of Korea Telecom was replaced after the union's recent sit-in is testament to the fact that industrial relations will play a critical role in the future of Korea Telecom.

Prospects for New Industrial Relations and Human Resource Management Policies

Since its transformation from a government agency to a public enterprise, Korea Telecom's economic performance has been very strong. Total sales, profits, and labor productivity all increased significantly after 1983.

---

14. In Korea Tobacco and Ginseng, which was also transformed from a government ministry to a public enterprise in 1987, more than 1,000 workers took the benefit of the early retirement plan in 1987 and 1988.

However, Korea Telecom's human resources are not being used in an efficient way, in part because the management of the company has not been granted the authority to make critical human resource decisions. Limits on wage increases have been set prior to the wage negotiations between the union and management of the company. For decisions concerning organizational restructuring and workforce size, Korea Telecom needs the approval of government officials.

Other problems at Korea Telecom include the fact that work procedures at the company are still very bureaucratic and centrally managed. Furthermore, neither the employees nor the union participate in decision making or problem solving at the workplace. Things are not any better at higher levels as the union is not allowed to participate in strategic decision making at Korea Telecom.

Human resource management problems at Korea Telecom include the fact that tenure matters most in promotions. The compensation scheme does not adequately reflect either the performance of individual workers or the company although employees do benefit from extensive employment security. Management has not recognized the importance of human resource management issues when formulating Korea Telecom's business strategies. In short, Korea Telecom is to a large extent still managed like a government agency.

These policies are to a large extent a product of the monopoly position held by Korea Telecom which helped produce a strong demand for the services provided by the company. The situations will be different in the coming years. Korea's telecommunications market will be open to foreign competitors as well as to domestic ones. Korea Telecom will no longer be able to enjoy a monopoly in the long distance service market, its most profitable business sector. A further complication arises from the fact that the union at Korea Telecom recently was taken over by younger and more militant leaders. Many of Korea Telecom's employees as well as the company's management recognize the need for reforming Korea Telecom's human resource management system, and there are plans underway for major changes in that system in 1996.

The biggest challenge in the reform of Korea Telecom's human resource practices will be development of a healthy relationship between the company and the government. If the government continues to intervene extensively in Korea Telecom's human resource management practices as it does now, corporate efforts to boost the efficiency are unlikely to be successful.

It appears that government policies toward industrial relations and human resource issues within public enterprises including Korea Telecom will not change much in the near term. The government has delayed considering reforms in Korea's basic labor laws. This delay makes it more likely that the government will continue to try to use the public sector as a means to influence industrial relations policy in the private sector.

However, there is a possibility that the recent changes that occurred in the leadership of the union at Korea Telecom might make a difference. If the new union leadership is able to propose a reasonable reform policy which reflects not only its members' interests but also the public interest, this reform policy might be supported by the management of Korea Telecom, which would put pressure on the government to go along with such reforms. This is the scenario that took place at Pohang Iron and Steel, a large public enterprise which successfully implemented a new human resource management system similar to the one which is now being considered by the management of Korea Telecom.[15]

It is unclear how the current confrontation between Korea Telecom's union and the Korean government in the 1995 wage negotiations will affect the union's efforts to reform Korea Telecom's human resource practices. In the face of the enormous impact the recent strike at Korea Telecom exerted on the Korean economy, it is impossible for the government to ignore the existence of a strong and militant union at Korea Telecom, a factor reflected in the government's most recent willingness to resume negotiations with the union.

Korea Telecom will be forced by heightened competition to become more efficient. To accomplish this objective it will be necessary to improve the industrial relations and human resource management practices at the firm. While the management of the company appears to recognize the need for the reform of its human resource systems the success of future reforms will depend heavily on Korea Telecom's relationship with the government.

15. It should be noted that the employment stability of Korean workers has been made possible partly due to the good performance of the Korean economy. The unemployment rate dropped under 5% in the early 1970s, and from then on, employment opportunities have been good for most Korean workers.

References

ABA. 1991. "Telecommunications Equipment." *Australian Business Profiles*, Australian Business Analysis 5-035, September, pp. 1–4.

Albert, M. 1991. *Capitalisme contre capitalisme*. Paris: Seuil.

Allen, Robert. 1993. Chairman of the Board and Chief Executive Officer, AT&T. Statement 24 March, 1993. Hearings before the House Subcommittee on Telecommunications and Finance. U.S. Congress. Edward Markey, Chairman. *National Information Infrastructure*. Serial No. 103-12, pp. 170–90.

Allen Consulting Group. 1991. *Developing Telecommunications Industry Strategies in Australia: Market Opportunity, Industry Capability, and Government Role*. Report to the Department of Industry, Technology, and Commerce, Melbourne.

AOTC. 1992. *Annual Report*. Australian & Overseas Telecommunications Corporation, Melbourne.

Arbeidsmiljø. 1994. *Nye muligheter for dem som må bort*. Oslo: Arbeidsmiljøsenteret, p. 8.

Armaroli, V. 1994. "Un anno di lavoro con l'Osservatorio Europeo." *Notiziario del lavoro SIP*, 65.

ATC. 1991. *Annual Report*. Australian Telecommunications Corporation, Melbourne.

ATEA. 1988. *The Communications Challenge: The Role of Telecom in Australia's Future*, 2d ed. Australian Telecommunications Employees' Association, Melbourne.

ATEA. nd. *The Great American Telephone Disaster: A Lesson for Australia*. Australian Telecommunications Employees' Association, Melbourne.

AT&T. 1982. *Bell System Statistical Manual, 1950–1980*. AT&T Comptrollers' Office. New York: AT&T, June.

Babe, Robert E. 1990. *Telecommunications in Canada.* Toronto: University of Toronto Press.

Bamber, G. J. 1986. *Militant Managers?* Aldershot: Gower.

Bamber, G. J., and R. D. Lansbury. 1987. *International and Comparative Industrial Relations: A Study of Developed Market Economies,* 1st ed. Sydney: Allen & Unwin.

———. 1993. *International and Comparative Industrial Relations: A Study of Industrialised Market Economies,* 2d ed. Sydney: Allen & Unwin.

Bamber, G. J., and R. B. Sappey. 1996. "Industrial relations reform and organisational change: Towards strategic human resource management in Australia?" In B. Towers, ed., *The Handbook of Human Resources Management,* 2d ed. Oxford: Blackwell.

Barnard, Chester. 1938. *The Functions of the Executive.* Cambridge: Harvard University Press.

Barrett, Martin, and Edmund Heery. 1995. " 'It's good to talk'? The reform of joint consultation in British Telecom." *Industrial Relations Journal* 26 (March): 57–64.

Batstone, Eric, Anthony Ferner, and Michael Terry. 1984. *Consent and Efficiency: Labour Relations and Management Strategy in the State Enterprise.* Oxford: Blackwell.

Batt, Rosemary. 1993. "Work Reorganization and Labor Relations in Telecommunications Services: A Case Study of BellSouth Corporation." MIT IPC Working Paper 93-04WP. August.

———. 1995. "Performance and Welfare Effects of Work Restructuring: Evidence from Telecommunications Services." Ph.D. dissertation, Sloan School of Management, MIT.

———. 1996. "From Bureaucracy to Enterprise? The Changing Jobs and Careers of Managers in Telecommunications Services." In Paul Osterman, ed., *Broken Ladders: Managerial Careers in the New Economy.* Oxford: University Press.

BC Telecom Inc. 1994. *1993 Annual Report.*

Bell Canada. 1993. *Shaping the Future, Balancing the System.* Report of the CEP/Bell Canada Task Force on Workplace Reorganization. (23 August). 58 p.

———. 1994. *1993 Annual Report.*

Bernard, Elaine. 1982. *The Long Distance Feeling: A History of the Telecommunications Workers' Union.* Vancouver, B.C.: New Star Books.

Berry, Jon. 1993. "Recent Developments in National Level Collective Bargaining and Employment Relations at British Telecom." Unpublished MAIR dissertation. University of Warwick, Coventry.

Boldizzoni, D. 1989. "Trasformazioni organizzative e relazioni industriali in SIP." In R. Nacamulli, ed., *Relazioni sindacali ed iniziativa manageriale.* Milan: Angeli. Pp. 284–335.

Bolter, Walter. 1990. *Telecommunications Policy for the 1990s and Beyond.* New York: M. E. Sharpe.

Bolton, Brian, et al. 1993. *Telecommunications Services: Negotiating Structural and Technological Change.* Geneva: International Labour Office.

Boroff, Karen, and Jeffrey H. Keefe. 1992. *AT&T Employment Security Survey.* New Brunswick, N.J.: Institute of Management and Labor Relations, Rutgers University.

Bourette, Susan. 1995. "Bell to Eliminate up to 20% of Staff." *The Globe and Mail.* Report on Business, Section B. (Wednesday, 15 March), pp. B1, B4.

British Telecom. 1992. *Agreement between Personnel Communications Division and the National Communications Union on ETG Field Skilling.* March.

Buchanan, D. A. 1994. "Principles and practices in work design." In K. Cession, ed., *Personnel Management.* Oxford: Blackwell. Pp. 85–116.

Büchner, Lütz-Michael. 1993. "The German Case." *Bulletin of Comparative Labour Relations,* special issue on telecommunications, 25, pp. 269–331.

Bureau of Industry Economics. 1992. *International Performance Indicators: Telecommunications.* Research Report 48. Canberra: Australian Government Publishing Service.

——. 1995. *Telecommunications 1995. International Performance Indicators* (Research Report 65). Canberra: Australian Government Publishing Service.

Butera, F. 1985. "Tecnologia e organizzazione: impatti e opzioni." *Industria e Sindacato* 43.

Castro, M. 1993. "The Spanish Case." *Bulletin of Comparative Labor Relations,* special issue on telecommunications, 25. Pp. 345–86.

Censis. 1994. Gli effetti del cambiamento organizzativo sul piano delle esigenze formative e del ruolo della formazione. Rome: Censis.

Chaykowski, Richard P. 1995. "Innovation and Cooperation in Canadian Industrial Relations: Preparing for NAFTA. Paper Prepared for the Canada–United States–Mexico Conference on Labor Law and Industrial Relations. Washington, D.C. (19–20 September 1994).

Chaykowski, Richard P., and Anil Verma. 1992. "Canadian Industrial Relations in Transition." In R. Chaykowski and A. Verma, eds., *Industrial Relations in Canadian Industry.* Toronto: Holt, Rinehart, and Winston.

Cheap, C. W. 1991. "Trade in telecommunications services in the ASEAN region." CIRCUIT, Working Chapter no. 6, Centre for International Research on Communication and Information Technologies, Melbourne.

Cilas, A. C. 1994. "Estudio Económico, Financiero, Productivo y Salarial de la Empresa Teléfonos de México." Unpublished paper. Mexico, 25 February.

CIRCUIT. 1989. "Women and the telephone." *Newsletter* (September). Centre for International Research on Communication and Information Technologies, Melbourne.

CITCA. 1980. *Technological Change in Australia,* vol. 2, chap. 11, Committee of Inquiry into Technological Change in Australia, Canberra.

Clark, Jon, Ian McLoughlin, Howard Rose, and Robin King. 1988. *The Process of Technological Change. New Technology and Social Choice in the Workplace.* Cambridge: Cambridge University Press.

Colling, Trevor, and Anthony Ferner. 1992. "The Limits of Autonomy: Devolution, Line Managers and Industrial Relations in Privatized Companies." *Journal of Management Studies* 29 (2):209–27.

Cruz, César. 1990. "Condiciones de trabajo en la industria telefónica." In Alejandro Alvarez, coord., *La Clase Obrera y el Sindicalismo Mexicano,* Economy Department, UNAM.

Danielian, N. R. 1939. *A.T.&T.: The Story of Industrial Conquest.* New York: Vanguard Press.

Darbishire, Owen. 1993. "Structure, Strategy and Bargaining: The Case of the Tele-communications Industry in Britain and America." M.Sc. thesis, Cornell University.

———. 1995: "Switching Systems: Technological Change, Competition, and Privatisation." *Industrielle Beziehungen* 2 (2): 156–79.

Darbishire, Owen, and Harry C. Katz. In process. "Converging Divergences: The Growing Variation in Employment Relations." Unpublished manuscript, NYS-SILR, Cornell University.

Davis, E. M., and R. D. Lansbury. 1989a. "Consultative Councils: The Cases of Telecom Australia and Qantas Airways Ltd." *Employee Participation Research Report No. 9*. Department of Industrial Relations, Industrial Relations Development Division, AGPS, Canberra.

———. 1989b. "Worker Participation in Decisions on Technological Change in Australia." In G.J. Bamber and R.D. Lansbury, eds., *New Technology: International Perspectives on Human Resources and Industrial Relations*. Sydney: Allen & Unwin.

De la Garza, Enrique. 1989. "Quién gano en Telmex?" *El Cotidiano*, No. 32, UAM-A, Mexico.

———. 1990. "Telefonistas y Electricistas." *El Cotidiano*, No. 41, UAM-A, Mexico.

———. 1993. *Productive Restructuring and Union Response in Mexico*. Instituto de Investigaciones Economicas, UNAM.

Department of Communications and Transportation. 1992. *Report Document*. Mexico City.

Doeringer, Peter, and Michael Piore. 1971. *Internal Labor Markets and Manpower Analysis*. Lexington, Mass.: D.C. Heath.

DTI (Department of Trade and Industry). 1994. *Study of the International Competitiveness of the UK Telecommunications Infrastructure*. Robert Harrison, PA Consulting Group, for DTI.

Dubb, Steve. 1992. "Trozos de cristal: privatización y política sindical en Telmex." Unpublished manuscript, UCLA, La Jolla.

Dunlop, John T. 1990. *The Management of Labor Unions: Decision Making with Historical Constraints*. Boston: Lexington Books.

Eaton, Adrienne, Michael Gordon, and Jeffrey Keefe. 1992. "The Impact of Quality of Work Life Programs and Grievance System Effectiveness on Union Commitment." *Industrial and Labor Relations Review* 45, no. 3 (April): 591–604.

Engelstad, Fredrik. 1990. *Oppsigelser ved driftsinuskrenkinger*. En analyse av fordeling og rettferdighet. Oslo: Tidskrift for samfunnsforskning.

———. 1994. "The emergence of the seniority criterion by work force reductions in Norway." Working Paper. University of Oslo. Institute for Social Research, Department of Sociology.

Eurostrategies. 1990. *Employment Structures and Trends in Telecommunications*. Brussels: DGXIII.

Fabela, Enrique, and G. Sánchez. 1986. "La digitalización del Telmex y sus efectos sobre los telefonistas." CIC-UAP, Cuadernos de Trabajo, Mexico.

Falck, Sturla. 1978. *Endring og Iojalitet*.

FDR. 1994: *Germany's Telecommunications Infrastructure in International Comparison*.

Federal Communications Commission. *Statistics of Communications Common Carri-*

ers. 1993/1994 edition. Washington, D.C.: Superintendent of Documents, Government Printing Office.

Ferner, Anthony, and Trevor Colling. 1991. "Privatization, Regulation and Industrial Relations." *British Journal of Industrial Relations* 29 (3): 391–409.

——. 1993. "Privatization of the British Utilities: Regulation, Decentralization, and Industrial Relations." In Thomas Clarke and Christos Pitelis, eds., *The Political Economy of Privatization.* London: Routledge, 125–41.

Fondazione Seveso/SIP. 1991. *Relazioni di lavoro e telecomunicazioni in Europa.* Milan: Angeli.

Gabrielli, G. 1993. "La comunicazione interna per lo sviluppo organizzativo e la qualita del servizio: il caso SIP." In Santoro, G.M., ed. *La farfalla e l'uragano,* Rome.

Gabrielli, G., and L. Canu. 1993. "The Italian Case." *Bulletin of Comparative Labor Relations,* special issue on telecommunications, 25, pp. 47–95.

Geary, J. F. 1994. "Task participation: Employees' participation enabled or constrained?" In K. Cession, ed., *Personnel Management.* Oxford: Blackwell, pp. 634–61.

Gemini Consulting. 1992. *Telekommunikasjoner I endring.* Nye arbeidsbetingelser for Televerket. Rapport utarbeidet på oppdrag for Televerket, Oslo.

Gerpott, Torsten J., and Rudolf Pospischil. 1993. "Internationale Effizienzvergleiche der DBP Telekom: Ergebnisse eines Benchmarking-Projektes zur Unterstützung von organisatorischem Wandel in einem staatlichen Telekommunnikationsunternehmen." *Zeitschift für betriebswirtschaftliche Forschung* no. 4, pp. 366–89.

Gilman, Mark. 1993. "Performance Related Pay in Practice: A Case Study of BT." MAIR dissertation, University of Warwick, Coventry.

Globe and Mail. 1994. *The Globe and Mail Report on Business Magazine,* vol. 11, no. 1 (July).

Goulden, Joseph. 1968. *Monopoly.* New York: G.P. Putnam's Sons.

Gouldner, A. W. 1954. *Patterns of Industrial Bureaucracy.* London: Collier-Macmillan.

Government Invested Enterprises Performance Evaluation Committee, ROK. 1984–94. *Report on Government Invested Enterprises Performance Evaluation.* Seoul.

Granovetter, Mark. 1985. "Economic Action and Social Structure: The Problem of Embeddedness." *American Journal of Sociology* (November): 481–510.

Gustavsen, Bjørn, and Gerry Hunnius. 1981. *New Patterns of Work Reform: The Case of Norway.* Oslo: Universitetsforlaget.

Herbst, Philip G. 1977. *Alternativ til hierarkisk organisasjon.* Oslo: Tanum.

Hernández, Francisco. 1990. "Profundización sindical." STRM, Mexico.

Hernes, Gudmund. 1978. *Forhandlingsøkonomi og blanadingsadministrasjon.* Oslo: Universitetsforlaget.

Honda, J. 1977. "Hageshii Gijutsu Kakusin to Gorika to Chingin" (The Rapid Technological Innovation and the Rationalization and the Wage in NTTPC). In *Koza Gendai no Chingin 3 Kan: Sangyo betsu Chingin no Jittai (2)* (Wages by Industries Part 2: Series on Wages in the Present Age, 3). Edited by S. Ujihara, S. Kurano, N. Funahashi, H. Matsuo, and T. Yoshimura. Tokyo: Shakai Shisosha. pp. 61–105.

Houghton, J. W. 1991. "Outsourcing information technology services." CIRCUIT, Policy Research Chapter no. 17. Centre for International Research on Communication and Information Technologies, Melbourne.

Houghton, J. W., and S. Paltridge. 1991. "Telecommunication equipment manufacturing in Australia: Opportunities and policy options," CIRCUIT, Policy Research Chapter no. 15. Centre for International Research on Communication and Information Technologies, Melbourne.

Howard, Ann, and Douglas Bray. 1988. *Managerial Lives in Transition: Advancing Age and Changing Times.* New York: Guilford Press.

Hughes, J. 1967. *Trade Union Structure and Government Part One: Structure and Development.* Royal Commission on Trade Unions and Employers' Associations Research, Chap. 5, London: HMSO.

IDS (Income Data Services). 1988. "Agreement and Implementation of Flexibility at British Telecom." *IDS Report* 531 (October): 27–28.

IRS (Industrial Relations Services). 1993. "Natural Selection: BT's programme of voluntary redundancy." *IRS Employment Trends* 533 (April): 11–15.

——. 1994. "Individualised pay and flexible benefits at Mercury." *IRS Pay and Benefit Bulletin* 365 (December): 4–9.

——. 1995. "Customer service drive brings new working time patterns to BT." *IRS Employment Trends* 579 (March): 10–16.

ISTUD. 1993. "Trasformazioni organizzative e relazioni industriali in SIP." Case study elaborated by D. Boldizzoni and M. Balconi, Stresa.

Ito, N., and T. Imagawa. 1993. "Wagaguni ni okeru Denki Tsuushin Sangyo no Seisansei Bunseki" (Analysis of the Growth of Total Factor Productivity in the Japanese Telecommunications Industry: Measurement and Factor Decomposition). *Institute for Posts and Telecommunications Policy Review,* no. 4, 1–20.

Iusacell: Cellular. 1992. Mexico City, May, p. 17.

Joho Tsuushin Sogo Kenkyusho. 1994. *Joho Tsuushin Hando Bukku 1993* (Handbook of Information and Communication 1993). Tokyo: Joho Tsuushin Sogo Kenkyusho.

JTWU. 1962. *Choki Undo Hoshin* (A Long-term Union Policy of JTWU). Tokyo: JTWU.

——. 1978. *Zendentsu Rodo Undoshi: Showa 40 nendai no Shuyo na Ayumi* (The History of JTWU: 1965–75). Tokyo: JTWU.

——. 1979. *Zendentsu Rodo Undoshi* (The History of JTWU), vol. 3. Tokyo: JTWU.

——. 1981. *Zendentsu Rodo Undoshi* (The History of JTWU), vol. 5. Tokyo: JTWU.

——. 1982. *Zendentsu Rodo Undoshi* (The History of JTWU), vol. 6. Tokyo: JTWU.

——. 1986a. *Dai 40 Kai Teiki Taikai Kettei Shu* (Proceedings of the 40th Congress). Tokyo: JTWU.

——. 1986b. *Dai 96 Kai Chuo Iinkai Kettei Shu* (Proceedings of the 96th Meeting). Tokyo: JTWU.

——. 1987. *Dai 41 Kai Teiki Taikai Kettei Shu* (Proceedings of the 41st Congress). Tokyo: JTWU.

——. 1988. *Zendentsu Rodo Undoshi: Kosha Seido Kaikaku Toso* (The History of JTWU: Struggle for Reform of NTTPC). Tokyo: JTWU.

——. 1990. *Zendentsu Rodo Undoshi* (The History of JTWU), vol. 8. Tokyo: JTWU.

——. 1991. "Collective Minutes of Collective Agreements and Collective Bargaining." No. 246, July.

——. 1992a. *Zendentsu Rodo Undoshi* (The History of JTWU), vol. 9. Tokyo: JTWU.

——. 1992b. *Zendentsu Rodo Undoshi* (The History of JTWU), vol. 10. Tokyo: JTWU.

——. 1993a. *Joho Annai Sa-bisu Bumon no Kongo no Jigyo Unei ni tsuite: Totatsu*

Naiyo to Kaisetsu (Promoting Business of the Information Service Division in the Future: Goals Achieved and Explanation). Tokyo: JTWU.

——. 1993b. *Aratana Keiei Kaizen Shisaku ni tsuite no Totatsu Naiyo to Kaisetsu* (Goals Achieved and Explanation of New Policies for Management). Tokyo: JTWU.

——. 1993c. "Business of Information Service Division in the Future." In "Collective Minutes of Collective Agreements and Collective Bargaining," no. 257, January.

Kalleberg, Ragnvald. 1993. "Implementing Work-Environment Reform in Norway. The Interplay between Leadership and Law." In *International Handbook of Political Participation in Organisations*. Oxford: Oxford University Press.

Kang, Shin Il. 1988. *Korea's Privatization Plans and Past Experiences*. Seoul: Korea Development Institute.

Kanter, Rosabeth Moss. 1990. *The Change Masters*. London: Cox and Wyman Ltd.

Katz, Harry C. 1985. *Shifting Gears: Changing Labor Relations in the U.S. Automobile Industry*. Cambridge, Mass.: MIT Press.

——. 1993. "The Decentralization of Collective Bargaining: A Literature Review and Comparative Analysis." *Industrial and Labor Relations Review* 47 (October): 3–22.

——. Forthcoming. "Downsizing and Employment Security." In Peter Cappelli, ed., *Change at Work*. London: Oxford University Press.

Katzenstein, Peter J. 1987. *Policy and Politics in West Germany: The Growth of a Semisovereign State*. Philadelphia: Temple University Press. Ithaca: Cornell University Press.

——. 1989. *Industry and Politics in West Germany: Toward the Third Republic*. Ithaca: Cornell University Press.

Keefe, Jeffrey. 1989. "Measuring Wage Dispersion: An Application of Entropy Measures to Analyze the Former Bell System's Pay Structure." *Proceedings of the Forty-First Annual Meeting of the Industrial Relations Research Association*, pp. 539–48. Madison, Wisc.: IRRA.

——. 1995. "Telecommunications: Where Are the Jobs on the Information Highway?" Unpublished manuscript, Rutgers University.

Keefe, Jeffrey, and Karen Boroff. 1994. "Telecommunications Labor-Management Relations: One Decade After the AT&T Divestiture." In Paula Voos, ed., *Contemporary Collective Bargaining in the Private Sector*. 1994. IRRA Research Volume, Cornell University. Ithaca: ILR Press.

Kerr, Clark, et al. 1964. *Industrialism and Industrial Man*. New York: Oxford University Press.

Kim, Hoon, and Joon-shil Park. 1994. *The Practice of HRM/IR in the Korean Steel Industry: A Case Study of POSCO*. Seoul: Korea Labor Institute.

Kiss, Ferenc, and Bernard Lefebvre. 1987. "Econometric Models of Telecommunications Firms." *Revue Economique* 2 (March): 307–74.

Koch, Marianne, David Lewin, and Donna Sockell. 1988. "The Effects of Deregulation on Bargaining Structure: The Case of AT&T." *Advances in Industrial Relations* 4.

Kochan, Thomas A., Harry C. Katz, and Robert B. McKersie. 1994. *The Transformation of American Industrial Relations*, 2d ed. Ithaca: ILR Press.

Kochan, Thomas A., R. Locke, and M. Piore. 1995. "Introduction." In Richard M. Locke et al., eds., *Employment Relations in a Changing World Economy*. Cambridge, Mass.: MIT Press.

Kohl, George. 1993. "Information Technology and Labor: A Case Study of Telephone Operators." *Workplace Topics* 3(1):101–111.

Kojo, M. 1994. "Akusesu Chaaji no Yakuwari to Kyoso heno Eikyo" (The Role of Access Charge and Its Impact on Competition). In *Gendai Terekomu Sangyo no Keizai Bunseki* (An Economic Analysis on Telecommunications Industry), edited by S. Nagai, pp. 166–82. Tokyo: Hosei University Press.

Kojo, M., and T. Nanbu. 1993. "Denki Tsuushin Kisei no Rekishi to Nichibei Kisei Hikaku" (The Comparative History of the Regulation in Telecommunication Industry in Japan and the U.S.). In *Nihon no Denki Tsuushin: Kyoso to Kisei no Keizaigaku* (Telecommunications Industry in Japan: Economics on Competition and Regulation), edited by M. Okuno, K. Suzuki, and T. Nanbu, pp. 27–73. Tokyo: Nihon Keizai Shinbunsha.

Komori, M. 1988. *Imadakara Katarou Denden Minei-ka no Butai-ura* (Now I Can Talk about the Background to Privatization of NTTPC). Tokyo: Godo Tsuushinsha and Orenji Shuppan.

Korbøl, Aud. 1977. *Telefonautomatisering I etterkrigstida.* Sosiologiske undersøkelser i Televerket, rapport nr. 1. Oslo: Institutt for samfunnsforskning.

Korea Labor Institute. 1993. *Quarterly Labor Review* 4,4. Seoul: Korea Labor Institute.

Korea Telecom. 1984–94a. *Report on Management Performance.* Seoul: Korea Telecom.

——. 1984–94b. *Annual Report.* Seoul: Korea Telecom.

——. 1994. "A Proposal for Korea Telecom's New Personnel Management System" (mimeo).

Korea Telecom Trade Union. 1994. "Wage Offensive News." 13 October.

Korea Tobacco and Ginseng Corp. 1988–91. *Report on Management Performance.* Daejeon, Korea: Korea Tobacco and Ginseng Corp.

Kuyek, Joan. 1979. *The Phone Book: Working at the Bell.* Kitchener: Between the Lines.

Labour Law, 5th ed. 1991. Kingston, Ont.: Industrial Relations Centre, Queen's University.

Lansbury, R. D., and E. M. Davis. 1984. *Technology, Work, and Industrial Relations.* Melbourne: Longman Cheshire.

Lara, Miguel Angel. 1992. "Labor and Automation Process: The Case of Telmex." Bachelor's thesis in Economics, UNAM, Mexico.

Lee, Geoff. 1990. "Full Circle or Revolution?" *Training & Development* 8 & 9 (September): 18–22.

Lee, M. 1994. "Telecommunications Policy Review Set to Begin." *Ministerial News Release,* 31 May.

Leonardi, S. 1993. "Relazioni sindacali e lineamenti di partecipazione alla SIP." Materiali IRES.

Locke, Richard M. 1992. "The Decline of the National Union in Italy: Lessons for Comparative Industrial Relations Theory." *Industrial and Labor Relations Review* 45 (January): 229–49.

Locke, Richard M., Thomas A. Kochan, and Michael J. Piore. 1995. *Employment Relations in a Changing World Economy.* Cambridge, Mass.: MIT Press.

Lynch, Lisa, and Paul Osterman. 1989. "Technological Innovation and Employment in Telecommunications." *Industrial Relations* 28 (Spring): 188–205.

Lyon-Caen, A. 1993. "The French Case." *Bulletin of Comparative Labor Relations*, special issue on telecommunications, 25.

Maina, Benson. 1993. "Skill Formation and Development in a Rapidly Changing Environment: The Case of Technician Training in British Telecom." M.A. dissertation. University of Warwick, Coventry.

Management and Coordination Agency. 1990. "NTT no Genjo to Kadai" (The Present Condition and the Issues of NTT). Administrative Inspections Bureau. June. Tokyo: Ministry of Finance.

Mathews, J. 1987. "Technological change and union strategy." In *Union Strategy & Industrial Change*, ed. S. Frenkel, pp. 134–54. Sydney: New South Wales University Press.

Matsuura, K. 1994. "Denki Tsuushin no Sangyo Soshiki" (The Industrial Organization in the Telecommunications Industry). In *Koteki Kisei to Sangyo 3: Denki Tsuushin* (Series in Public Regulation and Industries vol. 3: Telecommunications Industry), ed. T. Hayashi, pp. 15–53. Tokyo: NTT Shuppan.

Melody, W. H. "Telecommunication: Policy directions for Australia in the global information economy." CIRCUIT Policy Research Chapter no. 7, Centre for International Research on Communication and Information Technologies, Melbourne.

Merton, Robert K. 1976. "The Ambivalence of Organisational Leaders." In R. K. Merton, *Sociological Ambivalence and Other Essays*. New York: The Free Press.

Milkman, Ruth, and Cydney Pullman. 1991. "Technological Change in an Auto Assembly Plant." *Work and Occupations*, 2 (May):123–47.

Ministry of Posts and Telecommunications. 1991. "Telecommunications Statistics." Communications Policy Bureau, Tokyo, Japan.

———. 1993. "Telecommunications Statistics." Communications Policy Bureau, Tokyo, Japan.

———. 1994. "Telecommunications Statistics." Communications Policy Bureau, Tokyo, Japan.

———. 1995a. "Telecommunications Statistics." Communications Policy Bureau, Tokyo, Japan.

———. 1995b. "White Paper on Communications." Tokyo, Japan.

Mintzberg, Henry. 1989. "The Manager's Job." In H. Mintzberg, *Mintzberg on Management Inside Our Strange World of Organisations*. London: Macmillan Publishers.

———. 1990. "Management Mania." In *Scanorama*, an interview with Mintzberg by John Burton, September 1990.

Mitchell, J. 1991. "Quality of service—the missing link in telephone regulation?" CIRCUIT Policy Research Chapter no. 11, Centre for International Research on Communication and Information Technologies, Melbourne.

Morgan, Kevin, and Douglas Webber. 1986: "Divergent Paths: Political Strategies for Telecommunications in Britain, France, and West Germany." *West European Politics* 9 (October):72.

Muller, B. 1980. "Bureaucracy, Job Control, and Militancy: The Case of Telecom." In S. Frenkel, ed., *Industrial Action*, pp. 103–31. Sydney: Allen & Unwin.

Nagai, S. 1994. "Denki Tsuushin Sangyo ni okeru Kyoso to Ryokin Kisei" (Competition and Price Regulation in Telecommunications Industry). In *Gendai Terekomu Sangyo no Keizai Bunseki* (An Economic Analysis on Telecommunications Industry), edited by S. Nagai, pp. 83–109. Tokyo: Hosei University Press.

NCU. 1992. *Telecoms Privatization: The British Experiment.* Geneva: PTTI.

———. 1993a. *Survey of BT Customer Service Centre Employees 1993.* London: NCU.

———. 1993b. *Review of Telecommunications Operators in the UK.* July. London: NCU.

Negrelli, S. 1985. "Le relazioni industriali in un'azienda post-industriale." *Industria e sindacato* 43.

Negrelli, S., and T. Treu. 1993. "State, Market, Management, and Industrial Relations in European Telecommunications." *Bulletin of Comparative Labor Relations,* special issue on telecommunications, 25, pp. 3–46.

———. 1994. "Industrial Relations, Human Resources Practices, and Economic Performance." Conference on Managing Human Resources, Labor Relations, and Diversity for Global Competitiveness. McMaster University, Hamilton. 22–24 May.

Newell, Helen, and Sue Dopson. 1995. "Middle Management Careers: A Case Study of the Experience of Middle Managers in British Telecom." Warwick Papers in Industrial Relations, No. 51. Coventry: IRRU.

Nicolaides, Athina. 1993. "The New BT: Responses of the Organization to Challenges: A Case Study of the Work Organization and Employee Involvement Initiatives Taken by Management: Empirical Evidence from the Operators." MAIR dissertation, University of Warwick, Coventry.

Noam, Eli. 1992. *Telecommunications in Europe.* New York: Oxford University Press.

Normann, Richard. 1991. *Service Management.* Oslo: Bedriftøkonomenes Forlag A/S.

Norwegian Telecom. 1993. *Annual Report.* Oslo.

Norwood, Stephen. 1990. *Labor's Flaming Youth: Telephone Operators and Worker Militancy, 1878–1923.* Urbana: University of Illinois Press.

NTI Update. 1994. *New Magazine.* Oslo: Telenor International. June, p. 2.

NTT. 1986. *Nihon Denshin Denwa Kosha Shashi* (History of NTTPC). Tokyo: Joho Tsuushin Sogo Kenkyusho.

———. 1992. Personnel and Salary Systems. Unpublished internal report. April.

———. 1993. *NTT Data Book. 1993.*

———. 1994. *NTT Data Book. 1994.*

———. Undated. Outline of Expert College. Unpublished internal report.

NTT-JTWU. 1994. "Collective Agreements on Wages." March.

NTTPC. 1977. *Nihon Denshin Denwa Kosha 25 Nenshi* (Twenty Five Years of NTTPC), Part Two. Tokyo: Denki Tsuushin Kyokai.

———. 1978. *Nihon Denshin Denwa Kosha 25 Nenshi* (Twenty Five Years at NTTPC), Appendix, Tokyo: Denki Tsuushin Kyokai.

Official Journal of the Federation. 1990. 29 October.

———. 1990. 10 December.

Okuno, M., and K. Suzumura. 1993. "Denki Tsuushin Jigyo no Kisei to Seifu no Yakuwari" (The Regulation in Telecommunications Industry and the Role of the Government). In *Nihon no Denki Tsuushin: Kyoso to Kisei no Keizaigaku* (Telecommunications Industry in Japan: Economics on Competition and Regulation), edited by M. Okuno, K. Suzuki, and T. Nanbu, pp. 75–104. Tokyo: Nihon Keizai Shinbunsha.

Oniki, H., T. H. Oum, and S. Stevenson. 1993. "Mineika de NTT no Seisansei ha

Kojo Shitaka" (Has Privatization Increased the Productivity in NTT?). In *Nihon no Denki Tsuushin: Kyoso to Kisei no Kiezaigaku* (Telecommunication Industry in Japan: Economics on Competition and Regulation), edited by M. Okuno, K. Suzuki, and T. Nanbu, pp. 169–96. Tokyo: Nihon Keizai Shinbunsha.

Økonomisk Rapport. 1992. "Naeringslivet." Norges 300 største bedrifter, p. 11. Oslo: A/S Fagpresseforlaget.

Optus Communications. 1992a. *Optus Enterprise Agreement.* Sydney.

——. 1992b. *The Power of Choice in Long Distance and Mobile Communications.* Sydney.

——. 1992–1994. *Billabong* (Optus internal newsletter—various editions). Sydney.

——. 1994a. *Employee Survey Results.* Sydney.

——. 1994b. *Enterprise Flexibility Agreement.* Sydney.

Organization for Economic Co-Operation and Development (OECD). 1992. *Telecommunications and Broadcasting: Convergence or Collusion?* Information Computer Communications Policy 29. Paris: OECD.

Ortiz, Rosario. 1993. "Productividad y concertación? El caso de los trabajadores telefonistas." In *Productividad: diversas experiencias,* ed. Enrique de la Garza. Fundación Ebert, Mexico.

Osterman, Paul. 1988. *Employment Futures: Reorganization, Dislocation, and Public Policy.* New York: Oxford University Press.

Oxley, A. 1991. "International Trade in Telecommunication Services: The Pressure of Free Trade Paradigms." CIRCUIT Policy Research Chapter no. 12, Centre for International Research on Communication and Information Technologies, Melbourne.

Parasuraman, A., V. A. Zeithaml, and L. L. Berry. 1985. "A conceptual model of service quality and its implications for future research." *Journal of Marketing* 49 4: 41–50.

Park, Young-bum. 1988. *Study on Investment Efficiency in Government Invested Enterprises.* Seoul: Korea Institute for Economics and Technology.

Park, Young-bum, and Michael Byungnam Lee. 1995. "Economic Development, Globalization, and Practices in Industrial Relations and Human Resource Management in Korea." In A. Verma, T. Kochan, and R. Lansbury, eds., *Employment Relations in the Growing Asian Economies.* New York: Routledge.

——. 1993a. *Public Sector Adjustment through Privatization: The Republic of Korea.* Geneva: International Labor Office.

——. 1993b. "Public Sector Industrial Relations in Korea." In *Public Sector Industrial Relations In Selected Countries: with Special Reference to Korea's Reform Policies,* edited by Young-bum Park and Carmelo Noriel, pp. 3–34. Seoul: Korea Labor Institute.

——. 1993c. "Industrial Relations and Labor Law Developments in the Republic of Korea." *International Labour Review* 132 (5–6).

——. Forthcoming. *Public Sector Pay in Korea.* Geneva: International Labor Office.

Park, Young-bum, and Sang-duck Lee. 1990. *Public Sector Industrial Relations in Korea,* Seoul: Korea Labor Institute.

Park, Young-bum, and Y. Lee. 1994. "Industrial Relations and Human Resource Practices in the Korean Automotive Industry: Recent Development and Policy Options." Seoul: Korean Labor Institute.

Penn, Roger. 1990. "Skilled Maintenance Work at British Telecom: Findings from the

Social Change and Economic Life Research Initiative." *New Technology, Work and Employment,* 5 (2):135–44.

Philipson, G. 1992. "How Optus Created its IS." *Managing Information Systems* (August): 28–34.

Pickard, Jane. 1990. "When Pay Gets Personal." *Personnel Management* (July): 41–45.

Plunkett, S. 1993. "Optus, Building Rome in a Day. Australia's New Telecommunications Carrier, Fourteen Months On." *Business Review Weekly,* pp. 22–25.

PMSC. 1992. "Information Technology and Telecommunications Looking to the Year 2000." A chapter prepared by an independent working group for consideration by the Prime Minister's Science Council at its sixth meeting, AGPS, Canberra.

Pospischil, Rudolf. 1993: "Reorganisation of European Telecommunications: The Cases of British Telecom, France Télécom, and Deutsche Telekom." *Telecommunications Policy* (November): 603–21.

Reinecke, I. 1985. *Connecting You.* Fitzroy: McPhee Gribble/Penguin.

Reinecke, I., and J. Schultz. 1983. *The Phone Book: The Future of Australia's Communications on the Line.* Ringwood: Penguin.

Roethlisberger, F. J., and William J. Dickson. 1939. *Management and the Worker.* Cambridge: Harvard University Press. Eighth Printing.

Rosenberg, Nathan. 1994. *Exploring the Black Box.* New York: Cambridge University Press.

Salina de Gortari, Carlos. 1992. *Fourth Presidential Report.* Mexico City.

Sánchez, Germán. 1993. "Una reestructuración global: el sector de telecomunicaciones." In María E. Martínez et al., eds., *El Proceso de Reestructuración de México,* UAP.

Sánchez, Germán, and Enrique de la Garza. 1988. "La digitalización en Telmex, una transformación global." *El Cotidiano,* no. 21, UAM-A, Mexico.

Schacht, John. 1985. *The Making of Telephone Unionism, 1920–1947.* New Brunswick, N.J.: Rutgers University Press.

Schmidt, Susanne K. 1991. "Taking the Long Road to Liberalization: Telecommunications Reform in the Federal Republic of Germany." *Telecommunications Policy* (June): 209–22.

——. 1993. "Reforming the Federal Post and Telecommunications Services: The Second Wave." Unpublished paper presented at workshop "German Public Sector Reform in the Light of the British Experience," London School of Economics, 17–18 September.

Schuler, R. S. 1992. "Strategic Human Resources Management: Linking People with the Strategic Needs of the Business." *Organizational Dynamics* 21 (1):18–32.

Shadur, M. A., and G. J. Bamber. 1994. "Towards Lean Management? The Transferability of Japanese Management Strategies to Australia." *International Executive* vol. 36, no. 3: 343–364.

Shinto, H. 1983. *Watashi no Sanpo Ichi-ryo Toku Ron* (My Win-Win Theory). Tokyo: NTT Shuppan.

Simmons, D. E., M. A. Shadur, and G. J. Bamber. 1996. "Optus: New recruitment and selection in an enterprise culture." In *Blackwell Cases in Human Resource and Change Management,* ed. J. Storey. pp. 147–159. Oxford: Blackwell.

SIP. 1992. "Politiche di gestione e sviluppo dei quadri, 1993–95." Rome.

Sivesind, Karl Henrik, et al. 1995. "A Social-democratic Order Under Pressure. Norwegian Employment Relations in the Eighties." In R. Locke, T. Kochan, and M. Piore, eds., *Employment Relations in a Changing World Economy*. Cambridge: MIT Press.

Smith, Jill, and Michael Terry. 1993. "The English Case." *Bulletin of Comparative Labour Relations*, special issue on telecommunications 25, pp. 3–46, 185–267.

Solbraekke, Sidsel K. 1993. *VI og kundene. Serviceproduksjon og marketdsorientering i en offentlig virksomhet*. PSO-rapport: 32. University of Oslo, Department of Sociology.

——. 1995. "TELEVERKET: i gode og onde dager." Rapport fra prosjektet "Samfunnsbedrift og markedsaktør." University of Oslo, Department of Sociology.

Solis, Vicente. 1992. "El cambio estructural y la respuesta sindical en Telmex." Bachelor's thesis in Economics, UNAM.

Souter, David. 1993. *Regulation Telecommunications. The British Experience*. Report for PTTI.

Spalter-Roth, Roberta, and Heidi Hartmann. 1993. *Women in Telecommunications: Exception to the Rule of Low Pay for Women's Work*. Washington, D.C.: Institute for Women's Policy Research.

——. 1995. *Women in Telecommunications: Exception to the Rule*. Washington, D.C.: Institute for Women's Policy Research.

Stanislawski, Stefan. 1993. "What Is the Best Way to Organise the Telecommunication Sector?" in Analysys Ltd. 8/9 Jesus Lane, Cambridge CB5 8BA, UK.

Stentor. 1994. *Statistics (Annual: 1993). Ottawa: Stentor*.

Storey, John. 1992. *Developments in the Management of Human Resources*. Oxford: Blackwell.

Surtees, Lawrence. 1994. *Wire Wars: The Canadian Fight for Competition in Telecommunications*. Scarborough, Ont.: Prentice Hall Canada Inc.

——. 1995a. "CRTC Inquiry to Shape Canada's Broadcast Future." *The Globe and Mail*. Report on Business, Section B. (Monday, 6 March, pp. B1–B2.

——. 1995b. "Bell Slashing 10,000 Jobs." *The Globe and Mail* (Tuesday, 28 March), p. 1.

TD-bladet. 1993. "Organ for Tele-og Dataforbundet." Oslo. Tele-og Dataforbundet, p. 7.

Telecom Italia. 1995. "Telecom Italia perche." Speciale Dialogo, Rome.

Telenor. 1995. "In Step with the Future. An Introduction to Telenor." Oslo: Telenor AS, KI.

Telmex. 1994. *Annual Report*. Mexico.

Telstra. 1994. "Participative Implementation Framework." October. Melbourne.

——. 1995a. *Annual Report*. Melbourne.

——. 1995b. "Corporate Kit: Joint Awareness Sessions on Testra Participative Approach." February. Melbourne.

Teske, Paul. 1990. *After Divestiture*. Albany, N.Y.: SUNY Press.

Thelen, Kathleen A. 1991. *Union of Parts: Labor Politics in Postwar Germany*. Ithaca: Cornell University Press.

Tishima, A. 1982. "Denden Kosha no Chingin Kettei to Roshi Kankei" (Wage Determination and Industrial Relations in NTTPC). In *Denden Kosha no Roshi Kankei to Rodo Kumiai* (Industrial Relations and Trade Union in NTTPC), edited by JTWU and Nihon Rodo Chosa Kyogikai, pp. 73–99. Tokyo: Japan Institute of Labor.

Tong, Yee Mei. 1993. "Changing Working Practices in a Context of Labour Cuts. A

Case Study of Labour Flexibility in BT." MAIR dissertation, University of Warwick, Coventry.

Torres, María Teresa. 1990. "Historia del sindicato telefonista." Bachelor's thesis in Sociology, UAM.

Turner, H. A. 1962. *Trade Union Growth, Structure and Policy: A Comparative Study of the Cotton Unions.* London: Allen & Unwin.

U.S. Congress. 1993. *Pulling Together for Productivity: A Union-Management Initiative at US West, Inc.* Washington, D.C.: Office of Technology Assessment. September.

Vallas, Steven Peter. 1993. *Power in the Workplace: The Politics of Production at AT&T.* Albany: State University of New York Press.

van Haaren, Kurt, and Detlef Hensche, ed. 1995. *Multimedia: Die schöne neue Welt auf dem Prüfstand.* Hamburg: VSA-Verlag.

Vardy, Jill. 1995. "Bell TV Anxious for Home Approval." *Financial Post*, 18 March, p. 7.

Vázquez, Pilar. 1988. "Los telefonistas al filo de la navaja." *El Cotidiano*, no. 25, UAM-A, Mexico.

———. 1990. "El telefonista sostiene su apuesta." *El Cotidiano*, no. 35, UAM-A, Mexico.

Verma, Anil. Forthcoming. "From POTS to PANS: The Evolution of Employment Relations in Bell Canada under Deregulation." In Anil Verma and Richard P. Chaykowski, eds., *Contract and Commitment: Workplace Change and the Evolution of Employment Relations in Canadian Firms.* Kingston, Ont. Queen's IRC Press.

Verma, Anil, Thomas A. Kochan, and Russell D. Lansbury. 1995. "A Conceptual Framework." In A. Verma, T. Kochan, and R. Lansbury, eds., *Employment Relations in the Growing Asian Economies.* New York: Routledge.

Verma, Anil, and Joseph Weiler. 1992. "Industrial Relations in the Canadian Telephone Industry." In R. Chaykowski and Anil Verma, eds., *Industrial Relations in Canadian Industry.* Toronto: Holt, Rinehart and Winston.

Vérut, Caroline. 1993. *The Mexican Market of Telecommunications Equipment.* New York: B. Brisson.

Vickers, John, and Yarrow, George. 1988. *Privatization. An Economic Analysis.* Cambridge, Mass.: MIT Press.

Visser, J., and P. V. Besselaar. 1993. "The Dutch Case." *Bulletin of Comparative Labor Relations*, special issue on telecommunications 25.

Vittiglio, A. 1993. "Le retribuzioni nell'esperienza di relazioni industriali SIP." Notiziario del lavoro SIP 62, pp. 12–26.

Walton, Richard E., Joel E. Cutcher-Gershenfeld, and Robert B. McKersie. 1994. *Strategic Negotiations: A Theory of Change in Labor-Management Relations.* Boston: Harvard Business School Press.

Wash, Michael. 1991. "Quality Through Leadership." *Managing Service Quality* 1(2):83–86.

Witte, E. 1966. *Die öffentliche Unternehmung im Interessenkonflikt.* Berlin.

Womack, James P., Daniel T. Jones, and Daniel Roos. 1990. *The Machine that Changed the World.* New York: Rawson Associates.

Xelhuantzi, María. 1989. *Doce años. Sindicato de Telefonistas de la República Mexicana, 1976–1988.* STRM, Mexico.

Yamagishi, A. 1989. "NTT ni Asu wa Aruka" (Does NTT have a Future?). Tokyo: Nihon Hyoronsha.

Yoon, Seong-cheun, Sun Lee, and Jeong-han Kim. 1990. *A Study on Korea's Collective Agreements*. Seoul: Korea Labor Institute.

Zuboff, S. 1988. *In the Age of the Smart Machine: The Future of Work and Power*. New York: Basic Books.

Contributors

GREG J. BAMBER is Director of the Graduate School of Management, Griffith University

ROSEMARY BATT is Assistant Professor at the New York State School of Industrial and Labor Relations, Cornell University

RICHARD CHAYKOWSKI is Associate Professor at the Centre for Industrial Relations, Queen's University

OWEN DARBISHIRE is Rhodes Lecturer in Management Studies and Fellow of Pembroke College, Oxford University

ANTHONY FERNER is Principal Research Fellow, ESRC Centre for International Employment Research, Industrial Relations Research Unit, Warwick Business School, University of Warwick

ENRIQUE DE LA GARZA is Professor, Graduate Program in the Sociology of Work, Metropolitan University of Mexico

FERNANDO HERRERA is Professor, Graduate Program in the Sociology of Work, Metropolitan University of Mexico

SHIN'O HIRAKI is a graduate student at the University of Tokyo

HARRY C. KATZ is the Jack Sheinkman Professor of Collective Bargaining and Director of the Institute of Collective Bargaining at the New York State School of Industrial and Labor Relations, Cornell University

JEFFREY H. KEEFE is Associate Professor at the School of Management and Labor Relations, Rutgers University

KEISUKE NAKAMURA is Associate Professor at the Institute of Social Science, University of Tokyo

SERAFINO NEGRELLI is Professor of Industrial Relations, University of Brescia

YOUNG-BUM PARK is a senior fellow at the Korea Labor Institute, Seoul

MARK SHADUR is Principal Research Fellow, Australian Centre in Strategic Management, Queensland University of Technology

DAVID SIMMONS is Research Officer, Australian Centre in Strategic Management, Queensland University of Technology

SIDSEL K. SOLBRAEKKE is Lecturer, Department of Social Science, Vestfold College

MICHAEL TERRY is Reader in Industrial Relations and Organisational Behavior, Industrial Relations Research Unit, Warwick Business School, University of Warwick

ANIL VERMA is Associate Professor in the Faculty of Management and the Centre for Industrial Relations, University of Toronto

Index